To Stephen and Pauline,

whose friendship, support and
immeasurable enthusiasm for the
project I shall always treasure. And
with thanks for the beautiful Foreword!

Michael

The Authentic
Magic Flute Libretto

Mozart's Autograph or the
First Full-Score Edition?

Michael Freyhan

THE SCARECROW PRESS, INC.
Lanham • Toronto • Plymouth, UK
2009

Published by Scarecrow Press, Inc.
A wholly owned subsidary of The Rowman & Littlefield Publishing Group, Inc.
4501 Forbes Boulevard, Suite 200, Lanham, Maryland 20706
http://www.scarecrowpress.com

Estover Road, Plymouth PL6 7PY, United Kingdom

British Library Cataloguing in Publication Information Available

Library of Congress Cataloging-in-Publication Data

Freyhan, Michael.
   The authentic Magic Flute libretto : Mozart's autograph or the first full-score edition?
/ Michael Freyhan.
      p. cm.
   Includes bibliographical references and index.
   ISBN 978-0-8108-6657-7 (cloth : alk. paper) — ISBN 978-0-8108-6967-7 (ebook)
   1. Mozart, Wolfgang Amadeus, 1756–1791. Zauberflöte. Libretto. I. Mozart,
Wolfgang Amadeus, 1756–1791. Zauberflöte. Libretto. English & German. II. Title.
ML410.M9F825 2009
782.1026'8—dc22   2009014492

∞ ™ The paper used in this publication meets the minimum requirements of American
National Standard for Information Sciences—Permanence of Paper for Printed Library
Materials, ANSI/NISO Z39.48-1992.

Printed in the United States of America

In grateful memory of my parents, Hans and Kate

Contents

Abbreviations

AMZ	*Allgemeine Musikalische Zeitung.* Leipzig, 1798–1848.
Briefe	*Mozart: Briefe und Aufzeichnungen. Gesamtausgabe*, 7 vols. Edited by W. A. Bauer, O. E. Deutsch, J. H. Eibl. Kassel, 1962–1975.
Dokumente	*Mozart. Die Dokumente seines Lebens* (*Neue Mozart Ausgabe*, x/34). Edited by O. E. Deutsch. Kassel, 1961. *Addenda und Corrigenda.* J. H. Eibl. Kassel, 1978.
Grove	*The New Grove Dictionary of Music and Musicians*, 2nd ed. Edited by Stanley Sadie, John Tyrrell. London, 2000.
NMA	*Wolfgang Amadeus Mozart: Neue Ausgabe sämtlicher Werke.* Kassel, 1955–1991.

Preface

This book is the result of a chance encounter with the 1814 Simrock first full-score edition of *The Magic Flute* in the Rowe Music Library of King's College, Cambridge, in 1959. To my undergraduate eye the text changes to the familiar libretto were surprising. Nevertheless it seemed that the "wrong" libretto produced a powerful bond with Mozart's music. In an instant the impression that they were linked became overwhelming, and after fifty years' reflection my first impression remains undiminished.

For this reason I have focused first on the relationship between words and music in the first-edition score. Secondly, I have sought to discover whether this text originated at the time of the opera's composition and to investigate its performance and publication history. The trail of evidence has led through fifteen countries, but the authenticity of the first-edition text remains a hypothesis. The reader may judge for himself whether publication at this interim stage is justified, but it is my hope that in future years more evidence will appear, enabling further links to be inserted into the chain.

The manuscript source used by Simrock for the first edition was retained by the publisher and seen by the Mozart scholar Otto Jahn in 1862, who reported that it came from Constanze. A hundred years later the Simrock Archive, then housed in Leipzig in the former East Germany, comprised two thousand packets. But it was unavailable to researchers from the West. Today, only its printed editions have resurfaced and musical scholarship still awaits recovery of the Archive's manuscripts.

The introductory chapter outlines some of the issues raised by the first edition, drawing attention to the significance of its text and the probable reasons for its neglect. Chapter 2 offers a detailed investigation of the libretto divergences between Mozart's autograph and the first edition, supported by musical examples comparing the word setting. This is followed by an examination of the two libretti as literary texts.

The ownership of Mozart's autograph in the years immediately following the opera's composition is explored in chapter 3. Performances in Bonn and Hamburg in 1793 appear to have used the first-edition text twenty-one years before its publication by Simrock. The evidence for this is discussed in chapter 4, followed in chapter 5 by a review of *The Magic Flute* editions published by Simrock between 1793 and 1862.

Text deviations in printed and manuscript sources are not confined to the first edition. The question posed in chapter 6 is whether the earliest version of the libretto lies preserved in it, perhaps drafted by a member of Schikaneder's theatre company, Karl Ludwig Giesecke. This could explain his reported claim to authorship of the libretto.

Chapter 7 looks at accounts by Mozart's contemporaries of surviving and lost sketch material. What was the libretto text put in front of Süssmayr when Mozart instructed him to start copying the opera from his as yet incomplete short score, and did this copy become the manuscript source of the first edition? The final chapter summarizes the evidence presented in the book, concluding with documents from the Sächsisches Staatsarchiv, Leipzig, relating to the postwar survival of the Simrock Archive.

Appendix A is devoted to Karl Ludwig Giesecke, who has been widely portrayed in the musicological literature as a liar and a man of little consequence. After leaving Vienna, he won respect among scientists for the integrity of his geological work. His dogged seven-year exploration of Greenland and his scientific achievements are recorded in numerous documents of the time, including his own diaries, offering a picture of his character and personal qualities far more comprehensive than any assessment based only on the slender surviving details of his early theatrical career.

Appendix B contains the complete first-edition libretto, with a literal English translation. The autograph version is shown alongside, wherever it deviates, illustrating the differences at a glance.

Chapter One

Introduction

The final months of Mozart's life continue to exercise a peculiar fascination. Speculation that he did not die of natural causes is a theme that has enjoyed revival in modern times.[1] The circumstances surrounding the composition and completion of the Requiem remain unsolved. These are old problems, researched and investigated over many years. But there is a new question, one that has almost entirely escaped attention. It concerns the libretto of *The Magic Flute*: Which is the original German text, that in Mozart's autograph score or that printed in the first full-score edition?

At first sight it looks like a nonissue. A first edition assumes importance where no autograph survives or where it is known to embody a composer's corrections. *The Magic Flute* falls into neither of these categories, for Mozart's autograph score is in the Staatsbibliothek zu Berlin, available in facsimile[2] and online at http://digital-b.staatsbibliothek-berlin .de/digitale_bibliothek/zauberfloete.html (10th August 2009) and the first edition, published in Bonn by N. Simrock (also online at http://pds .harvard.edu:8080/pdx/servlet/pds?id=2573661 [10th August 2009]), did not appear until 1814, twenty-three years after Mozart's death. In seeming defiance of these facts the musician is presented with an unbridgeable chasm of credibility. For here in the first edition is a purity of word-music relationship of highest Mozartian quality. The music illuminates the text by melodic outline, by harmonic color, by orchestration, and by the unfailing subtlety of speech and musical rhythms. This can be demonstrated, but not proven. Artistic quality, transcending academic reasoning, reaches out to our emotions. Joseph Kerman has written:

> There is a widely held conviction that musicologists are . . . persons who know a lot of facts about music and very little about "the music itself." That could be

1

true of certain musicologists. But with the majority of them, in my experience, it is not so much a matter of inherent unmusicality as of a deliberate policy of separating off their musical insights and passions from their scholarly work. I believe this is a great mistake; musicologists should exert themselves towards fusion, not separation.[3]

The origin of this investigation is an intuitive conviction that the hand of Mozart can be recognized in the first edition. Proof remains elusive; neither is there any evidence, however, eliminating the possibility. In the following pages an attempt is made to draw in the threads from widely scattered sources. With the story still incomplete the authenticity of the first edition text remains hypothetical. Since no firm conclusion can be reached expectations may be disappointed, but it is hoped that the book contains enough of interest to stimulate wider discussion. The author's intention has been to document the trail he has followed, so that one day, when new material comes to light, the gaps in the story can be filled in.

The title page of the first edition (see photo 1) offers no clue as to the origin of the libretto, nor is the author's name given. It will be seen that the Italian title precedes the German. In the text underlay it is the reverse, the Italian translation being shown in italic type beneath the German words. Since no English translation of the libretto appears to exist, the English version used throughout this book is supplied by the author, as are all English translations not otherwise acknowledged.

The divergences from Mozart's autograph text are much in evidence throughout the opera, with the exception only of three short numbers in the second act—No. 10 (Sarastro with Chorus "O Isis und Osiris, schenket der Weisheit Geist dem neuen Paar!"), No. 11 (Duet for 2 Priests "Bewahret euch vor Weibertücken"), and No. 18 (Priests' Chorus "O Isis und Osiris, welche Wonne!"). The numbers quoted here and throughout are in accordance with the *Neue Mozart-Ausgabe* (*Die Zauberflöte II:5/xix* [Kassel, 1970] and online at http://dme.mozarteum.at/DME/nma/nmapub_srch.php [10th August 2009]).

The first edition adopts the numbering system seen in Mozart's autograph; the Overture is numbered No. 1, the Introduction (Tamino and the Three Ladies) No. 2, and so on.

The first-edition text is not so much in conflict as in parallel with that of Mozart's autograph. The two versions read like a paraphrase of each other. Comparison with German Masonic songbooks of the time[4] confirms the Masonic character of both texts. The language of the first edition is more colloquial, the autograph more dignified. But throughout the opera the music appears to draw inspiration from the colorful imagery of the first-edition text.

Simrock did not trouble themselves to have a new Italian translation made of their text. An operatic translation cannot be too literal, for the words must of necessity fit the musical rhythms. Giovanni de Gamerra's widely used 1794 Italian version was therefore acceptable. It is worth noting, too, that just as in Mozart's autograph, no dialogue is included in the first edition. This was, however, available with the complete libretto (published by Alberti) on sale at the first performance, which took place on 30th September 1791 at the Freihaus-Theater auf der Wieden, Vienna. This text differs only in minor detail from that of Mozart's autograph.[5]

There are two factors that may account for the surprising lack of interest shown in the first full-score edition. The first is the late date of its publication; the second is its concealment among a proliferation of alternative libretti, parodies, and travesties.[6] Particularly notorious is Ludwig Wenzel Lachnith's *Les Mistères d'Isis*, with libretto by E. Morel, a compilation deriving from this and other Mozart operas and published in Paris in full score in 1801. Berlioz does not mince his words:

> Then, when this appalling concoction was cobbled together, it was given the name *The Mysteries of Isis*, opera; in this state the said opera was performed, engraved, and published in full score; and the arranger put the name of Lachnith, cretin, desecrator, next to that of Mozart. . . . Mozart has been assassinated by Lachnith.

> Puis, quand cet affreux mélange fut confectionné, on lui donna le nom de *les Mmystères* [sic] *d'Isis,* opéra; lequel opéra fut représenté, gravé et publié en cet état, en grande partition; et l'arrangeur mit, à côté du nom de Mozart, son nom de crétin, son nom de profanateur, son nom de Lachnith. . . . Mozart a été assassiné par Lachnith.[7]

Compounding the problem is the fact that the first edition is entered in the Köchel catalog (even in the 1964 sixth edition, revised by Giegling, Weinmann, and Sievers [latest unaltered reprint, 1983]) without any mention of text changes. Today the first edition is widely accessible. Not only is it found in the collections of leading European and American research libraries, but it can be downloaded from the Harvard University website in the Digital Scores Collection of the Loeb Music Library (see p. 1).

Many uncertainties still surround the history of *The Magic Flute*. It was commissioned by Emanuel Schikaneder, writer, singer, actor, and director of the Freihaus-Theater. He arrived in Vienna in the summer of 1789, having been forced to leave Regensburg on account of scandal in his private life. At

the same time his Masonic membership was suspended for six months. The
decision of the lodge was announced to him in a letter dated 4th June 1789.

> It has therefore been unanimously decided at the present meeting to inform
> Brother Schikaneder by means of the lodge minute that on account of the uproar
> caused by what has taken place he should refrain from attending the forthcom-
> ing Feast of St. John and from further visits to the lodge for six months.

> [E]s ist dahero bey gegenwärtigen Versammlung einmüthig beschlossen wor-
> den, dem Br. Schikaneder durch einen Logenextract wissen zu machen dass
> sich selbigen wegen dieses viel Aufsehens machenden Vorfalles sowohl die
> Beiwohnung vor seyenden Johannis-Festes als auch der weitern □ besuchung
> auf sechs Monate enthalten mögte.[8]

In a disarming letter he apologizes for his moral shortcomings (actresses, it
seems, were his weakness) and points out that his sins are older than the very
Brotherhood itself.[9]

Schikaneder's departure from Regensburg may well have been a cloak-
and-dagger affair. All comings and goings were monitored at the town gates
and reported in the *Regensburgisches Diarium*.[10] For example, arrivals: 24th
February 1787, "Herr Schikaneder, Direktor der teutschen [*sic*] Schauspielergesellschaft."[11] But there is no record of his departure. Could he have slipped
out in disguise among the "20 common people" (20 gemeine Personen) who
took the boat to Vienna along the Danube on 17th May 1789,[12] the date of
his resignation letter? In the letter he declares his intention to remain in
Regensburg, and he wrote another letter dated the following day (quoted in
Egon Komorzynski's biography of Schikaneder),[13] but that could have been a
stratagem to cover his tracks. According to Komorzynski, Schikaneder must
have left Regensburg for Vienna by the beginning of June.

Although it has been generally assumed that Schikaneder and Mozart were
fellow Masons, recent research has failed to find any evidence that Schikaneder ever took up membership of a Viennese lodge following his suspension in Regensburg. Commenting on a list of members of the New Crowned
Hope Lodge published in 1872 by Ludwig Lewis, Paul Nettl writes: "In any
case it is wrong that Lewis includes Schikaneder among the most prominent
members." (Jedenfalls ist es unrichtig, wenn Lewis unter den hervorragend-
sten Mitgliedern der Loge "Zur neugekrönten Hoffnung" auch Schikaneder
anführt.)[14] Otto Erich Deutsch says of Schikaneder, "but he appears—after
his short membership of a Regensburg lodge 1788/9)—not to have belonged
to any Viennese lodge" (der aber—nach seiner kurzen Zugehörigkeit zu einer Regensburger Loge (1788/9)—keiner Wiener Loge angehört zu haben
scheint).[15] H. C. Robbins Landon reaffirms, too, in *Mozart and the Masons*

(1982), that Schikaneder's name "is not listed in any of the lodge protocols in Vienna," though, in the preface to the second edition (1991), he reports that Schikaneder was still listed as a member of his Regensburg lodge in 1791.[16] Moreover, this lodge appears to have had an "offshoot," the Viennese lodge for which Mozart wrote the Kleine Freimaurer-Kantate K623 for performance on 17th November 1791 (this date was confirmed by Cliff Eisen in 1991).[17] Claims for Schikaneder's and Karl Ludwig Giesecke's authorship of the text have been made. An announcement in the *Wiener Zeitung* of 25th January 1792 declares that the words of the cantata were written by a member of the lodge. According to the recently discovered Alberti edition of the words of the cantata, published even before Mozart had completed the music, the author was "Brother S . . . r," with music by "Brother M . . . t." Philippe A. Autexier[18] proposes the name of Ignaz von Schäffer as librettist, on the grounds that he was the only current member of the lodge whose name started with *S* and ended with *r*. But Schikaneder's name also fits the bill, and if relations between his Regensburg lodge and its alleged Viennese offshoot were close, perhaps the case for his authorship ought not to be dismissed out of hand.

Schikaneder and Mozart became acquainted when Schikaneder brought a company to Salzburg in 1780, offering a variety of operas, Singspiele, ballets, and plays. Mozart wrote an aria ("Warum, o Liebe . . . Zittre, töricht Herz" K365a) for inclusion in one of these productions, a German version of Carlo Gozzi's *Le Due Notti Affannose*.[19] Eleven years later, when Schikaneder approached Mozart in Vienna, he had in mind a Singspiel, based probably on a fairy tale, *Lulu oder die Zauberflöte*, from Wieland's collection entitled *Dschinnistan*. The performance in Vienna of another opera deriving from the same story, Müller's *Kaspar der Fagottist*, is assumed to be the reason for a hasty revision of the plot. In a letter to his wife dated 12th June 1791 Mozart reports:

> to cheer myself up I then went to the Kasperl Theatre to see the new opera der "Fagottist," which is causing such a stir—but there is nothing in it.

> ich gieng dann um mich aufzuheitern zum Kasperl in die neue Oper der "Fagottist," die so viel Lärm macht—aber gar nichts daran ist.

Kasperl was a comic character identified with Marinelli's Leopoldstadttheater, where this performance took place.[20] If Mozart was so unconcerned, it was probably Schikaneder, with responsibility for box office success and the reputation of his theatre, who favored a change. It is not known how the transformation of *The Magic Flute* into a deeply Masonic work came about, but Schikaneder's checkered history can hardly have endeared him to the Masons.

The libretto, in the form in which it finally emerged, became the subject of widespread criticism. An early example is the brief review sent by a correspondent in Vienna to the *Musikalisches Wochenblatt* of Berlin just nine days after the first performance. Ignoring the music, it focuses its attack on the libretto. It is quoted here complete.

> *Vienna*, 9th October. The new comedy with stage-works, *The Magic Flute*, with music by our Kapellmeister *Mozard* [sic], which is presented at great expense and with splendid scenery, didn't meet with the hoped-for approval because the content and language of the piece are much too poor.

> *Wien*, den 9ten Oktob. Die neue Maschienenkomödie: *Die Zauberflöte*, mit Musik von unserm Kapellmeister *Mozard* [sic], die mit grossen Kosten und vieler Pracht in den Dekorationen gegeben wird, findet den gehoften Beifall nicht, weil der Inhalt und die Sprache des Stücks gar zu schlecht sind.[21]

Few of the early published alternative versions offer any serious improvement. The one written by Vulpius, Goethe's brother-in-law, and performed at Weimar in 1794 does raise the language to a more sophisticated level, but its purpose is literary rather than musical. The existence of so many different texts should not blind us to the special and outstanding quality of the word-music relationship evident in the first edition. But how can the twenty-three years from composition to first edition be bridged? A long-ignored review, published in Leipzig in the *Allgemeine Musikalische Zeitung* of 13th September 1815, Jahrgang XVII, columns 625–27, provides a startlingly direct answer (see photo 2). Praising the accuracy of the edition and the enterprise of the publisher in offering for the first time the full score of *The Magic Flute*, the reviewer, Gottfried Weber, continues:

> The German text is in many places not quite the one in use on most German stages; the differences, however, are insignificant and neither worse nor better than the normal version. In any event the whole thing is in accordance with Mozart's own wishes, because Mr. Simrock's edition, by his assurance, is taken from an original manuscript score which the former Elector of Cologne, Max Franz of Austria, had obtained from Mozart himself.

> Der deutsche Text ist an manchen Stellen nicht ganz der, auf den meisten deutschen Bühnen eingeführte; die Varianten sind aber unbedeutend, und weder schlimmer, noch besser, als die *vulgata*. Auf jeden Fall ist das Ganze der Absicht Mozarts selbst entsprechend, da Hrn. Simrocks Ausgabe, nach dessen Versicherung, von einer handschriftlichen Originalpartitur genommen ist, welche der vorige Kurfüst von Cölln, Max Franz von Oesterreich, von Mozart selbst erhalten hatte.

The reported existence of "an original manuscript score" in the possession of the Elector of Cologne is both surprising and illuminating. Let us start, however, by examining the German text for which so much is claimed, investigating its relationship both to the music and to the German words in Mozart's autograph score of the opera. An assessment will then be made of the available historical data.

NOTES

1. An article on the history of poisoning by *aqua toffana*, published in 1791, suggests that this may have been a popular topic of conversation among the chattering classes around the time of Mozart's death (see *Le Fameux Poison Nommé Aqua Toffana. Almanac de Gotha pour l'Année MDCCXCI*, rear section 22–23, British Library P.P.2422.a). If the colorful reports are to be believed, suspicions, once aroused, were hard to extinguish, not least in Mozart's mind. "I won't last much longer: surely I've been poisoned! I can't free myself of that idea.—" (mit mir dauert es nicht mehr lange: gewiss, man hat mir Gift gegeben! Ich kann mich von diesem Gedanken nicht los winden.—). Franz Xaver Niemetschek, *Lebensbeschreibung des k. k. Kapellmeisters Wolfgang Amadeus Mozart. 2. Aufl.* (Prague, 1808), 51, British Library X.439/12075; and Georg Nikolaus von Nissen, *Biographie W.A.Mozart's.* (Leipzig, 1828), 563, British Library 785.g.28; also *Dokumente*, 439. And again: "'I know I must die,' he [Mozart] exclaimed, 'someone has given me acqua [*sic*] toffana and has calculated the precise time of my death—for which they have ordered a Requiem, it is for myself I am writing this.'" Rosemary Hughes, ed., *A Mozart Pilgrimage. Being the Travel Diaries of Vincent and Mary Novello in the year 1829. Transcribed by Nerina Medici di Marignano* (London, 1955), 125, British Library 7901.e.30; also *Dokumente, Addenda und Corrigenda*, 98.

2. Facsimile edition by Bärenreiter. *Documenta Musicologica. Zweite Reihe: Handschriften-Faksimiles VII* (Kassel, 1979).

3. Joseph Kerman, *Musicology* (London, 1985), Introduction, 18–19.

4. Some examples (with their shelf-marks) to be found in the British Library are as follows: *Freymäurerlieder mit Melodien, gedruckt bey G.L.Winter* (Berlin, 1771), C.424; *Allgemeines Gesangbuch für Freymäurer* (Danzig, 1784), 4785. bb. 61; *Gesänge für Frey-Maurer* (Leipzig, 1798) and *Sammlung auserlesener Freymaurer-Lieder* ([Kempten], 1790), 4785. aa. 48. (1–2); *Vollständige Samlung von Freymaurerliedern zum Logengebrauch* (Leipzig, 1791–92), 4785. bb. 60; *Gesangbuch für Freymäurer* (Königsberg, 1800), 4785. bbb. 52.

5. For a comparison of the first printed libretto with Mozart's autograph, see Peter Branscombe, "Die Zauberflöte: Some Textual and Interpretative Problems," in *Proceedings of the Royal Musical Association*, 92nd Session (1965/66).

6. See Peter Branscombe, *W. A. Mozart. Die Zauberflöte*, Cambridge Opera Handbooks (Cambridge, 1991), 165–66.

7. Hector Berlioz, *Mémoires de Hector Berlioz, 1803–1865* (Paris, 1870), chap. 16.

8. Paul Nettl, *Musik und Freimaurerei* (Esslingen, 1956), 92.

9. Ibid., 93. English translation *Mozart and Masonry* (New York, 1957), 62. See also Egon Komorzynski, *Emanuel Schikaneder. Ein Beitrag zur Geschichte des deutschen Theaters*, 2. Auflage (Wien, 1956), 127.

10. *Regensburgisches Diarium*, Staatliche Bibliothek Regensburg, 99 ZM Rat. civ. 439.

11. Ibid., Num. IX. Dienstags, den 27 Feb. 1787, 69.

12. Ibid., Num. XX. Dienstags, den 19 May 1789, 156.

13. Egon Komorzynski, *Emanuel Schikaneder. Ein Beitrag zur Geschichte des deutschen Theaters*, 2. Auflage (Wien, 1956), 128–30.

14. Paul Nettl, *Musik und Freimaurerei* (Esslingen, 1956), 77.

15. *Dokumente,* 361.

16. H. C. Robbins Landon, *Mozart and the Masons* (London, 1982), 52, and ibid., 2nd ed. (London, 1991) 6.

17. Cliff Eisen, *New Mozart Documents: A Supplement to O.E.Deutsch's Documentary Biography* (London and Basingstoke, 1991), 71, no. 112.

18. Philippe A. Autexier, *La Lyre Maçonne* (Paris: Detrad/A.V.S., 1997)*,* 140–41.

19. See Dexter Edge, "A Newly Discovered Autograph Source for Mozart's Aria, K365a (Anh. 11a)," *Mozart-Jahrbuch* (1996): 177–96. I am indebted to Neal Zaslaw for drawing my attention to this article.

20. E. M. Batley, *A Preface to The Magic Flute* (London, 1969), 74–75. For a comparison of the plots of Lulu, Kaspar, and die Zauberflöte see Branscombe, *W. A. Mozart, Die Zauberflöte*, 29–34.

21. F. Ae. Kunzen and J. F. Reichardt, eds., *Studien für Tonkünstler und Musikfreunde. Musikalisches Wochenblatt* (Berlin, 1793). Erstes Heft. Stück I–XII, 79. British Library, Hirsch IV. 1125. See also *Dokumente*, 358; and *Chronologisch-Thematisches Verzeichnis sämtlicher Tonwerke Wolfgang Amadé Mozarts*. Ludwig Ritter von Köchel, ed. Giegling, Weinmann and Sievers. Achte, unveränderte Auflage (Wiesbaden, 1983), Anmerkung 713.

Chapter Two

Comparison of First Full-Score Edition with Mozart's Autograph

The ensuing examination of the relationship of words to music is taken number by number, starting with the first scene. The musical examples follow the first-edition phrasing and dynamics, which are, of course, at times inappropriate to the autograph words.

ACT I

No. 1: Little musical significance in the changes.

No. 2: Little musical significance in the changes.

No. 3: In the dialogue preceding this aria, Tamino is given a portrait of Pamina. According to the stage direction printed in the Alberti libretto of 1791, "Tamino ist gleich bey Empfang des Bildnisses aufmerksam geworden; seine Liebe nimmt zu, ob er gleich für alle diese Reden taub schien" (On receiving the portrait Tamino's attention is immediately drawn to it; his love takes hold, and he appears oblivious to everything being said).

Example 1. Act I, No. 3, Bar 2

Translation

1st ed.: So charmingly lovely, so magically beautiful, I never yet saw such a
   woman, truly, it is the image of a goddess,
Autograph: This portrait is bewitchingly beautiful, such as no eye has ever
   seen before. I feel how this goddess . . .

The first edition text conveys a sense of wonder and growing ecstasy. The
realization "es ist ein Götterbild" (it is the image of a goddess), with its dramatic switch from first to third person, is reinforced by Tamino's climactic
A-flat, the highest point of the melodic line. The autograph text seems, by
contrast, more factual, more impersonal, with brittle vowel sounds and con-
sonants. As Tamino imagines what he would do should he find Pamina, the
music warmly describes "umschlingen sie" (embrace her), the bass clinging
to a tonic pedal and the tender violin phrase encircling tonic and dominant
harmony four times before finally breaking free to press down ("drücken")
with a D-flat onto the subdominant tonality.

Example 2.   Act I, No. 3, Bar 43

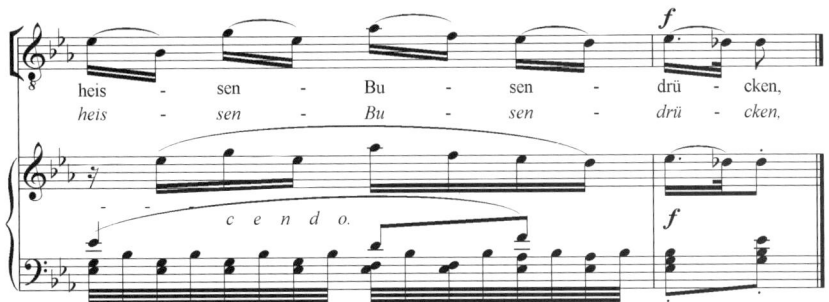

Translation

1st ed.: What would I do? Embrace her, press her, full of rapture, warmly to my bosom,

Autograph: What would I do? I would press her, full of rapture, warmly to my bosom,

In the autograph text the words "umschlingen sie" do not appear. But were they in Mozart's mind when he wrote these four bars?

No. 4: Little musical significance in the changes.

No. 5

Example 3.   Act I, No. 5, Bar 101

Translation

1st ed.: It melts to joy every sorrow,

Autograph: The sad person will be joyful

The violin figuration depicting joy occurs, in the first edition, after "Freude"; but in the autograph, before "freudig." Both settings have merit here. It could be said that the bass slipping away and the compact triad dissipating outward represents "schmilzt" (melts) of the first-edition text; on the other hand, the autograph version scores points by settling on the minor for "der Traurige" (the sad person) and returning to the major with "freudig" (joyful).

Neither first edition nor autograph hold back when it comes to describing the hazards of being apprehended by Sarastro.

Example 4.   Act I, No. 5, Bar 147

Translation

1st ed.: Thanks truly, I'll stay here! For you told me yourselves that he, oh I'm no fool, beats in the brains and wrings the neck of every stranger that he spies, then throws him to the dogs.

Autograph: No thanks very much. For I heard from you yourselves that he is like a tiger. Without mercy Sarastro would certainly have me plucked, roasted, and put out for the dogs.

In the first edition Papageno's words are an awkward, if amusing, tongue-twister (not so far in spirit from a Gilbert and Sullivan patter song), while the autograph presents a fate not only simpler to describe but more specifically tailored to a feathered visitor such as Papageno. Modern editions show "rupfen, braten" repeated three times, but in the autograph the words are spicily reversed the second time, a humorous touch of Mozart's own, presumably, since "rupfen, braten" appears only once in the Alberti printed edition of 1791.

No. 6 Terzetto: Little musical significance in the changes.

No. 7: A report published anonymously in the *AMZ* of 10th April 1799, Jahrgang I (column 448) and taken up by subsequent commentators, describes Schikaneder's interference in Mozart's work and his insistence on no fewer than five attempts at the Duet "Bei Männern." Whether true or false, there can be no doubt about the remarkable change of heart exhibited in Mozart's autograph with regard to the placing of the 6/8 meter (see photo 3). The whole number has been re-barred, with the bar lines shifted a half bar earlier, but only after Mozart, having reached the final bar, had failed to find a satisfactory ending. Certainly this re-barring is a delicate refinement adding poise and buoyancy to the rhythm. Beethoven, in his 1801 cello variations on this theme, makes the point abundantly clear with a strong chord to indicate the beginning of the bar. Similar examples of bar line adjustment may be found in Mozart's autograph of the slow movement of the String Quartet in E-flat K428 (see *British Library Music Facsimiles IV, with an Introduction by Alan Tyson* [London, 1985]) and in the Quartet No. 22 "La mano a me date" from the Second Act of *Così fan Tutte* (autograph in the Staatsbibliothek zu Berlin, Preussischer Kulturbesitz). But in both cases the decision to alter is made within no more than two phrases. Mozart's alteration in the slow movement of the Piano Concerto in F K459 is in a different category (see photo 4).[1] It appears to be triggered not by dissatisfaction with the barring as it originally stood but by a decision to interpolate a half-bar bare octave sustained *forte* by strings and horns. This is a strong, defining moment in the music that interrupts the prevailing calm with a gesture of command and authority. The alteration is seen in both exposition and recapitulation, indicating that the change was an afterthought. Only after thirteen bars does Mozart reach a suitable point of adjustment where he may revert to the original barring.[2]

What is it about the Pamina-Papageno Duet that should have caused Mozart to alter the barring of the entire number? The answer may lie not in the music but in changes to the words.

Example 5. Act I, No. 7, Bar 2

PAMINA

1ST ED. Der Lie - be hol - des Glück - emp - fin - den,

PAMINA

AUTOGRAPH Bey Män - nern wel - che Lie - be füh - len

Translation

1st ed.: To feel the pure joy of love,
Autograph: With men who feel love

In the phrase "Der Liebe holdes Glück" the stress falls on "*holdes* Glück," the genitive "Der Liebe" (of love) representing, in musical terms, an upbeat. In the alternative "Bei Männern welche Liebe fühlen," "*Männern*" is strong, requiring a downbeat, and this was how it originally stood in Mozart's autograph, with the subsidiary "welche" in the middle of the bar. So why did Mozart deliberately destroy such natural and correct word setting?

The last half bar seems to have created problems for him. It was only half filled in, then firmly crossed out. If the music had been conceived in Mozart's mind to the Simrock text, where there is no hint of conflict between words and music, a displacement of a half bar resulting from a text change would have necessitated a compensatory lengthening or shortening of the final phrase, to avoid damaging the orchestral postlude's sensitive relationship to the bar line. After writing three perfect cadences within two bars, Mozart abandoned the struggle, introducing poor word setting at the beginning of the duet, not present initially, as a solution to the problem. The alterations in the autograph may record, therefore, not uncertainty or a change of heart but the restoration of his original musical idea, in defiance of a new and inappropriate text. In a letter to his wife, written immediately after a performance of the opera on 7th October 1791, he reports that "The Duet *Mann* und *Weib* . . . was, as usual, encored" ("Das Duetto *Mann* und *Weib* . . . wurde wie gewöhnlich wiederhollet"). He means, of course, the Duet "Bei Männern." But he uses a little phrase in the middle that happens to be common to both texts. Was the opening an embarrassment to him? A further problem arises in connection with the autograph's final "reichen an die Gottheit an" (reach up to the deity; see photo 3). The recurring five-syllable "an die Gottheit an" causes Papageno to commence his phrase at the very moment where Pamina needs to breathe after her melisma; there are balance problems, too, especially the second time where she descends to a low C while Papageno sings an A-flat in a powerful part of his register. (In photo 3 Pamina's part is written in the soprano clef.) The first edition's "reihen sich den Göttern an" (join up with the gods) requires only a four-syllable repetition, "den Göttern an." In the first-edition full score Papageno enters, therefore, a quarter note (crotchet) later, with Pamina's top A-flat, which is musically more satisfying.

No. 8 Finale: The content of the opera's story remains virtually unaffected by the stylistic changes, though in the 1st Act Finale, No. 8, Scene 18, the first edition's persuasive combination of words and music serves to clarify Sarastro's personal feelings for Pamina. As she kneels before him, admitting that she tried to escape in order to avoid the unwelcome attentions of Mono-statos, Sarastro indicates in words common to both texts that he knows the secrets of her heart. The autograph then continues "du liebest einen andern sehr" (you love another very much), but the first edition dwells specifically on her relationship to him—"es ist für mich von Liebe leer" ([*your heart*] is empty of love for me).

Example 6. 1st Act Finale, No. 8, Scene 18, Bar 412

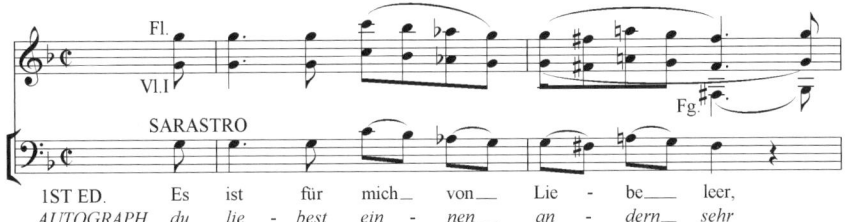

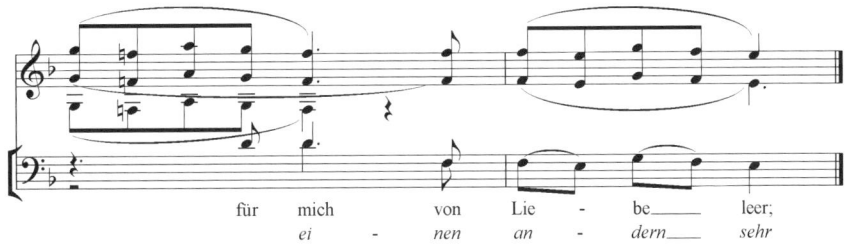

Translation

1st ed.: [Your heart] is empty of love for me;
Autograph: You love another very much

The sudden switch to the minor and the bleak octave doublings express emptiness and disappointment rather than the fullness of Pamina's love for Tamino.

ACT II

No. 9 Priests' March: No words.
No. 10 Aria with Chorus: No change.
No. 11 Duet: No change.
No. 12 Quintet: Little musical significance in the changes.
No. 13 Aria: Little musical significance in the changes.

No. 14 Aria: The violence of the dynamic markings suggests the buffeting of storm and rage (first edition) rather than simply the heat of fire (autograph). The irregularity of the orchestral accents culminates in climactic syncopation, coinciding with "toben" (rage).

Example 7. Act II, No. 14, Bar 1

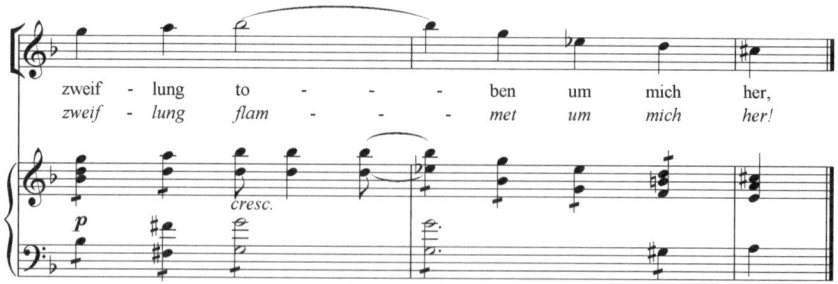

Translation

1st ed.: The vengeance of hell boils in my heart; death and despair, death and despair rage around me,

Autograph: The vengeance of hell boils in my heart, death and despair, death and despair burns around me!

A few bars later Mozart appears to have added a deviation of his own to the libretto. Attention was drawn to this passage in an article written in 1856 by Schnyder von Wartensee, who had the benefit of Mozart's autograph score before him (see photo 5).

> In the great bravura aria of the Queen of Night where D-minor vengeance beats in her heart there is a place that is often quoted as proof of how dreadfully Mozart sometimes abused our language. It is as follows: "so bist du mein', meine Tochter nimmermehr" (So you are my, my daughter nevermore). . . . But what he wrote was "so bist du, nein! meine Tochter nimmermehr" (So you are, no! my daughter nevermore).

> In der grossen Bravourarie der Königin der Nacht, wo die D moll Rache in ihrem Herzen pocht, ist eine Stelle, die man oft als Beweis anführte, wie heillos unsere Sprache manchmal von Mozart misshandelt wurde. Es ist folgende: "so bist du mein', meine Tochter nimmermehr" . . . . Er schrieb aber: "so bist du, nein! meine Tochter nimmermehr."[3]

Example 8.   Act II, No. 14, Bar 20

Translation

1st ed.: You are my child, my daughter no more,
Autograph: So you are, No! my daughter nevermore

The faulty version, with the unsatisfactory cutting-off of the feminine ending and the repetition "mein', meine," is still preserved in many modern editions, though not in the NMA (1970). Mozart appears to have created his own problems by writing a quarter (crotchet) rest after the first four syllables of "So bist du meine Tochter nimmermehr"—that is, between the two syllables of "meine." Though these words are repeated several times in succession, only once does the intrusive rest occur. The monosyllabic "nein!" is not found in the Alberti printed libretto of 1791. It is needed to solve the problem of the discrepancy between words and music and looks therefore like a composer's addition to the text. Did Mozart make a mistake and try to cover it up by changing the words rather than the music? The first-edition text offers a better answer, for here the words divide naturally exactly where Mozart placed the rest: "Bist du mein Kind, bist mir nicht Tochter mehr" (You are my child, my daughter no more). If this were his original text, there was no error on his part. But the substitution of an alternative text would account for the barely concealed incompatibility between words and music that we see in the autograph.

No. 15 Aria: The solemnity of this aria is in no way diminished by moments of extraordinary brightness, where the 1st violins ascend the E-major scale to a point two and a half octaves above any other instrument.

Example 9.   Act II, No. 15, Bar 11

Translation

1st ed.: 1. Then, clearer in understanding, he walks the path of light on the hand of a friend, 2. To forgive your enemy his guilt, what can be more worthy of a wise man,

Autograph: 1. Then he makes his way, on the hand of a friend, cheerful and happy into the better land. 2. He who does not rejoice in such teachings does not deserve to be a man.

This striking passage conveys perfectly the first-edition imagery of walking "den Weg des Lichts" (the path of light). Perhaps, too, the musical sophistication of the contrapuntal bass line reflects "Verstand" (understanding). In the second verse, the words at this point in the music show a significantly milder, more forgiving Sarastro than is depicted in the autograph text. At the end of the aria it is more likely to have been the rounded vowel sounds of "Freundes" and "Weisen" than the short *e* of "bess're" and "Mensch" that inspired Mozart to descend to the resonant depths of a low F-sharp.

Example 10. Act II, No. 15, Bar 23

Translation

1st ed.: 1. On the hand of a friend. 2. More worthy of a wise man?
Autograph: 1. Into the better land. 2. To be a man.

No. 16 Terzetto: Little musical significance in the changes.
No. 17 Aria

Example 11.   Act II, No. 17, Bar 8

Translation

1st ed.: You will never return to me, rapturous hours of sublime joy.
Autograph: You will never come back to my heart, rapturous hours!

In her mood of despair, Pamina's richly poignant rising melisma in B-flat major is deeply expressive. This inspired melodic line, though not inappropriate to the autograph "meinem Herzen" (to my heart), describes the first-edition "hoher Freuden" (of sublime joy [*lit.* of high joys]) precisely. A few bars further on the music is once again explicit to the first-edition text, Pamina's falling "herab" (down) drawing a sensitive echo from the orchestra.

Example 12.   Act II, No. 17, Bar 19

Translation

1st ed.: Hot tears stream down my cheek,
Autograph: These tears flow for you alone, my beloved,

In the last twelve bars the music identified in the first-edition text with the words "hoher Freuden" returns in the minor, to the words "gut, ich kenn' den Weg ins Grab."

Example 13.   Act II, No. 17, Bar 30

Translation

1st ed.: All right, I know the path to the grave.
Autograph: So there will be peace in death!

"Grab" (grave) in the first edition evokes powerful harmonies, followed by disturbing vacillations of E-flat/E-natural, contradicting the mood of the autograph's "Ruh im Tode" (peace in death). Pamina's striking upward leap of an octave—the only moment of its kind in the entire aria—reinforces the first-edition "ja, ich kenn'" (yes, I know), words expressing her positive determination to die. The orchestral postlude, abounding in chromaticism and cross rhythms, tellingly depicts the tortuous descent to the grave.

No. 18: No change.
No. 19: Little musical significance in the changes.
No. 20

Example 14.   Act II, No. 20, Bar 32

Translation

1st ed.: Poor me, my eyes already break [with tears];
Autograph: If a woman's mouth should kiss me

In the third verse the autograph is entertaining in the breaking-up of the word "weibli-cher." But the first edition, whether by chance or design in this strophic aria, offers the absolutely appropriate "brechen."

No. 21

Example 15.   2nd Act Finale, No. 21, Scene 27, Bar 75

Translation

1st ed.: Better to leave this life quickly than to languish in long drawn-out sorrow,
Autograph: Better to die by this iron [dagger] than to waste away in love-sickness.

The contrast of "schnell" and "lang" (first edition) is apparent in the music.

Example 16.   2nd Act Finale, No. 21, Scene 27, Bar 158

Translation

1st ed.: They hold firm in pain and sorrow. Their bond is the bond of eternity.
Autograph: In vain is the enemies' effort, the gods themselves protect them.

For the word "fest" (firm) in the first edition Pamina climbs to a high B-flat, a
beacon that dominates for nearly four bars. The dramatic descent "in Schmerz

und Leid" (in pain and sorrow) takes in almost her entire vocal range. "Bund der Ewigkeit" (bond of eternity) finds expression in a layer-by-layer succession of endlessly unfolding harmonies. The four syllables of "der Ewigkeit" (one more than the autograph "schützen sie") ensure a continuity of musical line uninterrupted by rests.

As the different branches of the story fall into place, the message of the opera begins to emerge. Tamino and Pamina, now united, are to undergo the trials together. For the first and only time, she speaks of her father and the origin of the magic flute itself. Avoiding the obvious, Mozart calls for oboe and bassoon solo, in a gesture of extreme sensitivity that allows him to save the flute for the mystical march to follow, with accompaniment of brass and timpani. With mention of the magic flute the music becomes suddenly more spacious. The long words of the first-edition text are subtly matched with predominantly long note values. Even the two short sixteenth-note (semiquaver) groups carry only one syllable each. The autograph text, with its many monosyllabic words, is by comparison a disappointment.

Example 17.   2nd Act Finale. No. 21, Scene 28, Bar 306

Translation

1st ed.: May the heavenly sound of the magic flute ease our heroic path: In the abyss of his magic cave my father once cut it, deep in the hour of the spirits, from an eternal cedar,

Autograph: Play the magic flute, may it protect us on our journey. My father cut it in a magic hour from the profoundest depths of the thousand-year-old oak

Here, in the autograph, is the most uncomfortable word setting to be found in the opera, producing vocal writing quite uncharacteristic of Mozart. "Schnitt" (cut) is given the status of a half note (minim), and its object, "sie," separated from it and placed the other side of a quarter (crotchet) rest. The autograph reveals that this was not his first attempt at setting these words (see photo 6). A consistent feature of Mozart's handwriting is that he writes his half notes (minims) to the left of the stem, irrespective of whether the stem goes up or down. The half-note (minim) "schnitt," however, is a wide loop to the right; what is more, one can clearly see the dark blob of a quarter note (crotchet) underneath,[4] followed by what might be the remnant of a smudged-out quarter (crotchet) rest and a small pen stroke over which has been written an eighth (quaver) rest. The final eighth note (quaver) is the upbeat "in." The first edition has a dotted quarter note (crotchet) followed by three eighth notes (quavers), with word setting that flows naturally and without strain. The fact that the autograph shows alteration indicates that Mozart was experiencing a problem. The end result is a poor one. Why was he suddenly unable to write music to fit a given text? Would not a last-minute change of text account for the clumsiness? Incidentally, a similar rhythmic alteration (quarter note [crotchet] to half note [minim]) has been made at the end of the same sentence, on the word "Braus." But here there is no discrepancy between autograph and first-edition text (see photo 6). The change appears to have been made in order to allow Pamina to sustain the final note of her phrase against the violins after all the other instruments have been silenced.

In the next example, the exceptional smoothness of the phrasing may have arisen from the idea of "bezähmten" (tamed) in the first edition; certainly not from the autograph "bekämpften" (fought).

Example 18.   2nd Act Finale, No. 21, Scene 28, Bar 371. March

Translation

1st ed.: We walked through burning fires, bravely tamed the danger.
Autograph: We walked through burning fires, bravely fought the danger

Papageno's colorful language provides plenty of opportunity for musical word painting.

Example 19. 2nd Act Finale, No. 21, Scene 29, Bar 439

Translation

1st ed.: I already grabbed her, I already grabbed her by her round chin; I chattered, my sweetheart was gone, I chattered, my sweetheart was gone. I sipped a true wine of the gods,

Autograph: I chattered—chattered, and that was bad, and so it serves me right!—Since I tasted this wine—

The *mfp* chord in the third bar reinforces the first-edition "schon fasst' ich sie" (I already grabbed her). The badly stressed "ich plauder*te*" is the only such example in the first edition. In the context of Papageno's tragi-comic situation it serves to raise a smile. In the next phrase the slippery nature of the violin figuration is suggestive of wine (not of the nonalcoholic variety) slipping down Papageno's throat—"ich schlürfte ächten Götterwein" (I sipped a true wine of the gods) in the first edition. "Seit ich gekostet diesen Wein" (since I tasted this wine) is the more sober offering of the autograph text, similar in meaning but less closely linked to the character of the music. On the other hand, a few bars later it is for once the autograph text that is the more fitting, with "hier" and "da" tossed from strings to wind.

Example 20.   2nd Act Finale, No. 21, Scene 29, Bar 455

Translation

1st ed.: My heart is now full of the pain of love, and I want to see nothing but girls.

Autograph: So it burns in the chamber of my heart, so it pinches here, so it pinches there!

Papageno and Papagena look forward to producing a large family. In the first-edition text their offspring are to be "der Seegen froher Eltern" (the blessing of happy parents). In the autograph version expectation runs only to "der Eltern Segen" (the blessing of the parents), but the music produces a joyful flourish on the first edition "froher."

Example 21.   2nd Act Finale, No. 21, Scene 29, Bar 697

Translation

1st ed.: (If many Papageno°ₐ}s) should be the blessing of happy parents.
Autograph: (If many Papageno°ₐ}s) will be the blessing of the parents.

Curiously, it seems to have been Mozart himself who omitted the word from his manuscript, for the Alberti printed libretto of 1791 has exactly the same text here as the first edition.

As a final example, the last bars of the opera show a remarkable instance of orchestration in support of the first-edition text, the words "in himmlischem Glanz" (in heavenly brightness) drawing flutes and violins up to a high tessitura on a chord of sustained brightness and intensity.

Example 22.   2nd Act Finale, No. 21, Scene 30, Bar 868

Translation

1st ed.: Truth triumphed, in heavenly brightness
Autograph: Strength triumphed and crowns, as the reward

The intimacy of the word-music relationship in the first-edition full score lies at the heart of this investigation. If this is merely another spurious libretto, how is one to account for the empathy that exists between its verbal images and Mozart's music? The first-edition word setting appears to demonstrate Mozartian perfection; it is a model of sustained high quality, arguably superior to the autograph version. The links forged flow from words to music. To maintain that the first-edition text was falsely implanted into Mozart's music after he had composed it to another libretto is to maintain that the descriptive power of Mozart's music is not only undamaged by the substitution of a wrong text but can be enhanced by it—an idea that sends Mozart right to the bottom of the class in vocal setting.

Another important relationship is that of the two texts to each other, without reference to the music. Certain first-edition words, for example, are entirely absent in the autograph text—words of high emotional appeal, such as "Seele," "Menschheit," "Erdenleben," "Grab," "Leid," "Zärtlichkeit" (soul, humanity, earthly life, grave, sorrow, tenderness), words to whose intensity the music responds. A factor in their exclusion from the final autograph text may, of course, be the Masonic resonance they evoked. It is difficult, however, to see a consistent pattern in this theory, for similar words are excluded at one particular moment but included elsewhere in the text. "Freude," for example, so perfectly described in the first edition by Mozart's melisma in Pamina's G-minor Aria "Ach ich fühl's" (Act II, No. 17 [see example 11]), has no place in the autograph text at this point, but it is present in the previous number, the Terzetto of the Three Boys (Act II, No. 16), where the first edition does *not* have it.

1st ed.: Ist Freiheit eures Muthes Lohn, (Freedom will be [is] the reward for your courage,)
Autograph: Ist Freude eures Muthes Lohn! (Joy will be [is] the reward for your courage!)

Obviously, the context may have a bearing, but the word itself is not taboo and cannot be listed among the excluded words.

If there is any consistent pattern, it has to do with style and language rather than with vocabulary. The first-edition text is more colloquial, the autograph more dignified and respectful of grammar. The use of "wie" in Tamino's Portrait Aria (Act I, No. 3) provides a typical example.

1st ed.: Fürwahr es ist ein Götterbild, wie's meine ganze Seele füllt (Truly it is the image of a goddess, how it fills my whole soul)
Autograph: Ich fühl' es, wie dies Götterbild mein Herz mit neuer Regung füllt (I feel how this image of a goddess fills my heart with new excitement.)

Later in the same aria Tamino asks, "was würde ich?" In answer, the first edition leaps straight to the infinitive.

1st ed.: Umschlingen sie, voll Entzücken an diesen heissen Busen drücken,
(Embrace her, press her, full of rapture, warmly to my bosom,)

In the autograph he answers in full.

Autograph: Ich würde sie voll Entzücken an diesen heissen Busen drücken,
(I would press her, full of rapture, warmly to my bosom,)

The addition of "Ich würde sie" has, however, resulted in the omission of "Umschlingen sie," for whoever was responsible for the alterations seems to have been at pains to retain an equal number of syllables, despite an overall looseness in the metrical scansion; this suggests that the changes were designed to fit music which was already in existence. The musical implications of the absence of "Umschlingen sie" have already been discussed (see example 2).

There is a noticeable tendency for the verbs in the first edition to be more frequently in the first or second person, those in the autograph more frequently in the third (see opening of example 1). In the following extract from the 1st Act Quintet (No. 5), where the 1st Lady offers Tamino the magic flute, the choice is between "von unsrer Fürstin bring ichs dir" (I bring it to you from our princess) and "dies sendet unsre Fürstin dir" (our princess sends it to you).

1st ed.: Hier Prinz, nimm dies Geschenk von mir; von unsrer Fürstin bring ichs dir. Die Zauberflöte wird dich schützen, und tobt um dich ein Heer von Blitzen. (Here, prince, take this present from me, I bring it to you from our princess. The magic flute will protect you, even though a host of lightning flashes rage around you.)
Autograph: O Prinz! nimm dies Geschenk von mir dies sendet unsre Fürstin dir. Die Zauberflöte wird dich schützen im grössten Unglück unterstützen (Oh prince! Take this present from me, our princess sends it to you. The magic flute will protect you, support you in the greatest adversity)

Even the small changes reflect the increased refinement of the autograph text: first edition, "Hier Prinz"; autograph, "O Prinz." Dignity can, however, prove the enemy of poetic imagery. "Ein Heer von Blitzen" (a host of lightning flashes) is far more vivid than "im grössten Unglück" (in the greatest adversity).

It is in Papageno's nature to use more colloquial language than that of the other characters in the opera. The first-edition text exaggerates this feature even more than the autograph does, sailing, at times, remarkably close to the wind. In example 4 the first phrase, "Dank ergebenst, bleibe hier!" lacks the subject "ich." In the autograph it is supplied: "Nein, dafür bedank ich mich." A few lines later the first-edition "Dass doch der Prinz beym Henker wäre" (The prince can go to the hangman) becomes, more conventionally, "Dass doch der Prinz beym Teufel wäre" (The prince can go to the devil); and "Kömmt nur Gefahr, bei meiner Ehre! er trollt ab, wie ein Dieb" (should there be any danger, on my honor, he would skedaddle like a thief) converts to the more normal "Am Ende schleicht bey meiner Ehre er vor mir wie ein Dieb" (when it comes to it, on my honor, he would sneak past me like a thief). Neither is there a place in the autograph for the somewhat naive rhyme with which he receives the glockenspiel from the Three Ladies: "O lasst doch hören, holde Schönen!" (Oh, let's hear them, my lovely beauties). Instead he simply asks, "Werd ich sie auch wohl spielen können?" (Shall I also be able to play them?).

In keeping with the autograph's preference for the less intimate third person, Pamina sings in the Terzetto No. 6:

1st ed.: nur du, o Mutter dauerst mich; der Schmerz um mich, er tödtet dich.
(Only you, oh mother, have my pity; grief for me will kill you.)
Autograph: nur meine Mutter dauert mich, sie stirbt vor Gram ganz sicherlich.
(Only my mother has my pity, she will quite certainly die of sorrow.)

As Papageno catches sight of Pamina, his idiomatic "Ein Mädchen, jung und fein, traun, keine üble Beute" (A girl, young and handsome, how's this for a catch) in the first edition is restored to respectability in the autograph with "Schön Mädchen jung und rein, viel weisser noch als Kreide." (Lovely girl, young and pure, much whiter even than chalk.)

The Pamina-Papageno Duet No. 7 has a certain naïveté of expression in the first edition, rendered characteristically more dignified, even more aloof, in the autograph, with a view of woman's role that raises eyebrows in today's politically correct world.

1st ed.: **Pamina.** Der Liebe holdes Glück empfinden, kann nur der gute Mann allein. **Papageno.** Ach, an ein gutes Weib sich binden, das lasst mir eine Freude seyn! (**Pamina.** Only a good man can feel the pure joy of love. **Papageno.** Ah, to be tied to a good woman, that's what I call joy!)
Autograph: **Pamina.** Bey Männern welche Liebe fühlen fehlt auch ein gutes Herze nicht. **Papageno.** Die süssen Triebe mitzufühlen ist dann der Weiber erste Pflicht. (**Pamina.** With men who feel love a good heart is not lacking either. **Papageno.** To share these sweet impulses is then a woman's first duty.)

The question of the acceptance of women in Freemasonry in Mozart's era is discussed by Philippe A. Autexier in *La Lyre Maçonne* (1997).[5]

Sometimes the changes are concerned primarily with word order.

1st Act Finale, No. 8, Scene 15

1st ed.: **Priest.** Sobald dich an der Weisheit Band in's Heil geführt der Freundschaft Hand. (As soon as the hand of friendship has led you on wisdom's bond to holiness.)

Autograph: **Priest.** Sobald dich führt der Freundschaft Hand ins Heiligtum zum ewgen Band. (As soon as the hand of friendship leads you into the sanctuary to eternal bond.)

Learning that Pamina is still alive, Tamino is allowed, in the first edition, to be exultant; the autograph, however, requires him to be ever mindful of his heroic dignity.

1st ed.: Sie lebt? sie lebt? O tausend Dank dafür. O! dass mir doch ein Ton gelänge, der euch den Dank des Herzens sänge; der meine Adern all' durchfliesst, in Freudenthränen, in Freudenthränen sich ergiesst. (She lives? She lives? Oh, a thousand thanks for that. Oh! If only I could find the sound to sing the thanks in my heart, which flows through all my arteries, pouring forth in tears of joy.)

Autograph: Sie lebt, sie lebt! ich danke euch dafür O wenn ich doch im Stande wäre, Allmächtige, zu eurer Ehre, mit jedem Tone meinen Dank zu schildern, wie er hier [*aufs Herz deutend*] hier—entsprang. (She lives, she lives! I thank you for that. If only I were truly able, Almighty, in your honor, to describe my thanks with every sound that I make, as it here, [*pointing to his heart*] here—arose.)

Dignity of language leads once again to a reduction in feeling in the autograph text where Papageno sends Monostatos and his slaves away, dancing in ecstasy at the sound of the magic bells.

1st ed.: **Pamina–Papageno.** Ja sanft mildert Harmonie jegliche Beschwerden, schmilzt das Herz zur Sympathie, sagt zur Freude: Werde! (Yes, harmony gently smoothes every trouble, melts the heart to sympathy, says to joy: arise!)

Autograph: **Pamina–Papageno.** Nur der Freundschaft Harmonie mildert die Beschwerden ohne diese Sympathie ist kein Glück auf Erden (Only the harmony of friendship softens troubles, without this sympathy there is no happiness on earth)

In the Queen of Night's Aria No. 14 the repetition of "bist" and the tautological reference to both "Kind" (child) and "Tochter" (daughter) is found only in the first edition.

1st ed.: bist du mein Kind, bist mir nicht Tochter mehr, (you are my child, my daughter no more,)
Autograph: so bist du, Nein! meine Tochter nimmermehr (so you are, No! my daughter nevermore)

In No. 16 the Three Boys come to return the magic flute and bells to Tamino and Papageno. They promise on their next meeting the reward of "Freiheit" (freedom) in the first edition or "Freude" (joy) in the autograph. The use of the word "Freude" has already been discussed in the context of vocabulary. From the point of view of language and meaning it is an improvement here on the ambiguous "Freiheit," which might misleadingly suggest release from Sarastro's power, rather than "freedom of spirit."

No. 17 Aria (example 11) drew attention to the musical response to the phrase "Wonnestunden hoher Freuden" in the first edition. From the literary viewpoint the accusation of tautology could once again be made, since "Wonne" (rapture) and "hoher Freuden" (of sublime joy) mean almost the same thing. The autograph offers "Wonnestunden meinem Herzen" (rapturous hours to my heart).

The opening of the 2nd Act Finale finds the Three Boys startled to observe Pamina, dagger in hand, preparing for suicide.

1st ed.: **Pamina.** Du also bist mein Bräutigam? Willkommen! ende meinen Gram. **Three Boys.** Seht ihre Blicke wild und stier, vernahmt ihr's? Wahnsinn sprach aus ihr. (**Pamina.** Are you then my bridegroom? Welcome! End my grief. **Three Boys.** See her looks, wild and staring, did you observe? There was madness in her speech.)
Autograph: **Pamina.** Du also bist mein Bräutigam—durch dich vollend ich meinen Gram! **Three Boys.** Welch dunkle Worte sprach sie da! Die Arme ist dem Wahnsinn nah! (**Pamina.** You are then my bridegroom—through you I end my grief! **Three Boys.** What dark words she spoke there! The poor girl is near to madness!)

The relative formality of the autograph text's "Welch dunkle Worte sprach sie da!" (Three Boys), as against the directly personal "Seht ihre Blicke wild und stier, vernahmt ihr's?" of the first edition, sums up the essential difference in style and approach between the two libretti. Similarly, some bars later, when the Three Boys try to persuade Pamina to give up her suicide attempt, the direct appeal in the first edition gives way to a mere statement of the religious position in the autograph, once again in the third person.

1st ed.: Wirf den Mörderstahl von dir. (Throw the murder weapon away.)
Autograph: Selbstmord strafet Gott an dir! (God will punish you for suicide!)

Some of the "refinements" of the autograph text are concerned only with linguistic detail. The repetition of "an" is avoided in the passage where Pamina prepares to accompany Tamino on the trials (2nd Act Finale, scene 28).

1st ed.: Ich werd' an allen Orten an deiner Seite sein. (I will be at your side in all places.)
Autograph: Ich werde aller Orten an deiner Seite sein. (I will be at your side in all places.)

Be it on biblical or Masonic grounds, there is disagreement on the wood used for the making of the magic flute (see example 17). The first edition has it fashioned out of an "ew'gen Zeder" (eternal cedar) while the autograph is content with the relatively youthful "tausenjähr'gen Eiche" (thousand-year-old oak). Sacred or secular is the choice; cedar was used in the building of Solomon's temple, while oak is traditionally a stout wood. Since "Zeder" and "Eiche" are both of two syllables, with the stress on the first, there can be no musical reason for the change.

The couple emerge from the trials of fire and water to a triumphant chorus.

1st ed.: geläutert bist du licht und rein! (you are purified, bright and clear!)
Autograph: Der Isis Weihe ist nun dein! (The initiation of Isis is now yours!)

Tautology has already been mentioned as a characteristic of the first-edition text that is carefully avoided in the autograph. The words "geläutert," "licht," and "rein" are so close in meaning as to be virtually identical. There are good poetic reasons for using all three, but the autograph prefers a more prosaic welcome to the newly initiated couple. In fact, the first edition quotes from the Chorale of the Armed Men at the beginning of scene 28 "er wird verklärt, geläutert, licht und rein, sich den Mysterien der Isis ganz zu weih'n" (he becomes transfigured, purified, bright and clear, to dedicate himself completely to the mysteries of Isis). Here, too, the autograph goes its own way with "Erleuchtet wird er dann im Stande seyn sich den Mysterien der Isis ganz zu weihn" (enlightened, he will then be able to dedicate himself completely to the mysteries of Isis).

There is a distinctly biological flavor to the first-edition language as Papageno prepares to take leave of life (scene 29). Starting with "Kinn" (chin), he proceeds through "Herz," "Augen," "Hals," and "Nase" to "Blase" (heart, eyes, neck, nose, bladder). "Blase" belongs in the expression "springt die Blase" (the bubble bursts). Whether or not there is humorous intent in the double entendre of "Blase" is not clear, but the falling sixth in the music, which serves to point the rhyme with "Nase," is suggestive of a little harmless impropriety.

Example 23.   2nd Act Finale, No. 21, Scene 29, Bar 483

1ST ED.   schiebst mein Glück mir vor   die   Na - se,   da ich's   fas - se, springt die Bla - se,
AUTOGRAPH weil   du   bö - se   an   mir han -delst mir kein schö -nes Kind zu - ban -delst

Translation

1st ed.: You push happiness before my nose, as I grasp it the bubble (bladder) bursts,

Autograph: Because you treat me badly and don't send me a pretty young thing

Of the catalog of parts of the body, only "Herz" and "Hals" survive in the autograph version.

Such, then, is the nature of the two texts. The first edition is fresh, direct, even raw, and alive with imagery; the autograph tidier, more dignified, and a little remote. But in the operatic context the stylistic shortcomings, if such they are, of the first edition are of little consequence, for the powerful magnetism of the music predominates over the refinements of language. It could be argued that simplistic words are often better suited to musical setting, especially if they are rich in emotive vocabulary. Schubert's inspiration responded as much to the poetry of Wilhelm Müller, author of "Die schöne Müllerin" and "Die Winterreise," as to the more sophisticated literary style of Goethe and Heine.

The reader may well complain of the inference that the autograph is an altered version of the first-edition text—an apparent contradiction of historical facts. This is not, however, an assumption that has been lightly made; rather, it arises out of the text comparison. What purpose would there be in turning a libretto that is reasonably refined in language and grammar into a less cultured, more colloquial piece of writing? If it were only a question of altered speech rhythms, it would perhaps be possible to believe that changes had been made in order to improve the relationship to the musical rhythms. But we have seen the sensitivity of the music of *The Magic Flute* to so many significant details of the first-edition text. A melisma, a surprising turn of harmony, a sudden brightness of orchestration, a deep bass note, a long held top note—can these be given new meaning by the substitution of a text never known to the composer? On the contrary, the process is the other way around, the music arising out of the words. On these grounds, and on the grounds of its comparatively naive literary style, it would seem probable that the first-edition text came first.

In "separating off their musical insights and passions from their scholarly work" (Joseph Kerman, see p. 2), musicologists are avoiding important responsibilities. One is entitled to look to an expert for an opinion—to date a painting, to authenticate a Chippendale chair, a Stradivarius, an unsigned manuscript. He is expected to draw on his knowledge *and* experience. The exercise of artistic judgment is a valid first stage in the quest for objective truth. Even in science it is acceptable practice to propose a theory and then search for the evidence to prove it. There exists documentation in support of the authenticity of Simrock's *Magic Flute* first edition from which cautious conclusions may be drawn. Cliff Eisen has written, in another context,

> An overwhelming reliance on Mozart's autographs does not do full justice to the wide range of authentic and potentially authentic sources of evidence for the attribution, chronology, text, and performance practice of his works. . . . For while autographs may be primary sources, they represent only one element in a complex web of evidence.[6]

The evidence should be carefully weighed, not for the sake of historical knowledge alone, but because the first edition represents what appears to be the original version of an opera whose timeless truths enrich our quality of life.

As we reflect on the implications to Mozart of an altered libretto, we would do well to recall his own views on operatic text, expressed ten years before *The Magic Flute* was written in a letter to his father in connection with *Die Entführung aus dem Serail*.

> *Vienna*, 13th October 1781. . . . Now about the text of the opera.—so far as Stephani's work is concerned you are quite right.—but the poetry exactly fits the character of the stupid, uncouth and spiteful Osmin.—and I am well aware that the kind of verse it contains is not of the best—but it was so in tune with my musical ideas |: which were already going around in my head before :| that I couldn't help liking it;—and I would bet that when it is performed no one will feel the lack of anything . . . in an opera poetry must absolutely be the obedient

daughter of the music . . . an opera must succeed all the better when the plot is
well worked out, with the words, however, written entirely for the music and
not here and there to satisfy some miserable rhyme |: God knows, they don't
contribute to the value of a theatrical performance, whatever it may be, rather
they do damage :| . . . it is verse which is most indispensable to the music—but
rhyme—for rhyme's sake, is most harmful;—those gentlemen who go to work
so pedantically will inevitably come to grief, together with the music.—

Vienne ce 13 d'octobre 1781. . . . Nun wegen dem text von der opera.—was
des Stephani seine arbeit anbelangt, so haben sie freylich recht.—doch ist die
Poesie dem karackter des dummen, groben und boshaften osmin ganz angemes-
sen.—und ich weis wohl dass die verseart darinn nicht von den besten ist—doch
ist sie so Passend, mit meinen Musikalischen gedanken |: die schon vorher in
meinem kopf herumspatzierten :| übereins gekommen, dass sie mir nothwendig
gefallen musste;—und ich wollte wetten dass man bey dessen auführung—nichts
vermissen wird . . . bey einer opera muss schlechterdings die Poesie der Musick
gehorsame Tochter seyn . . . um so mehr muss Ja eine opera gefallen wo der Plan
des Stücks gut ausgearbeitet; die Wörter aber nur blos für die Musick geschrie-
ben sind, und nicht hier und dort einem Elenden Reime zu gefallen |: die doch,
bey gott, zum werth einer theatralischen vorstellung, es mag seyn was es wolle,
gar nichts beytragen, wohl aber eher schaden bringen :| . . . verse sind wohl für
die Musick das unentbehrlichste—aber Reime—des reimens wegen das schäd-
lichste;—die herrn, die so Pedantisch zu werke gehen, werden immermit sammt
der Musick zu grunde gehen.—

NOTES

1. Facsimile edition, Bärenreiter 1988. See also facsimile in Eva and Paul Badura-
Skoda, *Mozart-Interpretation* (Vienna, 1957); *Notenanhang* and NMA V:15/v, XXII
(showing part of Mozart's alterations).

2. I am indebted to Martin Outram, Christoph Wolff, and Alan Tyson for pointing out the barring adjustments Mozart made in the autographs of the String Quartet
K428, Così fan Tutte, and the Piano Concerto K459 respectively.

3. Schnyder von Wartensee, "Notizen über die Zauberflöte von Mozart." *Neue
Zeitschrift für Musik* (Leipzig, 25th July 1856). Band 45, no. 5, 43. British Library
P.P. 1946.

4. An exact analogy is found in the string quintet K614 (1st viola part, four bars
before the end of the Minuet—see *British Library Music Facsimiles V, with an Introduction by Alan* Tyson [London, 1987], 140). Initially Mozart probably wrote a dotted
quarter note (crotchet) here, matching the 2nd viola.

5. Philippe A. Autexier, *La Lyre Maçonne* (Paris: Detrad/A.V.S., 1997), 117–22.

6. Cliff Eisen, ed., "The Mozarts' Salzburg Copyists." *Mozart Studies* (Oxford,
1991), 298–99.

Chapter Three

Negotiations to Buy
the *Zauberflöte* Manuscript

MAX FRANZ, ELECTOR OF COLOGNE

The evidence in favor of the authenticity of the first-edition text starts with the review in the *AMZ* of 13th September 1815 attributing the source to "an original manuscript score which the former Elector of Cologne, Max Franz of Austria, had obtained from Mozart himself" (see p. 6 and photo 2). What might be the meaning of "an original manuscript score"? It is surely straining credulity to its limits to imagine that Mozart should have had the time and will, in the last months of his life, to make a second *Magic Flute* full score for the sake not of the music, but of an alternative libretto. Gottfried Weber, who wrote the review, was not of a naive disposition. Though devoted to music, his real profession was law, in which he achieved considerable distinction. Details of his career are given in his 1831 autobiography, published in 1839, three months after his death.[1] As founder and editor of the music journal *Cäcilia*, published in Mainz, he launched a vigorous campaign in 1825 to alert the public to the extent of Franz Xaver Süssmayr's work on the completion of Mozart's Requiem. A wide-ranging controversy ensued. Ten years earlier, however, his natural skepticism was not aroused by Simrock's claims for the Elector of Cologne's *Magic Flute* manuscript.

The elector was known to Mozart; the youngest son of the Empress Maria Theresa, he had been present when Mozart appeared as a prodigy at the Viennese court. Il Rè Pastore had been commissioned on the occasion of his visit to Salzburg in 1775. Their childhood acquaintance (they were both the same age) was carried through into adulthood. On 23rd January 1782 Mozart wrote, in a letter to his father,

> [A]bout him I can say that he values me highly—he puts me forward at every opportunity—and I would say almost certainly, that if he were already Elector of Cologne, I should be his Kapellmeister.

> [B]ey diesem kann ich sagen dass ich alles gelte—er streicht mich bey allen gelegenheiten hervor—und ich wollte fast gewis sagen können, dass wenn er schon Churfürst von kölln wäre, ich auch schon sein kapellmeister wäre.

Mozart was evidently somewhat impulsive in his reactions to people, for just two months earlier, in a letter of 17th November 1781, he had complained to his father that the future elector seemed to have lost his wit and intelligence.

> You should see him now!—stupidity stares out from his eyes.—he talks and speaks away to all eternity, and everything in falsetto.—he has a swollen throat.—in a word it's as if the man were turned totally upside down.

> sie sollten ihn izt sehen!—die [dumheit] guckt ihm aus den augen heraus.—er redet und spricht in alle Ewigkeit fort, und alles in falset.—er hat einen geschwollnen hals.—mit einem wort als wenn der ganze herr umgekehrt wär.

In 1784 Max Franz took up his position in Cologne, but Mozart never followed him. The new elector proved a great stimulus to musical life in the Rhineland, drawing on his Viennese connections. He received Haydn and provided active encouragement and sponsorship for Beethoven, who traveled to Vienna with his blessing. Beethoven's teacher, Christian Gottlob Neefe, wrote enthusiastically of his beneficial influence.

> Our capital is becoming increasingly attractive to music lovers through the benevolent support of our dearest Elector. He has a large collection of the finest musical material and is dedicated every day to enlarging it. Through him we frequently have the opportunity to hear good virtuosi on various instruments. Good singers come rarely.

> Unsere Residenzstadt wird jetzt immer anziehender für Musikliebhaber durch den gnädigsten Vorschub unsers theuersten Churfürstens. Er hat eine grosse Sammlung von den schönsten Musikalien, und verwendet täglich noch viel auf Vermehrung derselben. Durch ihn haben wir Gelegenheit, öfters gute Virtuosen auf mancherley Instrumenten zu hören. Gute Sänger kommen selten.[2]

In his manuscript autobiography, revised in 1789, Neefe testifies to the elector's personal qualities.

It is my pride and pleasure to serve one of the most enlightened German princes. It can be said of him truthfully, without flattery (of which he has sworn eternal hatred), that he fulfils every duty of his high rank completely and with joyfulness. . . . His energetic example gives life and success to all business affairs. . . . He encourages all true merit. His subjects have access to him every day, even the humblest of them, and he helps them promptly if their grievances are well founded. He knows, however, how to get rid of good-for-nothings quickly. He is a connoisseur, friend and rewarder of the art of music; it is one of his favorite forms of relaxation. Who, then, would not serve a regent such as *Maximilian Franz* with joy?

Es ist mein Stolz und mein Vergnügen, einem der aufgeklärtesten teutschen Fürsten zu dienen. Von ihm kann mit Wahrheit, ohne Schmeichelei, (dieser hat er einen ewigen Hass geschworen) sagen, dass er jede Pflicht seiner hohen Staffeln ganz und mit Freudigkeit erfüllt. . . . Sein thätiges Beispiel giebt allen Geschäften Leben und Gedeihen. . . . Er ermuntert jedes wahre Verdienst. Täglich haben seine Unterthanen, auch die geringsten, bei ihm Zutritt, und er hilft ihnen schleunig, wenn ihre Beschwerden gegründet sind. Taugenichts weiss er aber bald von sich zu entfernen. Er ist Kenner, Freund und Belohner der Tonkunst; sie ist eines seiner liebsten Erholungsmittel. Wer sollte denn einem solchen Regenten, wie *Maximilian Franz* ist, nicht mit Freuden dienen?[3]

Neefe elaborated on the elector's commitment to music in the Gotha *Theater-Kalender* for the year 1791.

The Elector is not merely a friend of the stage and of the art of music, as are most of his kind, but he earns his place among connoisseurs. He knows how to judge plays, actors, musical compositions, and practical musicians with insight and taste. He himself possesses a considerable stock of the newest and best opera scores (which he continually augments), which he reads very fluently and with which now and then in the afternoon he entertains himself in his room after the anxieties of government affairs. He then sings the arias himself; piano, one cello, two violins, and a viola accompany him. Part-songs are distributed among those accompanying him who can sing . . . . For the rest his genial bearing must delight every artist.

Der Kurfürst ist nicht blos ein Freund der Bühne und der Tonkunst, wie die Meisten seines gleichen; sondern er verdient unter den Kennern seinen Platz. Er weiss Stücken [*sic*], Schauspieler, musikalische Kompositionen und praktische Tonkünstler mit Einsicht und Geschmack zu beurtheilen. Er besitzt selbst einen ansehnlichen Vorrath (den er immer noch vermehrt) der neuesten und besten Opernpartituren, die er sehr fertig liesst [*sic*] und womit er sich zuweilen Nachmittags nach besorgten Regierungsgeschäften im Kabinet amusiert. Die Arien singt er dann selbst: das Klavier, ein Violoncell, zwei Violinen und eine Viola begleiten ihn. Mehrstimmige Gesänge vertheilt er unter die Accompagnateurs, die singen können. . . . Uebrigens muss sein leutseeliges Betragen jeden Künstler entzücken.[4]

At the end of 1791 the elector took steps to acquire Mozart's latest operas.

> Vienna
> to Monsieur
> Monsieur Louigi Simonetti
> First Tenor of His Highness
> The Elector of Cologne
> *in Bonn*

Monsieur!
    You can have both la Clemenza di Tito and die Zauberflöte from me very soon, as soon, that is, as the copyist can complete the copy. For one score I ask 100 imperial ducats and await your speedy decision which, if either, you will take, so that the copyist may begin at once. Be so kind as to arrange the order in such a way that the money may be drawn as soon as the required score is handed over, for it is all the property of my sons, who are not yet of age. I am respectfully
    Monsieur
    Your humble servant
    Constanza Mozart, née Weber
    Vienna
    28th December *1791*

Vienne / à Monsieur / Monsieur Louigi Simonetti / primo Tenore di Sua Altezza / Elettorale di Cologna / *à* / *Bonn*. Monsieur! Sie können sowohl la clemenza di Tito als die Zauberflöte sehr bald von mir erhalten, sobald nämlich der Kopist die Abschrift vollenden kann. Ich verlange für eine Partitur 100 Kaiser Dukaten, und erwarte nächstens Ihren Entschluss, ob, und welche Sie nehmen, um den Kopisten sogleich anfangen zu lassen. Die Anweisung belieben Sie so einzurichten, dass man gegen Uibergabe der allenfalls verlangten Partitur zugleich das Geld beheben könne, denn es ist Alles Eigenthum meiner noch unmündigen Söhne. Ich bin mit Hochachtung / Monsieur / Ihre ergebene Dienerin / Constanza Mozart / geborne Weber. Wien den / 28ten Xbris *1791*.[5]

Simonetti, a favorite singer of the elector, was apparently handling the transaction. In vol. 6, 430, of *Briefe*, published in 1971 under the editorship of Joseph Heinz Eibl, attention is drawn to the misreading "Kremnizer Dukaten" (Kremniz ducats) for "Kaiser Dukaten" (imperial ducats) in the version of the letter in *Dokumente* (377). Eibl is also of the opinion that the handwriting, which is found in three other letters of the period, is not Constanze's. He writes, "It may be assumed (with due caution) that they were written on Constanze's instructions by Sophie Weber" (Es darf [mit allem Vorbehalt] vermutet werden, dass diese von Sophie Weber im Auftrag Constanzes geschrieben sind).[6] The letter is listed in the catalog of the *Mozart en France* exhibition published by the Bibliothèque Nationale, Paris, in 1956.[7] I was informed in a private telephone conversation in the late 1980s with François Lesure, head keeper of the Music Department, Bibliothèque Nationale, Paris, that the collection had been sold and the letter's whereabouts was no longer known.

The date, 28th December, is of great interest. Mozart had died on 5th December. The elector himself was in Vienna at that time. Here, with documentation, is the chronology of events.

1791, 6th November, Morning

The Elector of Cologne arrives in Vienna. His visit is announced in Latin in *Ephemerides Politico-Litterariae*, Budapest, and in German in the *Wiener Zeitung*.

Documentation

"Vienna, 5th November. The Elector of Cologne, Archduke of Austria, is expected in Vienna."

"Vienna, 10th November. The feast of the order of St. Stephen was celebrated in the court chapel on 6th November . . . Archduke Maximilian, Elector of Cologne, arrived on the same day."

Vienna 5ta Novembris. Elector Coloniensis Archi Dux Austriae Viennam expectatur.

Vienna 10ma Nov. Die 6ta Novembris festum Ordinis Equitum S. Stephani in Sacello Aulico celebratum est . . . Eadem die Archi Dux Maximilianus Elector Coloniensis advenit.[8]

"The feast-day of St. Stephen was solemnly celebrated at court on Sunday the sixth of the month. . . . His Royal Highness the Archduke Maximilian, Elector of Cologne, arrived here on the morning of the very same day."

Sonntags den 6.d.M. wurde das Titularfest des St. Stephansordens bey Hofe feyerlich begangen. . . . An eben diesem Tage des Morgens sind Se K.H. der Erzherzog Maximilian, Kurfürst von Kölln, hier eingetroffen.[9]

6th November, Evening

On the day of the elector's arrival Count Zinzendorf attended the twenty-fourth performance of *The Magic Flute*. Its success in Vienna may be measured by the fact that only thirty-eight days had elapsed since the first performance on 30th September 1791.

Documentation

"At 6.30 to the *Starhemberg Theatre* in the suburb by the river Wien in M. and Mme. d'Auersperg's box, to hear the 24th performance of *The Magic Flute*. The music and designs are pretty, the rest an incredible farce. Huge audience."

A 6h½ au *Théatre de Starhemberg* au fauxbourg de la Vienne dans la loge de M. et M*e* d'Auersperg, entendre la 24*me* representation *von der Zauber-flöte*. La musique et les decorations sont jolies, le reste une farce incroyable. Un auditoire immense.[10]

Second Week of November

Ephemerides Politico-Litterariae reports the elector's attendance at public performances.

Documentation

"Vienna 13th November . . . The Elector of Cologne was greeted with warm applause when he appeared at public performances."

Vienna 13tia Nov. . . . Elector Coloniensis laeto cum adplausu in spectaculis publicis exceptus est.[11]

17th November

Mozart leaves his house to conduct the first performance of the Masonic Cantata K623 at his lodge Zur (neu)gekrönten Hoffnung ([New] Crowned Hope). The event was reported in *Das Wienerblättchen* and, posthumously, in the *Wiener Zeitung* and in a Masonic oration on Mozart's death.

Documentation

"On the 17th, the Viennese Lodge 'New Crowned Hope' celebrated the inauguration of its temple with an oration, procession, and a cantata composed by Herr Mozart. Printed, public admission tickets were distributed."[12]

"*Announcement of a cantata by the deceased great artist, Mozart* . . . a work . . . which he himself conducted at a performance two days before his final illness, in the company of his best friends."

Ankündigung einer Cantate des verstorbenen grossen Künstlers Mozart . . . eines Werkes . . . dessen Ausführung er zwey Tage vor seiner letzten Krankheit, im Kreise seiner besten Freunde selbst dirigirt hat.[13]

"Hardly have a few weeks elapsed since he stood here in our midst, glorifying with the magic of his music the dedication of our Masonic temple. Which one of us, my brothers!—would then have measured the thread of his life so short?—Which one of us would have believed that after three weeks we would mourn him?"

Kaum sind einige Wochen vorüber, und er stand noch hier in unsrer Mitte, verherrlichte noch durch seine zauberischen Töne die Einweihung unseres Maurertempels.

Wer von uns, meine Brüder! hätte ihm dazumahl den Faden seines Lebens so kurz ausgemessen?—Wer von uns hätte gedacht, dass wir nach drey Wochen um ihn trauern würden?[14]

5th December

Death of Mozart. The *Wiener Zeitung* obituary recognizes the magnitude of music's loss.

Documentation

"The court composer Wolfgang *Mozart* passed away in the night of 4th to 5th of this month. Since his childhood he was famous in all Europe for the rarest of musical talent, attaining the level of the greatest masters by the most fortuitous development of his outstanding natural gifts and by persistent application; witness to this his widely loved and admired works, which give the measure of the irreplaceable loss which the noble art of music suffers through his death."

In der Nacht vom 4. zum 5. d. M. verstarb allhier der K.K.Hofkammerkompositor Wolfgang *Mozart*. Von seiner Kindheit an durch das seltenste musikalische Talent schon in ganz *Europa* bekannt, hatte er durch die glücklichste Entwickelung seiner ausgezeichneten Natursgaben und durch die beharrlichste Verwendung die Stufe der grössten Meister erstiegen; davon zeugen seine allgemein beliebten und bewunderten Werke, und diese geben das Mass des unersetzlichen Verlustes, den die edle Tonkunst durch seinen Tod erleidet.[15]

13th December

The only recorded official engagement of the elector's visit—he performed the christening of the infant Maria Ludovica, attended by the *Wiener Zeitung*'s reporter.

Documentation

"The solemn christening took place yesterday afternoon at 5 o'clock at court in the great front chamber. . . . His Majesty the Elector of Cologne performed the christening. Her Majesty the Empress held the newborn Archduchess, who received the names Maria Ludovica."

Gestern, Nachmittags um 5 Uhr, ist bey Hofe, in dem grossen Vorgemach, die feyerliche Taufhandlung vor sich gegangen . . . . Se Kurfürstl. Durchl. von Köln verrichteten die Taufe. I. Maj. die Kaiserinn, hielten die neugeborne Erzherzoginn, welcher die Nahmen Maria Ludovica beygelegt wurden.[16]

18th December

The elector leaves Vienna, but not, according to *Ephemerides Politico-Litterariae*, before making a donation to Mozart's widow.

Documentation

"Archduke Maximilian, Elector of Cologne, left Vienna on 18th. Before departing he granted the sum of 1,335 royal florins per annum to his former tutor, B. Rottenburg. He gave 24 gold coins to the widow of the very famous musician Mozart."

Archi Dux Maximilianus Elector Coloniensis 18va Vienna discessit. Ante abitum suo olim Institutori B. Rottenburg 1335 R fl. annum solutionem resolvit. Viduae vero celebris Musici Mozart 24 aureos donavit.[17]

28th December

Constanze writes to Simonetti at the Elector's court, offering to have a copy made of *Titus* or *The Magic Flute*, according to his choice.

Documentation

See letter quoted above, on p. 42.

We learn, therefore, from these reports that the elector arrived in Vienna a month before Mozart's death. It was evidently a private and family visit, almost devoid of official business. Within a week he was attending public performances. It is not known what they were, but *The Magic Flute* had been enjoying great popular success in Vienna.

> The acclaim which greeted it ["The Magic Flute"] in Vienna . . . was exceptionally great. It was performed sixty-two times consecutively and never failed to attract a crowd. Theatres in Vienna start at 7 o'clock, but in the first two weeks of *The Magic Flute* performances one had to be there as early as 5 o'clock in order to get a seat, for a little later people were turned away in their hundreds because the house was full. Only by the third week did it become possible, with difficulty, to fight your way to a seat at 6 o'clock.

Der Beyfall, den es ["Die Zauberflöte"] in Wien erhielt war . . . ausserordentlich gross. Zwey und sechzigmal nach einander ward es aufgeführt, und immer blieb der Zulauf derselbe. Um sieben Uhr fangen in Wien die Schauspiele an, doch in den ersten vierzehn Tagen der Vorstellung der Zauberflöte, musste man schon um fünf Uhr seinen Platz suchen, denn etwas später mussten die Menschen zu Hunderten abgewiesen werden, weil das Haus voll war. Erst in der dritten Woche konnte man es so weit bringen, dass man um sechs Uhr mit Mühe ein Plätzchen sich erkämpfte.[18]

With his days so tragically numbered, Mozart was still well enough, as late as 17th November, to leave the house to conduct a performance of his Masonic Cantata K623, eleven days after the elector's arrival. No meeting has been recorded between the two men, but the elector responded to Constanze's financial needs within less than two weeks of her widowhood. Furthermore, her letter offering *Titus* or *The Magic Flute* reads like a continuation, or written confirmation, of a matter already under discussion. Perhaps the twenty-four gold coins represented not just a gift but a down payment on a score. With whom had this discussion taken place—with Constanze, with Mozart, or with both? It would be surprising if the elector's intense musical interest had not drawn him to see *The Magic Flute* and subsequently renew contact with the composer, his admired friend.[19] Is this, therefore, the meaning of Simrock's claim that the elector had acquired his score "from Mozart himself"?

JOHANN JAKOB HAIBEL

Constanze's asking price, 100 ducats, seems to have originated with Mozart. Letters from Johann Jakob Haibel to Baron Wolfgang Heribert von Dalberg, director of the Mannheim Theatre, quoted in Friedrich Walter's *Archiv und Bibliothek des Grossh. Hof- und Nationaltheaters in Mannheim* (1899), reveal something of the early dissemination of the opera.

On 10th December 1791: "Regarding the Egyptian Mysteries, known here under the name of *The Magic Flute*, I have to inform you that I am not yet able to get hold of the opera, since Mr. *Mozart* has died, and while still alive set a price of 100 ducats (500 fl.) on the *score*; I will, however, send *Your Excellency* the libretto." On 29th February 1792 he writes: "I have also to report to *Your Excellency* that *The Magic Flute* is now available, but for a minimum of around twenty ducats." And on 30th March 1792 he sends *The Magic Flute* with the words: "I must only ask *Your Excellency* that, if the *opera The Magic Flute* is to be *copied*, the *copyists* should be forbidden in the strongest terms from copying the *score* secretly and selling it elsewhere, since this would hurt me very much, because the *score* cost me over a hundred ducats to buy, for no-one other than *Your Excellency* possesses it yet."

Am 10. Dez. 1791: "Betreffend die Egyptischen Geheimnisen [*sic*], die unter dem Namen der Zauberflöte hier bekannt sind, muss ich die Ehre haben, zu berichten, dass ich bis itzt die Oper noch nicht erhalten kann, indem H. *Mozart* gestorben und er bey seinen Lebzeiten noch die *Partitur* davon auf 100 Dukaten (500 fl.) angeschlagen, indessen werd ich *Euer Excellenz* das Buch davon überschicken." Am 29. Febr. 1792 schreibt er: "Auch hab ich die Ehre, *Euer Excellenz* zu berichten, das [*sic*] die Zauberflöte dermalen schon zu haben ist, aber nicht leichter als um Zwanzig Ducaten." Und am 30. März 1792 überschickt er die Zauberflöte mit den Worten: "Nur muss ich noch bitten, dass *Euer Excellenz,* wenn die *oper* Die Zauberflöte zum *copiren* gegeben wird denen *copisten* auf das schärfste möchten verbitten lassen, solche *Partitur* etwa heimlich abzuschreiben und anderer Orten zu verkaufen, indem es mir einen grossen Schaden verursachen würde, weil mich die *Partitur* im Ankauf über hundert Dukaten kam, denn noch besitzt sie niemand ausser *Euer Excellenz.*"[20]

Immediately above the quotations from Haibel's letters Walter has listed the prices of the operas known to have been sold by Haibel to von Dalberg during the five years from 1791 to 1796; he points out that the prices are for a copy of the score. At 90 florins, *The Magic Flute* is easily the most expensive, the nearest contender being Wranitzky's *Das Marokkanische Reich*, at 70 florins The original sources used by Walter from the Mannheim Theatre records did not survive the Second World War.

The letter of 10th December 1791 also appears in *W. A. Mozart, Die Dokumentation seines Todes,* published by Dalchow, Duda, and Kerner in 1966 (p. 183). Haibel is misleadingly described by the authors as Mozart's brother-in-law. Sixteen years after the letter was written, he did indeed marry Constanze's sister Sophie. However, his connection with *The Magic Flute* at the time of the letter was not Mozart, but Schikaneder, in whose theatre troupe he was employed as actor, singer, and composer. One infers from this letter, written just five days after Mozart's death and presumably on Schikaneder's authority, that the music of the opera cannot be made available because it has become the property of the deceased's estate. The propriety of this answer is in marked contrast to the well-known story that Schikaneder refused to return the score to Mozart, thus depriving him of the opportunity to make any profit from it, while he himself sold it here, there, and everywhere. The story appears in the biography of Mozart written by Constanze's second husband, Georg Nikolaus Nissen, and published in 1828. But the diligent reader of the *AMZ* will discover that it has merely been copied verbatim from the series Authentic Anecdotes (*Verbürgte Anekdoten*) from Mozart's Life, published thirty years earlier by Breitkopf and Härtel under the editorship of Friedrich Rochlitz.

In his introduction to the series (10th October 1798) Rochlitz claims to have verified the stories personally with Mozart's widow and former close friends. Some of the anecdotes, though not this one, are attributed directly to her. They have long been regarded as suspect, however. Maynard Solomon, in a penetrating article, has reexamined the veracity of the tales, as well as their supposed authentication by Constanze.[21] Constanze was, of course, responsible for the account in Nissen's book, for she herself saw his work through to publication following his death in 1826. However, the task of completing the book was performed not by her but by Johann Heinrich Feuerstein, a man with medical rather than musical qualifications, who may, as Solomon's article suggests, "have been recommended by . . . Breitkopf and Härtel" (p. 52). The use of the Rochlitz anecdotes could have been an expedient—not sanctioned by Nissen—to prepare the book quickly for publication.

It appears, from the evidence of Haibel's letters, that *The Magic Flute* was not made available to von Dalberg until exactly two months after Constanze offered it to Simonetti, the elector's leading tenor. Haibel himself purchased *The Magic Flute* score for "over a hundred ducats." One hundred ducats (500 fl.) was, of course, Mozart's and Constanze's price. Yet he was prepared to sell to von Dalberg for only "around twenty ducats." This would seem to indicate that he bought the autograph and had a copy made for von Dalberg. But was his purchase made from Constanze or from Schikaneder? If from Schikaneder, this would explain not only Constanze's fury against Schikaneder for failing to yield up the score to her, but her need to seek another source for the preparation of the elector's copy.

Haibel's first letter was written on the day of the memorial service for Mozart—held at the Michaelerkirche, Vienna, at Schikaneder's instigation—which included music from the Requiem before its completion by Süssmayr. Schikaneder showed his concern for Constanze's financial situation by arranging a benefit performance of *Die Zauberflöte* for her.[22] Did he perhaps consider that this relieved him of further obligation and he was now entitled to retain Mozart's autograph score?

In any case, Haibel's apparent acquisition of the autograph would have removed it definitively from Constanze's possession. We do not know whether the elector accepted Constanze's terms. He would certainly have been justified in refusing to pay 100 ducats (500 fl.) for a copyist's work.[23]

JOHANN ANTON ANDRÉ

The anecdote referring to Schikaneder's alleged "theft" of *The Magic Flute* score appeared on 7th November 1798. Constanze had just opened negotiations over the sale of her late husband's still unpublished manuscripts, first with Breitkopf and Härtel of Leipzig, then with Johann Anton André of Offenbach. Karl-Heinz Köhler, editor of the 1979 Bärenreiter facsimile edition of *The Magic Flute* autograph score, draws attention, in his introduction, to Constanze's sale of manuscripts to André at the turn of the century, implying that *The Magic Flute* was among them.

> Mozart left 280 manuscripts to his wife Constanze, who however parted with them round about 1800 to the publisher Anton André of Offenbach on the Main for the sum of 1,000 ducats. André's ambitious plans for the publication of Mozart's works were never fully realised, and on his death André's effects went in 1842 to his five sons. . . . The manuscript of "The Magic Flute" went to the oldest of the five sons, Julius André in Frankfurt on the Main, and was still in his possession around 1860.[24]

But nowhere in Constanze's published correspondence with André—nor with Breitkopf—is *The Magic Flute* score on offer.[25] In a more recent publication Köhler goes further, without identifying the source of his information.

> In the meantime the precious autograph of the work lay slumbering in one of Johann Anton André's cupboards virtually untouched for a good four decades, and probably all too rarely would a friend have been allowed to set eyes on it.

> Indes schlummerte die kostbare Urschrift des Werkes reichlich vier Jahrzehnte in einem der Schränke Johann Anton Andrés nahezu unberührt und war wohl allzu selten den Blicken eines Freundes zugänglich.[26]

André did at some time acquire it, for in 1829 he published a remarkable edition of the Overture, showing, by means of black and red ink, Mozart's process of composition (British Library e.57.h and Hirsch IV. 1643). As is clearly evident, even in the facsimile edition, Mozart wrote the string parts and important wind solos in heavy ink, the rest in paler ink, which André represented in red. It may well be true that Schikaneder retained possession of the score, perhaps at first for reference, since the work was being performed almost nightly at his theatre. But its near-perfect condition today suggests it was unlikely ever to have been in regular use as a rehearsal or performance score. Significantly, von Dalberg considered it appropriate to seek to purchase the score from Haibel, a member of Schikaneder's company, rather than from Mozart. The Elector of Cologne's direct dealings with Constanze may well reflect his personal relations with the Mozart family. Von Dalberg, it should be recorded, had in earlier times also had communication with Mozart, who, in a letter of 24th November 1778, offered "to write a Monodrama for 25 louis d'or" ("um 25 louis d'or ein Monodrama zu schreiben"). The work, *Semiramis*, was probably completed but is now lost (see *Dokumente*, 162). His interest in acquiring *The Magic Flute* at such an early stage may have been motivated by the fact that he, too, was a Freemason.[27] The same is true of André, who, as noted by Philippe A. Autexier,

> officiated as venerable master of the lodge Charles-et-Charlotte-à-la-fidélité.

> officiait comme vénérable maître de la loge Charles-et-Charlotte-à-la-fidélité.[28]

After Haibel's death on 24th March 1826, and Nissen's on the same day, the two widowed Weber sisters, Sophie and Constanze, set up house together in Salzburg. They were visited by Vincent and Mary Novello in 1829. Mary Novello reported:

> Madame took us to the grave of Mr. Nissen. . . . By a singular coincidence the husband of the sister who lives with her at present, and who appears very amiable, died the same day as Mr. Nissen, a circumstance which must unite them closer from sympathy.[29]

If Haibel had retained *The Magic Flute* autograph throughout his life, the last twenty years of which were spent in Djakovar (now Dakovo, Croatia), it would have been a logical step for the sisters to offer it to André at this time. There is no evidence to support this theory, but it has the attraction of explaining the gap of nearly three decades that elapsed between André's original purchase of Mozart manuscripts from Constanze and his unique publication of *The Magic Flute* Overture in accordance with Mozart's autograph.

The fact that Constanze reopened correspondence with André on 28th October 1825, after an interval of twenty-two years, makes such speculation less implausible. Writing from Salzburg, she declared: "I had hoped to find all kinds of things with my sister-in-law and in the birthplace of my late husband" (Ich habe hoffen dürfen, bei meiner Schwägerinn und in der Geburtsstadt meines sel. Mannes Allerhand zu finden). The few originals she discovered did indeed belong to Mozart's sister. "The poor 75-year-old lady [she was in fact 74] is, however, blind. She won't part with anything that is original, we will have to wait" (Die arme 75jährige ist aber blind. Was Original ist, giebt sie nicht her, es müsste gewartet werden). The published correspondence between Constanze (often written by Nissen but signed by her) and André continued over the next two years, with more works sent or offered to André. Though *The Magic Flute* is not mentioned, it is indicated in *Briefe* IV (475 and 481), that the surviving correspondence from this period is incomplete.

André wrote a preface to his two-color Overture edition drawing attention to the insights into Mozart's working methods that his edition affords. He does not indicate how or when Mozart's autograph came into his possession, but he writes with the enthusiasm of one who is proud to be able to offer the public something new and unusual. Curiously, the idea may have arisen indirectly from Constanze, who suggested to him, in a letter dated 1st January 1826, that he make an edition of the Requiem

> in two different types, one for Mozart's handwriting, the other for Süssmayr's.

> mit 2 verschiedenen typis herausgeben, die eine für die Mozart'sche, die andere für die Syssmayr'sche Handschrift.[30]

In his Requiem score of 1827 André marks the handwriting changes with the letters M and S, in accordance with the annotated Breitkopf score, which Constanze had sent him as early as 26th January 1801. André's vocal score of the Requiem, published in that year, made no use of the annotations that indicated how much of the Requiem was authentic Mozart, and how much Süssmayr. The reason, as he explained in his preface to the 1827 score, was that the information had been given to him "under the seal of secrecy" (unter dem Siegel des Geheimnisses)—Vorbericht, VI. Since no reason or excuse for delayed publication is given in the preface to the *Zauberflöte* Overture edition of 1829 one may surmise that the *Zauberflöte* autograph was a relatively recent acquisition. If, as suggested, Constanze regained control of the *Zauberflöte* autograph in or around 1826, the moment was opportune to offer it to André. It would then have been out of circulation for about thirty-five years, unavailable to Simrock or anyone else interested in the text of the opera for performance or publication during that time.

André's interest in Mozart's working methods dated back a quarter of a century. In a preface to his 1805 printed edition of Mozart's thematic catalogue for the years 1784–1791, he commented:

> It is very interesting reading his original scores, for one can clearly see in them the initial plan and the further working-out of his ideas.

> Sehr interessant ist es, seine Originalpartituren zu lesen, indem man darin die erste Anlage und weitere Ausführung seiner Ideen am besten einsehen kañ.[31]

Claiming furthermore to own some 250 original manuscripts of works not in Mozart's catalog, he waited, regrettably, until 1841—the year before he died—before publishing a complete list of those in his possession.[32] That list includes *The Magic Flute*, but here too there is no indication when it was acquired. Writing in the 1968–1970 *Mozart-Jahrbuch*, Wolfgang Plath notes that works that were missing or incomplete in the autograph were delivered or completed from whatever copies were available from Constanze or Nissen, first from Vienna, later also from Salzburg.

fehlende oder im Autograph unvollständig vorliegende Werke wurden von Constanze bzw. Nissen erst von Wien, später auch von Salzburg aus soweit wie irgend möglich in Form von anderweitig beschafften Kopien nachgeliefert oder komplettiert.[33]

Plath's article details various manuscript sources used in the compilation of André's 1841 "Verzeichniss," which are now in the Stadt- und Universitäts-bibliothek, Frankfurt am Main. They are found in the Nachlass of Heinrich Henkel (1822–1899), who assisted André in preparing the list for publication. In the earliest of them (Mus Hs 778/2) *The Magic Flute* was entered (on folio 31) by Henkel, not by André. Henkel came to Offenbach in 1839. In a signed preface to the document, Henkel identified those folios in which André's hand is found (and that of his son Julius André) and those he himself contributed. There is no indication when André began to catalog his Mozart autographs. Henkel's preface states only that "this list is the first draft in the process of recording those original manuscripts by W. A. Mozart which Councillor Anton André in Offenbach possessed" (Dieses Verzeichniss ist der erste Entwurf, resp. Aufstellung derjenigen Originalhandschriften von W.A.Mozart welche Hofrath Anton André in Offenbach besass). A further draft was made by Henkel before the list was printed.

The first draft, which includes incipits, contains 218 works to which Köchel numbers can be attributed. But only some 47 of them are referred to, directly or obliquely, in Constanze's published letters to André. From the surviving correspondence it seems that Constanze supplied the material for little more than 20 percent of these works, but the true figure is perhaps higher.

The first page of the *Zauberflöte* autograph shows evidence of various catalog numbering systems. At the top, in duplicate on both left and right side, stands "N.13." crossed out and replaced by "N.11." Below, on the right, is the figure "141," matching the number in André's 1805 printed edition of Mozart's thematic catalog (but not in the catalog itself, where a penciled numbering system in an unknown hand, not Mozart's, introduces an inaccuracy of one by the inadvertent repetition of no. 30). Near the bottom of the page stands "46," the number in André's 1841 "Verzeichniss" under the classification "B. Opern und TheaterMusik." The words "Mozarts eigne Handschrift" appear at the top of the page in a hand seen on innumerable Mozart autographs and widely acknowledged to be Nissen's. The autograph must therefore have been seen by him. The question is, when? A reasonable guess would be after Haibel married Sophie Weber in 1807, though probably not during the decade following 1810, when Constanze and Nissen were living in Copenhagen. From the facsimile reproductions available in the NMA one discovers that the autograph of *Così fan tutte* was at first numbered 18, but this was subsequently crossed out and replaced by 16; *la Clemenza di Tito* was given the number 20, later crossed out and replaced by 18. *Die Zauberflöte*, sandwiched between them in order of composition, ought therefore to be 19, crossed out and replaced by 17. But these numbers appear on the autograph of *Der Schauspieldirektor*, completed a few months before *Figaro*, in 1786. There cannot have been any doubt about the true chronology of Mozart's late operas in the immediate years after Mozart's death, especially as they are listed in Mozart's own *Verzeichnüss aller meiner Werke* (1784–1791). It seems likely that the *Zauberflöte* autograph was numbered at a different time from its immediate neighbors, with the numbering perhaps reflecting the chronology of the currently available autograph manuscripts. All the above autographs carry Nissen's handwritten authentication on the title page. In the Henkel numbering (first draft) *Die Zauberflöte* appears where its chronology requires, as number 17, between *Così* (16) and *la Clemenza* (18). In his list number 11 is given not to *Die Zauberflöte* but to the *Idomeneo* ballet music. *Der Schauspieldirektor* receives number 14.

These figures have something to tell us about the early cataloging history and ownership of Mozart's autographs, but their interpretation is by no means straightforward. In her correspondence with Breitkopf and Härtel, Constanze refers to a "Verzeichniss" she sent on 25th March 1799,[34] but her letter is lost. A discrepancy of two in the numbering system is also seen in a letter to Breitkopf of 11th November 1799, in which she writes of

> your no. 6, which is no. 8 in my numbering.

> Ihr N.6., welches bey mir N.8 hat.[35]

Constanze and Breitkopf must therefore at first have applied themselves separately to the task of cataloging Mozart's compositions. Three days earlier she entered into a contract with André, offering him, among other works, Mozart's string quartets and quintets. Again, using readily available facsimile reproductions (NMA and British Library Music Facsimiles), it emerges that Constanze's numberings of all ten of Mozart's last quartets, 28 to 37 on her list, are matched by the numberings on the autographs. The same is true of the three quintets that can be checked in this way: K406, K515, and K614. But here the original autograph numberings have been crossed out and raised by a factor of one. This is seen, too, in the autograph of the string quartet K499. In her letter to André of 8th November 1799 Constanze uses the corrected numbers, which suggests that the alterations were by then already in place. Among the late quartets and quintets, the only one to be included in André's 1841 printed Verzeichnis of the manuscripts in his possession is the quintet K515. It is cataloged as number 185, and this number is written at the bottom of the first page of the autograph. The ten late string quartet autographs were sold by André to Johann Andreas Stumpff "some time after 1810," according to Alan Tyson's introduction to the British Library facsimile edition.[36]

Yet another numbering system makes an appearance in three of the string quartet autographs. K387, K421, and K428 are given numbers 175, 176, and 177, respectively, which is of particular interest because in Mozart's autograph they are called Quartetto I, II, and IV. Constanze's list preserves this order, with 28, 29, and 31, respectively. But IV (K428) was composed more than a year before III (K458 "The Hunt"), and the additional numbering system therefore reflects the correct chronology. The six "Haydn" quartets, to which they belong, were published as early as 1785 by Artaria as Opera X, with K458 before K428. The same order and opus number are seen in *The Breitkopf Thematic Catalogue, 1762–1787.*[37]

A further matching of numbers can be observed in some of the early opera autograph facsimiles in the NMA; this time they conform with Henkel's "first draft" list. They are as follows—*Apollo et Hyacinthus* 172, *Bastien und Bastienne* 141, *Ascanio in Alba* 173, *Il Sogno di Scipione* 142, and *Il Ré Pastore* 200. These numbers differ from André's 1841 printed Verzeichnis. André used opus numbers for some of his Mozart publications, which were adopted by Constanze in her communications with him. Nissen's *Biographie W. A. Mozart's* (1828) has a supplement that includes four lists of Mozart's works (Anhang 3–23). They start with Leopold Mozart's catalog of his son's compositions up to the age of twelve (see also *Briefe* I, 287–89), continue with Mozart's own thematic catalog for the years 1784–1791, followed by a catalog of the fragments and, finally, a catalog of the remaining completed works. It would probably be fair to say that these numbering systems at present raise more questions than they solve. They merit wider investigation, but that lies outside the scope of this *Zauberflöte* study.

Though Nissen himself authenticated the *Zauberflöte* autograph, one can only speculate when this might have occurred and whether the manuscript was relinquished at some time by Haibel or whether it passed to Constanze via her sister Sophie after his death, as suggested above. Cordial relations must certainly have existed between the Haibels and the Nissens, judging from the opening paragraph of Sophie's well-known letter to her brother-in-law and sister of 7th April 1825, containing a moving account of Mozart's final illness. André at first employed Franz Gleissner to help cataloging the Mozart Nachlass (around 1800), but no *Zauberflöte* entry can be expected here since Gleissner left off essentially where Mozart's own Verzeichnis (1784–1791) began.[38]

On 29th March 1800 Constanze sent André a memorandum asking for a list of all the Mozart autographs he had acquired from her.

> NB.NB.NB.NB. Hr. André has acquired all my catalogs and has promised me in return a complete thematic catalog of all Mozart's works. The sooner the better, as I could use it.—In the meantime I would be happy if Hr. André would at least send me *immediately* either all my (former) thematic catalogs, or, in addition, detailed notification of each and every composition *with keys* that he has received from me *in the original*, arranged by type, containing in particular all *major* works and indicating the number of acts and the number of pages. I might perhaps put a detailed announcement about it in an esteemed and well-read journal, which would lend honor, respect, and merit to his edition.

> NB.NB.NB.NB. Hr. André hat alle meine Verzeichnisse bekommen, und mir dagegen ein ganz vollständiges thematisches Verzeichniss aller Werke Mozarts versprochen. Ich könnte dieses, je eher je lieber, brauchen.—Indessen wollte ich schon froh seyn, wenn Hr. André mir *itzt gleich* entweder meine (gewesenen) thematischen Verzeichnisse alle oder auch eine blosse specielle Anzeige einer jeder Composition *mit der Tonart*, welche er *im Original* von mir bekommen hat, nach den Fächern eingerichtet, senden wollte, worin auch alle *grossen* Werke namentlich mit der Anzahl ihrer Acte und der bogenzahl angeführt wäre. Ich werde vielleicht darüber in einem sehr geschäzten und gelesenen Journale eine detaillirte Anzeige machen, die seiner Ausgabe Ehre, Respect und Vorzug verschaffen kann.[39]

Later that year, on 4th October 1800, Constanze again raised the matter with André.

> What is your intention with regard to the thematic Catalog? Do you want to publish a catalog of only the original manuscripts you purchased from me? I imagine that is the case, since you say:
>   "as closely as I can accomplish it by means of the estate which I bought."
>   But according to your letters to me it is to be a catalog of all those works known to you. That would be preferable to me and altogether more interesting for the general public. *It would then be up to you* to indicate by an x or some other sign which of the works you possess in the original.

> Was ist Ihr Zwek in Ansehung des thematischen Catalogs? Wollen Sie nur das Verzeichniss aller Sachen herausgeben, die Sie von mir im Original gekauft haben? Das müsste ich fast glauben, weil Sie sagen:
>   "so gut ich ihn durch den an mich gekauften Nachlass besorgen kann."

Nach ihren briefen [*sic*] an mich soll es aber das Verzeichniss aller Ihnen bekannten Sachen seyn. dies [*sic*] ist mir auch lieber und überhaupt für das Publicum interessanter. *Es steht dann auch bey Ihrem Gutbefinden,* durch ein x oder andres Zeichen anzumerken jedes Stük, das Sie im Original besizen.[40]

Constanze's instinctive foresight for the requirements of future musicologists was on this occasion stronger than André's. After further attempts (*Briefe* IV, 381, 11th October–12th November 1800; 417–18, 3rd April 1802; 423–24, 16th July 1802; 430, 13th January 1803), she gave up. Twenty-four years later, on 3rd November 1827, eager to prepare Nissen's *Biographie W. A. Mozart's* for posthumous publication, she tried again.

[A]nd now I would like to take the liberty of asking you to send me the catalog which you yourself so kindly promised me and to which I have looked forward for so long with such great longing; I need it most urgently to finish off the Biography.

[U]nd nun bin ich so freu [*sic*] Sie zu bitten, mir den Catalog den Sie selbst so gütig waren mir zu versprechen und dem ich mit so grosser sehntsuch [*sic*] so lange entgegen sehe mir zu Schicken; indem ich ihn zur Verferdigung der Biographie sehr Nothwendig brauche.[41]

It was another six years before André completed his *Thematisches Verzeichniss W. A. Mozartscher Manuskripte, chronologisch geordnet von 1764–1784,* which remained in manuscript. Constanze died in 1842, exactly one month before André. They therefore both lived to see the printed 1841 *Thematisches Verzeichniss derjenigen Original-Handschriften von W. A. Mozart, welche Hofrath André in Offenbach besitzt,* but, poignantly, it was to be a sale catalog in anticipation of his death. Unfortunately it shows neither the source nor date of acquisition of Mozart's compositions. Details of the distribution of André's Mozart autographs between his sons are given in Wolfgang Rehm, *Mozarts Nachlass und die Andrés. Dokumente zur Verteilung und Verlosung von 1854. Musikverlag Johann André* (Offenbach am Main, 1999). It lists all the works, with their numbers, appearing in the 1841 Verzeichnis (see 45–64), and includes the ownership history of every manuscript from 1854 until 1999. Dokument II/Seite I (see 16, 24–25) reveals the prices asked for individual works. Among the more expensive operas are *Die Zauberflöte* (250 Carolin), followed by *Idomeneo* and *Così* (150 each), and, in the bargain basement, *La Clemenza di Tito* at 40 Carolin. But *Don Giovanni* leads the field with 350 Carolin (see 12).

André was open to higher bids, but not lower ones, as he makes clear in his preface (Vorbericht) to the 1841 "Verzeichniss." It shows the motivation behind the catalog and demonstrates his desire for the greatest possible accuracy. The Vorbericht is given here complete.

In response to the widely expressed wishes of Mozart's devoted admirers the owner of the immortal composer's *Original Manuscripts* shown in the present catalog has finally decided to offer them for sale. Consequently he has divided these manuscripts into categories, with groups of works in each category organized chronologically, and in this last regard has used the thematic catalog written in Mozart's own hand, as well as reproducing word for word the remarks found on most of these manuscripts, whenever they stem from Mozart or his father.

The owner (Councilor André) has set a price, either for the whole collection or for any individual work, which is very modest relative to the value of a *Mozart manuscript*, but below which he will not sell; on the other hand anyone who puts in the highest bid before 31st December of the current year can purchase either the whole collection or a single manuscript of his choice. All those who wish to avail themselves of a free printed copy of the above-mentioned price list should send a postage-paid letter to the music shop of *Johann André. Offenbach a. M., 1st May 1841.*

Den vielseitig geäusserten Wünschen der Verehrer Mozart's endlich zu entsprechen, hat sich der Besitzer der in gegenwärtigem Catalog verzeichneten *Original-Handschriften* des unsterblichen Tondichters zu deren Verkauf entschlossen. Er hat daher diese Manuscripte in Classen abgetheilt und sämmtliche Werke einer jeden Classe chronologisch geordnet, und in letzterer Beziehung den von Mozart eigenhändig geschriebenen thematischen Catalog, sowie auch die auf den meisten dieser Manuscripte befindlichen Bemerkungen hierzu benutzt, und diese Bemerkungen selbst, soweit solche von Mozart oder von seinem Vater herrühren, wörtlich mit abdrucken lassen.

Der Besitzer (Hofr. André) hat nun sowohl für die ganze Sammlung, als für jedes einzelne Werk einen bestimmten, und im Verhältniss zu dem hohen Kunstwerthe eines *Mozart'schen Manuscriptes* sehr mässigen Preis festgesetzt. unter welchem aber auch keines derselben abgegeben wird; dagegen jedermann, welcher bis zum 31. December 1. J. das höchste Mehrgebot thut, entweder die ganze Sammlung oder das zu bezeichnende einzelne Manuscript käuflich beziehen kann. Von dieser erwähnten Preisansetzung steht allen denjenigen ein gedrucktes Exemplar gratis zu Diensten, welche sich dessfalls in portofreien Briefen an die Musikalien-Handlung von *Johann André* dahier wenden wollen. *Offenbach a. M. den 1. Mai 1841.*[42]

André also supplied an incipit to every work, a necessity before the existence of the Köchel catalog. The layout of his Verzeichnis and the kind of detail he included are shown in photo 7.

As we have seen, Constanze's failure to persuade André to catalog in detail the acquisition of his Mozart manuscripts has left gaps in our knowledge today. Wolfgang Plath has summed up the situation as follows:

> It remains no easier to understand why none of the known Mozart catalogues from the house of André (Gleissner-Verzeichnis with Commentary, Gleissner-André-Verzeichnis, manuscript André-Verzeichnis 1833, printed André-Verzeichnis 1841)—and, furthermore, none of the newly presented catalogs that follow here—catalog the Mozart-Nachlass as it stood when it was originally acquired. From the very beginning the work was in part imprecise and summary, but later it was in part characterized by the familiar effort to separate the authentic from the unauthentic, the important from the unimportant.

> Weniger leicht verständlich bleibt, dass keines der bisher bekannt gewordenen Mozart-Verzeichnisse des Hauses André (Gleissner-Verzeichnis nebst Kommentar, Gleissner-André-Verzeichnis, handschriftliches André-Verzeichnis 1833, gedrucktes André-Verzeichnis 1841)—und übrigens auch keines der hier im folgenden neu vorzustellenden Verzechnisse—den ursprünglich erworbenen Mozart-Nachlass in seinem faktischen Bestand katalogisiert. Von Anfang an ist teils ungenau und summarisch, teils späterhin mit dem erkennbaren Bestreben gearbeitet worden, Echtes von Unechtem, Wichtiges von Unwichtigem zu trennen.[43]

In his *Grove* article on André, Plath acknowledges André's pioneering groundwork in Mozart scholarship, declaring that he "deserves to be called 'the father of Mozart research.'" But Ignaz Moscheles, who visited André in 1823 "in order to feast on Mozart manuscripts" (um in Mozart'schen Manuscripten zu schwelgen) found André's appreciation of Mozart seriously wanting, in one respect at least.

> I, who revere every note of Mozart, who consider him the greatest musical genius, how should I respond to Councilor André's assertion that Mozart didn't understand declamation at all, since words that have the opposite meaning from his opera texts would fit his music just as well as those which he set! This accusation seemed to me not even worth defending—I held my tongue!

> Was sollte ich, der ich jede Note von Mozart verehre, der ich ihn für das grösste Musikgenie halte, aber dazu sagen, dass der Hofrath André behauptete, Mozart habe die Declamation durchaus nicht verstanden, da Worte, die den entgegengesetzten Sinn seiner Operntexte hätten, ebenso gut unter seine Musik, als die von ihm componierten passen würden! Diese Beschuldigung schien mir keiner Vertheidigung würdig—ich schwieg![44]

EMANUEL SCHIKANEDER

By late 1798, with plans in hand to make a great deal of money from her late husband's works, Constanze's frustration with Schikaneder seems to have led her to resort to a public denunciation. Evidently the benefit performance of *The Magic Flute* that Schikaneder organized for her at the end of 1791 had not been enough. We do not, however, know the whole truth about Mozart's business arrangements with Schikaneder, for the story that has been generally accepted cannot be independently corroborated. This is how it originally appeared in the *AMZ*.

A certain theatre director, who deserves, really, to be identified by name—fell upon hard times, partly through his own fault, partly through lack of public support. In some despair he came to Mozart and explained his circumstances, determined that only he could save him.

"I?—How so?"—

"Write me an opera that will appeal to the public taste of today; you can also make it for connoisseurs and to the satisfaction of your own reputation, but have in mind especially the ordinary people of all classes. I will look after the libretto, stage designs etc., everything according to requirements"—

"Fine—I'll take it on!"

"What payment do you ask?"

"You're destitute! Right—we'll do it like this, so that it helps you and I get a little profit too. I will give you simply and solely my score; give me what you like for it: but on condition that you personally guarantee that no copies are made of it. If the opera is a success I will sell it elsewhere, and that will be my payment"—

Delighted, the theatre director gave his word of honor. Mozart worked hard, honestly, and according to the man's wishes. The opera was given; audiences poured in, its fame spread throughout Germany, and after only a few weeks it was performed in foreign theatres, even though not a single person had received a score from Mozart!—

Ein gewisser Schauspieldirektor, der allerdings genannt zu werden verdiente— war, theils durch eigene Schuld, theils durch Mangel an Unterstützung des Publikums, ganz heruntergekommen. Halb verzweifelnd kam er zu Mozart, erzählte seine Umstände und beschloss damit, dass nur Er ihn retten könnte.

"Ich?—Womit?"—

"Schreiben Sie eine Oper für mich, ganz im Geschmack des heutgen—er [*sic*] Publikums; Sie können dabei den Kennern und Ihrem Ruhme immer auch das Ihrige geben, aber sorgen Sie vornehmlich auch für die niedrigern Menschen aller Stände. Ich will Ihnen den Text besorgen, will Dekorationen schaffen u.s.w., alles, wie man's jetzt haben will"—

"Gut—ich will's übernehmen!"

"Was verlangen Sie zum Honorarium?"

"Sie haben ja nichts! Nun—wir wollen die Sache so machen, damit Ihnen geholfen und mir doch auch nicht aller Nutzen entzogen werde. Ich gebe Ihnen einzig und allein meine Partitur; geben Sie mir dafür was Sie wollen: aber unter der Bedingungen, dass Sie mir dafür stehen, dass sie nicht abgeschrieben werde. Macht die Oper Aufsehen, so verkaufe ich sie an andere Direktionen, und das soll meine Bezahlung seyn"—

Der Herr Theaterdirekteur schloss den Vertrag mit Entzücken und heiligen Betheuerungen. Mozart schrieb emsig, schrieb brav und ganz nach dem Willen des Mannes. Man gab die Oper; der Zulauf war gross, ihr Ruf flog in Deutschland umher, und nach wenigen Wochen gab man sie schon auf auswärtigen Theatern, ohne dass ein einziges die Partitur von Mozarten erhalten hätte!—[45]

The same year, 1798, saw Schikaneder's attempt to repeat the success of *The Magic Flute* with a sequel to the opera, entitled *Das Labyrinth, oder der Kampf mit den Elementen*, with music by Peter Winter. This must have been a thorn in Constanze's flesh, for, at the time of her courtship with Mozart, Winter had been responsible for creating a scandal by spreading malicious rumors and gossiping to her guardian about her association with Mozart. Forced, eventually, to sign a document declaring his intention to marry her within three years, Mozart was obliged to defend himself in a letter to his father dated 22nd December 1781.

Certain impertinent busybodies, such as Herr Winter, must have shouted all sorts of stories about me into the ears of this person |: who doesn't know me at all :|—that one should beware of me—that I have nothing secure behind me—that I have an intimate relationship with her—that I would perhaps abandon her—leaving the girl in a wretched position etc.

diesem |: der mich gar nicht kennt :| müssen so dienstfertige und Naseweisse herrn wie H: Winter und ihrer mehrere allerhand dinge von mir in die ohren geschrien haben—dass man sich mit mir in acht nehmen müsse—dass ich nichts gewisses hätte—dass ich starken umgang mit ihr hätte—dass ich sie vieleicht [*sic*] sitzen lassen würde—und das Mädchen hernach unglücklich wäre etc.[46]

Mozart reports in the letter that Constanze herself tore up the insulting document. Even with the passage of years her feelings toward Winter cannot have been warm, nor would she have been delighted with Schikaneder for his tactless choice of composer for the second part of *The Magic Flute*. Against this background comes the accusation of betrayal in the *AMZ*, reinforced the following month by further comment.

He [Mozart] did not allow himself to be bothered by ingratitude; he was hardly put out more than a few minutes by it. When he learned of the treachery of

that theatre director whom I mentioned in No. 11, all he said was: "the scoun-
drel!"—and with that it was forgotten.

Durch Undankbarkeit liess er sich darin nicht stören; Als er die Betrügerey jenes
Theaterdirektors, den ich unter No. 11 habe auftreten lassen, erfuhr, war alles,
was er sagte: "Der Lump!"—und damit war es vergessen.[47]

Schikaneder is, of course, not named, but no one can have been in doubt
about his identity. Was it mere coincidence that Schikaneder's vilification
should have taken place in the pages of the *AMZ*, published in Leipzig by
the same firm—Breitkopf und Härtel—that had just set its sights on the acquisition of Constanze's Mozart manuscripts? Schikaneder and Haibel were
at this time still in collaboration at the Freihaus-Theater auf der Wieden in
Vienna; was the purpose to put pressure on them to yield up *The Magic
Flute* manuscript?

Though Haibel had doubtless wished to sell more copies than just the one
bought by von Dalberg, the alleged immediate burgeoning of performances
all over Germany and abroad has not been recorded by history. According
to the listings in the 1978 edition of Alfred Loewenberg's *Annals of Opera*,
more than a year elapsed between the Viennese premiere of 30th September
1791 and its successor, a Prague production opening on 25th October 1792.
That year also saw a concert performance in Zittau. In January 1793 the
opera reached Augsburg, Leipzig, and Passau, followed in March and May
by performances in Budapest and Graz respectively. In June it was given in
Brünn (the present-day Brno, Czech Republic) and, thanks to Constanze's
cooperation, Bad Godesberg, near Bonn, in the presence of the Elector of
Cologne. In Maynard Solomon's article entitled "The Rochlitz Anecdotes"
(1991),[48] the list of early *Zauberflöte* performances is different. The first one
outside Vienna is given as Lemberg (September 1792), followed by Prague
(25th October 1792). All the others mentioned above are omitted. By 1794
the legendary popularity of *The Magic Flute* was well established. As a contemporary writer waggishly observed:

Never has a product of the theatre had more widespread success in any nation
than Mozarts immortal work *The Magic Flute*. England and France, of course,
had two no less well-known works in their time, the former the famous *Beggar's
Opera* . . . and the latter Beaumarchais' *Marriage of Figaro* . . . nevertheless I
certainly doubt whether either work made such a universal sensation in its own
country, and was produced, fashioned, trimmed, used and misused, arranged,
moulded, parodied, imitated and disfigured in such countless ways as Mozart's
Magic Flute in Germany. For the last few years it has been given ceaselessly on
every stage and stall which could muster just one and a half voices, a couple of
fiddles, a curtain, and six changes of scenery; it has drawn audiences from miles

around, as the magic drum of a shaman draws the sable, and has filled theatre tills. For our music engravers and music dealers it has been a veritable goldmine of Potosi; for it has been printed and hand-copied in all music businesses, partly complete, partly broken up into single arias and fragments in piano reduction, with or without vocal parts, arranged as variations and parodies, and available at all fairs and markets. It has given bread and livelihood to our town pipers, Prague [i.e., Bohemian] musicians, ballad singers, and marmot boys [a marmot was probably a cheap alternative to a monkey on a string], for at all fairs, in spas, gardens, coffeehouses, inns, masquerades, and serenades boasting just one fiddle, one hears nothing but *The Magic Flute*; yes, it has even been transplanted onto all the barrels of the barrel-organ and onto the magic lantern. It lies on all the pianos of our tinkling, young beginners, has given our lads, large and small, Papageno-pipes, and our lovely lasses new fashions, hairstyles and headbands, muffs and work bags *à la Papagena* . . . in short a universal commotion, activity, indecent greed, and profit in Germany. An object that can bring this about in a whole nation must be considered indeed among the most effective of the fermentations dropped by the goddess of fashion from time to time into the long-slumbering brain matter of poor mortals to get it going again and prevent it from sinking into total flabbiness.

Nie hat ein dramatisches Product bey irgend einer Nation ein allgemeineres Glück gemacht als Mozarts unsterbliches Werk, die *Zauberflote* [*sic*]. England und Frankreich hatte zwar zwey nicht minder zu ihrer Zeit berühmte Stücke, jenes seine Famose *Beggars Opera* . . . dieses aber Beaumarchais *Mariage de Figaro* . . . indessen zweifle ich doch dass beyde Stücke so allgemeine Sensation bey ihren Nationen gemacht, und auch so unzähliche Art produzirt, geformt, gestutzt, gebraucht und gemissbraucht, bearbeitet, gemodelt, parodirt, nachgeahmt, und verhunzt worden sind, als Mozarts *Zauberflöte* in Teutschland. Sie ist nun schon seit einem paar Jahren daher auf allen Bühnen und Buden, wo es nur noch anderthalb Kehlen, ein Paar Geigen, einen Vorhang und sechs Coulissen gab, unaufhörlich gegeben worden, hat die Zuschauer viele Meilen weit in die Runde, wie die Zaubertrommel eines Schamanen die Zobel, an sich gezogen und die Theater-Cassen gefüllt. Für unsere Notenstecher und Musikhändler war sie eine wahre Goldgrube von Potosi; denn sie ist in allen Noten-Offizinen theils ganz, theils *en hachis* in einzelnen Arien und Fragmenten im Clavier-Auszuge, mit oder ohne Gesang, variirt und parodirt, gestochen und geschrieben herausgekommen und auf allen Messen und Jahrmärckten zu haben. Unsern Stadpfeifern, Prager-Musikanten, Bänkelsängern, und Marmotten-Buben, hat sie Brod und Verdienst gegeben, denn auf allen Messen, in Bädern, Gärten, Caffeehäusern, Gasthöfen, Redouten und Ständchen, wo nur eine Geige klingt, hört man nichts als *Zauberflöte*, ja sie ist sogar auf alle Walzen der Dreh-Orgel und Laterne-Magique verpflanzt worden. Sie liegt auf allen Klavieren unsrer lernenden und klimpernden Jugend; hat unsren grossen und kleinen Buben Papageno-Pfeifchen, und unsern Schönen neue Moden, Coeffüren [*sic*] und Stirnbänder, Müffe und Arbeitsbeutel *à la Papagena* gegeben . . . kurz eine

allgemeine Bewegung, Thätigkeit, Lüsternheit und Genuss in Teutschland her-
vorgebracht. Wenn ein Gegenstand dies bey einer ganzen Nation bewürket, so
kann man ihn gewiss für eins der würksamsten Gährungsmittel halten, das die
Göttin-Mode zuweilen in den langeruhenden Stoff der Gehirnmasse der armen
Sterblichen tröpfelt, um ihn einmal wieder in Bewegung zu setzen, und ihn nicht
in eine gänzliche Atonie versinken zu lassen.[49]

If this report seems a little exaggerated, a second opinion, dating from the
same year, confirms the essential facts on which it is based.

In this year of 1794 nothing can or may be sung and played or listened to with
approval that doesn't carry the all-powerful, magic name of Mozart on its brow.
Operas, symphonies, quartets, trios, duets, piano pieces, songs, even *dances*,
everything that lays claim to general approval must be by Mozart. The musical presses have, for their part, omitted nothing in their effort to satisfy these
whims of amateurs. Through the great art of *arranging* we already possess
this composer's *Magic Flute* printed and engraved in all the above-mentioned
forms. Heaven knows how strangely many of these attempts have turned out,
and especially on account of the nature of this piece, had to turn out. It suffices
that one is playing or singing *Mozart*, and what's more, from his *Magic Flute*.
. . . Piano reductions of *Mozart's* Magic Flute in Maynz, Mannheim, Offenbach,
Leipzig, Berlin, and Braunschweig, published six times in one and the same
year, a hitherto unprecedented phenomenon in the history of musical literature,
adequately justifying what was said above about the general enthusiasm for
Mozart's work.

In diesem 1794sten Jahre kann und darf nun nichts gesungen und gespielt und
nichts mit Beifall angehört werden, als was den allgewaltigen Zaubernamen
Mozart, an der Stirn führt. *Opern, Sinfonien, Quartetten, Trios, Duetten, Klavi-
ersachen, Lieder*, sogar *Tänze*, alles muss von Mozart seyn, wenn es Anspruch
auf allgemeinen Beifall machen soll. Auch haben die Notenpressen an ihrer
Seite nichts unterlassen, diese Grillen der Dilettanten zu befriedigen. Vermittels
der grossen Kunst des *Arrangirens*, besitzen wir bereits *die Zauberflöte* dieses
Komponisten in allen oben genannten Formen gedruckt und gestochen. Der
Himmel weiss, wie abenteuerlich manche dieser Versuche ausgefallen sind,
und wegen der Natur dieses Stückes insbesondere, ausfallen mussten. Genug,
man spielt oder singt von *Mozarten*, und was noch mehr, aus seiner *Zauberflöte*.
. . . *Mozarts Zauberflöte* im Klavierauszuge, in Maynz, Mannheim, Offenbach,
Leipzig, Berlin und Braunschweig: Also sechsmal in einem und dem nemlichen
Jahre aufgelegt: eine bis itzo in der musikalischen Literaturgeschichte beispiel-
lose Erscheinung, welche dasjenige hinlänglich rechtfertiget, was oben von dem
allgemeinen Enthusiasmus für *Mozarts* Arbeit gesagt worden ist.[50]

The first Mannheim performance took place on 29th March 1794, using the
Vulpius libretto from the Weimar production of two months earlier. Accord-

ing to Friedrich Walter, this had been inserted in many places over the text in the theatre's archive copy.[51] There is no evidence to support the insinuation that Schikaneder was profiteering within Mozart's lifetime from the autograph score, though there may have been disagreements over ownership between him and Constanze after Mozart's death. Schikaneder himself lived on until 1812. Another possible, though less likely, scenario is that Haibel's business activities were undertaken not on his own behalf but on behalf of Schikaneder's company. In that event the score of *The Magic Flute* could only have been bought from Constanze, and her later machinations against Schikaneder would have been without foundation.

When Constanze's copyist sat down to make a score for the Elector of Cologne, it was clearly not Mozart's autograph that she put before him. What alternative source may have been available to her? Was Constanze herself aware that it differed from Mozart's own autograph text and the printed Alberti libretto? Above all, how did it come to surface in the first full-score edition of 1814? It will be helpful to follow Constanze's manuscript to the electoral court and try to reconstruct the events leading to its publication by Simrock.

NOTES

1. Robert Schumann, ed., *Neue Zeitschrift für Musik*, Leipzig, 17th December 1839. Band 11, No. 49, 195.

2. *Magazin der Musik*, ed. C. F. Cramer. Report from Bonn, 8th April 1787. Jahrgang 2, Band 2, 1385–86. British Library P.P. 1945. ap. Reproduced in Irmgard Leux, *Christian Gottlob Neefe (1748–1798). Mit zwei Bildnissen und einer Handschrift-Nachbildung. Veröffentlichungen des Fürstlichen Institutes für musikwissenschaftliche Forschung zu Bückeburg. Fünfte Reihe. Stilkritische Studien.* Zweiter Band. (Leipzig, 1925), 92. British Library M.G. 1400. London University Warburg Institute DBE 90.

3. Walther Engelhardt, "Christian Gottlob Neefens Lebenslauf von ihm selbst beschrieben Nebst beigefügtem Karackter 1789." See *Beiträge zur Rheinischen Musikgeschichte.* Heft 21. (1957), 22.

4. *Theater-Kalender auf das Jahr 1791.* Gotha, 13–14. Both the above quotations also appear in Walther Engelhardt, "Die Kieler Handschrift der Autobiographie Christian Gottlob Neefes 1748–1798." *Zeitschrift für Musikwissenschaft, herausgegeben von der Deutschen Musikgesellschaft.* Heft 8. Jahrgang VII. Mai 1925, 471, n7, and 472.

5. *Briefe* IV (1963), 177–78.

6. Ibid. VII (1975), 607.

7. *Mozart en France,* Bibliothèque Nationale, Paris, 1956 (no. 176, 51)—"Lettre de Constance Mozart au ténor italien Luigi Simonetti, Vienne, 28 octobre [*sic*, recte décembre] 1791.- Ms. autogr.- Paris, Collection Roger de Garate."

8. *Ephemerides Politico-Litterariae.* Pest. 11th November 1791, 291 and 15th November 1791, 299. Országos Széchényi Könyvtár FM3/8111.

9. *Wiener Zeitung.* 9th November 1791. No. 90, 2864.

10. Zinzendorf's Diary. 6th November 1791. Quoted in *Dokumente.* Joseph Heinz Eibl, *Addenda und Corrigenda* (1978), 72.

11. *Ephemerides Politico-Litterariae.* Pest. 18th November 1791, 309.

12. *Das Wienerblättchen*, Vienna 26th November 1791. Quoted in Cliff Eisen, *New Mozart Documents. A Supplement to O.E.Deutsch's Documentary Biography* 71, no. 112 (1991). This source, discovered by Dexter Edge, corrects the date 18th November given by Deutsch.

13. *Wiener Zeitung.* 25th January 1792. No. 7, 217. Quoted in *Dokumente*, 385–86.

14. Masonic oration on Mozart's death (Alberti, 1792). Quoted in *Dokumente*, 392.

15. *Wiener Zeitung.* 7th December 1791. No. 98, 3122. Quoted in *Dokumente*, 369.

16. Ibid. 14th December 1791. No. 100, 3185.

17. *Ephemerides Politico-Litterariae.* Pest. 30th December 1791, 394.

18. From *Geheime Geschichte des Verschwörungssytems der Jakobiner in den Österreichischen Staaten. Für Wahrheitsfreunde* (London, 1795), 47f. Quoted in *Dokumente*, 415.

19. It may not be altogether irrelevant to note, in this context, that ten years later the elector's presence was recorded by Zinzendorf at the first performance of Haydn's *The Seasons.* See H. C. Robbins Landon, *Haydn. Chronicle and Works. The Late Years 1801–1809* (1977), 42.

20. Friedrich Walter, *Archiv und Bibliothek des Grossh. Hof- und Nationaltheaters in Mannheim* (1899), Bd. I, 460, n1. British Library 011907.e.2.

21. Maynard Solomon, "The Rochlitz Anecdotes: Issues of Authenticity in Early Mozart Biography." *Mozart Studies* ed. Cliff Eisen (Oxford, 1991), 1–59.

22. See p. 157. See also Christoph Wolff, *Mozart's Requiem* (Oxford, 1994), 120–21. Benefit performances were given by Schikaneder in 1791 and 1792 for Gerl and Schack, joint composers of *Die Wienerzeitung* and *Das Schlaraffenland*. Josepha Hofer (the first Queen of Night and Mozart's sister-in-law) was included as a beneficiary. See Heinz Schuler, "Das 'Zauberflöte'—Ensemble des Jahres 1791: Biographische Miszellen," *Mitteilungen der ISM* (1991): vol. 39, 118.

23. We may gain some idea of its purchasing power in Vienna from a letter Haydn sent to the Elector of Cologne on 23rd November 1793, requesting further financial support for his pupil Beethoven. "100 ducats were allotted to him for the past year. Your Electoral Highness will be well aware that this sum was insufficient, even just for living expenses" (Für das verflossene Jahr waren ihm 100 # angewiesen. Dass diese Summe nicht hinreichend war, auch nur um bloss zu leben, daran sind Eure Churfürstliche Durchlaucht wohl selbst überzeugt). "Neues zu Beethovens Lehrjahr bei Haydn. Fritz von Reinöhl." *Neues Beethoven-Jahrbuch*, ed. Adolf Sandberger. Vierter Jahrgang. Augsburg (1930, reprinted 1980), 45. See also H. C. Robbins Landon, *The Collected Correspondence and London Notebooks of Joseph Haydn* (1959), 142.

24. Karl-Heinz Köhler, *Documenta Musicologica. Zweite Reihe: Handschriften-Faksimiles VII. Mozart, Die Zauberflöte.* Beiheft zur Faksimile-Ausgabe, trans. George Baurley (Bärenreiter, 1979), 16.

25. See *Briefe* IV (1963).

26. Karl-Heinz Köhler, *Das Zauberflötenwunder: eine Odyssee durch zwei Jahrhunderte* (Wartburg Verlag, 1996), 66.

27. See Gotthold Deile, *Freimaurerlieder als Quellen zu Schillers Lied "An die Freude"* (Leipzig, 1907), 10, n3. Warburg Institute Library, University of London FDD 352. See also Ludwig Keller, "Schillers Stellung in der Entwicklungsgeschichte des Humanismus." *Vorträge und Aufsätze aus der Comenius-Gesellschaft.* Dreizehnter Jahrgang. 3. Stück (Berlin, 1905), 17 and 49. British Library Ac. 2622.

28. Philippe A. Autexier, *La Lyre Maçonne* (Paris: Detrad/A.V.S., 1997), 225–26.

29. Rosemary Hughes, ed., *A Mozart Pilgrimage. Being the Travel Diaries of Vincent and Mary Novello in the year 1829*, transcr. Nerina Medici di Marignano (London, 1955), 110.

30. *Briefe* IV, 474, 1st January 1826. Quoted in Vorbericht to André's 1827 Requiem score, VI. British Library Hirsch IV. 875. See also Wolff, *Mozart's Requiem* (Oxford, 1994), 166. Originally published in German as *Mozarts Requiem: Geschichte-Musik-Dokumente-Partitur des Fragments* (München and Kassel, 1991).

31. Vorerinnerung, *Thematisches Verzeichniss sämmtlicher Kompositionen von W. A. Mozart. Nach dem Original-Manuscripte herausgegeben von A.André.* (1805). British Library Hirsch IV. 1062 and M.e.1.(2).

32. *Thematisches Verzeichniss derjenigen Originalhandschriften von W.A.Mozart . . . welche Hofrath André in Offenbach a. M. besitzt* (1841). British Library Hirsch IV. 1064.

33. Wolfgang Plath, *Mozartiana in Fulda und Frankfurt. Mozart-Jahrbuch* 1968/70 (Salzburg, 1970), 334.

34. See *Briefe* IV, no. 1245, 15th June 1799, lines 119–22; and no. 1267, 17th November 1799, line 58.

35. *Briefe* IV, no. 1264, 11th November 1799, line 16.

36. Alan Tyson, *British Library Music Facsimiles, with an Introduction*, IV (1985) introduction, xi; and V (1987) introduction, 13; see also the *Köchel Verzeichnis*, 6th ed. (1964), XXXI.

37. *The Breitkopf Thematic Catalogue 1762–1787 (Catalogo delle Sinfonie, che si trovano in manoscritto nella officina musica di Giovanno Gottlob Immanuel Breitkopf, in Lipsia)*, Supplemento XVI, col. 9, ed. B. S. Brook (1966), col. 849, British Library MUS780.216.

38. The only works listed by both Mozart and Gleissner are K468, K546, and K564. I am indebted to Faye Ferguson for this information.

39. *Briefe* IV, 344.

40. Ibid., 373–74.

41. Ibid., 493.

42. Vorbericht to *Thematisches Verzeichniss derjenigen Originalhandschriften von W. A. Mozart . . . welche Hofrath André in Offenbach a. M. besitzt* (1841).

43. Wolfgang Plath, *Mozartiana in Fulda und Frankfurt. Mozart-Jahrbuch 1968/70* (Salzburg, 1970), 334.

44. *Aus Moscheles' Leben nach Briefen und Tagebüchern herausgegeben von seiner Frau* (Leipzig, 1872), 79. British Library 10705.ff.16 or Hirsch 3742. See also *Life of Moscheles, By His Wife*, adapted from the original German by A. D. Coleridge (London, 1873), 82–83.

45. *AMZ.* 7th November 1798. Jahrgang I. Column 83, section 11.

46. In a parallel, though not equivalent, situation, Haydn too signed a document of intent. "I, the undersigned, promise to *Signora* Loisa Polzelli (in case I should consider marrying again) to take no wife other than the said Loisa Polzelli, and should I remain a widower, I promise the said Polzelli to leave her, after my death, a pension for life of three hundred Gulden (in figures 300 fl.) in Viennese currency . . . Vienna, 23rd May 1800." (Io qui in fine Sottoscritto prometto alla Signora Loisa Polzelli [in caso ch'io pensasse di rimaritarmi] io nissuna altra prenderei per mia moglie, che Suddetta Loisa Polzelli; e se io resto vedovo, prometto alla Suddetta Polzelli di lasciar dopo la mia morte ogni anno una pensione di tre cento fiorini, cioè 300 fl. in monetta di Vienna durante sua vita . . . Vienna ai 23. di Maggio 1800.) H. C. Robbins Landon, *The Collected Correspondence and London Notebooks of Joseph Haydn* (London, 1959), 169; original Italian in C. F. Pohl, *Joseph Haydn* (Berlin, 1875). Zweiter Band, 92. British Library 2268.c.7.

47. *AMZ.* 5th December 1798. Jahrgang I. Column 147.

48. Maynard Solomon, "The Rochlitz Anecdotes: Issues of Authenticity in Early Mozart Biography." *Mozart Studies,* ed. Cliff Eisen (Oxford, 1991), 23.

49. F. J. Bertuch and G. M. Kraus, eds., *Ueber Mozarts Oper die Zauber-Flöte. Journal des Luxus und der Moden* (Weimar, August 1794), 9ter Band, 364–65. Russian State Library, Moscow, A 17/31. Reproduced in part in *Dokumente.* Joseph Heinz Eibl, *Addenda und Corrigenda* (1978), 80, and in Franz Grandaur, *Der Text zu Mozart's "Zauberflöte" und Johann Georg Karl Giesecke.* (Separat-Abdruck aus den" Bayerischen Literaturblättern") 1–2. Wienbibliothek im Rathaus (formerly Wiener Stadt- und Landesbibliothek) 31497A.

50. "*Teutschlands Annalen des Jahres 1794*" (Chemnitz, 1795). Quoted in *Dokumente,* 413–14.

51. See Friedrich Walter, *Archiv und Bibliothek des Grossh. Hof- und National-theaters in Mannheim,* Bd. II, 179. The Mannheim production was clearly a lavish affair. In his *Chronik des Grossherzoglichen Hof- und National-Theaters in Mannheim* (Mannheim, 1879), 132, Anton Pichler quotes from the *Mannheimer Theaterkalender* of 1795: "This opera was given with a splendour which surpassed anything yet seen on our stage" (Diese Oper wurde mit einem Pomp gegeben der alles übertraf, was man je auf unserer Bühne gesehen). In footnote *** on the same page, one learns that "[t]he score of *The Magic Flute* was procured from the Bonn music publisher Simrock for 26 fl." (Die Partitur der Zauberflöte war von dem Musikverleger Simrock in Bonn für 26 fl. bezogen.) Since twenty years had still to pass before the score of *The Magic Flute* first appeared in print, this must have been a manuscript made by a professional copyist. Simrock sold hand-copied music as well as printed editions (see

Sieghard Brandenburg, *Die Gründungsjahre des Verlags N. Simrock in Bonn. Bonner Geschichtsblätter* [1977], Bd. 29, 30). The Mannheim Theatre already possessed the Haibel copy, bought in 1792 for 90fl. Clearly Haibel had been able to capitalize on its rarity value at the time. Incidentally, the price of the printed first edition score of 1814 was even lower, at 48 francs, or 22fl. (see photo 1 and p. 93). Owing to the loss of archive material from the Mannheim Theatre during the Second World War, it is no longer possible to establish whether the Vulpius text was inserted into the Simrock copy or into the manuscript score acquired from Haibel in 1792.

Chapter Four

Two 1793 Productions Linked to the First-Edition Text

PERFORMANCES AT THE COURT OF THE ELECTOR OF COLOGNE UNDER CHRISTIAN GOTTLOB NEEFE

The June 1793 performance at Bad Godesberg took place under the direction of Christian Gottlob Neefe and Herr Ries, the court violinist Franz Anton Ries (father of the composer Ferdinand Ries). Neefe himself reviewed it in the *Berlinische Musikalische Zeitung* of 19th October 1793.

> *Mozart's The Magic Flute* (for me the most beautiful and my favorite work of his) was performed in June in the large ballroom at Godesberg, directed by Mr. *Ries* and myself, to wholehearted acclaim in front of the Elector, all the nobility, and an altogether glittering assembly. Many strangers had come a long way to hear this music. Only the trombones were missing, but they have now arrived and are to be used in a second performance in September. The panpipes (*Syrinx*) had been really well made out of tin by the local organ builder. Instead of the glockenspiel I hastily had a keyed glockenspiel made, of two octaves only, which is supposed to have done the job well. I couldn't judge that because, playing it myself, I was too close to the sound. I had to alter a certain amount to fit the reduced compass, as you can imagine, especially if you know the music. A third octave is now added below so that the whole range now consists of c c c. . . .

> Im Junius ward zu Godesberg im grossen Redoutensaale *Mozarts Zauberflöte* (mir das schönste und liebste Werk von ihm) unter Herrn *Riesens* und meiner Direktion mit ungetheiltem Beifalle vor dem Churfürst, dem ganzen Adel, überhaupt vor einem sehr glänzenden Auditorium aufgeführt. Es waren viele Fremde weiten wegs gekommen, diese Musik zu hören. Es fehlten nur die Posaunen, die nun aber auch da sind, und im September bei einer zweiten Aufführung

gebraucht werden sollen. Die Panspfeiffe *(Syrinx)*, hatte der hiesige Orgelbauer
von Zinn recht gut gemacht. Statt des Glockenspiels liess ich ein Stahlklavier
in der Geschwindigkeit nur von zwei Octaven machen, welches sich gut ausge-
nommen haben soll. Ich konnte nicht davon urtheilen, weil ich es selbst spielte,
und mir der Ton zu nahe war. Ich musste freilich manches ändern, wie sich bei
einer solchen Einschränkung leicht denken lässt, besonders wenn man die Musik kennt. Nun kommt noch eine dritte Octave unten darzu, so, dass das Ganze
nun aus c c c besteht. . . .[1]

This performance was in all likelihood a direct result of the elector's acquisition of the score from Constanze. There seems little justification for the
doubts expressed by Gernot Gruber in *Mozart and Posterity* about the outcome of Constanze's offer:

> . . . Constanze offered copies of *La Clemenza di Tito* and *Die Zauberflöte* to the
> tenor Luigi Simonetti who was working in Bonn; she demanded an excessive
> price, and was unsuccessful.[2]

The connection between Constanze's "excessive" asking price and the price
paid by Haibel for Mozart's autograph is particularly significant. Hardly less
so is the use of Constanze's copy as the manuscript source for Simrock's
1814 first-edition full score, but neither here nor in Gruber's preface to the
NMA *Zauberflöte* volume II:5/xix (1970) are these issues brought to light.

The performance at Bad Godesberg, as well as the high asking price in
Constanze's letter (see p. 42), attracted the attention of Otto Erich Deutsch.

> *The Magic Flute* was performed in June 1793 at the large ballroom in Godes-
> berg.—The asking price was probably much too high.

> *Die Zauberflöte* wurde im Juni 1793 im grossen Redoutensaal zu Godesberg
> aufgeführt.—Der verlangte Preis war wohl viel zu hoch.[3]

But the elector's performance was ignored by Joseph Heinz Eibl, who wrote:
"The negotiation [*with Constanze*] seems to have come to nothing" and "Per-
formances of *The Magic* Flute by the Böhm troupe . . . were given in Aachen
(first Rhineland performance of the work in the summer of 1794), Cologne,
Düsseldorf and Krefeld" (Das Geschäft scheint nicht zustande gekommen
zu sein. [and] Aufführungen der *Zauberflöte* durch die Truppe Böhm sind in
Aachen [erste Rheinische Aufführung des Werks im Sommer 1794], Köln,
Düsseldorf und Krefeld . . . nachgewiesen).[4]

Bad Godesberg, a health resort near Bonn, was developed by the elector
and much frequented by him. According to the information sheet handed out

to visitors to the Redoutensaal (ballroom) before its conversion to a restaurant in recent times, the building was constructed between August 1790 and Whit Monday 1792, when it was formally opened by the elector. One may reasonably speculate that the text used at his *Magic Flute* performance was the one that survives in the 1814 first full-score edition, deriving from Constanze's copy. Some months after the performance Simrock published a vocal score of the opera, eagerly awaited by Neefe, judging by his comment in the *Berlinische Musikalische Zeitung* in the week following his review:

> Mr. *Simmrock* [sic] is engraving the *complete vocal score of The Magic Flute* and it is very nearly finished.

> Hr. *Simmrock* [sic] sticht den *ganzen Klavierauszug von der Zauberflöte* und ist schon weit damit fertig.[5]

This edition (British Library Hirsch IV 186) can now be seen in many libraries. The piano reduction is by Fridrich Eunike, and all the vocal parts, male and female, are written in the treble clef. It carries the autograph text, without Italian translation. It would have been helpful to know Neefe's opinion of the text of this edition, in view of his involvement in the elector's performance. Unfortunately, however, it attracted but a brief mention by another reviewer, identified only by the initials J.F., after which the *Berlinische Musikalische Zeitung* went out of business.

> This complete vocal score of Mozart's last and best vocal music is the best and most suitable that the reviewer has seen until now.

> Dieser vollständige Clavierauszug von Mozarts letzter und bester Singmusik ist bis jetzt noch der beste und zweckmässigste, der Rec. zu Gesicht gekommen ist.[6]

There is in the Wienbibliothek im Rathaus (formerly Wiener Stadt- und Landesbibliothek) a manuscript vocal score of the opera (MH 10632) bearing not the autograph text but the first-edition version in all but a few details (see photo 8a). It is described by the library in a letter in my possession dated 18th April 1990 as

> a contemporary copy . . . which, according to the original binding, paper and character of the handwriting was made c.1790/1800. The copyist/author of the piano reduction cannot be traced, since there is neither a signature nor initials visible at the end of the manuscript. The paper used (of medium thickness, the staffs ruled, with the watermark D ? C DLAU W in rough capital letters and with a fragmentary coat-of-arms) indicates German provenance.

Eine zeitgenössische Abschrift . . . , die nach dem Original-Einband, dem ver-
wendeten Papier und dem Schriftduktus um 1790/1800 angefertigt wurde. Der
Kopist/Verfasser des Klavierauszuges lässt sich leider nicht eruieren, da weder
ein Namenszug noch eine Paraphierung am Ende des Manuskriptes sichtbar ist.
Das verwendete Papier (mittlere Stärke, rastriert mit Wasserzeichen—D ? C
DLAU W in groben Blockbuchstaben, fragmentarischer Wappenschild) lässt
auf deutsche Provenienz schliessen.

I am indebted to Johann Ziegler of the Wienbibliothek im Rathaus for the
above observations.

The watermark comes in fact from the Dutch firm of papermakers D&C
BLAUW. It can be seen on plate 254, no. 1828, of *Monumenta Chartae
Papyracae Historiam Illustrantia, vol. I,* ed. E. J. Labarre, *Watermarks by
Edward Heawood, M.A.*, The Paper Publications Society (1950), British Library RAR 676.209 (open shelves), and 1950 [1957] offset reprint, corrected,
L.R.402.f.12. The author observes: "[I]n the 18th C., native makers like . . .
the Blauws and others came more and more to the fore" (Introduction, Holland, p. 26). Heawood found this watermark on "flyleaves to J.J.B.D'Anville:
Atlas Nouveau de la Chine. The Hague '1737' (some sheets have w-ks with
'1746')" (see p. 105 of *Monumenta Chartae Papyracae Historiam Illustrantia, vol. I*). Other examples of Blauw watermarks are shown on plates 418–19,
nos. 3267–68 (used in publications in "Amsterdam c.1769," "Paris ?early
19th C," and "England c.1769," ibid., p. 137).

I am very much indebted to Dr. Erich Duda for making a tracing of the
somewhat faint watermark of manuscript MH 10632 in the Wienbibliothek
im Rathaus. It is shown on photo 8b. The coat of arms comes from pp. 1–4
and the name D&C BLAUW from pp. 9–12 (each page being a quadrant of a
single large sheet). Below it, for comparison, is the example of a Blauw watermark given on plate 254 of Heawood's *Monumenta Chartae Papyracae.*

The fact that this manuscript vocal score predates the first-edition full score
by so many years, yet bears its text, suggests a connection with the original
source used by Simrock. The use of Dutch paper strengthens the possibility
that this manuscript originated in Bonn (which is joined to Holland by the
Rhine waterway). It is worth noting that Blauw paper does not appear in David Buch's *Musical Quarterly* study of Viennese copies of *Die Zauberflöte.*[7]
However, the assumption that Dutch paper did not travel as far as Vienna
would be incorrect, since paper by C & I Honig was used extensively by
Beethoven in his late works,[8] not to speak of other examples of Dutch paper
in his Bonn compositions.[9]

From the handwriting the manuscript may be the work of Neefe. Among
the sources used for comparison of his handwriting are an undated fragment

(eight pages) from his melodrama *Sophonisbe* (Deutsche Staatsbibliothek Mus. ms. autogr. Neefe, Chr.G. 1); two letters dated 18th December 1792 and 21st December 1773, respectively (Deutsche Staatsbibliothek Mus. ep. Chr. G.Neefe, 1, 2); and a letter dated 22nd December 1778, reproduced by permission of the Universitätsbibliothek Leipzig in a book by Irmgard Leux entitled *Christian Gottlob Neefe (1748–1798).*[10] According to *Grove*, *Sophonisbe* dates from 1776. *The Magic Flute* piano reduction, if by Neefe, must have been made sometime between 1792, when Constanze's score was sent to the Elector of Cologne, and 1797 (Neefe died on 26th January 1798 after an illness). The letter of 1792 is therefore of special significance in identifying his handwriting. It is shown in photo 8a with the manuscript of Tamino's Portrait Aria Act I, No. 3, possibly also in his hand. The word "Gefühl," which appears at the end of the musical extract and at the beginning of the letter, makes a useful point of comparison. Differences in the form of clefs, especially the treble clef, used in *Sophonisbe* and *The Magic Flute* need not invalidate the attribution of both manuscripts to Neefe. For example, Cliff Eisen has shown that the Salzburg court copyist Joseph Richard Estlinger changed his clef forms during the early 1760s, with alternative forms sometimes used within the same manuscript during the years 1760–1764.[11] Paralleling this kind of flexibility, the tempo directions in *The Magic Flute* piano reduction show two different forms of capital *A*. Both are seen on p. 41—Allegretto and Allegro—but, perversely, on p. 7 the rounded *A* of "Allegro" (the form used in the *Sophonisbe* manuscript) matches the *A* of p. 41's "Allegretto," not "Allegro." Further facsimiles of Neefe's handwriting may be seen in *Christian Gottlob Neefe* (Chemnitz, 1997).[12]

Neefe died sixteen years before publication of the first full-score edition. Not only were Simrock and Neefe colleagues together at the electoral court, but both had been prominent members of the Masonic movement in Bonn since the early 1780s. *The Magic Flute* would thus have aroused their interest as Masons as well as musicians. Known as the Minervalkirche zu Stagira, the Bonn group was disbanded in April 1785 but resurfaced in 1787 under the title Bonner Lesegesellschaft.[13] Neefe seems to have regarded the break as a suspension rather than a cessation of activities, for in a letter of 27th August 1786 to the writer and theatre director Gustav Friedrich Wilhelm Grossmann he still considered himself to be a lodge member.[14] Recently discovered documents in the Universitätsbibliothek, Bonn, (Handschrift S 444) establish the existence of the earlier Bonn group, and Neefe's membership, as early as 1781. In a document of June 1783 Neefe was listed as "1. Vorsteher" (Head) and Simrock as "C.M." (Master of Ceremonies).[15] The documents, covering the years 1781–1784, expose secret criticism of Neefe's character by some members, including Simrock. But if personal tensions existed between Neefe and Simrock at this time, there was no lasting damage to their professional or personal relationship. Among Simrock's earliest publications were Neefe's piano variations "Das Frühstück schmeckt viel besser hier" from Dittersdorf's opera *Das rote Käppchen* and Neefe's piano reduction of the overture to Dittersdorf's Singspiel *Hocus Pocus*.[16]

Criticism of Neefe came not only from within the Masonic movement. His position at court was initially in jeopardy with the arrival of the new elector, Max Franz, in 1784. There was talk of replacing him with his pupil, the young Beethoven, and one may even cautiously wonder, in the absence of any evidence, whether it was not Mozart's expectation of a job in the Rhineland (see p. 40) that lay behind the frosty treatment Neefe received from Max Franz at the time of his accession. However, after a difficult period for Neefe some measure of financial security was guaranteed him and he remained in Bonn.[17]

Simrock remained a friend until Neefe's death. On 22nd September 1797, with Neefe's final illness already beginning to take hold and his wife, too, gravely ill, Simrock wrote to him sympathetically, with apologies for delayed payment of money owed.

> I am sorry from the bottom of my heart for having given you cause for further discontent, of which you have so much.

> Herzlich leid ist es mir, dass ich Ihnen auch noch Ursache zum Missvergnügen gegeben, dessen Sie soviel haben.[18]

It is tempting to imagine that this manuscript vocal score was made as a rehearsal score for the June 1793 performance. However, Neefe musical autographs are not sufficiently numerous to permit definitive identification of his hand in this manuscript, especially in view of the substantive changes in his handwriting to be observed in his letters. Many numbers from the opera—carrying, of course, the autograph text—were already available in vocal score from other publishers. Would Neefe have been so pleased to welcome Simrock's imminent publication of Eunike's piano reduction if a version of his own had been ready at this time? On the other hand, why would he have taken the trouble to make his own version after Eunike's had appeared in print? In the *Theater-Kalender auf das Jahr 1794*, published in Gotha, there is a list of members of the Kurfürstliches Hoftheater in Bonn. Neefe was employed as Opern-Regisseur (opera producer) and Eunike as Schauspieler (actor).

Between the years 1796 and 1800 Simrock published Neefe's vocal scores of *Die Entführung aus dem Serail*, *Figaro*, *Don Giovanni*, *Così fan tutte*, and *La Clemenza di Tito*. The piano writing in *The Magic Flute* manuscript shows important differences from these publications, for it is not so much a practical, sensible reduction as a representation of the score squeezed onto two staffs. Indeed it is at times unplayable. Yet it was once considered material for publication because on the outside page is the instruction, possibly in another hand, "NB. To be engraved only in the treble and bass clef" (NB. Nur im Violin und Bassschlüssel zu stechen). The manuscript uses C clefs for the vocal parts, as is found in the first-edition full score and in Mozart's autograph.

The first of Neefe's five Mozart opera reductions to be published by Simrock was *Figaro* (1796), British Library R.M.9.e.18. It carries on the back page the printed observation:

The instrumental accompaniment has been altered as little as possible and now and then the necessary indication of obbligato wind entries shown so that this piano reduction can be used for want of a full score for conducting and study purposes. For the same reason pizzicato, col'arco, con sordini etc. are also shown. Several piano reductions have already been produced by the present publisher in this manner and future ones will appear in the same form.

Die Instrumental Begleitung ist so wenig als möglich verändert worden und hin und wieder die nöthige Anzeige der eintretenden obligaten Blasinstrumente geschehen, damit dieser Klavierauszug in Ermangelung einer vollständigen Partition zum Dirigieren und einstudieren gebraucht werden könne. Eben darum hat man auch das pizzicato, col'arco, con sordini &c: angezeigt. Auf diese Art sind schon mehrere Klavierauszüge im gegenwärtigen Verlage herausgekommen, so wie die künftigen in gleicher Gestalt erscheinen werden.

The faithful representation of the orchestral score at the expense of playing comfort is far more exaggerated in *The Magic Flute* manuscript than in Simrock's vocal scores of *Figaro* and in his other Mozart operas published in this format. This is not to belittle it, for it is finely worked and originates unmistakably from the hand of an accomplished musician. The reason for its nonpublication need not concern us here, but it is worth noting that various piano compositions and arrangements by Neefe based on music from *The Magic Flute* were published by Simrock. The reader is referred to *Christian Gottlob Neefe. Ein sächsischer Komponist wird Beethovens Lehrer* (Schlossbergmuseum Chemnitz, 1997), 74–75, 111; Beethoven-Haus, Bonn, Me 8 NEEF c / 1997 Schlo; and *VI Pièces d'une exécution facile tirées de l'operette* [sic] *Die Zauberflœte de Mr Mozart arrangées . . . arrangées à 4 mains pour le Clavecin ou le Fortepiano . . . par C. G. Neefe.*, British Library e.379.k.(2.). No. 2 in this collection is a four-hand transcription of the "Bei Männern" Duet (Act I, No. 7). In the closing phrases Neefe's Secondo part follows Papageno's four-syllabic repetition (see discussion of example 5 in chapter 2), in accordance with the first edition and Wienbibliothek im Rathaus manuscript MH 10632. Neefe was evidently familiar with the first-edition text, as yet unpublished, and chose it in preference to the five-syllable repetition of Mozart's autograph. This does not in itself prove his authorship of manuscript MH 10632, but it strengthens the case for it, as well as for the use of this text in *The Magic Flute* performances given under his direction at the electoral court.

We may reflect that, from their viewpoint within the Masonic movement, discussions could have taken place between Neefe and Simrock about the authenticity of Constanze's text.[19] Neefe's concern for the word-music relationship in opera was expressed in a letter to Grossmann dated 8th November 1791. Complaining that his *Don Giovanni* translation had been plagiarized by Schröder, he wrote:

> He made some expressions more poetic that were more musical in my version. If it sounds better when sung I will often choose a prosaic word in preference to a poetic one. And I take a lot of trouble over this, to which other people are indifferent. Singing is, in my opinion, the most important aspect of opera.

> Manchen Ausdruck hat er poetischer gemacht, der bei mir musikalischer war. Ich nehme oft ein prosaisches Wort vor einem poetischen, wenn jenes im Gesang wohlklingender ist. Und dies macht mir oft viel Mühe, worüber andere Herren hinwegsehen. Singen ist, mein' ich, doch die Hauptsache der Oper.[20]

It seems that Neefe would not have been "indifferent" to the sensitive relationship between words and music in Constanze's *Magic Flute* manuscript, which was on offer to Bonn only a few weeks later.

PERFORMANCES IN HAMBURG
INSTIGATED BY CARL DAVID STEGMANN

Simrock's "conversion" to this text many years later remains as yet unexplained. There is an important clue in an exchange of letters between Mendelssohn and Nicolaus Simrock's son Peter Joseph. I am indebted to Neal Zaslaw for drawing my attention to this correspondence. Mendelssohn wrote from Leipzig on 12th June 1843:

> Some time ago Mr. Herrmann made enquiries on my behalf regarding *The Magic Flute* score engraved by you; however, I would like you to let me know once more directly whether any copy exists with the *original* German text? Whether any ever existed? And if neither is the case I would very much like to ask whether you would not be willing to substitute the right text in your plates and make a few proof copies of them? It seems to me almost a duty to see that

such a work is handed down to posterity unaltered; *we* all know very well, of course, that there is an aria, for example, starting with the words "Dies Bildniss ist bezaubernd schön," but if after several years younger musicians see only "so reizend hold, so zaubrisch schön" in print, they will get a false idea of Mozart's thoughts, and I would go so far as to maintain that even the categorically *worst* places in such a text deserve to be preserved, since they were composed by Mozart and have therefore become native to the whole of Germany. If one wants to suggest improvements—fine; but they should be placed *next to* the original, which should in no circumstances be allowed totally to disappear, otherwise faithfulness to this great musician of the past is sacrificed. Please mention it to Mr. Herrmann when you write to him; and should you decide to alter the plates I will be the first purchaser to thank you, though certainly not the last.

Herr Herrmann hat schon vor einiger Zeit einmal in meinem Namen wegen der bei Ihnen gestochenen Partitur der *Zauberflöte* angefragt; doch möchte ich noch einmal bei Ihnen direkt erkundigen, ob kein Exemplar mit dem *ursprünglichen* deutschen Text existirt? Ob keines je existirt hat? Und wenn beides nicht der Fall ist, so möchte ich fast fragen, ob Sie nicht in Ihren Platten dann den richtigen Text substituiren, und einige Abzüge davon machen lassen wollten? Es erscheint mir fast, wie eine Verpflichtung, dass ein solches Werk unverändert auf die Nachwelt komme; *wir* wissen zwar noch alle recht gut, dass z.B. die Arie mit den Worten anfängt: "Dies Bildniss ist bezaubernd schön," aber wenn in mehreren Jahren die jüngeren Musiker immer nur gedruckt sehen "so reizend hold, so zaubrisch schön" bekommen sie doch eine unrichtige Idee von dem mozartischen Gedanken, und ich gehe sogar soweit zu behaupten, dass selbst die entschieden *schlechtesten* Stellen in einem solchen Text beibehalten zu werden verdienen, seit sie von Mozart componirt und dadurch in ganz Deutschland einheimisch wurden. Will man Verbesserungen vorschlagen—recht gut; aber sie müssten dann mit dem Original *zugleich* dastehen, in keinem Fall dürfte dies ganz verschwinden, sonst ist der Treue gegen den grossen dahingegangenen Musiker kein Genüge geschehen. Bitte sagen Sie mir hierüber einige Worte, wenn Sie an Herrn Herrmann schreiben; und entschliessen Sie sich zu einer Veränderung der Platten, so bin ich der erste Abnehmer, der es Ihnen dankt, aber gewiss nicht der letzte.[21]

Peter Joseph Simrock's reply is dated 30th June 1843.

So far as my memory serves me from earlier times the publication of Mozart's *Magic Flute* in a full score edition, which had always been my father's intention along with The Marriage of Figaro and The Abduction, was put off until around 1812, when Steegmann, the Hamburg musical director and a personal friend of my father, settled in Bonn . . . it was he, indeed, who induced my father to base the edition on the new, improved text, as given at that time in Hamburg and on leading German stages—my father conceded, thereby taking account more of the judgment of this otherwise generally honest man than following his own opinion—certainly it remains regrettable that the original text was not at least printed with it. The plates have long ago been melted down and I see no possibility of complying with your request other than by prefixing the complete older text as a special supplement at the beginning of the score, which I am very ready to do.

Wie ich mich aus jener frühern Zeit zu erinnern glaube, verzögerte sich die Herausgabe der Mozartschen Partitur der *Zauberflöte*, welche mein Vater so wie jene von Figaro's Hochzeit und Entführung stets beabsichtigte, bis etwa ums Jahr 1812, in welchem der Musikdirektor Steegmann aus Hamburg, persönlich mit meinem Vater befreundet, in Bonn sich ansiedelte . . . er war es auch der meinem Vater vormagte bei dieser Herausgabe den neuen verbesserten Text wie er damals in Hamburg und auf den ersten Bühnen Deutschlands gegeben wurde, zu Grunde zu legen—mein Vater ging darauf ein und mogte dabei wohl mehr das Urtheil des sonst allerdings wackern Mannes berücksichtigt haben als seiner eigenen Meinung gefolgt seyn—gewis bleibt es zu bedauern, dass nicht wenigstens der Original Text mit abgedruckt wurde. Nun sind die Platten längst verschmolzen und ich sehe keine Möglichkeit Ihrer Aufforderung auf andere Weise zu entsprechen als durch Vordrucken des vollständigen ältern Textes zu Anfang der Partitur auf einem besondern Bogen, wozu ich sehr gern bereit bin.[22]

Peter Joseph Simrock evidently accepts Mendelssohn's assumption that the first-edition text is not in any way connected with Mozart. He appears to be unaware that it derives from a manuscript sent by Constanze. His investigation of the matter was probably only superficial, for, according to the information given in volume (Band) 13 of the Simrock records in the Oesterreichische Nationalbibliothek, Vienna (Mus Hs 36 601), the plates of the *Zauberflöte* first full-score edition (number 1092) were melted down on 24th November 1870 ("verschm. 24/11.70"). They should therefore still have been available to Simrock in 1843.

Carl David Stegmann (1751–1826) was a singer, actor, harpsichordist, and composer. His friendship with Nicolaus Simrock probably dated from 1783, when he joined the Grossmann theatre company in Bonn, where Neefe was kapellmeister. Stegmann sang Papageno at the first Hamburg performance of *The Magic Flute*. This took place on 15th November 1793, just five months after the performance directed by Neefe for the Elector of Cologne. It was reviewed in the *Privilegirte Wöchentliche gemeinnützige Nachrichten von und für Hamburg* of 29th March 1794:

Among the most recent performances . . . in the Hamburg Theatre **The Magic Flute**, a singspiel with **Mozart's** music, first given on 15th November last year, has become the object of universal attention . . . . Within the domestic circle Hamburg's virtuosi have been playing the enchanting, ravishingly beautiful arias and duets of **Mozart's** swan song for a long time. The theatre was extraordinarily full (on the first night of this production). But initially **The Magic Flute** didn't achieve the expected and hoped-for sensation . . . . However, this **Magic Flute** was accompanied by music that to connoisseurs and amateurs was instantly delightful, intelligible, and rich in fine, original features; and the libretto was likewise a model of jollity, abnormality, magic and delusion, illustrated by more than one new (if not exactly wonderfully picturesque) set and thoroughly beautiful, appropriate costumes. . . . Among the singers who are called upon to serve up this feast for the eye and the ear Mr. **Stegmann** as Papageno, Mad. **Langerhans** as Papagena (artists who know how to enliven even the silliest roles with admirable acting and singing), acquitted themselves with distinction. Mlle. **Stegmann** makes a conscientious Pamina, and sings agreeably. . . . But **The Magic Flute** is often so ravishing to the listener, through the magic of expressive, deeply felt musical numbers, that he temporarily forgets to lament how much the immortal composer wasted his talent on a text that wasn't worth the effort.

Unter den neuesten Vorstellungen des . . . Hamburgischen Theaters, ist die am 15 November vorigen Jahrs zuerst gegebne **Zauberflöte**, Singspiel mit **Mozarts** Musik, ein Gegenstand allgemeiner Aufmerksamkeit geworden. . . . Die Virtuosen und Virtuosinnen in Hamburgischen Familienzirkeln spielten schon lange zuvor die bezaubernden, hinreissend schönen Arien und Duette dieses **Mozartschen** Schwanengesanges. Das Schauspielhaus war an den ersten (dieser Vorstellung gewidmeten Spielabenden ungemein voll.) Doch machte die **Zauberflöte** anfangs nicht die erwartete und gehoffte Sensation. . . . Und doch war diese **Zauberflöte** mit einer, für Kenner und Dilettanten gleich entzückenden, fasslichen und an feinen, originellen Zügen reichen Musik begleitet; und doch war auch dieser Opertext eine Musterkarte von Lustigkeit, Unnatur, Zaubereien und Blendwerken, durch mehr als eine neue (wenn gleich nicht durchaus mahlerisch schöne) Dekoration und durchaus schöne passende Prachtgewänder versinnlicht. . . . Unter den Sängern und Sängerinnen, welche dies Augen- und Ohrenmahl aufzutischen berufen sind, zeichnet sich Herr **Stegmann** als Papageno, Mad. **Langerhans** als Papagena (Artisten, die auch die albernsten Rollen, Arien und Duette, durch trefliches Spiel und Gesang zu beleben wissen) . . . vorzüglich aus. Demois. **Stegmann** giebt ihre Pamina mit Fleiss, und singt sie angenehm. . . . Die **Zauberflöte** aber reisst oft durch den Zauber ausdruckvoller [*sic*] empfindungsreicher Sätze den Hörer so sehr hin, dass er es für den Moment zu beklagen vergist [*sic*], wie sehr der unsterbliche Komponist sein Talent an einen Text verschwendete, der so vielen Aufwandes nicht wehrt war.[23]

Johann Friedrich Schink comes to a similar conclusion to the above in his review of the Hamburg premiere:

> . . . if *The Magic Flute* were an even more senseless opera than it is, Mozart's splendid music would make us forget it.

. . . wenn die Zauberflöte eine noch Sinnlosere Oper wäre, als sie ist, Mozarts
vortrefliche Musik würd' es uns vergessen lassen.[24]

Neither reviewer points to any discrepancies in the libretto. But the original
surviving performance material from the Stadttheater, Hamburg, reveals that,
twenty-one years before its publication by Simrock, the text of the first full-
score edition was sent from Bonn to be used in performance on the Hamburg
stage (see photos 13–15).

The manuscript score (Staats- und Universitätsbibliothek Hamburg Carl
von Ossietzky, NDVII 256) is entitled "Die Zauber-Flöte / Eine grosse Oper
in 2 Aufzügen / In Musik gesezt von Herrn Wolfgang Mozart." Beneath are
the words "bey Hofmusikus Simrock in Bonn." The copyists at first underlaid the autograph version of the libretto, which is not particularly surprising,
since, as we have seen, Simrock published his vocal score of the opera with
autograph text at almost exactly this time. However, in this manuscript score
the autograph text has been firmly crossed out throughout the entire opera,
and the first-edition text inserted. The orchestral parts show the underlay for
the accompanied recitative of the 1st Act Finale. Here only the first-edition
text is given; this text must therefore have been the one used in performance.
The numbering system in both score and parts follows the first edition and
autograph, with the curtain rising, after the Overture, on number 2. No Italian
translation is given. The material was returned to Hamburg from St. Peters-
burg in 1991, having resurfaced in Russia after the Second World War.[25]

Advertisements in Hamburg journals of the time offer various numbers
from the opera for sale, in accordance with the current production (see
photo 9).

Musical Announcement. Available from the latest opera *The Magic Flute*: 1)
The lovely Duet: Der Liebe holdes Glück empfinden, etc. 2) The comic Duet
between Papageno and Papagena. 3) The comic Aria: Ein Mädchen oder Weibchen. 4) The favorite Aria: In diesen heiligen Hallen etc. All completely in accordance with the present performance and text; available from Hermann at the
Fish Market and at all the usual places for 8 shillings.

Musikalische Anzeige. Aus der neuesten Oper, die *Zauberflöte*, sind zu haben:
1) Das schöne Duett: Der Liebe holdes Glück empfinden, etc. 2) Das comische
Duett zwischen Papageno und Papagena. 3) Die comische Arie: Ein Mädchen
oder Weibchen. 4) Die beliebte Arie: In diesen heiligen Hallen etc. Alle ganz
nach der hiesigen Vorstellung und dem Texte; sind bey Hermann am Fischmarkt
und an allen gewöhnlichen Orten für 8 sch. zu haben.[26]

The above quotation from the *Privilegirte Wöchentliche gemeinnützige Nachrichten von und für Hamburg* gives the first edition words in number 1, "Der

Liebe holdes Glück empfinden," confirming the use of this text in Hamburg in 1793. The opening lines of the other numbers mentioned in the advertisement are common to both first-edition and autograph text. Within two days the *Staats- und Gelehrte Zeitung des Hamburgischen unpartheyischen Correspondenten* (Staatsarchiv, Hamburg, Z900 702) carried a similar advertisement (Anno 1793. [Am Freytage, den 20 December] Num. 203. Beylage. 3rd column), and two weeks later the *Hamburgischer Briefträger* confirmed that the advertisement was for printed rather than handwritten copies.

> Musical Announcement. A skilful local musician has edited from . . . *The Magic Flute*: Ein Mädchen oder Weibchen etc.—Pa-pa Pa-pagena—In diesem [*sic*] heilgen Hallen, and the Duet: Der Liebe holdes Glück empfinden: as they are sung and played in the present performances; there are 2 sheets and each costs 8 shillings. The print and paper are good, and we can recommend it to the public for its accuracy.

> Musikalische Anzeige. Ein geschickter Musikus hieselbst hat aus . . . der *Zauberflöte*: Ein Mädchen oder Weibchen etc.—Pa-pa Pa-pagena—In diesem [*sic*] heilgen Hallen, und das Duett: Der Liebe holdes Glück empfinden: so wie sie bey den hiesigen Vorstellungen gesungen und gespielt werden, herausgegeben; Es sind 2 Bogen und kostet jeder 8 Schilling. Druck und Papier sind gut, und ihrer Richtigkeit halber können wir sie beym Publikum empfehlen.[27]

Part, at least, of Simrock's first-edition text was therefore in print two decades before the 1814 full score was published. Whether this was the publication *Melpomene*, to which Kurt Stephenson refers in *Mozarts Meisteropern im aufklärerischen Hamburg* (1938), has not been possible to ascertain, since no extant copy of any of the printed musical material mentioned in the above quotations has been traced.

> The monthly periodical "Melpomene" ("für Verstand und Herz") carries a detailed and very skilful summary of the opera, including a printed copy of the texts of favorite arias; in the first place, of course, Papageno's "Der Vogelfänger bin ich ja," but also Tamino's Portrait Aria (at that time "So reizend hold, so zaubrisch schön . . .") and the Eb Pamina-Papageno Duet (at that time "Der Liebe holdes Glück empfinden . . .") etc.

> Die Monatschrift "Melpomene" ("für Verstand und Herz") bringt eine ausführliche und sehr geschickte Inhaltsangabe der Oper, und darauf die Texte der beliebtesten Arien zum Abdruck, in erster Stelle natürlich Papagenos "Der Vogelfänger bin ich ja," dann aber auch schon Taminos Bildnis-Arie (damals: "So reizend hold, so zaubrisch schön . . .") und das Es-dur-Duett Pamina-Papageno (damals: "Der Liebe holdes Glück empfinden . . .") usw.[28]

The first-edition text also appeared on a copper engraving now in the Hamburg University Theatersammlung (see photo 10 and front cover). The picture shows Pamina kneeling before Sarastro in the 1st Act Finale, No. 8, Scene 18. Below is a quotation, giving, in the fourth line (bar 412), the first-edition "Es ist für mich von Liebe leer" (it is empty of love for me) rather than the Mozart autograph version "du liebest einen andern sehr" (you love another very much). The engraving is headed "Aus der Zauberflöte, Zweÿter Aufzug" (from *The Magic Flute*, Second Act), which is not a mistake, since in the Hamburg score and parts, Mozart's two acts have been changed to four acts. Underneath are the words "Hamburg, zu bekommen bey dem Buchbinder J. C. Zimmer in der Altstädter Fulentwiete" (Hamburg, available at the bookbinder J. C. Zimmer in the Altstädter Fulentwiete).

Stegmann, to whom the text probably owes its survival, had been a familiar figure on the Hamburg stage since 1778, but it was not until 1798 that he was appointed codirector, a position he retained until 1811. In view of Gottfried Weber's observation that "the German text is in many places not quite the one in use on most German stages" (*AMZ* review of 13th September 1815 [see p. 6 and photo 2]), the Hamburg version was evidently exceptional. However, Peter Joseph Simrock confirms in his correspondence with Mendelssohn (see pp. 79–80) that it was not unique.

NOTES

1. *Berlinische Musikalische Zeitung.* 19th October 1793. 38tes Stück, 150. British Library Hirsch IV, 1133.
2. Gernot Gruber, *Mozart and Posterity*, trans. R. S. Furness (1991), 15. Originally published in German as *Mozart und die Nachwelt* (1985).
3. *Dokumente,* 377.
4. *Briefe.* Bd. VI ed. Eibl (1971), 430; and Bd.V ed. Eibl (1971), 574.
5. *Berlinische Musikalische Zeitung.* 26th October 1793. 39tes Stück, 153.
6. Ibid. 4th January 1794. Nachtrag zum 52ten Stück, 209.
7. David J. Buch, "Eighteenth-Century Performing Materials from the Archive of the Theater an der Wien and Mozart's Die Zauberflöte," *Musical Quarterly*, vol. 84, no. 2 (Summer 2000): 287–322.
8. See Joseph Schmidt-Görg, "Die Wasserzeichen in Beethovens Notenpapieren." Beiträge zur Beethoven-Bibliographie, hrsg. Kurt Dorfmüller (München, 1978), 180–81, 192. British Library X.431/2997.
9. See Neal Zaslaw, *Mozart's Symphonies: Context, Performance Practice, Reception* (Oxford, 1989), 326.
10. *Christian Gottlob Neefe (1748–1798).* Mit zwei Bildnissen und einer Handschrift-Nachbildung. (Veröffentlichungen des Fürstlichen Institutes für musikwissenschaftliche Forschung zu Bückeburg. Fünfte Reihe. Stilkritische Studien. Zweiter

Band.) Irmgard Leux (Leipzig, 1925), facing p. 64. British Library M.G. 1400. London University Warburg Institute DBE 90.

11. Cliff Eisen, "The Mozarts' Salzburg Copyists," *Mozart Studies*. ed. Cliff Eisen (Oxford, 1991), 259–64.

12. *Christian Gottlob Neefe. Ein sächsischer Komponist wird Beethovens Lehrer.* (Schlossbergmuseum Chemnitz, 1997). Beethoven-Haus, Bonn, Me 8 NEEF c/1997 Schlo.

13. See Walther Ottendorff-Simrock, *Das Haus Simrock* (Ratingen, 1954), 18–19; and Karl Heinz Kobé, ed., *Bonner Geschichtsblätter* (1937), Bd. 1, 328, Stadtarchiv und Stadthistorische Bibliothek Bonn I e 303.

14. See Walther Engelhardt, "Die Kieler Handschrift der Autobiographie Christian Gottlob Neefes (1748–1798)." Zeitschrift für Musikwissenschaft, herausgegeben von der Deutschen Musikgesellschaft. Heft 8. Jahrgang VII. Mai 1925, 470, n2. Attention is also drawn to the letter in Alfred Becker, "Christian Gottlob Neefe und die Bonner Illuminaten." *Bonner Beiträge zur Bibliotheks- und Bücherkunde*, herausgegeben von Richard Mummendey. Bd. 21. Veröffentlichungen aus den Beständen der Universitätsbibliothek Bonn. 3 (Bonn, 1969), 3.

15. See Becker, "Christian Gottlob Neefe und die Bonner Illuminaten," 4, 13–14.

16. See *Bonner Geschichtsblätter* (Bonn, 1977), Bd. 29, 30–31, Sieghard Brandenburg, *Die Gründungsjahre des Verlags N.Simrock in Bonn*.

17. See Irmgard Leux, *Christian Gottlob Neefe (1748–1798)*. Mit zwei Bildnissen und einer Handschrift-Nachbildung. (Veröffentlichungen des Fürstlichen Institutes für musikwissenschaftliche Forschung zu Bückeburg. Fünfte Reihe. Stilkritische Studien. Zweiter Band.) (Leipzig, 1925), 87–90.

18. Letter of 22nd September 1797. Quoted in ibid., 112.

19. Neefe himself wrote Masonic songs. As a side issue one might also speculate on the influence of Neefe's philosophical thinking on the young Beethoven. The text of Schiller's *Ode to Joy*, for example, which Beethoven selected for the 9th Symphony Finale, appeared anonymously in a Masonic songbook in a specifically Masonic version while Beethoven was still in Bonn. By way of comparison here is verse 1 of the original nine verses in both versions.

An die Freude.	Ermunterungen zur Freude.
Freude, schöner Götterfunken,	Freude, schöner Götterfunken,
Tochter aus Elisium,	Tochter aus Elysium,
Wir betreten feuertrunken,	Maurer singen feuertrunken,
Himmlische, dein Heiligthum,	hier dein Lob im Heiligthum,
Deine Zauber binden wieder,	zu des grossen Meisters Füssen,
was der Mode Schwerd getheilt,	wo nichts unsre Ruhe theilt,
Bettler werden Fürstenbrüder,	wo sich Hoh' und Niedre küssen,
wo dein sanfter Flügel weilt.	und die goldne Gleichheit weilt.
Chor.	Chor.
Seid umschlungen Millionen!	Seyd umschlungen, theure Brüder!
Diesen Kuss der ganzen Welt!	freut Euch Gottes schöner Welt!

Brüder—überm Sternenzelt
muss ein lieber Vater wohnen.

Maurer, seht, vom Sternenzelt
schwebt die Freude zu Euch nieder.

THALIA. herausgegeben von Schiller.
Erster Band. Zweites Heft 1786, 1.
Leipzig, bey Georg Joachim

VOLLSTÄNDIGE SAMLUNG VON
FREYMAURERLIEDERN ZUM
LOGENGEBRAUCH. Erstes Bänd
chen.

Göschen, 1787.

Leipzig. Gedrukt bey W.G.Sommer,
1791, 191.

(British Library P.P.4737.d.)

(British Library 4785.bb.60.)

To Joy

Exhortation to Joy

Joy, beautiful spark divine,
daughter from Elisium,
drunk with fire we enter,
heavenly one, your sanctuary.
Your magic spells bring together
what the sword of fashion sternly divided;
Beggars become princes' brothers
wherever your soft wing lingers.
  Chorus.
Be embraced, millions!
This kiss of the whole world!
Brothers—above the canopy of stars
a dear Father must dwell.

Joy, beautiful spark divine,
daughter from Elisium,
drunk with fire, Masons sing
your praise here in the sanctuary,
at the feet of the grand master,
where nothing divides our peace,
where mighty and lowly kiss,
and golden equality dwells.
  Chorus.
Be embraced, dear brothers,
rejoice in God's beautiful world!
Masons, see, from the canopy of stars
joy floats down to you.

A Freemason called Zerboni wrote to Schiller from Glogau on 14th December 1792: "Sir, I am here charged by the Golden Celestial Globe Masonic lodge to thank you in its name for the exalted, joyous sentiments which the chanting of your song *To Joy* in its dining lodges has hitherto awakened in every individual, and to inform you at the same time that, irrespective of whether you are perhaps a member of our brotherhood or not, we never omit to drink a *toast* to your *genius*, with sincere brotherly love for the eternal *energy* of your spirit, at every masonic feast." (Die hiesige Maurerloge zur goldenen Himmels- Kugel hat mir den Auftrag gemacht Ew. Wohlgeborhen in ihrem Nahmen für die erhaben frohen Empfindungen zu danken, welche die Absingung Ihres Liedes an die Freude bei ihren Tafellogen bisher in jedem Individuo erweckt hat, und Ihnen zugleich zu melden: dass wir ohne Rücksicht, ob Sie vieleicht unseres Bundes sind oder nicht, nie unterlassen, bei jedem maurerischen Feste mit inniger Bruderliebe Ihrem *Genius* für die immerwährende *Energie* Ihres Geistes eine *Libation* zu bringen.) *Briefe an Schiller herausgegeben von L. Urlichs* (Stuttgart, 1877), 155–56, British Library 10910. cc. 10. Also quoted in Gotthold Deile, *Freimaurerlieder als Quellen zu Schillers Lied "An die Freude"* (Leipzig, 1907), 57. Warburg Institute Library, University of London, FDD 352.

The *Ode to Joy* was also used, in a modified version, in the Lodge Balduin zur Linde, Leipzig. Between 1786 and 1789 musical settings of the poem, adapted for Masonic use, were composed by Johann Christian Müller, Daniel Friedrich Schubart, Christian Jacob Wagenseil, and Carl Immanuel Engel (see Phillipe A. Autexier, *La Lyre Maçonne* [Paris: Detrad/A.V.S., 1997], 92 and 242–43).

20. Quoted in Irmgard Leux, *Christian Gottlob Neefe (1748–1798).* Mit zwei Bildnissen und einer Handschrift-Nachbildung. (Veröffentlichungen des Fürstlichen Institutes für musikwissenschaftliche Forschung zu Bückeburg. Fünfte Reihe. Stilkritische Studien. Zweiter Band) (Leipzig, 1925), 116, n2.

21. *Felix Mendelssohn Bartholdy. Briefe an Deutsche Verleger.* Gesammelt und herausgegeben von Rudolf Elvers (Berlin, 1968), letter 270, 237–38. London University Library [S] 780.92. Autograph: Otto Lobbenberg, New York.

22. Ibid., 238, n3. Original in M.Deneke Mendelssohn collection, Bodleian Library, Oxford, Vol. 17, no. 314.

23. *Privilegirte Wöchentliche gemeinnützige Nachrichten von und für Hamburg.* 26. Stück. Sonnabend, den 29 März 1794. Cols. 205–8. Staatsarchiv, Hamburg, Z900 704. Essentially the same report appears in Johann Friedrich Schütze, *Theater- Geschichte* (Hamburg, 1794). Reprinted Zentralantiquariat der Deutschen Demokratischen Republik (Leipzig, 1975), 684–89. London University Institute of Germanic Studies C 38.53109 HAM 5 Scu.

24. Johann Friedrich Schink, *Laune, Spott und Ernst* (Hamburg, 1793), auf Kosten des Verfassers und in Kommisssion bei J.F.Hammerich zu Altona. Zweiter Band, 807. Landesbibliothek und Murhardsche Bibliothek der Stadt Kassel II 40a2/10.

25. Some details of the recent history of Hamburg's archive material are found in an article by Jürgen Neubacher on the Staats- und Universitätsbibliothek Hamburg Carl von Ossietzky, in *Musik in Geschichte und Gegenwart,* ed. Ludwig Finscher (1995). Sachteil 3, Col. 1774.

26. *Privilegirte Wöchentliche gemeinnützige Nachrichten von und für Hamburg.* 101. Stück. Mittewochen, den 18 December 1793, Col. 831. Staatsarchiv, Hamburg, Z900 704.

27. *Hamburgischer Briefträger.* Vierter Jahrgang. Erstes Quartal. Siebenter Bogen. Hamburg, den 4ten January 1794, 104–5. Staatsarchiv, Hamburg, Z900 57, and Staats- und Universitätsbibliothek Hamburg Carl von Ossietzky X6565.

28. Kurt Stephenson, *Mozarts Meisteropern im aufklärerischen Hamburg* (Weimar, 1938), 17. Staats- und Universitätsbibliothek Hamburg Carl von Ossietzky B1947/302. There is a footnote (p. 22, n22), giving the source as *"Melpomene. Eine Monatschrift für Verstand und Herz.* Drittes Heft, erstes Bändchen. Hamburg 1793. Gedruckt bey Johann Peter Treder. In Commission bei Bachmann und Gundermann. S. 161 ff. und später."

Chapter Five

Simrock Editions

It is not known exactly when Nicolaus Simrock first became aware of the existence of the elector's score. The text alterations in the Hamburg manuscript score must have been made sufficiently in advance of the opening night (15th November 1793) to enable the parts to be copied and the opera rehearsed. The 1793 Simrock vocal score was published, however, in the autograph text. Perhaps Stegmann was more enthusiastic to secure the elector's version, acquired from Constanze, for Hamburg than Simrock was to publish it at this time. Simrock dedicated his vocal score to the elector.

Most Serene Elector, Most Gracious Sovereign and Master.
   To whom else than to Your Electoral Highness, my most gracious Master, who by his keen interest encourages all useful art, all artistic endeavor, should I dedicate my first attempt at music printing? Yes, I dare to lay this sample at the feet of Your Electoral Highness, encouraged by the knowledge that, even though of humble typographical merit, its primary task will be to make better known Your Highness' favorite music, the last and perhaps most beautiful masterpiece of Mozart.
   I remain, with deepest reverence and loyalty, the most humble servant of Your Electoral Highness,
   Simmrock [*sic*]

Durchlauchtigster Kurfürst,
   Gnädigster Fürst und Herr.
   Wem sonst, als Ewr: Kurfürstlichen Durchlaucht, meinem gnädigsten Herrn, der jede nützliche Kunst, und jeden Kunstfleiss seiner höchsten Aufmerksamkeit würdigt, sollte ich diesen ersten Versuch meines Notenstiches widmen? Ja, ich wage es um so muthiger, diese Probe Ewr: Kurfürstlichen Durchlaucht zu Füssen zu legen, da sie, wenn sie auch an sich wenig typographisches Verdienst

hätte, doch das Verdienst hat, Höchst Dero Lieblingsmusick, das letzte und vielleicht das Schönste Meisterstück Mozarts zuerst bekannter zu machen.
Ich ersterbe mit der tiefsten Ehrfurcht und Treue
Ewr: Kurfürstlichen Durchlaucht
untherthänigster Knecht
    Simmrock [*sic*]

Most examples of this edition lack the dedication, but it can be seen in a
copy in the Bibliothek der Internationalen Stiftung Mozarteum, Salzburg
(Rara 620/22) and in one in the R. Conservatorio di Musica Luigi Cherubini,
Florence (D.I. 424). It gives added testimony to the elector's personal involvement in the arts. It also appears to identify the launching of the Simrock
music-publishing business.

The Simrock records in the Oesterreichische Nationalbibliothek (mentioned on p. 80 in connection with the melting down of the first-edition plates)
consist of copybooks ("Copierbücher") of business letters for the years 1799,
1822–1825, 1834, 1846, 1848–1849, 1851, 1862, 1866, and 1868. Band 13,
undated, contains a typewritten list of Simrock publications from number 1 to
number 1,998. Dates of publication are not shown. It is headed "Abschrift des
Plattenbuches beginnend mit Nummer 1 unter gleichzeitiger Hinzuziehung
des Auflagenbuches, ebenfalls Beginn mit Nummer 1" (Copy of the plate
register beginning with number 1, with simultaneous inclusion of the edition
register, likewise starting at number 1). Nevertheless the list has substantial
gaps. The 1793 *Magic Flute* vocal score does appear, however. According to
Simrock it was his first publication, but it is entered as number 4 on the list,
and indeed the edition bears the plate number 4 at the foot of each page. It
is preceded by Beethoven Variat. Nr. 1 Rothkäppchen (No. 3) and Maurer,
Romanze: Ritter, etc. (No. 2). No. 1 is not identified. The plate number 4
was retained in subsequent vocal score editions of *The Magic Flute* up to and
including that of c.1820. As we have seen, the first full-score edition of 1814
(plate No. 1092) is also listed.

In an illuminating article entitled *Die Gründungsjahre des Verlags N.
Simrock in Bonn*,[1] Sieghard Brandenburg shows (p. 31) that the 1793 *Magic
Flute* was in fact the first publication to be produced by Simrock from his
own printing press and that the dedication page was included only in the first
print run ("erste Auflage").[2]

The Simrock archive in the Stadtarchiv, Bonn, contains more than 220 different Simrock editions. However, to put it in perspective, this represents less
than 1.5 percent of all Simrock publications. Nicolaus Simrock, the founder
of the firm, was born in Mainz in 1751.[3] He started his professional life as
a horn player, joining the court orchestra of the then Elector of Cologne,
Maximilian Friedrich, in 1775. In 1784 the new elector, Max Franz, granted

him an additional contract as official supplier of musical material. He also ran his own business, which included not only selling music and instruments but trading in wine. One is reminded of Joseph Leutgeb, Mozart's horn-playing friend, who kept a cheesemonger's shop. Simrock continued to play the horn until 1792, which means that he would not himself have taken part in the elector's *Magic Flute* performance of June 1793. Nevertheless, his close ties with the musical activities of the court may have influenced his decision to publish a vocal score of the opera. The elector was to remain in power only one more year before being driven out in 1794 by the arrival of French troops in the Rhineland. He died in Vienna in 1801. Simrock, on the other hand, stayed on and his business in Bonn prospered. He was still in control when the first-edition full score was produced. Stegmann must have been a persuasive advocate for the former elector's manuscript, which contradicted the text not only of the Simrock vocal scores of 1793 and c.1800 but of the original printed libretto of 1791. Stegmann and Simrock were probably unaware of the purchase of Mozart's autograph by Johann Jakob Haibel in 1792 (see pp. 47–49).

Did the evidence available to Simrock and Stegmann lie exclusively in their memory of events twenty years past (both men were the same age)? Or did they have recourse to written documentation? It is, in any case, unlikely to have been a frivolous decision. Two years later Simrock made known his intention, in the pages of the *AMZ*,

to make available Mozart's major works in score,

Mozarts Meisterwerke in Partituren weiter zu verbreiten[4]

demonstrating a certain seriousness of purpose. Skeptics could, however, point to a lapse in strict authenticity in the 1815 Simrock edition of the Kleine Freimaurer–Kantate K623. This is the work written at the end of Mozart's life in celebration of the dedication of a new temple at his Masonic lodge (Zur neugekrönten Hoffnung [New Crowned Hope]), and, as already mentioned, conducted by him within two and a half weeks of his death (see pp. 5 and 44–45). In 1800 it acquired a new text at the hands of Breitkopf und Härtel. This was their explanation, in a preface given in some, though not all, editions:

The present Cantata, Mozart's last composition, completed shortly before his death, was until now available only in score and, on account of the text, of use mainly for Masonic gatherings.

We wanted to present it, so far as possible, for the enjoyment of the public at large, and we believe we have successfully achieved this objective in supplying it in piano reduction with a new text underlay especially prepared for it by Mr.

D. Jäger, who has already proved his worth in similar undertakings by virtue of his poetic talent and musical feeling.

Nevertheless, in order to avoid damaging the original conception of this Cantata by the substitution, we include here the original text.

The score of this Cantata is available from us for 2 Rthlr.

Breitkopf und Härtel

Die gegenwärtige Cantate, Mozarts letzte, kurz vor seinem Tode beendigte Composition—war bisher blos in Partitur vorhanden und dem Texte zufolge zunächst für Freymaürergesellschaften [*sic*] brauchbar.

Wir wünschten sie auch dem grössern Publicum soviel als möglich geniessbar zu machen, und glauben unsere Absicht glücklich erreicht zu haben, indem wir sie hier im Klavierauszug mit einem neuunterlegten, und für diese Composition absichtlich gearbeiteten Texte von Hr. D. Jäger liefern, welcher sich von Seiten seines Dichtertalents und musikalihcsen Gefühlss chon [*sic*] durch ähnliche Proben legitimirt hat.

Um indes der ersten Bestimmung dieser Cantate durch die getroffene Abänderung keinen Eintrag zu thun, fügen wir den Originaltext hier bey.

Die Partitur dieser Cantate ist bey uns geschrieben für 2 Rthlr. zu haben.

Breitkopf und Härtel[5]

There followed the original Masonic text. Clearly there was no intention to deceive, and the explanation for the new text was repeated in a review that appeared in the *AMZ* of 12th March 1800 (p. 423). The work apparently gained popularity in this form, for even Nissen's biography of 1828 uses Breitkopf's title "Das Lob der Freundschaft" in place of the original "Laut verkünde unsre Freude." But it is disappointing that in the year following Simrock's publication of a completely unknown *Magic Flute* text, by virtue of its claim to authenticity, he should have seen fit to perpetuate the spurious Breitkopf version of the Cantata.

As far as *The Magic Flute* is concerned, Simrock kept faith with the first-edition text, reprinting it c.1820 in two separate editions. One was a full score using the same plates with the substitution only of a new title page (British Library Hirsch II, 681); the other was a new vocal score by Stegmann, replacing Eunike's (British Library E 1050 c, New York Public Library *MS Krehbiel Collection 1230694—plate No. 4, as mentioned above). It carries the first-edition text except, inexplicably, in Tamino's Portrait Aria (Act I, No. 3), which still adheres to the autograph text. A few misprints have been corrected. For example, in the recitative between the Priest and Tamino (1st Act Finale) the Priest asks, "What do you seek here in the sanctified place?" (Was suchst du hier im Heiligthum?). "The possession of love and virtue" (Der Lieb' und Tugend Eigenthum), in the autograph and c.1820 Simrock vocal score, is a more natural answer than "The sanctified place of love and virtue" (Der Lieb' und Tugend Heiligthum), in the first edition. Yet another vocal score based on the first edition was published c.1830 (British Library G. 260. f.). It bears the plate number 191.

A particular curiosity is the vocal score edition to be seen in the Bibliothek der Internationalen Stiftung Mozarteum, Salzburg (Rara 620/65) and in the Simrock archive in the Stadtarchiv, Bonn (Simrock Noten 4). Both these examples use the 1793 Eunike piano reduction, including treble clef for all the male vocal parts. An index has been added, showing the autograph text. However No. 3 ("Dies Bildniss"), No. 7 ("Bey Männern"), and No. 15 ("In diesen heil'gen Hallen") turn out to be underlaid not with the autograph text but with the first-edition text. The Salzburg and Bonn copies are to all intents and purposes identical, though there are minor printing differences on just three pages (107, 115, and 117), arising from the use of different plates.[6] The date of publication must lie between 1814 and c.1820. It cannot be earlier than 1814 on account of the announcement on the index page:

The whole complete full score of this opera has been produced by this publishing house cleanly and correctly printed, with German and Italian text. The shop price is 22 florins net. The scores of MOZART's Idomeneo und *The Abduction* from the Seraglio likewise.

Die ganze vollständige Partitur dieser Oper ist im saubern Abdruck und correcktem Stich, mit deutsch und italienischem Text, in diesem Verlag erschienen. Der Ladenpreis ist 22 Gulden rhein: Die Partituren von MOZART's Idomeneo und *der Entführung* aus dem Serail, eben so.

It would not have been later than c.1820 because an edition that adheres for the most part to the autograph text is hardly likely to have been published later than Stegmann's vocal score with first-edition text, especially since even the three numbers underlaid with first-edition text use not the Stegmann but the 1793 Eunike piano reduction.

Critical comment on the Simrock first-edition text is extremely rare. After Mendelssohn's correspondence with Nicolaus Simrock's son Peter Joseph, there appears to be nothing until 1861, when Alfred Freiherr von Wolzogen observed in the *Deutsche Musik-Zeitung*:

in the Simrock full score, published in Bonn, as in many vocal scores, the words are often . . . arbitrarily and incomprehensibly altered.

sowohl in der bei Simrock in Bonn gestochenen Partitur, als in vielen Clavierauszügen sind die Worte öfter . . . willkürlich und unverständig geändert.[7]

In fact the Simrock first-edition text was to survive only one more year for in 1862 Simrock, still under the control of Peter Joseph, issued a revised score (unfortunately too late for Mendelssohn, who died in 1847). It carries the same plate number, 1092, as the first-edition score of 1814. It is a somewhat rare edition, but it may be seen in the Eda Kuhn Loeb Music Library, Harvard (Mus. 745.1.666 [Hollis 001602006]), in the Bayerische Staatsbibliothek, Munich (2 Mus. pr. 10784) and in the Archiv der Gesellschaft der Musikfreunde, Vienna (IV 7888 H 29118).[8] The editor, Otto Jahn, proving better informed than the head of the firm, writes in his preface (photo 11):

> The first edition of the full score of Mozart's *Magic Flute* was made from a copy the publisher had acquired from Mozart's widow in 1792. The present new edition is based on an accurate revision in accordance with Mozart's original autograph, in the course of which isolated mistakes have been corrected and in particular the expression marks given more precisely. All divergences of the present from the earlier edition hark back, therefore, to the authority of the Mozart autograph, from which departure has been made, intentionally, in just one place.

> Die erste Ausgabe der Partitur von Mozarts *Zauberflöte* wurde nach einer Abschrift gemacht, welche der Verleger von Mozarts Wittwe im Jahr 1792 erworben hatte. Der gegenwärtigen neuen Ausgabe liegt eine genaue Revision nach Mozarts Originalmanuscript zu Grunde, durch welche einzelne Fehler verbessert und namentlich die Vortragsbezeichnungen genauer gegeben werden konnten. Alle Abweichungen der jetzigen von der früheren Ausgabe sind daher auf die Gewähr des Mozartschen Autographs zurückzuführen, von welchem mit Absicht nur an einer Stelle abgewichen ist.

Jahn has in mind the omission of two wind chords from the introduction to the Pamina-Papageno Duet (Act I, No. 7). He says:

> They cannot be left out and do in fact appear in the above-mentioned copy.

> Sie können nicht fehlen und stehen auch in der obenerwähnten Abschrift.[9]

It seems that Jahn had before him the copy sent by Constanze in 1792. His preface provides definitive corroboration that this was indeed the source of the Simrock first-edition score, and that Constanze's offer, in her letter of 28th December 1791, was accepted by the elector. Jahn assumes, however, that the copy went directly to Simrock. In one sense this is true, for Nicolaus Simrock was responsible for supplying the court with its musical material. It is not clear why Constanze's letter was addressed to Simonetti rather than to Simrock. Some kind of breakdown in communication at court is indicated because Simrock's 1793 vocal score, with its autograph text, is obviously based on a different source.

Noting the re-barring of the duet, Jahn proposes the theory that confusion in Mozart's mind led to the oversight of the two wind chords. He then carefully reviews the autograph, concentrating on details of orchestration and ending with the words:

> Schikaneder's text, which underwent various alterations in the first edition, has now been restored to its original form.
>
> Bonn, December 1862

> Der Schikandersche Text, welcher in der ersten Ausgabe mancherlei Veränderungen erfahren hatte, ist jetzt in seiner ursprünglichen Gestalt wieder gegeben worden.
>
> Bonn, December 1862

But the last word went to the Simrock printers, for Sarastro's "In diesen heil'gen Hallen" (Act II, No. 15) remains defiantly faithful to the first-edition text, a reflection, doubtless, of Jahn's faulty proofreading rather than of his editorial policy.

Constanze's *Magic Flute* copy, seen by Jahn in 1862, cannot now be traced. Despite the knowledge that it came from Constanze within just months of the opera's completion, Jahn was not persuaded to retain it. There cannot, therefore, have been conclusive written evidence in favor of its authenticity. Jahn, of course, had access to Mozart's own autograph. If, as has already been proposed, it had become available only after the death of Haibel in 1826, Nicolaus Simrock, at the time of the first edition, would not have had this advantage. Simrock's handling of another question of authenticity in Mozart can be seen in a letter he wrote to the musical magazine *Cäcilia* (edited, as mentioned on p. 39, by Gottfried Weber), defending his decision to publish a certain Mozart Mass No. 7. He claimed to have heard a movement from it in the distant days of the electorate.

> Declaration of the publishing firm of N. Simrock regarding the authenticity of the Mozart Mass No. 7.
>
> In the 17th issue of *Cäcilia* I was invited by the esteemed editorship of *Cäcilia* to make a clear statement on the matter of the scruples about the authenticity of the above work expressed there by the court kapellmeister Mr. *von Seyfried*.
>
> Accordingly I declare that I obtained the score of the abovementioned Mozart work from Mr. *Carl Zulehner*, on whose integrity I knew I could rely and therefore needed to demand no further guarantee of the authenticity of the work than that granted by his very quality. Moreover I still remember from the old days of the Electorate that the Fugue *"Cum sancto spiritu,"* which Mr. *von Seyfried*

himself considers worthy of Mozart was performed in a Mozart Mass given in the Electoral Chapel . . .

Bonn, Nov. 1826.
N. Simrock

Erklärung der Verlagshandlung von N. Simrock betreffend die Echtheit der Mozartschen Messe Nr. 7.

Im 17. Hefte der *Cäcilia* werde ich, auf die, dort von Herrn Hofcapellmeister *v. Seyfried* gegen die Echtheit des obengenannten Werkes geäusserten Scrupel, von einer geschätzten Redaction der *Cäcilia* aufgefordert, mich offen über die Sache zu erklären.

Ich erkläre demnach, dass ich die Partitur des genannten Mozartschen Werkes von Herrn *Carl Zulehner* erhalten habe, auf dessen mir bekannte Rechtlichkeit ich mich verlassen, und daher für die Echtheit des Werkes keine noch weitere Bürgschaft verlangen durfte, als welche mir auch dessen innere Beschaffenheit gewährte. Überdies erinnere ich mich noch aus alten Kur–Köllnischen Zeiten her, dass die Fuge *"Cum sancto spiritu,"* welche Herr *von Seyfried* selber Mozarts würdig hält, in der Kurfürstl. Capelle in einer Mozartschen Messe aufgeführt worden ist . . .

Bonn im Nov. 1826
N. Simrock[10]

It seems that, in principle, he was prepared to publish on the word of one trusted authority. In the case of *The Magic Flute* first full-score edition, that authority, according to his son Peter Joseph, was Stegmann. The Mass, incidentally, is not now regarded as authentic. Significantly, we learn that in his midseventies Simrock's memory was fresh enough to recall the performance of a fugue thirty-two years or more previously, in the days of the electorate. We may assume, therefore, that he would have had little difficulty at the time of the first edition (1814) in recalling to mind the events of only some twenty-two or twenty-three years earlier, when the Elector of Cologne acquired his *Magic Flute* score from Constanze. Whatever written evidence may have been available to Simrock has not come down to us, though the basic facts were known to Jahn. Neither the Simrock archive in the Stadtarchiv, Bonn, the Simrock copybooks in the Oesterreichische Nationalbibliothek, Vienna, nor the Simrockbriefe in the Goethe-Schiller-Archiv, Weimar, contain anything that can throw light on the question.

The Elector of Cologne's library is now in the Biblioteca Estense in Modena, Italy. But it forms only a very small part of this important and voluminous family archive. A handwriting and watermark study of the manuscripts might eventually provide information about the origin of the holdings, but that work has not yet been done. Of the many surviving historical catalogs in the collection, only one relates definitively to the Bonn court, the *Catalogus von der Kurfürstlichen theater-Bibliothek* (IMOe, Cat. 69.I). It is dated 1784, too early for *The Magic Flute*, unfortunately. Another (IMOe, Cat. 53.I-II) may in all likelihood have originated in Bonn, to judge from its character and content. It is a thematic catalog of instrumental music, undated. *The Magic Flute* is entered on folio 114 (modern pencil numbering) in German script: "Die Zauberflöte ein Klavierauszug/Von Mozart." There are no more details. The history of the musical collections in the Biblioteca Estense is yet to be fully investigated.[11] It is clear, however, that there were substantial gains and losses during the five centuries between 1400 and 1900.

An incomplete early manuscript score and parts of *The Magic Flute* found in the collection has been recognized in the NMA *Zauberflöte* preface as an important contemporary copy.

Among contemporary secondary sources the nearest to the autograph is an incomplete copy of the score in the Biblioteca Estense in Modena (Ms. Mus. F. 787).

Unter den zeitgenössischen Sekundärquellen steht eine unvollständige Partiturkopie der Biblioteca Estense in Modena (Signatur: Ms. Mus. F. 787) dem Autograph am nächsten.[12]

But there is no evidence linking this manuscript in any way to Bonn and the Elector of Cologne, nor to Constanze. It does not use the first-edition text but follows the autograph closely, even to the extent of omitting the opening wind chords in the "Bei Männern" Duet. They have, however, been added on top of the rests. In the second verse the orchestral material is not written out, but the words "come prima" have been inserted, exactly as in Mozart's autograph.

The Elector of Cologne's library passed first to his heir Franz IV before finally reaching its present home in Modena.[13] The date of its removal from Bonn is not known, though other more essential material seems to have left Bonn even before the elector. Thayer reports that the French armies came so close in October 1792 that

on the 24th and and 25th the archives and funds of the court at Bonn were packed up and conveyed down the Rhine. On the 31st the Elector, accompanied by the Prince of Neuwied, reached Cleve on his first flight from his capital. It was a time of terror. All the principal towns of the Rhine region, Trèves, Coblenz, etc., even Cologne, were deserted by the higher classes of the inhabitants.[14]

Documents relating to the elector's estate are housed in the Haus-Hof-und Staatsarchiv in Vienna. The history or present whereabouts of Constanze's copy is not divulged here either. Much documentary material may have been sold or lost.

NOTES

1. Sieghard Brandenburg, "Die Gründungsjahre des Verlags N. Simrock in Bonn." *Bonner Geschichtsblätter* (1977), Bd. 29, 28–36.

2. Lists of Simrock publications are also given in Otto Erich Deutsch, *Musikverlags Nummern* (Berlin, 1961), 26, British Library Mus. 338.47; and *Musikverlag N.Simrock, Katalog Nr. 191, Musikantiquariat Hans Schneider* (Tutzing, 1975).

3. According to the 1928 *Simrock-Jahrbuch*, vol. 1, ed. Erich H. Müller, which gives details of his life and career, his dates were 1752–1833. Other sources, including *Grove*, give 1751–1832. A letter from Mendelssohn to Nicolaus Simrock's son Peter Joseph dated 28th July 1832, in which Mendelssohn offers his sympathy "on the loss of Herr Simrock" (über den Verlust des Herrn Simrock), confirms 1832 as the year of Simrock's death. See Rudolf Elvers, ed., *Felix Mendelssohn Bartholdy. Briefe an deutsche Verleger* (Berlin, 1968), 180. Further information about Nicolaus Simrock may be found in the following publications: Theodor Anton Henseler, "Das musikalische Bonn im 19. Jahrhundert," *Bonner Geschichtsblätter* (1959), Bd. XIII, 36–42, A. Bonn, chez N. Simrock; Sieghard Brandenburg, "Die Gründungsjahre des Verlags N. Simrock in Bonn," *Bonner Geschichtsblätter* (1977), Bd. 29, 28–36; Walther Ottendorff–Simrock, *Das Haus Simrock* (Ratingen, 1954).

4. *AMZ*, 7th August 1816, Jahrgang XVIII, column 551.

5. Preface to *Das Lob der Freundschaft*. Vocal score, Breitkopf und Härtel. 1800. Example in the Lilly Library, Bloomington, Indiana (Lilly M 1533. M 939 K.623 1800), also in the Bibliothek der Internationalen Stiftung Mozarteum, Salzburg (Rara 441/2) and Muzeum ceské hudby, Prague (XLVI. C, 144). The preface is not included in the British Library copy of the edition (Hirsch IV, 869).

6. Comparison with the 1793 Simrock vocal score, also available in the Bibliothek der Internationalen Stiftung Mozarteum, Salzburg (Rara 620/61), reveals, in addition to the six pages of first edition text in Rara 620/65, the use of different plates in twenty-six of the autograph text pages. The price of 18 Francs has been added above the original 7½ fl. on the title page (the French occupied Bonn in 1794 and in 1802 Simrock opened a branch in Paris). For a discussion of the typographical differences in early Simrock editions see Sieghard Brandenburg, "Die Gründungsjahre des Verlags N. Simrock in Bonn," *Bonner Geschichtsblätter* (1977), Bd. 29, 28–36.

7. *Deutsche Musik–Zeitung*, Vienna, 12th August 1861, 252.

8. The Vienna copy was once owned by Brahms (stamped "Aus dem Nachlass von Johannes Brahms"). Brahms also possessed the first edition score (Mozart, Partituren—*Zauberflöte*, [Simrock] alte u. neue Ausg. See Kurt Hofmann, *Die Bibliothek von Johannes Brahms. Bücher–und Musikalienverzeichnis* [Hamburg, 1974], 157). In the manuscript jottings Brahms made of fifths and octaves in the music of well-known composers he quotes twice from *The Magic Flute*, using the first-edition page numbering. See Johannes Brahms, *Oktaven und Quinten u. a.,* ed. H. Schenker (Vienna, 1933); see also *The Music Forum*, vol. V (1980), 40–43, and *Music and Letters* (February 1992), 57. In his hot pursuit of fifths and octaves Brahms makes no mention of first-edition text differences.

9. For another opinion about the missing wind chords see Horst Seeger, "Die Originalgestalt des Es-Dur-Duetts Pamina/Papageno in der Zauberflöte." *Beiträge zur Musikwissenschaft.* 5. Jahrgang. Heft 1 (Berlin, 1963), 65–68.

10. *Cäcilia.* Sechster Band. Mainz, 1827, 129.

11. There are various studies on this topic. The swings of fortune suffered by the collection were outlined by A. G. Spinelli in "Della Raccolta Musicale Estense," an article that precedes an alphabetical list of the composers represented. It was published in 1893 in the series *Memorie della Regia Accademia di Scienze, Lettere, ed Arti in Modena,* Serie II, Volume IX (I-MOe, S.C. Cat. 47 [Mus]). A more recent study by Alessandra Chiarelli appeared in 1987, entitled "I Codici di Musica della Raccolta Estense" and published in *Quaderni della Rivista Italiana di Musicologia, Società Italiana di Musicologia,* 16. Biblioteca Estense Universitaria Modena CFI0050530.

12. *NMA II:5/xix. Die Zauberflöte,* 1970, ed. Gernot Gruber, preface, XI.

13. See A. G. Spinelli, "Della Raccolta Musicale Estense," in *Memorie della Regia Accademia di Scienze, Lettere, ed Arti in Modena,* 1893, Serie II, vol. IX, XXV (I-MOe, S.C. Cat. 47 [Mus]).

14. Alexander Wheelock Thayer, *The Life of Ludwig van Beethoven* . . . edited, revised, and amended from the original English manuscript by Henry Edward Krehbiel (New York, 1921), vol. I, 125.

Chapter Six

Sources and Reports Relating to the *Zauberflöte* Text

NON-SIMROCK APPEARANCES
OF THE FIRST-EDITION TEXT

The manuscript vocal score in the Wienbibliothek im Rathaus (MH 10632), which has already been discussed in chapter 4 (see pp. 73–78 and photo 8), is an important source because it was produced before publication of Simrock's 1814 first-edition full score. There are two further sources, both undated, that could have been in existence before the first edition. One is a printed libretto and the other is a manuscript full score with a mixture of first-edition and autograph text.

The libretto, from the Hamburg publisher Friedrich Hermann Nestler, is rare, but there is a copy in the Staatsbibliothek zu Berlin Preussischer Kultur-besitz (Mus. T. 2077) and in the New York Public Library (+ZB *MG p.v. 285 [no. 6]). The title page reads:

Arien und Gesänge
aus
der Oper
Die Zauberflöte
in vier Acten
Die Musik ist von Mozart
Hamburg
gedruckt bey Friedrich Hermann Nestler

Apart from minor aberrations the Simrock text is adhered to. Four lines are added, however, which appear neither in the Simrock nor in Mozart's autograph text, but are to be found in the 1791 Alberti printed libretto, forming the conclusion to the Papageno-Papagena Duet (2nd Act Finale, Scene 29).

If the little ones, then, are playing around them,
The parents feel the same joy,
Take pleasure in the likeness of themselves.
Oh, what happiness can be greater!

Wenn dann die Kleinen um sie spielen,
Die Aeltern gleiche Freude fühlen,
Sich ihres Ebenbildes freun.
O welch ein Glück kann grösser seyn!

In keeping with both first edition and autograph there is no dialogue, nor
would one expect it from the title "Arien und Gesänge." Each of the work's
two acts has been divided, Act I after the Quintet No. 5, Act II after Pamina's
G-minor Aria No. 17 (No. 16 in this edition, since the wordless Priests'
March No. 9 does not appear), making four acts in all. As already mentioned,
this was the practice in Hamburg (see p. 84).

> The last-named opera, like many others, for example "Don Juan," "The Magic
> Flute" etc., had to put up with being divided into four acts, which often weak-
> ened the overall impression. Why? The theatre bar was leased out, and this
> impermissible mutilation, which is unfortunately sometimes still retained in the
> older operas, arose for its benefit.

> Die letztgenannte Oper musste sich, nebst vielen anderen, wie z.B "Don
> Juan," "Die Zauberflöte" u.s.w., gefallen lassen, sich in vier Acte getheilt zu
> sehen, wodurch der Totaleindruck derselben oft sehr geschwächt wurde. Wes-
> halb? Die Theaterschenke war verpachtet, und ihr zu Gunsten entstand diese
> unerlaubte Verstümmlung, die in den älteren Opern leider noch jetzt zuweilen
> beibehalten ist.[1]

This observation from the 1841 *Jahrbuch für Theater und Theaterfreunde*
was reinforced in 1948 by Kurt Stephenson.

> To give the audience somewhere to go during the intervals a "punch-bar" was
> set up in the theatre, where it later became the custom to indulge in lively dis-
> cussion about the quality and presentation of the artistic productions. Schröder's
> wife sometimes managed the little business herself. The intimate character of
> a visit to the theatre in the first decades of Ackermann's management of the
> house found friendly expression in this way. As a gesture to the punch-bar and
> to the advantage and profit of the current lessee, singspiels and operas, provid-
> ing they filled an evening, were given in principle in four acts, therefore with
> three intervals—even Mozart's "Don Giovanni" and "The Magic Flute" and
> furthermore Rossini's "Barber of Seville" (from 1821) were "quartered" in this
> scarcely artistic fashion.

Für den Aufenthalt der Zuschauer während der Pausen wurde im Theater eine "Punschstube" eingerichtet, in der später eifriger Gedankenaustausch über Wert und Darstellung der Kunstwerke gepflogen wurde. Schröders Frau hat den kleinen Betrieb zuzeiten selbst bewirtschaftet. Der familiäre Charakter des Theaterbesuches in den ersten Jahrzehnten des Ackermannschen Hauses kam hierin zu freundlichem Ausdruck. Der Punschstube zuliebe und dem jeweiligen Pächter zu Nutz und Frommen wurden Singspiele und Opern, soweit sie den Abend füllten, grundsätzlich in vier Akten, also mit drei Pausen, gegeben—selbst Mozarts "Don Giovanni" und "Zauberflöte" und noch Rossinis "Barbier von Sevilla" (ab 1821) wurden auf diese wenig künstlerische Weise "gevierteilt."[2]

Ackermann opened a new house in 1765 and his stepson Schröder had three separate spells as director between 1771 and 1812.

In 1807 Nestler published samples of the typefaces used in his publications, entitled *Proben der Schrift-Sorten, welche in der Buchdruckerey von Friedrich Hermann Nestler wohnhaft in Hamburg auf den grossen Bleichen No. 323. [sic] befindlich sind* (Hamburg, 1807), Staatsarchiv, Hamburg, A902 342. Kleine Cicero Fractur appears to have been the one chosen for *The Magic Flute* libretto, so far as can be determined in a comparison with the New York Public Library microfilm, which may not have been reproduced in exactly the same size as the original. A similar publication twenty-seven years later shows Kleine Cicero Fraktur No. 1 and Kleine Cicero Fraktur No. 2, listed as Nos. 114 and 115 in *Proben der vorzüglichsten Lettern in der Buchdruckerey von F.H.Nestler & Melle* (Hamburg: Grosse Bleichen No. 29, 1834), Staatsbibliothek zu Berlin Preussischer Kulturbesitz 1939.8938. But here the print has changed marginally, and the firm now includes the name Melle, which is not the case on the title page of the libretto. It would be reasonable, therefore, to assign a pre-1834 date to the libretto. Unfortunately no address is shown so one cannot establish whether the move from Grosse Bleichen No. 323 to No. 29 had already been made by the time the libretto was published.

In 1800 Nestler started a theatre journal, *Raisonirendes Journal vom deutschen Theater zu Hamburg*. A review of a *Magic Flute* performance in Hamburg confirms the division into four acts.

On Wednesday, 1st October 1800, one of Mozart's best-loved masterpieces, *The Magic Flute*, with text by Schikaneder, was performed at Hamburg's German Theatre, and, in accordance with the alterations imposed by the management here, in 4 acts.

Mittwochs, den 1sten October 1800, wurde auf Hamburgs deutschem Theater, eines von Mozarts beliebtesten Meisterstücken, die *Zauberflöte*, nach Schikanederschem Text, und unter hier Directions- wegen getroffenen Abänderungen, in 4 Akten aufgeführt.[3]

Here too the typeface matches the libretto; likewise in Nestler's *Annalen des Theaters* (Staatsarchiv, Hamburg Z530 8), which started publication in January 1801. Nestler's activities in Hamburg may be traced back even earlier, however, from reports in the *Privilegirte Wöchentliche gemeinnützige Nachrichten von und für Hamburg* around the time of the city's first *Magic Flute* performance.

> Announcement. Messrs. Nestler and Rubien have now established their Readers' Library at the Fish Market. The most recent books are available there.

> Bekanntmachung. Herr Nestler und Rubien haben nun ihre Lesebibliothek am Fischmarkt etablirt. Man kann bey ihnen die neuesten Bücher haben.[4]

> After various requests to include journals with our Readers' Library (which we have now established at the Fish Market and where the most recent and best books are available for reading), we have decided to open a Readers' Club for journals from the end of January. Nestler and Rubin at the Fish Market.

> Nachdem wir verschiedentlich ersucht worden, neben unsrer Lesebibliothek (welche wir jetzt auf dem Fischmarkt etablirt haben und woselbst man die neuesten besten Bücher zu lesen bekommen kann) auch Journale zu halten; so sind wir entschlossen mit Ende Januars eine Lesegesellschaft für Journale zu eröffnen. Nestler und Rubin am Fischmarkt.[5]

From the foregoing one may propose the hypothesis that the Nestler libretto was based on the Simrock manuscript copy available in Hamburg since 1793, and may have been published even before the Simrock first-edition full score of 1814. The Berlin copy, undated, is cataloged as "[um 1800]."

The manuscript full score is found in the National Library, Budapest (Országos Széchényi Könyvtár), Ms. Mus. 4.647 1/2. The 1st Act follows the first edition text as far as the Finale, where the autograph text takes over. The 2nd Act opens with the first edition text, returning once more to the autograph with the Terzetto of the Three Boys, No. 16 ("Seyd uns zum zweitenmal willkommen"). Such a mixture from the same copyist is strange. An interesting feature is the tasteful ornamentation of Sarastro's aria "In diesen heil'gen Hallen" (Act II, No. 15). The title page bears the name of Carl Binder, who lived from 1816 to 1860 and worked as a kapellmeister at various theatres around Vienna in the first half of the nineteenth century. His ready access to theatre archives raises interesting questions about where he may have acquired this score. He was, for example, kapellmeister at a theatre managed by Schikaneder from 1801 to 1806, the Theater an der Wien. More significantly, perhaps, he was a pupil of Ignaz von Seyfried. Seyfried, who in his youth had taken rehearsals for the first performance of *Die Zauberflöte* in Vienna, appears to have had knowledge of the libretto's origins (see pp. 121–22). Seyfried left Binder "his musical collection" (see *Grove* article on Seyfried [where Carl Binder has been confused with his son Karl, as yet unborn at the time of Seyfried's death]). If Binder's copy was once owned by Seyfried it might have had connections with the early history of the opera.

An undated vocal score giving the first-edition text was published by Cranz, Hamburg. However, since the firm was founded in Hamburg in 1814 (see *Grove* article on Cranz), this vocal score is hardly likely to have predated the Simrock first-edition full score published in the same year. It is identical in almost every respect to the Simrock vocal score edition of c.1820, which bears the first-edition text. Even the page numbering is the same. The title pages are different, however, and only in the Simrock is Stegmann credited with the piano reduction. In both editions Tamino's Portrait Aria (Act I, No. 3) is printed in the autograph text "Dies Bildniss ist bezaubernd schön." But despite the remarkable similarity, Cranz has not used the Simrock plates. Cranz frequently omits the alla breve vertical stroke in the $\mathbb{C}$ time signature, and where Simrock uses wedges Cranz uses staccato dots. The British Library copy (Hirsch IV, 1218) is dated "1830?," but one cannot nevertheless be sure that the Simrock c.1820 is the earlier of the two. The Cranz exemplar in the Staats- und Universitätsbibliothek Hamburg Carl von Ossietzky (MB/4819) was at one time loosely dated "um 1800." As stated in a letter to me from the British Library, dated 15th May 1996: "The dating of the many early 19th century vocal scores of *Die Zauberflöte* is often merely a matter of educated guesswork. This is certainly the case with the two you mention, published by Simrock in Bonn and Cranz in Hamburg."

We can be confident, however, that the manuscript full score supplied by Simrock to the Hamburg theatre, and used for the first Hamburg production of *Die Zauberflöte* in 1793, predates the first-edition full score of 1814 by at least twenty-one years.

PERFORMANCE MATERIAL FROM THE
FIRST HAMBURG PRODUCTION

Documentary evidence for the use of the first-edition text on the Hamburg stage exists in the form of archive material from the Hamburg theatre. The Hamburg production was probably not the first to use this text. The Bad Godesberg performances for the elector of Cologne, which took place in June and September 1793 and are mentioned in the *Berlinische Musikalische Zeitung* of 19th October 1793 (see pp. 71–72), are likely to have been based on the text supplied by Constanze. However, we do not have the kind of evidence that exists in Hamburg to prove it.

The Hamburg score was made by four or more Simrock copyists. I am grateful to Dexter Edge for examining the *Zauberflöte* score and orchestral parts. It would appear that though the score and some of the parts date from the 1790s, other parts were copied in the nineteenth century. The score is bound in four volumes, each representing one act. There are many markings, additions, and alterations, as one might expect in a working theatre score. They have been made in faint ink, strong ink, and black and brown pencil. The libretto changes, marked in faint and strong ink, appear to be in the same hand throughout. Comparison with two letters written by Carl David Stegmann to Nicolaus Simrock (27th June and 12th October 1816, Stadtarchiv, Bonn, Musikverlag Simrock SN157, Nr. 79) in connection with the publication of his Masonic songs (evidently Stegmann too was a Mason) and two communications with a friend more than three decades earlier (19th July 1781 and 29th March 1783, Staats- und Universitätsbibliothek Hamburg Carl von Ossietzky, LA: Stegmann, Carl David: 1–3) suggests that this hand may have been Stegmann's. Photo 12 shows one example from 1783 and one from 1816. One may surmise that the alterations were entered in Bonn, since there is no known Hamburg source for the Simrock text. The orchestral parts lack the attribution to Simrock seen on the front page of the score. They may therefore have been copied in Hamburg, especially in view of the fact that they use the division into four acts.

The alterations in the score conform overwhelmingly with the first-edition text. Occasionally some words diverge, matching the version in the Wienbibliothek im Rathaus manuscript vocal score instead (henceforth Wienbibl. 10632). Particularly fascinating are those few places where alterations occur of which there is no sign in the first edition. Could those who prepared the first-edition full score for Simrock have inadvertently overlooked some details of Constanze's manuscript? Which is the more faithful to it, the Hamburg score or the first edition? An example is seen at the conclusion of the accompanied recitative in the 1st Act Finale. The phrasing given here is in accordance with the Hamburg score.

Example 24.   1st Act Finale, No. 8, Scene 15, Bar 167

Translation

Hamburg score: Sound forth, promised magic tone, conjure away sorrow and pain from Pamina's heart.

1st ed.-autograph: Is not your magic tone strong, because, noble flute, through your playing even wild animals feel joy.

Photo 13 shows the above in the original Hamburg score. "Kummer" and "Schmertzen" are conjured away in contrary-motion three-part eighth-note (quaver) writing whose smoothness is not particularly appropriate to "wilde Thiere" (wild animals). It will be noticed that the wild animals, which are a feature of most productions at this point, are crossed out in the Hamburg manuscript, both in the text and in the stage direction. The text of Wienbibl. 10632 agrees with the Hamburg score. Stage directions cannot be compared, however, since Wienbibl. 10632 dispenses with them entirely. The Hamburg manuscript, in common with Wienbibl. 10632, continues "doch sie hört nicht den Zauberton" (but she does not hear the magic tone), while the first edition and autograph offer "doch nur Pamina bleibt davon" (but only Pamina remains absent).

Another example of an altered text that does not appear in the first edition occurs a little later in the 1st Act Finale, immediately before the first meeting between Tamino and Pamina, where Sarastro recommends to Pamina that she needs not her mother, but a man, to guide her.

Example 25. 1st Act Finale, No. 8, Scene 18, Bar 438

SARASTRO

HAMBURG SCORE — des Man - nes Raths be -darf das Weib, soll's aus der
1ST ED.-AUTOGRAPH — *denn oh - ne ihn pflegt je - des Weib aus ih - rem*

Pflich - - ten Kreis nicht schrei - ten
Wir - - kungs - kreis zu schrei - ten.

Translation

Hamburg score: A woman needs a man's advice if she is not to step outside
   her sphere of duty

1st ed.-autograph: For without him every woman is apt to step outside her
   proper sphere.

The eighth-note (quaver) E on "nicht" is unique to the Hamburg score and is
probably a copyist's error. The Hamburg words are shared not only by Wienbibl. 10632 but by Nestler (in this case "des Mannes Rath"). While on the
subject of domestic bliss, Papageno and Papagena's many children, eagerly
anticipated in the duet toward the end of the 2nd Act Finale (see chapter 2,
example 21), are expected to prove, in Mozart's view, "der Eltern Seegen"
(the blessing of the parents), while the first edition and Nestler, thinking
positively, prefer "der Seegen froher Eltern" (the blessing of happy parents).
The Hamburg score and Wienbibl. 10632 opt for "der Eltern Sorgen" (the
parents' worries). Does this last version represent a healthy realism or is it
simply a misreading? In any case it was not the result of an alteration, for it
was entered by the original Simrock copyist into the text. "Sorge," in the singular, is printed in the Eunike vocal score (British Library, Hirsch IV, 186),
which Simrock published at almost exactly the same time as his manuscript
full score was first used in a Hamburg performance.

   One Hamburg alteration that is less than convincing is the passage where
Pamina, preparing to undergo the trials with Tamino, describes the making of
the magic flute by her father in a storm.

Example 26. 2nd Act Finale, No. 21, Scene 28, Bar 314

PAMINA

HAMBURG SCORE — In sei - ner Zau - ber - höh - le
1ST ED. — *In sei - ner Zau - ber- höh - le Schlun - de schnitt einst mein*

Translation

Hamburg score: In the abyss of his magic cave, deep in the hour of the spirits, my father once cut it in a raging storm from an eternal cedar.

1st ed.: In the abyss of his magic cave my father once cut it, deep in the hour of the spirits, from an eternal cedar, in lightning and thunder, storm and turbulence.

The autograph and first edition, though not the same throughout the passage (see chapter 2, example 17) agree on "bei Blitz und Donner, Sturm und Braus," supported by Mozart's string thirty-second-note (demisemiquaver) tremolo and two *fp*s. The Hamburg variant (also in Wienbibl. 10632 and Nestler), omitting "Blitz und Donner" and replacing "Sturm und Braus" with "Sturmgebraus," is, on this occasion, less satisfactory, since the two stormy bars in Mozart's music no longer coincide with the appropriate word.

A text change that is linked to a rhythmic change is sung by the chorus immediately before the concluding *Presto* of the 1st Act Finale.

Example 27.   1st Act Finale, No. 8, Scene 19, Bar 502

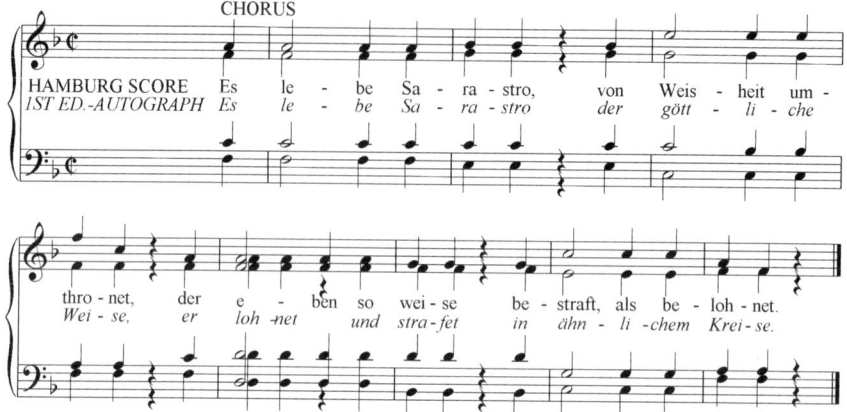

Translation

Hamburg score: Long live Sarastro, reigning in wisdom, who punishes just as wisely as he rewards.

1st ed.-autograph: Long live Sarastro, the divine sage, he rewards and punishes within the same orbit.

Wienbibl. 10632 and Nestler concur with the Hamburg score. The first "e" of "eben" becomes a half note (minim), with two quarter notes (crotchets) "ben so" to complete the bar more smoothly, but with less variety, than the first-edition/autograph rhythm.

Another alternative offered by the Hamburg score is the use of the first-edition words in a slightly different musical setting. It occurs in the final phrase of the 1st Act accompanied recitative.

Example 28.   1st Act Finale, No. 8, Scene 15, Bar 154

Translation

Hamburg score and 1st ed.: Oh! If only I could find the sound to sing to you the thanks in my heart which flows through all my arteries, pouring forth in tears of joy.

Wienbibl. 10632 follows the Hamburg score, not the first edition. Photo 13 shows the end of the passage in the Hamburg score. It is reproduced again in photo 14, as it appears in a bass part from the Hamburg orchestral material. The substitution of G for A at the beginning of the penultimate bar is probably the copyist's interpretation of an ambiguously written note in the Hamburg score.

A musical rather than textual alteration to Mozart's autograph at the start of the march that accompanies the fire and water trials (Act II Finale, Scene 28) is shared by the Hamburg score, the first edition, and Wienbibl. 10632. In the Hamburg manuscript full score a correction attempting—not altogether accurately—to restore the autograph version has been inserted above.

Example 29.   2nd Act Finale, No. 21, Scene 26, Bar 362

The version shown on the third staff is also found in Cranz and in the Sim-rock c.1820 vocal score, as well as in the vocal score with first-edition text published by Nicolaus Simrock's son Peter Joseph Simrock c.1830 (British Library G 260 f). The same musical deviation is encountered in the autograph version Simrock vocal scores of 1793 (British Library Hirsch IV, 186) and c.1800 (British Library E150 y).

In another small alteration the same music and words are used, but with an alternative verbal repetition.

Example 30.   2nd Act Finale, No. 21, Scene 26, Bar 43

Translation

Hamburg score and 1st ed.: How beautiful she herself is, even in grief!

The Hamburg score is supported by Wienbibl. 10632 in the repetition of "wie ist," while the first edition prefers the repetition of "im Schmerz." From such details one is drawn to speculate on the possibility that words and music in Constanze's manuscript might have been either separately written at times, or at least not fully and precisely underlaid, leaving the next copyist free to create the underlay in his own way.

Another instance where the Hamburg score and Wienbibl. 10632 agree with each other, but not with the first edition, occurs in the Quintetto No. 5. Tamino's third quarter (crotchet) in Bar 31 is clearly a C in Mozart's autograph. The first edition, in common with the NMA and countless other editions, gives B-flat. Why such an error (to which my attention was drawn by Nicholas McNair) should be so widespread is unexplained.

There is a moment in the 1st Act recitative where Wienbibl. 10632 offers a text that appears nowhere else. The Priest, responding to Tamino's outburst against Sarastro—"ich hass' ihn ewig, ja!" (I hate him forever, yes!)—sings

Example 31.   1st Act Finale, No. 8, Scene 15, Bar 114

	Und	kennst	du	die - sen	wei - sen	Mann?
WIENBIBL. 10632	Und	kennst	du	die - sen	wei - sen	Mann?
AUTOGRAPH	*Nun*	*gieb*	*mir*	*dei - ne*	*Grün - de*	*an!*
1ST ED.	*So*	*gieb*	*mir*	*dei - ne*	*Grün - de*	*an.*

Translation

Wienbibl. 10632: And do you know this wise man?
Autograph: Now give me your reasons!
1st ed.: So give me your reasons.

Not quite in the category of a text deviation, but nevertheless interesting, is the occasional underlining of words in the Hamburg score. It occurs, for example, at the beginning of the Pamina-Papageno Duet (Act I, No. 7—in the autograph text, "Bey Männern welche Liebe fühlen"), where a good man and a good woman are accorded this special treatment (see photo 15).

Pamina. Der Liebe holdes Glück empfinden kann nur der gute Mann allein.

Papageno. Ach! an ein gutes Weib sich binden, das lasst mir eine Freude seyn!

Another example is the underlining of the word "mich" in the 1st Act Finale (see chapter 2, example 6) where Sarastro admits (first edition, but not autograph text) that Pamina's heart is not for him: "es ist für mich von Liebe leer" (it is empty of love for me). The word "mich" is reiterated after two bars, where it is underlined again. The observant reader will already have noticed such an underlining in example 28, Hamburg score version: "O! dass mir doch ein Ton gelänge, der euch den Dank des Herzens sänge" (Oh! If only I could find the sound to sing to you the thanks in my heart). If the underlining of "mich" and "gute(s)" is deemed to have special significance, what possible reason could there be for granting a mere definite article such emphasis? The underlining of "den" is also found in Wienbibl. 10632, though, curiously, not the other underlinings quoted. A deviation concerning only the music occurs in the final bar of the 1st Act Terzetto, No. 6. In Mozart's autograph the music ends with three quarter-note (crotchet) wind chords. In the Hamburg score the last one is crossed out and replaced by a rest (see photo 15), bringing it into conformity with the first edition and Wienbibl. 10632. The effect of the three chords is to introduce a new rhythmical element. The final bar gains in weight but not necessarily in charm.

Example 32.   Act I, No. 6, Bar 71

There are small instances where first-edition text differences have not been entered either in the Hamburg score, Wienbibl. 10632, or Nestler. For example, Tamino, seeking directions from the Three Ladies for the forthcoming journey to Sarastro's realm (Quintet, Act I, No. 5, Scene 8, Bar 203) addresses them with the words, as in Mozart's autograph, "Doch schöne Damen saget an" (but, lovely ladies, say) instead of the first edition's "saget mir" (tell me). Nor do they follow the first-edition substitution of "Freiheit" (freedom) for the autograph's "Freude" (joy) in the Terzetto of the Three Boys (Act II, No. 16, Scene 16, Bar 19). (The ambiguity of the word "Freiheit" at this point in the plot was discussed on p. 34).

A comparison of different sources reveals which ones are linked. There are of course bound to be minor errors in copying, whether attributable to today's flickering computer screen or yesterday's flickering candlelight, as well as little adjustments that reflect the individuality of the copyist. But there remains the strong overall impression that the two earliest sources—the Hamburg score and Wienbibl. 10632—are closely related.

The *Zauberflöte* performances in Hamburg attracted considerable attention in the journals of the time. A report on the first performance that appeared in *Privilegirte Wöchentliche gemeinnützige Nachrichten, Hamburg* has already been quoted above (see pp. 81–82). The *Hamburgischer Briefträger* made the following observations.

On 15th November for the first time: **The Magic Flute**. A singspiel in 4 Acts. The music is by **Mozart**. So our public got what it had so long desired. We knew the piece, since we had seen it performed some time ago in another large town in our German fatherland. It wasn't the fault of our well-meaning, worthy management that it couldn't be given here in so complete a form as it was there. The situation—circumstances, or whatever you care to call it, changes matters. Many arias were omitted and necessarily so, due to a lack of facilities—many parts of the complete scenery were missing, thanks to the idiosyncrasies of this place and other circumstances. Nevertheless the present management spared no expense in this opera in giving the audience something really pleasing to the eye. The subject—as is well known, is a fairy tale of little significance. An Egyptian prince, in order to win a girl (in this country it doesn't apply anymore), has to go through fire and water—an undertaking by no means appropriate to everyone in their dealings with women—however, theatre fire doesn't burn and theatre water doesn't kill, and so Prince **Tamino** weathers these tests safely. Herr **Stegmann** is unsurpassed in the role of the bird-catcher **Papagena** [*sic*]; his daughter, in no way inferior to him in playing the part of **Pamina**, is developing worthily into one who deserves well of the noble art, as the noble art deserves of the girl. The singing of the Three Nymphs wasn't too pleasing . . . nor was Madame **Stegmann's** singing very successful. . . . The music is lovely . . . a masterpiece of the deceased [*vereinigeen* is probably a misprint for *verewigten*] **Mozart**. And if one chooses to say finis coronat opus [the last work is the crowning glory] it is justified in his case, for it was written shortly before his passing.

Am 15ten November zum erstenmale: **Die Zauberflöte**. Ein Singspiel in 4 Aufzügen. Die Musick ist von **Mozart**. So erhielt denn das hiesige Publikum, etwas darnach es so lange geschmachtet. Wir kannten das Stück, weil wir es schon vor einiger Zeit an einem andern grossen Orten unsers deutschen Vaterlandes hatten aufführen sehen. Dass es nun freilich hier nicht so complet als dort gegeben werden konnte, daran ist der gute Wille unsers verehrungswürdigen Direktion nicht schuld. Lage—Umstände und wie das alles heisst, verändern die Sache. Viele Arien blieben weg und mussten wegbleiben; weil es an Execution fehlte—vieles zur volständigen [*sic*] Decoration Gehöriges musste fehlen, weil es die Beschaffenheit des Orts und andere Umstände nicht zuliessen. Indessen hat die hiesige Direktion keine Kosten gespart, um dem Auge des Zuschauers ein wahres Vergnügen durch diese Oper zu verschaffen. Das Sujet ist—bekanntlich ein Feen Märchen und hat nicht viel zu bedeuten. Um ein Mädchen zu erobern muss ein egiptischer Prinz (hier zu Lande ist das der Fall nicht mehr) durch Feuer und Wasser—ein Unternehmen was nun für jeden dem es um eine Frau zu thun ist, wol [*sic*] nicht allezeit passlich wäre—doch das Theater- Feuer brennt und das Theater- Wasser tödtet nicht und so stehet der Prinz **Tamino** diese Proben glücklich aus. Herr **Stegmann** spielt seine Vogelfänger Rolle als **Papagena** [*sic*] unverbesserlich; so wie dessen Tochter als **Pamina** ihm in ihrem Spiele nichts nachgiebt, das wackre Mädchen macht sich immer mehr und mehr verdient um die edle Kunst und die edle Kunst ums Mädchen. Der Gesang der drey Nimpfen wollte uns gar nicht gefallen . . . Der Madame **Stegmann**

glückt ihr Gesang auch nicht. . . . Die Musik ist schön . . . ein Meisterstück des
vereinigeen [*sic*] **Mozart**. Und heisst es finis coronat opus; so heisst es bey
ihm mit recht so, denn er verfertiget sie kurz vor seinem Hinscheiden.[6]

One wonders whether the omission of the animals already noted in the Hamburg score (see example 24 and photo 13) was seen by the reviewer as an example of the production's incompleteness.

The original theatre bill is preserved in the Hamburger Theatersammlung of the Staats- und Universitätsbibliothek Hamburg Carl von Ossietzky (see photo 16). There is no indication who directed the performance. Opera culture was very much singer-oriented, as it is today. Thumbnail sketches of some of the singers who participated in the first Hamburg *Magic Flute* performance were published two years earlier in the *Hamburgischer Briefträger* of February 1791, contributed by an anonymous correspondent, and are quoted by Kurt Stephenson in *Mozart's Meisteropern im aufklärerischen Hamburg*.[7] Eule (Sarastro) was considered to have "a pure voice, scope and musical understanding" (eine reine Stimme, Umfang und Musikkenntnis); known as a comic, he was "sometimes funnier than he really ought to be" (zuweilen etwas komischer ist, als er billig sein sollte). Pleisner (Monostatos) had a voice that was "not unpleasant, but he ought to be very careful not to force, or his tone becomes rough and disagreeable on the ear" (nicht unangenehm, nur muss er sich vor aller Anstrengung derselben sehr in acht nehmen, weil sein Ton alsdenn rauh und dem Ohr widrig wird). Demoiselle Jaime (1st Lady), whose "good though not yet developed voice" (gute obgleich noch nicht ausgebildete Stimme) promised one day to be among the best, was "as yet not an actress of significance" (Als Schauspielerin bedeutet sie noch wenig). The Three Boys, played by women (Madame Löhrs, Demoiselle Schwarzenfeld, Demoiselle Wilken) get a brief mention, with particular praise for Madame Löhrs, who "plays soubrettes and peasant girls, leaving nothing to be desired" (spielt Soubretten und Bauernmädchen, so, dass sie nichts zu wünschen übrig lässt). Stegmann and his family, who played such an important part in the first *Magic Flute* production at the Hamburg theatre, were not in Hamburg in 1791.

But eight years later (*AMZ*, 1. Jhrg., July 1799 cols. 713–14) Stegmann was regarded as "a very estimable composer of much skill" (ein sehr achtungswerther Komponist von vielen Kenntnissen). He was criticized, however, for the "somewhat shrill tone of his voice" (seiner etwas kreischenden Stimme). His wife (3rd Lady), "whose singing has for some time been improving considerably" (deren Gesang seit einiger Zeit sich sehr bessert), fared better, better in any event than Madame Langerhans (Papagena): "It's a pity that Mad. Langerhans, who is, moreover a very meritorious and useful actress, absolutely cannot sing." (Schade, dass Mad. Langerhans, die übrigens eine sehr verdienstvolle und brauchbare Actrice ist, so ganz und gar eigentlich nicht—singen kann). Eule is criticised here, too, for his "completely inflexible voice" (gänzlich unbiegsame Stimme), though highly praised as a comic. In a later report from Hamburg (*AMZ*, 4. Jhrg., August 1802 col. 766) the writer declares himself "delighted with the fine ensemble of the excellent orchestra" (Ich . . . freue mich über das schöne Ensemble des braven Orchesters). Stegmann again finds favor as a composer—"splendid, highly original music" (vortreffliche, höchst originelle Musiken).

The *Hamburgischer Briefträger* kept a watchful eye on the progress of the *Magic Flute* production. On 25th November 1793, ten days after the opening, the theatre was so full that many were turned away. The correspondent, who managed to get a seat in a dress circle box, found

that the aroma here was of asiatic musk, rather than the domestic German variety which one often smells in the stalls and gallery. The artists, among whom the Bird-Catcher **Papageno** (Mr. **Stegmann**) was especially outstanding by virtue of his amusing acting and singing, acted very worthily on this occasion, completely making up for their errors last time. Even the waterfall, which broke down and stopped gushing on 21st, did its very best. On the whole it seems that in the course of time our good public acquires more and more taste for this piece. The artists themselves get increasingly familiar with it, and a certain fear and anxiety, which made them present and produce much of it rather stiffly at first, diminishes with every performance . . . only the Three Genii still have some of the stiffness: it shows a lot because when they appear one thinks of them as slim, merry youngsters, not little devils. There were at least some from Lübeck who didn't much care for what was in the middle of their costume—they found the position of the bunch of flowers rather shocking.

dass es hier nach asiatischen im Parteere [*sic*] und auf der Gallerie aber, nur oft nach deutschen—vaterländischen Moschus roch. Die Künstler, worunter sich der Vogelfänger **Papageno** (Herr **Stegmann**) vorzüglich seines drolligen Spiels und Gesanges halber ausgezeichnet, spielten an diesem Abend sehr brav und machten völlig wieder gut, was sie das letztemal versahen. Auch der Wasserfall, der am 21sten stockte und zu sprudeln aufhielt, that seine möglichsten Dienste. Ueberhaupt scheint es dass unser gutes Publikum von Zeit zu Zeit immer mehr Geschmack an diesem Stücke findet. Die Künstler selbst werden immer mehr und mehr bekannter mit demselben, und eine gewisse Furcht und Aengstlichkeit, die im Anfange sie vieles steif heraus und hervorbringen hiess, nimmt mit jeder neuen Vorstellung ab . . . nur die drey Genien will die Steifigkeit noch nicht ganz verlassen: sie fällt vorzüglich auf, weil man sich bey ihrer Erscheinung keine Vitzliputzli,[8] sondern schlanke und muntere Jungen denkt. Die Mitte ihres Anzuges wollte wenigstens einigen aus Lübeck auch nicht gefallen—sie fanden den Blumen- Cranz in seiner Stellung etwas auffallend.[9]

The reviewer evidently reflects the spirit of the *Hamburgischer Briefträger*'s droll subtitle:

> Writings containing history, town and country news, poems, letters, as well as theatre reports and humorous articles of all kinds to make you laugh or weep. A weekly paper for friends and enemies by A. F. Bonaventurus.

> Schriften, worin Geschichte, Stadt- und Landneuigkeiten, Gedichte, Briefe, auch Theaternachrichten und launige Aufsätze allerley Art zum Lachen und Weinen enthalten sind. Eine Wochenschrift für Freunde und Feinde von A. F. Bonaventurus.

Bonaventurus is identified by Kurt Stephenson as Adam Friedrich Schulze, who died in 1800.[10]

Two and a half weeks later a correspondent of the *Hamburgischer Briefträger* again attended a *Magic Flute* performance.

> 12th [December]: **The Magic Flute**. This opera, which begins to be appreciated more and more, was given today with improved new sets, which are very beautiful.

> Am 12ten [December]: **Die Zauberflöte**. Es wurde diese Oper, die immer mehr und mehr zu gefallen anfängt, heute mit verbesserten neuen Decorationen gegeben, die sehr schön sind.[11]

Its increasing favor with the public was again confirmed following a performance on 13th January 1794, with interesting additional, if gratuitous, comments on the clientele, as well as on traffic conditions around the theatre.

> This opera begins more and more to rise to a position among the public's favorite . . . various people were present who lacked only a dressing-gown, since their head was covered with a nightcap. The people of Israel seem to have a great preference for this piece, at least they would rather see it than the **Merchant of Venice**. . . . Pedestrians, or those coming and going on foot to the theatre, also thank the worthy management for the new arrangements now in place with regard to carriages; for from this evening the barrier was closed for the first time, so that coaches could not proceed until pedestrians had passed through the narrow exit. Everyone is now assured that the nightly danger of injury to arms and legs has passed.

> Diese Oper fängt immer mehr und mehr an zu den Lieblingsstücken unsers Publikums hinaus zu schwinge . . . verschiedene Leute, denen weiter nichts als der Schlafrock fehlte, denn die Nachtmütze bedeckte ihr Haupt, waren gegenwärtig. Vorzüglich scheint dem Volke Israel dies Stück mehr als ein anderes zu

behagen, wenigstens sehen sie es lieber als den **Kaufmann von Venedig**. . . .
Auch danket das wandelnde, oder zum Schauspielhause hin und weggehende
Publikum der würdigen Direction für die neue nun ganz complete Anordnung in
Absicht der Wagen; denn mit diesem Abend wurde zum erstenmal der Baum ge-
schlossen, damit die Kutschen nicht eher vorfahren können, bis die Fussgänger
den schmalen Ausgang passiret sind. Jeder ist doch nun für Verletzung seiner
Arme und Beine versichert, die sonst an jedem Abend in Gefahr waren.[12]

Three weeks later the *Hamburgischer Briefträger* again reviewed a *Magic
Flute* performance—or rather, matters peripheral to it.

On 10th February: **The Magic Flute**. A singspiel in 4 acts. Music by Mozart.
This evening we saw how business was flourishing, as Papageno's bird-whistle
was offered for sale outside the theatre for 12 sh. in brass, and for 4 sh. made of
quill. We have long wondered at the fact that **Papageno** used a substitute piper,
especially as his bird-whistle is becoming so common that **young** gentlemen
greet each other in the street with it. We saw the former Miss **Wilcken** for the
first time as Mrs. **Hönicke**, both on the playbill and on the stage. Yesterday the
dear girl was joined in marriage with the music director of our orchestra Mr.
Hönicke, and so furthered her destiny, for it seems to me that the aforesaid good
lady is on the whole made more for marriage than for the theatre. Her voice is
as little captivating as her figure is good and beautiful. We wish her, in view of
her agreeable personality and especially her virtuous character, the best of luck
in her new situation! . . . The house was very full again, by the way, and people
of all races with and without nightcaps clapped **Papageno**.

Am 10ten Februar: **Die Zauberflöte**. Ein Singspiel in 4 Aufzügen. Die Musik
von Mozart. Wie sehr die Handlung hier im Flor ist, sahen wir auch an diesem
Abend, denn des Papageno Vogelpfeife wurde schon für 12 sch. in Messing,
und zu 4 sch. aus Federspulen nachgemacht vor dem Schauspielhause zum
Kauf angebothen. Wir haben es schon lange bewundert: dass **Papageno** sich
bey seinem Pfeifen einen Substituten gehalten hat, zumal da seine Vogelpfeife
so gemein wird, dass die **jungen** Herrn auf den Strassen einen damit salutiren.
Noch sahen wir in der ehemaligen Demoiselle **Wilcken**, heute Abend die
Madame **Hönicke**, sowohl auf dem Zettel, als auf der Bühne zum erstenmale.
Am gestrigen Tage verband sich das liebe Mädchen mit dem beym hiesigen
Orchester angestellten Musikdirektor Hrn. Hönicke, und kam also dadurch ihrer
Bestimmung näher, denn für den Ehestand scheint uns, überhaupt genommen,
die gegenwärtige gute Dame mehr als für's Theater geschaffen zu seyn. So gut
und schön ihr Körperbau ist, so wenig ist ihre Stimme einnehmend. Wir wünschen ihr zu ihrem neuen Stande ihrer angenehmen Person und vorzüglich ihres
tugendhaften Characters wegen, das beste Glück! . . . Das Haus war übrigens
wieder sehr besetzt, und Leute aus allerley Volk mit und ohne Nachtmützen
beklatschten den **Papageno**.[13]

Further entertainment followed for the readers of the *Hamburgischer Briefträger* in the form of a peasant's comments on *The Magic Flute*, conveyed in broad dialect[14] and quoted as "proof that even a peasant thinks" (einen Beweis, dass der Bauer auch denkt). The *Briefträger* then left the opera to fend for itself for a bit, merely noting (three times in August 1794—2nd, 9th, and 23rd, pp. 566, 587, and 618, respectively) its continued popularity. In October, however, it was unable to resist a bizarre incident.

> On 13th October *The Magic Flute* was performed. The lion got too close to the prompter's light and caught fire.—A boy who made up the lion's tail end noticed it and, seeing the fire, detached himself from the body.—It was an amusing procession.

> Am 13ten October wurde die *Zauberflöte* aufgeführt. Der Löwe kam dem Licht des Souffleurs zu nahe und verbrannte sich.—Ein Knabe der den Schweif des Löwen machte merkte es und als er den Brand sahe trennte er sich von dem Körper.—Es war ein amüsanter Aufzug.[15]

Five years later the *AMZ* was not so easily amused.

> If it can't be given any better than we have seen it here up to now, an opera like *The Magic Flute* should best be left alone.

> Eigentlich sollte man eine solche Oper, wie die *Zauberflöte*, wenn sie nicht besser gegeben werden kann, als wir sie bis jetzt hier gesehen haben, lieber ganz weglassen.[16]

Comments on the text used are sadly absent in the reviews of Hamburg performances. A critic writing about a performance that took place on 1st October 1800 refers to the duet "Bey Männern welche Liebe fühlen etc.," which seems to indicate a performance employing the autograph version (the first-edition text of the duet is "Der Liebe holdes Glück empfinden"). He describes it as being "in the first act" (im ersten Akt), but this is a direct contradiction of his opening statement that the opera was "performed in accordance with the alterations imposed by the management here, in 4 acts" (unter hier Directions- wegen getroffenen Abänderungen, in 4 Akten aufgeführt),[17] since the Hamburg score and parts, as well as the Nestler libretto, place this duet in the second act. He continues, however, with references to scenes in the third and fourth acts, suggesting that the production did, after all, conform with the normal Hamburg four-act format. If opera singers' diction was no clearer then than it is today, critics can hardly be blamed for ignoring text variants in performance; their apparent indifference is more understandable than the neglect of the first edition itself over almost two centuries. Despite the critics' silence we have it on the word of Peter Joseph Simrock, in his letter to Mendelssohn of 30th June 1843 (see p. 79), that the first-edition text was still in use "in Hamburg and on leading German stages" in 1812, one year after Stegmann had left Hamburg for Bonn.

One should not leave the subject of the first Hamburg performances of the opera without mentioning that there was a small appetizer to the official premiere.

> On 3rd [November], i.e. on Sunday, the second concert took place. It consisted of two parts. In the first the most pleasing item was the symphony by Mr. **Stegmann**, and in the other that by Mr. **Mozart** from **The Magic Flute**. The house was very full.

> Am 3ten [November], als [*sic*, probably a misprint for "also"] am Sonntage war die zwote [*sic*] musikalische Akademie. Sie bestand aus 2 Theilen. Im erstern [*sic*] gefiel die Sinfonie von Herrn **Stegmann**, und im andern die vom Herrn **Mozart** aus der **Zauberflöte** am besten. Das Haus war sehr besetzt.[18]

It would seem that Hamburg heard the overture one and a half weeks before the curtain rose on the full production.

THE CLOSE CIRCLE AROUND MOZART

It is hard to separate fact from fiction in the accounts that have reached us from those present in Mozart's circle when the opera came into being. Ignaz von Seyfried, for example, delves deeply into his memory of the past in a letter to Georg Friedrich Treitschke of around 1840. But one should bear in mind that, at the age of about sixty-four, he was describing events that took place some forty-nine years earlier when he was but a boy of fifteen.

> *Schikaneder* got to know *Mozart* . . . in a Freemasons' Lodge,—not the very famous one to which *Born* belonged, . . . but simply a so-called private or banqueting lodge, where in the weekly evening meetings the members occupied themselves with games, music, and the many pleasures of a well-stocked dining-table, as *Gieseke* often told me, who was the one to draw *Schikaneder's* attention to *Wieland's Dschinnistan*, the source of material for several of his operas. The composition of *The Magic Flute* was started very probably only in spring 1791, because *Mozart* never took long and above all worked quickly. He wrote mostly in *Gerl's* apartment, or in *Schikaneder's* garden, just a few steps from the theatre; I myself was often a guest at the same table and took many rehearsals in that room, or, to be more exact, wooden hut. The prompter *Haselbeck* had the task of putting *Schikaneder's* prose sketches into verse; much may

have been made up by him, rhymes such as "schön Mädchen jung u: fein—viel weisser noch als Kreide," or the preceding "Aha! hier seh ich Leute,—gewagt, ich geh' hinein!"—The libretto was finished as far as the 1st Act Finale when "*Die Zauberzither*," or "*Kaspar der Fagottist*" appeared in the Leopoldstadt Theatre. *Perinet* had used the very same *Wieland* fairy-tale, keeping closely to the original, but conforming with the requirements of his theatre. That didn't bother our Emanuel too much; for he knew exactly what to do, changing the whole plan around, much to the benefit of the whole, for *Mozart* could otherwise scarcely have left us, in his last stage work, such a ravishing model of poetry and romanticism . . . when he set out on the journey to Prague at the official invitation of the Bohemians, all the ensemble pieces, up to the concluding Finale of *The Magic Flute*, were already complete, that is, vocal parts, bass line, and, in addition, the important motifs were indicated; from this short score my good friend *Henneberg* rehearsed hard. After *Mozart's* return—10th or 12th September, he got on quickly with the orchestration and completion of the smaller pieces that still remained to be done; on 28th, as his own thematic catalogue shows, he wrote the Priests' March and Overture, the parts for the latter arriving still wet for the dress rehearsal.

Schikaneders persönliche Bekanntschaft mit *Mozart* . . . datirt sich aus einer Freymaurer Loge her,—freylich nicht jene hochberühmte *Born'sche*, . . . sondern schlechtweg eine sogenannte Winkel- oder Fress-Loge, woselbst man sich in den wöchentlichen Abendzusammenkünften mit Spiel, Musik, u: den vielen Freuden einer wohlbesetzten Tafel beschäftigte, wie *Gieseke* mir oftmals erzählte, der auch *Sch: Wieland's Dschinnistan* mittheilte, woraus derselbe den Stoff zu mehreren seiner Opern entlehnte. Sehr wahrscheinlich begann die Composition der *Zauberflöte* erst im Frühjahr $\overline{791}$, weil *M:* nie lange an dem nehmlichen Werke, u: überhaupt schnell arbeitete. Meistens schrieb er in *Gerl's* Wohnung, oder in *Sch:s* Garten, nur wenige Schritte am Theater; ich selbst war auch Gast an demselben Tische, u: hielt viele Proben im nehmlichen Salon, oder auf deutsch: Holzhütte. Der Souffleur *Haselbeck* musste *Sch's* prosaische Entwürfe versifiziren; manches möchte auch wohl aus eigener Fabrik herstammen, wie solche Reime: "schön Mädchen jung u: fein—viel weisser noch als Kreide," zum vorhergehenden: "Aha! hier seh ich Leute,—gewagt, ich geh' hinein!"—Das Textbuch war bis zum ersten Finale vollendet, als in der Leopoldstadt: "Die *Zauberzither*," oder: "*Kaspar der Fagottist*" erschien. *Perinet* hatte ebenfalls dasselbe *Wieland*'sche Märchen benützt, war aber, den lokalen Zuschnitt abgerechnet, dem Originale treu gefolgt. Das genirte wohl etwas weniges unsern Emanuel; doch wusste er bald Rath dafür, durch Herumdrehen des ganzen Plan; zum Heil u: Glück des Ganzen, weil uns sonst *M:* schwerlich in seinem dramatischen Schwanengesang ein also wunderherrliches, poetisch romantisches Vorbild hätte hinterlassen können . . . als er, der Einladung der böhmischen Stände entsprechend, die Prager Reise antrat, waren bereits alle Ensemblestücke, bis zum letzten Finale, der *Zauberflöte* fertig, versteht sich:

Singstimmen, Grundbass, nebst angemerkten Hauptmotiven; aus welchen Parti-
cello mein Gevatter *Henneberg* inzwischen fleissig einstudierte. Nach *Mozart's*
Rückkunft—10t oder 12t Sept:—gieng es rasch zum instrumentiren, u: nachho-
len der fehlenden kleineren Piecen; am 28ten entfloss erst, wie der eigenhändige
themat: Katalog ausweisst, der Priestermarsch u: die Ouverture seiner Feder;
letztere kam sogar in nassen Auflagparten zur Generalprobe.[19]

This interesting account, not accurate in every respect, may nevertheless convey something of the atmosphere in which Mozart worked. Seyfried himself
was employed by Schikaneder as a conductor from 1797, moving with him
to the new Theater an der Wien in 1801. He must have been something of a
prodigy to have been entrusted at the age of fifteen with the first rehearsals
of the new opera. Gerl, in whose apartment Mozart worked, sang Sarastro
at the first performance. Schikaneder is affectionately referred to as "our
Emanuel." As has already been indicated (pp. 4–5), the supposed blossom-
ing of friendship between Mozart and Schikaneder behind the closed doors
of a Masonic lodge is not confirmed in the Viennese membership lists. The
earlier acquaintance of Mozart and Schikaneder in Salzburg days ought not
to be overlooked.

KARL LUDWIG GIESECKE

Mention of Giesecke raises once again the much-discussed but still unre-
solved question of his part in the writing of the libretto. His theatrical career
is only sketchily documented. He seems to have joined Schikaneder's company for a short time in Augsburg in June 1786, having worked as an actor
in Regensburg until the end of May 1786.[20] In the month of his departure
from Regensburg he published the *Regensburgisches Theater-Journal von
1784–1786* (Stadtarchiv Regensburg. 332 Theatersammlung. Blank 3. Sign.
1872). An intelligent and cultured man, he later turned to science, undertaking mineralogical research in Greenland. Subsequently he was appointed professor of mineralogy to the Royal Dublin Society. On 30th September 1791,
however, he was employed in the role of 1st Slave at the first performance
of *The Magic Flute*. From the evidence of a copy of the 1791 Alberti printed
libretto in the National-Bibliothek, Vienna (685928-A. Musik-Abt.), he may
also at some time have been involved in production work, for the essential
stage directions have been copied in his own hand onto blank pages (once
double pages, but now, unfortunately, cut in half) that opened out between the
pages of printed text. Like Mozart, he was a Freemason. More than a quarter
of a century later he reappeared in Vienna.

In the summer of 1818 in Vienna a distinguished old gentleman in a blue coat
and white cravat and wearing a decoration, came and sat down at the restaurant
table where Ignaz von Seyfried, Korntheuer, Jul. Laroche, Küstner, Gned, and
I were in the habit of lunching. His venerable snow-white head, refined speech,
and whole manner made a favorable impression on us all. It was the former
chorus singer Giesecke, who, now a professor at Dublin University, came to
Vienna directly from Iceland and Lapland with a natural history collection of the
plant, mineral, and animal world, in order to incorporate it in the Imperial Natural History Collection: *Seyfried* was the only one to recognize him. The delight
which the old man took in Vienna and in his acknowledgement by the emperor
Franz (who presented him with a truly valuable gold box overflowing with
gems, and full of the latest Kremnitz coins) was the reward for many years of
privations and sufferings. And so it came about that we learned so much about
the old times; among other things we discovered that he (a member of the then
victimized order of Freemasons) had been the real author of "The Magic Flute"
(which Seyfried had already suspected). I report this from his own words, which
we had no reason to doubt. . . . Many thought that the prompter, Helmböck, had
been Schikaneder's assistant. But Giesecke put us right about this too, attributing to Schikaneder only the character of Papageno and his lady.

Im Sommer des Jahres 1818 zu Wien, setzte sich einst ein feiner alter Herr im
blauen Frack und weissem Halstuch, mit einem Orden geziert, zu uns an den
Wirthstisch, an welchem sich Ignaz von Seyfried, Korntheuer, Jul. Laroche,
Küstner, Gned und ich täglich zum Mittag versammelten. Der ehrwürdige
schneeweisse Kopf, die gewählte Art zu sprechen, das ganze Benehmen
machte einen angenehmen Eindruck auf uns alle. Es war der ehemalige Chorist
Giesecke, der jetzt als Professor an der Universität Dublin, mit einer naturhistorischen Sammlung aus dem Pflanzen-, Mineral- und Thierreich direkt von
Island und Lappland nach Wien kam, um dieselbe dem kaiserlichen Natural-
cabinette einzuverleiben: *Seyfried* war der Einzige, der ihn erkannte. Die Freude
des alten Herrn über Wien und seine Anerkennung vom Kaiser Franz—(der
ihn mit einer von Solitären strotzenden, wirklich kostbaren Golddose voll der
neuesten Kremnitzer beschenkte) war der Lohn vieljähriger Entbehrungen und
Leiden. Bei dieser Gelegenheit erfuhren wir denn so vieles aus der alten Zeit;
unter Andern lernten wir auch in Ihm, (der zu dem damals hochverpönten Orden
der Freimaurer gehörte), den eigentlichen Verfasser der "Zauberflöte" kennen,
(wovon Seyfried allerdings eine Ahnung hatte.) Ich erzähle dies nach seiner
eigenen Aussage, welche zu bezweifeln wir keine Ursache hatten. . . . Viele
meinten der Souffleur Helmböck sei Schikaneders Mitarbeiter gewesen. Aber
auch hierüber enttäuschte uns Giesecke, nur die Figur des Papageno und seiner
Frau gestand G. dem Schikaneder zu.[21]

In this eyewitness account, from Julius Cornet's *Die Oper in Deutschland*
(1849), it appears that Seyfried was not at all surprised to learn of Giesecke's

"authorship" of the libretto. As a boy, Seyfried had himself been close to the center of events. His opinion of the first-edition libretto would have been worth hearing, though we cannot be sure that he was acquainted with it. But his challenge to Simrock to explain the origin of the Mass No. 7 (see pp. 95–96) was supported by the editor of *Cäcilia*, Gottfried Weber, the man who eleven years earlier had reviewed *The Magic Flute* first edition for the *AMZ*, giving credence to Simrock's claims for its authenticity. Weber was a persistent investigator. His detailed examination of the problems surrounding the Mozart Requiem text was mentioned at the head of chapter 3. His handling of the voluminous correspondence it inspired is recorded in the pages of *Cäcilia*. In the following year came the airing of Seyfried's scruples over the Mass and Simrock's response, naming Carl Zulehner as his authority. Weber immediately reacted by inviting Zulehner to add his voice to the discussion, albeit without success so far as the pages of *Cäcilia* are concerned. It is deeply regrettable that he was never especially exercised over the question of *The Magic Flute* first edition, having recognized its uniqueness. One of the prime witnesses could of course no longer be summoned (the Elector of Cologne had died in 1801), but Constanze was available, especially after 1820, when she settled in Salzburg with her husband Nissen following his retirement from diplomatic life after ten years in Copenhagen. Having dismissed the text differences as "unbedeutend" (insignificant), that, apparently, is where he was content to let the matter rest.

Giesecke's bearing impressed his erstwhile Viennese friends. If anything they understated his qualities. His scientific work earned him respect throughout Europe. Details of his pioneering exploration of Greenland are given in appendix A. It is hard to believe that a man deeply motivated by the quest for knowledge and truth should have attempted to perpetrate a totally outrageous lie, especially in the presence of Seyfried, who had himself been actively engaged in the preparation of the first performance of *The Magic Flute*. They had also collaborated artistically, with Seyfried providing music for four of Giesecke's texts between the years 1797 and 1799.[22] Giesecke's testimony is still regarded with suspicion by many musicologists because it does not fit comfortably into the accepted wisdom. Indeed one might say that, without any attempt at a new investigation, he has been declared guilty until proved innocent.

> It is to be hoped that at last Karl Ludwig Gieseke and other "genuine" librettists may finally be laid to rest.

> Es steht zu hoffen, dass nun endlich Karl Ludwig Gieseke und andere "wahre" Librettisten ad acta gelegt werden.[23]

Gernot Gruber's view is widely shared. H. C. Robbins Landon dismisses him with the single epithet, "notorious,"[24] while Volkmar Braunbehrens, in a book on Mozart claiming on the flyleaf to have "stripped away the sentimental myths and accretions" calls him a "botanist" (Botaniker) and labels his evidence "this bit of barroom claptrap" (dieses kleine Stammtischgeschwätz), quoting the errors in Seyfried's letter to Treitschke of c.1840 to further discredit him.[25] But in a carefully balanced study of Giesecke, Otto Erich Deutsch concludes that he was "an honorable man" (ein ehrenwerter Mann).[26]

Since Cornet's book and Seyfried's letter to Treitschke convey Giesecke's words at second hand, the accuracy of these reports cannot be guaranteed. But an impressive body of nineteenth-century scientific opinion (available in printed editions in the British Library) regarded Giesecke as a man of integrity. Failure to notice this has led some musical commentators to indulge in a character assassination of Giesecke that has no basis in the written opinions of his contemporaries nor in the evidence of Giesecke's own writings. For example, from Komorzynski's *Emanuel Schikaneder* (1956):

> He was a good-for-nothing . . . who "*studied*" law in Göttingen from 1781 to 1783, but who, like so many idlers in those days, preferred to be an actor. . . . He traveled to Bremen with the theatre company of the manager Karl Ferdinand Abt, but made off after a few weeks and was henceforth a member of various companies. *Reichards Theaterkalender* for 1785 contains the information that in 1784 a "*Herr Giesike*" secretly "*absconded*" from the Grossmann company (which at that time was playing in Mainz and Frankfurt am Main). . . . He had a very broad conscience and always did what was useful to him. In May 1800 he became a dealer in minerals and through his cunning achieved the position of Professor of Mineralogy at the University of Dublin.

> Er war ein Taugenichts . . . der 1781 bis 1783 in Göttingen Jus "*studierte*," aber, wie so viele Bummler damals, lieber Schauspieler wurde. . . . Mit der Gesellschaft des Prinzipals Karl Ferdinand Abt reiste er nach Bremen, lief aber nach wenigen Wochen davon und war fortan Mitglied verschiedener Gesellschaften. *Reichards Theaterkalender* für 1785 enthält die Mitteilung, es sei 1784 von der Grossmannschen Gesellschaft (die damals in Mainz und Frankfurt am Main spielte) ein "*Herr Giesike*" heimlich "*entwichen.*" . . . Er hatte ein sehr weites Gewissen und tat jederzeit, was ihm nützte. Im Mai 1800 wurde er Mineralienhändler und hat es durch seine Schlauheit bis zum Professor der Mineralogie an der Universität Dublin gebracht.[27]

Komorzynski's scornful attitude toward Giesecke for abandoning a career in law is hardly justified. It was not "cunning" (Schlauheit) that secured him his position in Dublin, but acknowledged scientific achievement. His written application, with supporting testimonials, is published in *The Proceedings of the Dublin Society*, vol. 50, 1813–1814, 32–35 (National Library of Ireland IR 506 R9). The procedures leading up to Giesecke's appointment are described in detail in the *Dublin University Magazine*, February 1834, 166–68 (British Library P.P. 6155). Advertisements were placed in Dublin, London, Edinburgh, and Vienna. Nine candidates applied and the "committee of mineralogy" short-listed four for consideration. In a final ballot on 2nd December 1813, it was down to just Thomas Weaver and Giesecke, the other candidates having withdrawn. Giesecke won by 152 votes to 106. Thereafter he continued to be honored and respected in Dublin. He was elected a member of the Royal Irish Academy in 1817[28] and in 1831 became its vice president.[29] A document signed by Giesecke on 30th November 1832 in his capacity as vice president (granting honorary membership of the Royal Irish Academy to Henry Ellis, principal librarian of the British Museum) is preserved in the British Library, Add. 36658 f.13 (see photo 17). Details of Giesecke's career are also found in the preface by K. J. V. Steenstrup to Giesecke's Greenland diary, *Meddelelser om Grønland*.[30] Incidentally, both Neefe and Grossmann rejected law in favor of music and the theatre.[31] It is fascinating to reflect that, seven years before *The Magic Flute* was written, Giesecke, as a member of the Grossmann company operating at that time in Frankfurt, Mainz, and Bonn, could have had contact with Neefe, Stegmann, and even perhaps Simrock, all of whom appear to have had knowledge of the first-edition text before publication.

Ludwig Wilhelm Gilbert's article in the 1819 edition of *Annalen der Physik* (see pp. 167–68 and 192n3) offers especially useful corroboration of Giesecke's standing in Vienna at the time his claims were made. Clearly Giesecke would have had much to lose if he had been caught compromising with the truth. It is of course not beyond the realms of human behavior that an honorable man, distinguished in one field, should seek to gain false credit in another, but there is nothing in Giesecke's record to suggest that he ever pursued this path.

A thorough study of Giesecke, based partly on material in Dublin, was undertaken by Edward J. Dent in 1913. He concluded:

> It has been necessary to trace the course of Giesecke's strange career in some detail, in order that the reader may be able to form some idea of his remarkable personality. This is important, because the case for his being the original author of "Die Zauberflöte" rests almost entirely upon his own statement. . . . If Giesecke was the real author, why did he allow his work to be published under Schikaneder's name? We know so little about the actual circumstances of the case that it is impossible to suggest a complete explanation of the mystery.[32]

Two years earlier Dent had drawn attention to Sigismund Neukomm's testimony to Otto Jahn.

> Cornet's statement was accepted by Jahn, and corroborated by that made to him personally by Neukomm, who had come to Vienna in 1798 to be a pupil of Haydn, and had known Giesecke himself.[33]

Dent evidently had in mind Jahn's comment

> Neukomm, too, confirmed to me that Giesecke, whom he had known as an actor at the Wieden Theatre, had a major share in the Magic Flute text.

> Dass Giesecke einen Hauptantheil an dem Text der Zauberflöte habe bestätigte mir auch Neukomm, der denselben als Schauspieler auf der Wieden gekannt hatte.[34]

The existence of the first-edition text points to an interesting, and obvious, solution. If there were not one, but two authentic libretti, there need be no conflict of truth in the respective claims of two different librettists. But who was responsible for which, and how much did their work overlap? Do we owe the popular comedy to Schikaneder, the man of the theatre? Was Giesecke, the committed Mason, the originator of the philosophic ideas that lie at the heart of *The Magic Flute*? In *Die Oper in Deutschland* (1849) Cornet states quite clearly that Giesecke was responsible for the original text and Schikaneder for the alterations, which might explain why Giesecke never pressed a claim to authorship of the libretto in its final form.

> Original German opera libretti were . . . the authentically German "Zauberflöte" by Schikaneder and his chorus member Giesecke, who did the design of the plot for him, the distribution of scenes and the well-known naive rhymes.
>   This Giesecke . . . was the author . . . of Die Zauberflöte (after Wieland's Lulu); Schikaneder only made alterations to it, cutting and adding, and claimed for himself the title of author.

> Original-deutsche Opernbücher waren . . . die ächt deutsche "Zauberflöte" von Schikaneder und seinem Choristen Giesecke, der ihm den Plan der Handlung, Scenen-Eintheilung und die bekannten naiven Reime machte.
>   Dieser Giesecke . . . war Verfasser . . . der Zauberflöte, (nach Wielands Lulu) woran Schikaneder nur änderte, strich und zusetzte, und sich den Autornamen vindicierte.[35]

There could be good reason to take note of Cornet's observations. In 1821, three years after his meeting with Giesecke, he sang Tamino in Hamburg.

The Magic Flute. Opera by Mozart. (Performed on 1st June.) . . . Mr. Cornet, leading tenor of the Braunschweig Theatre, appeared as guest artist in the role of Tamino. On first hearing, one concludes that he is a very fine singer, and he could become far better still in the future. His voice is pure and still in the full freshness of youth, very sonorous, of fairly considerable scope and very commendable even in tone, which can only have been acquired by diligent scale practice. His delivery bears witness to his culture and good knowledge of the material; in particular he kept scrupulously and strictly, in this Mozart part, to the instructions of the master himself, thus preserving the intended noble simplicity and dignity of the melodies. . . .

Die Zauberflöte. Oper von Mozart. (Aufgeführt am 1sten Juny.) . . . In der Rolle des Tamino trat Herr Cornet, erster Tenorist des Theaters zu Braunschweig, als Gast auf. Das ist, nach diesem ersten Anhören zu schliessen, ein sehr braver Sänger und wird für die Zukunft ein noch weit besserer werden können. Seine Stimme ist rein und noch in voller Jugendkraft, sehr wohlklingend, von ziemlich bedeutendem Umfang und von sehr empfehlender Gleichheit der Töne, welche nur durch eine fleissige Uebung der Scala erlangt werden konnte. Der Vortrag zeugt von Bildung, und guter Kenntnis des Satzes; insbesondre hielt er sich, in dieser Mozart'schen Partie mit Sorgfalt und Strenge an die Vorschrift des Meisters selbst und erhielt so den Gesang in seiner beabsichtigten, edlen Einfachheit und Würde. . . .[36]

Whether the first-edition version (by this time in print) was still in use in Hamburg is not clear from this review in *Dramaturgische Blätter für Hamburg*. The duet "Bey Männern, welche Liebe fühlen" is mentioned in the course of it, but that seems to be no proof, as we have seen in connection with the performance on 1st October 1800 (see p. 120), that the autograph text was the one chosen for the performance. Kurt Stephenson, in *Hamburgische Oper zwischen Barock und Romantik* (1948), adds that Cornet later became a director of the Hamburg theatre.

Julius Cornet, the important tenor and later codirector of the Hamburg Stadttheater, was first heard in Hamburg as Tamino in 1821.

Den bedeutenden Tenor Julius Cornet, späteren Mitdirektor des Hamburger Stadttheaters, hörten die Hamburger zuerst 1821 als Tamino.[37]

When he wrote his book Cornet could hardly have been unaware of the alternative text sent by Simrock and used in Hamburg from 1793 for about two decades (to the best of our knowledge), let alone of the first edition itself. One wonders whether a possible connection with Giesecke ever crossed his mind.

Schikaneder himself provides evidence in the preface to *Der Spiegel von Arkadien* that Giesecke's claim to have participated in the writing of the libretto must have been circulating in Vienna long before Giesecke's meeting with Cornet.

> . . . a certain theatre journalist in Regensburg had the nerve to inform some actors that he had been my collaborator on my *Zauberflöte*. Such impudence verges on knavery.[38]

Yet Schikaneder could not so easily throw off the charge of employing collaborators and assistants.

> Here, too, a rumour must be denied, one that has unjustly become almost universal, and would have it that Schickaneder [*sic*] is not the father and actual begetter of his theatrical children. . . . That Schickaneder [*sic*] did not write all the verses of his opera, however, he himself does not deny.[39]

> A priest, a friend of Schikaneder's, is said to write his plays for him, and the latter then published them under his own name.[40]

Citing the above three quotations in English in his book *W. A. Mozart, Die Zauberflöte* (Cambridge Opera Handbooks, 1991), Peter Branscombe puts the whole matter into perspective (p. 91).

> In a period in which copyright as we know it did not exist, and originality frequently meant no more than the ability to make good use in new ways of more or less familiar material, accusations of plagiarism were frequent, and doubtless justified. However, they become important only in the case of works which proved to be of more lasting value than the normal run of ephemera. That Schikaneder's success aroused jealousy as well as admiration is to be expected, but it is rare to find anyone bothering to doubt his rightful claim to authorship of his works other than *Die Zauberflöte*.

In the 1795 preface to *Der Spiegel von Arkadien*, Schikaneder asserts that *The Magic Flute* was "an opera which I thought through diligently with the late Mozart" (eine Oper, die ich mit dem seligen Mozart fleissig durchdachte). It would seem, therefore, that the libretto was the product of deliberation and discussion between librettist and composer. There could have been a third party present at these sessions, to whom Schikaneder might have delegated the writing of the first draft. In any event he surely reserved for himself the responsibility for improving and altering it before giving it the final stamp of approval—his name. If such a draft existed, and had been shown to Mozart as well as to Schikaneder, Mozart might well have overtaken Schikaneder in getting down to work on it. The idea of such a distribution of labor would appear in line with Schikaneder's working methods, if we accept that there is no smoke without fire. In such circumstances—and they are only conjectural—the libretto would have to be considered a committee effort, and it would be difficult to ascertain in later years exactly where credit for this, or blame for that, should lie.

Giesecke worked speedily for Schikaneder, producing, at times, a complete work, be it an adaptation or a translation, almost every month.

1794

31 May. Der bezauberte Baum
10 July. Hamlet, Prinz von Dänemark
14 August. Die Schule der Liebe

1795

3 March. Die Unterhaltung auf dem Lande
8 April. Das entdeckte Geheimnis
9 May. Idris und Zenide
18 August. Das Ungeheuer
19 September. Der Milzsüchtige

1796

4 June. Die zwölf schlafenden Jungfrauen. Part I
15 June. Die zwölf schlafenden Jungfrauen. Part II[41]

In "Das 'Zauberflöte'-Ensemble des Jahres 1791" (1991), Heinz Schuler lists twenty-five works written by Giesecke for Schikaneder between 1789 and 1800. *Die Zauberflöte* is not included. Giesecke's translations of *Figaro* (*Die Hochzeit des Figaro*) and *Così fan tutte* (*Die Schule der Liebe oder So machen sie's alle*) were used by Schikaneder. I am grateful to Neal Zaslaw for drawing my attention to this article.

Schikaneder's colorful charges of "impudence" and "knavery" seem to suggest that he was extremely sensitive on the question of his sole authorship. Yet if there had been a collaborator, no more likely candidate than Giesecke could be imagined. First, he was a Mason, listed as a member of Mozart's lodge Zur Gekrönten Hoffnung in 1790.[42] Second, he had already written three libretti for Schikaneder; a fourth, *Georg von Asten*, was evidently in hand, since it was performed a month before the *Zauberflöte* premiere.[43]

Schikaneder's preface to *Der Spiegel von Arkadien* is dated 14th June 1795. The list of Giesecke's works shows that he produced one text every month for Schikaneder in the three months leading up to that date. Is it not strange that Schikaneder should publicly denounce an active member of his own company while continuing to employ him? Giesecke's *Regensburgisches Theater-Journal* ran from 26th May 1784 until 28th May 1786. The description "a certain theatre journalist in Regensburg" was therefore nine years out of date. No one else appears to have kept a theatre journal in Regensburg subsequently. Schikaneder's scornful attack continues (Vorrede, V–VI):

—Mr. Journalist, I well remember that you once sent me an opera in which every scene was played in the clouds, and that I rejected it, indicating that you had no understanding of what is effective in the theatre!—You also had the audacity to say in Regensburg, where I have a certain reputation, that I am a trivial actor.—Beware of slinging mud at people against whom you cannot win; otherwise I shall be obliged to name you and ask you what you call *trivial*? I would prefer my Papageno to be played as a good-humoured fellow, not as a clown, as unfortunately happens on so many stages.

—Mein Herr Journalist, ich kann mich gar wohl erinnern, dass Sie mir einmal eine Oper zuschickten, in welcher jede Scene in den Wolken spielte, und dass ich Ihnen solche mit dem Bedeuten verwarf: Sie hätten keine Kenntniss von dem, was auf dem Theater Wirkung machen könnte!—Sie hatten auch die Dreistigkeit, in Regensburg, wo ich doch nicht unrühmlich bekannt bin, zu sagen, dass ich ein trivialer Schauspieler wäre.—Hüten Sie sich, Leuten, denen Sie nie die Spitze bieten können, die Ehre abzuschneiden; sonst seh ich mich genöthigt, Sie bey Namen zu nennen, und Sie zu fragen, was Sie *trivial* heissen? Ich wollte wünschen, man spielte meinen Papageno als einen launichten Menschen, nicht als einen Hannswurst [*sic*], wie es leider auf so vielen Bühnen geschieht.

There is no mention of Schikaneder in the *Regensburgisches Theater-Journal* (he was not in Regensburg during the period of its publication), nor has any other record of Giesecke's criticisms of Schikaneder come to light. Giesecke refers to him briefly in his *Salzburgisches Theater-Journal* (1787), reporting the fact that Schikaneder had been in Augsburg in August 1786.

. . . since most of them [members of the Regensburg Company] had traveled there [Augsburg] with Mr. Schikaneder . . . in order to profit from the presence of visitors who had come to see Mr. Lütgendorf's aerial flight [in an air balloon].

. . . weil die meiste derselben mit Hrn. Schikaneder . . . dahin abgereist waren, um von der Gegenwart der anwesenden Fremden, die die Himmelfahrt des Hrn. von Lütgendorfs sehen wollten, zu profitiren.[44]

I am indebted to Erich Duda for drawing my attention to this publication. If the unnamed enemy was indeed Giesecke (and in the absence of any other suitable candidate one is forced to believe it was) it seems nothing short of extraordinary that they should have continued to work so closely together.

Giesecke's first libretto for Schikaneder was a Singspiel with music by Paul Wranitzky entitled *Oberon, König der Elfen*. Like *Die Zauberflöte* it is based on Wieland, which tends to confirm the claim in Seyfried's letter to Treitschke of around 1840 that it was Giesecke who drew Schikaneder's attention to Wieland. (Schikaneder and Giesecke had recourse to Wieland again in 1795 with *Idris und Zenide*, composed by Süssmayr.) Oberon was first performed on 7th November 1789 at Schikaneder's Freihaus-Theater auf der Wieden in Vienna.[45] According to the Wranitzky article in *Grove* (by Milan Postolka/Roger Hickman):

> The enthusiastic reception of this work [Oberon] in Vienna prompted Schikaneder to conceive *Die Zauberflöte* for Mozart, whose setting shows certain striking resemblances to Wranitzky's work.

Though the Masonic language of *The Magic Flute* separates it from any other opera text, there are undoubtedly words and rhymes in Oberon that ring bells for those familiar with *The Magic Flute* libretto. Here are some examples. Unless otherwise indicated *The Magic Flute* quotations are common to Mozart's autograph text and the Simrock first full-score edition [S]. The Oberon text is published in the series *Die Oper, ed. Christoph-Hellmut Mahling and Joachim Veit* (München, 1993) [O]. Page references are also given for the vocal score edition by J. M. Götz (Worms, 1795?), British Library D.308 [G].

Oberon	**Magic Flute**
Act II, No. 15	*Act I, No. 2*
Heissa, lustig, ohne Sorgen,	stets lustig heissa hopsasa!
[O] 187 [G] 85	[NMA] 70
Act II, No. 17	*Act I, No. 3*
o welch Entzükken, sie an mein	voll Entzücken an diesen
klopfend Herz zu drükken.	heissen Busen drücken,
[O] 224–25 [G] 97	[NMA] 78–79
Act II, No. 18	*Act I, No. 5*
ist mir weit mehr als Kronen,	ist mehr als Gold und Kronen wert,
[O] 239 [G] 103	[NMA] 98

Oberon	**Magic Flute**
Act I, Neunter Auftritt	*Act I, No. 5*
Doch lass uns hier nicht länger weilen,	mit dem Prinzen ohn' Verweilen
auf, auf, lass uns nach Bagdad eilen,	nach Sarastros Burg zu eilen.
[O] 137 [G] 63	[NMA] 102
Act II, No. 17	*Act I, No. 8*
Sie lebt, sie ist's,	Sie lebt, sie lebt!
[O] 224 [G] 97 (Sie ist's! Sie ist's!)	[NMA] 144
So hab' ich ihn, so war's kein Traum.	Er ist's, ich glaub' es kaum,
Ich halte dich und glaub' es kaum.	sie ist's, es ist kein Traum.
[O] 223–24 [G] 96	[NMA] 172–73
Act II, No. 18	*Act II, No. 19*
halte dein Versprechen,	dich ruft dein Wort!
wir sehn uns wieder.	Die Stunde schlägt! Wir sehn uns
	wieder!
[O] 253 [G] 108	[NMA] 255–56
Act III, No. 25	*Act II, No. 21*
froh Hand in Hand hinübergehn	froh Hand in Hand in Tempel
	gehn.
[O] 373 [G] 150	[NMA] 297–98
Act II, No. 17	*Act II, No. 21*
Amande mein,	Tamino mein! . . .
	Pamina mein!
[O] 223 [G] 96	[NMA] 299
Act III, No. 20	*Act II, No. 21*
Komm her, mein liebes	Papagena! Herzensweibchen!
Herzensweibchen,	
[O] 314 [G] 126	[NMA] 317–18

In another passage the comparison with Oberon is specific to the first-edition text of *The Magic Flute*.

Act I, No. 3	*Act I, No. 5 (first-edition text)*
Wenn doch die Ritterehre	Dass doch der Prinz beym Henker wäre;
diesmal beim Henker wäre,	
[O] 52–53 [G] 23	[S] 83 [NMA] 104 (beim Teufel wäre.)

As has been pointed out on p. 32, Mozart's autograph (and NMA) reads "Teufel" instead of "Henker."

It would be foolish to interpret these few comparisons as proof of Giesecke's authorship of *The Magic Flute* libretto; on the other hand, there is evidently some relationship of phraseology between the two.

Giesecke's writing showed pre-echoes of *The Magic Flute* even before he had started to collaborate with Schikaneder. Here are some examples, many of them relating to the first edition rather than the autograph text, taken from the *Gelegenheitsgedichte* he published in the Anhang (supplement) to his *Regensburgisches Theater-Journal von 1784–1786.*

Gelegenheitsgedichte	*Magic Flute*
	Act I, No. 3 (first edition text)
es ist fürwahr das grösste Glück auf Erden	fürwahr, es ist ein Götterbild,
p. 77	[S] 60 [NMA] 75 (Ich fühl es, wie dies Götterbild)
	Act I, No. 7
Euer hoher Zweck	Ihr hoher Zweck
p. 64	[NMA] 124
	Act I, No. 8 (first edition text)
Tausend Dank für Eure Huld!	O tausend Dank dafür. O! dass mir doch ein Ton
p. 80	gelänge, der euch den Dank des Her zens sänge;
Wir danken Euch mit Freudenthränen p. 70	der meine Adern all' durchfliesst in Freudenthränen,
So dankt euch diese kleine Schaar mit Freudenthränen,	[S] 120 [NMA] 144–45 (Ich danke euch dafür. O
	wenn ich doch im Stande wäre, All mächtige, zu
p. 71	eurer Ehre, mit jedem Tone meinen Dank zu schildern)
	Act II, No. 15 (first-edition text)
Wir werden stets derselben würd'ger seyn— p. 72	was kann des Weisen würd'ger seyn? [S] 225–26 [NMA] 233–34 (verdienet nicht ein Mensch zu sein)

Gelegenheitsgedichte	*Magic Flute*
	Act II, No. 18
in düstrer Nacht.	Die düstre Nacht verscheucht der Glanz der Sonne!
p. 79	[NMA] 245–46
	Act II, No. 19
die Stunde, die uns scheiden soll, Naht sich schon:—wir sehn uns schwerlich wieder-	Die Stunde schlägt, nun müsst ihr scheiden, [NMA] 253 Wir sehn uns wieder! . . .
Gönner! Freunde! Lebet ewig wohl.-	Lebewohl! [NMA] 256
p. 80	
	Act II, No. 21 (first edition text)
Vernahmt ihr diesen Wink? p. 77	Seht ihre Blicke wild und stier, vernahmt ihr's? [S] 264 [NMA] 272 (Welch dunkle Worte sprach sie da!—Die Arme)
	Act II, No. 21 (first edition text)
Auf unsre Pfade streut, p. 71	sie streu' uns Rosen auf den Pfad, [S] 296 [NMA] 300 (Sie mag den Weg mit Rosen streuen,)
	Act II, No. 21 (first edition text)
nach einer bang durchwachten düstern Nacht p. 74	durch des Todes düstre Nacht. [NMA] 302–3
	Act II, No. 21 (first edition text)
So schlürft er p. 71	Ich schlürfte ächten Götterwein [S] 313 [NMA] 316–17 (Seit ich gekostet diesen Wein)
	Act II, No. 21
das höchste der Gefühle p. 63	das höchste der Gefühle, [NMA] 337

A common vocabulary does not necessarily indicate a common imagination and style. But nor, on the other hand, can the claim that Giesecke was incapable of writing *The Magic Flute* libretto be regarded as well substantiated. In any case, whoever wrote it was deeply indebted to both the ideas and language of Freemasonry.

Egon Komorzynski finds points of similarity between *Der Luftballon*—an earlier work of Schikaneder's, dating from 1786—and *Die Zauberflöte*.

> The fundamental thought of a test which must be undergone—in fact undergone by both lovers together—, so that love holds good and is worthy of reward; the same mix of serious and comic features; the promise of happy reunion after undergoing danger and the final chorus of rejoicing—all of that together proves the wondrous fact that Schikaneder as librettist, independently of Mozart, took a road that must lead finally to "*The Magic Flute*" . . . for verses such as "*Farewell, we shall soon meet with renewed joy!*" "*Now praise the lovely couple with a shout of joy!*" "*The danger is conquered with courage!*" "*The lovely couple is crowned!*" "*Love will strew roses for him!*" and many others reappear almost verbatim in "*The Magic Flute*"; certain individual words, too—"Harmony," "Beloved," "lovely" in its preferred form ["*hold*"]—are common to both works.

> Der Grundgedanke einer Prüfung, die bestanden werden muss—und zwar von beiden Liebenden gemeinsam bestanden—, damit die Liebe sich bewähre und des Lohnes würdig sei; das seltsame Gemisch von ernsten und komischen Zügen; die Verheissung des frohen Wiedersehens nach bestandener Gefahr und der Jubelchor zum Schluss—all das zusammen beweist die wundersame Tatsache, dass Schikaneder unabhängig von Mozart als Textdichter einen Weg einschlug, der schliesslich zur "*Zauberflöte*" führen musste . . . denn Verse wie: "*Lebt wohl, bald sehn wir uns mit neuer Freude!,*" "*Rühmt jauchzend nun das holde Paar!,*" "*Mit Mut besiegt ist die Gefahr!,*" "*Bekrönet ist das holde Paar!,*" "*Die Liebe wird ihm Rosen streun!*" und manche andere kehren fast wörtlich in der "*Zauberflöte*" wieder, wie auch gewisse einzelne Wörter—"Harmonie," "Trauter," das mit Vorliebe gebrauchte "hold"—beiden Stücken gemeinsam sind.[46]

Throwing circumspection to the wind, Komorzynski concludes that

> "*Der Luftballon*" is the irrefutable proof that Schikaneder is the author of the "*Magic Flute*" libretto.

> "*Der Luftballon*" ist der unwiderlegliche Beweis dafür, dass Emanuel Schikaneder der Verfasser des Textes der "*Zauberflöte*" ist.[47]

More cautiously, one may observe that a certain common currency of vocabulary and ideas, not necessarily confined to Schikaneder's theatrical productions, helped to blur the demarcation lines of authorship. Neither the vocabulary nor the style emanates from Christoph Martin Wieland, however, as a perusal of the original texts of *Lulu oder die Zauberflöte*[48] and *Oberon*[49] reveals.

NOTES

1. *Jahrbuch für Theater und Theaterfreunde* herausgegeben von C.Lebrün. Erster Jahrgang (Hamburg, 1841), 220. London University Institute of Germanic Studies C38.3 JTT1.

2. Kurt Stephenson, *Hamburgische Oper zwischen Barock und Romantik.* Hamburger Theaterbücherei, hrsg. Paul Th. Hoffmann. Bd. 6. (Hamburg, 1948), 25. Staats- und Universitätsbibliothek Hamburg Carl von Ossietzky X/8475–6.

3. *Raisonirendes Journal vom deutschen Theater zu Hamburg.* October. November/December (Hamburg, 1800). Bey Friedrich Hermann Nestler. Zweites Stük [sic]. Sonnabends, den 11ten October 1800, 22. Staatsarchiv, Hamburg, Z530 6.

4. *Privilegirte Wöchentliche gemeinnützige Nachrichten von und für Hamburg.* 96. Stück, Sonnabend, den 30 November 1793, col. 792. Staatsarchiv, Hamburg, Z900 704.

5. Ibid. Zweiter Jahrgang 1794, cols. 6–7. Staatsarchiv, Hamburg, Z900 704.

6. A.F.Bonaventurus, *Hamburgischer Briefträger.* Vierter Jahrgang, erstes Quartal, fünfter Bogen. Hamburg den 14ten December, 1793, 70–72. Staats- und Universitätsbibliothek Hamburg Carl von Ossietzky X6565 und Staatsarchiv, Hamburg, Z900 57.

7. Kurt Stephenson, *Mozart's Meisteropern im aufklärerischen Hamburg* (Weimar, 1938), 21–22, n10. Staats- und Universitätsbibliothek Hamburg Carl von Ossietzky B1947/302. The quotations are from the *Hamburgischer Briefträger* of 12th February 1791, 106f., and 19th February 1791, 120f.

8. Vitzliputzli (from *Aztec "Huitzilopochtli"*—see *Deutsches Wörterbuch, Wahrig*) seems to have been a topical allusion in Hamburg. *Marat und Orleans—Ein Dialog aus der Hölle*, in which a character named Vizlipuzli played the role of Satan's court jester, had been published only a week earlier. See Johann Friedrich Schink, *Laune, Spott und Ernst, auf Kosten des Verfassers und in Kommisssion bei J. F. Hammerich zu Altona* (Hamburg, Sonnabend, den 14. December, 1793), Zweiter Band, 785f., Landesbibliothek und Murhardsche Bibliothek der Stadt Kassel II 40a2/10.

9. A. F. Bonaventurus, *Hamburgischer Briefträger.* Vierter Jahrg., erstes Quartal, sechster Bogen. Hamburg, den 21sten December, 1793, 86.

10. Stephenson, *Mozart's Meisteropern im aufklärerischen Hamburg*, 10.

11. A. F. Bonaventurus, *Hamburgischer Briefträger.* Vierter Jahrgang, erstes Quartal, siebenter Bogen. Hamburg, den 4ten January, 1794, 102.

12. Ibid. Vierter Jahrgang, erstes Quartal, zwölfter und letzter Bogen. Hamburg, den 8ten Februar, 1794, 182–83.

13. Ibid. Vierter Jahrgang, zweites Quartal, dritter, sonst funfzehnter [sic] Bogen. Hamburg, den 1ten März, 1794, 231–32.

14. Ibid. Vierter Jahrgang, zweites Quartal, siebenter, sonst neunzehnter Bogen. Hamburg, den 29sten März, 1794, 294–97. Reproduced in Stephenson, *Mozart's Mei-*

steropern im aufklärerischen Hamburg, 22–23, n23. A small sample gives the flavor:
. . . "Met ens ging de Fortun (der Vorhang) up; un da kehm erst ehn dick bretschulle-riger Kerl so dick as unsen Herrn sien Kutscher:de gift sick vörn Prinzen uth un mackt so väl Schnacks von verlohren verlohren! halt halt! Und denn kümt ock ehn Schlang angahn, und beert as wenn se em bieten will. Wat is to dohn: met ens fallt he dahl as en Stück Holt. Nu kemen dree Schwarten uth ehn Kamienlock heruth un haren lange Stöcke un damet tick! tick! upde Schlang un weg is see. Dat seg vertrekt uth. Ock dät hät mi verdunnert gefal'n. . . ."

15. Ibid. Vierter Jahrgang, viertes Quartal, zwölfter, sonst acht und vierzigster und letzter Bogen dieses Quartals. Hamburg, den 25sten October, 1794, 764.

16. *AMZ*, 1. Jhrg., July 1799, col. 714.

17. See p. 103.

18. A.F.Bonaventurus, *Hamburgischer Briefträger*. Vierter Jahrg., erstes Quartal, vierter Bogen. Hamburg, den 7ten December, 1793, 59.

19. *Dokumente*, 471–72.

20. See Franz Grandaur, *Der Text zu Mozart's "Zauberflöte" und Johann Georg Karl Giesecke. Separat-Abdruck aus den "Bayerischen Literaturblättern"* (Wienbibliothek im Rathaus 31497 A). See also Friedrich Ratzel, *Jahresbericht der Geographischen Gesellschaft in München für 1877–1879. Zur Biographie des Augsburger Grönlandforschers Johann Georg Karl (oder Karl Ludwig) Metzler-Giesecke* (München, 1880), 159. British Library Ac.6059. Both authors give as their source F. A. Witz, *Versuch einer Geschichte der theatralischen Vorstellungen in Augsburg* (1876).

21. Julius Cornet, *Die Oper in Deutschland* (Hamburg, 1849), 24–25 (British Library 7896.bb.39). Reproduced in *Dokumente*, 475.

22. See Heinz Schuler, "Das 'Zauberflöte'-Ensemble des Jahres 1791: Biographische Miszellen," *Mitteilungen der ISM*, vol. 39 (1991), 120.

23. Review by Gernot Gruber of Peter Branscombe's *W. A. Mozart. Die Zauberflöte*. 1991. *Mozart-Jahrbuch* 1995, 218.

24. H. C. Robbins Landon, *1791. Mozart's Last Year* (1988), 141. But in *Mozart and the Masons* (2nd ed., 1991), 48, Robbins Landon concedes that he was "an interesting man."

25. Volkmar Braunbehrens, *Mozart in Vienna, 1781–1791*, trans. Timothy Bell (1990), 379. For the original German see the author's *Mozart in Wien* (1986), 401.

26. Otto Erich Deutsch, "Der rätselhafte Gieseke." *Die Musikforschung*. V. Jahrgang (1952), 152–60. British Library P.P.1946.aef.

27. Egon Komorzynski, *Emanuel Schikaneder. Ein Beitrag zur Geschichte des deutschen Theaters*. 2. Auflage (Wien, 1956), 158.

28. See Gilbert Waterhouse, "Goethe, Giesecke, and Dublin," *Proceedings of the Royal Irish Academy* 41C (1933): 213. National Library of Ireland IR 506.

29. See Gilbert Waterhouse, "Goethe, Giesecke, Schikaneder and 'Die Zauberflöte,'" *Hermathena* XCV (July 1961), 37 (National Library of Ireland G 8805 h1).

30. K. J. V. Steenstrup, *Meddelelser om Grønland*. Commmissionen for Ledelsen af de geologiske og geographiske Undersøgelser i Grønland (Copenhagen, 1910), XXV–XXVII. National Library of Ireland 549 G2.

31. See Irmgard Leux, *Christian Gottlob Neefe (1748–1798)*. Mit zwei Bildnissen und einer Handschrift-Nachbildung. Veröffentlichungen des Fürstlichen Institutes

für musikwissenschaftliche Forschung zu Bückeburg. Fünfte Reihe. Stilkritische Studien. Zweiter Band (Leipzig, 1925), 13–14 and 65.

32. Edward J. Dent, *Mozart's Operas. A Critical Study* (1913), 355. Some of Dent's handwritten and typewritten notes on Giesecke are preserved in The Papers of Edward Joseph Dent, '"Mozart's operas" notes.' King's College Library, Cambridge, EJD/2/3/1.

33. Edward J. Dent, *Mozart's Opera The Magic Flute. Its History and Interpretation* (Cambridge, 1911), 34.

34. Otto Jahn, *W. A. Mozart* (Leipzig, 1856–59). Vierter Theil, 603, n20.

35. Cornet, *Die Oper in Deutschland*, 24. British Library 7896.bb.39. Reproduced in *Dokumente*, 475.

36. *Dramaturgische Blätter für Hamburg*, hrsg. Fr.G.Zimmermann. Erster Band, no. 45 (Hamburg, 1821), 364–65. British Library P.P. 5243. i.

37. Kurt Stephenson. *Hamburgische Oper zwischen Barock und Romantik*. Hamburger Theaterbücherei, hrsg. Paul Th. Hoffmann. Band. 6 (Hamburg, 1948), 156. Staats- und Universitätsbibliothek Hamburg Carl von Ossietzky X/8475–6, 2.Ex.

38. Quoted in Peter Branscombe, *W. A. Mozart, Die Zauberflöte* (Cambridge Opera Handbooks, 1991), 89. The original German reads: "Unter andern hat ein gewisser Theater-Journalist in Regensburg die Frechheit gehabt, einige Schauspieler glauben zu machen, Er [sic] hätte an meiner Zauberflöte mit gearbeitet. Solche Dreistigkeiten gränzen an Büberey." Emanuel Schikaneder, Vorrede. *Der Spiegel von Arkadien* (Wien: bey Joseph Ochss, 1795), IV–V. Wienbibliothek im Rathaus 17909A 1.Ex.

39. Quoted in Branscombe, *W. A. Mozart, Die Zauberflöte*, 90. Joachim Perinet, *Theateralmanach auf das Jahr 1803*. *"Neuerbautes,"* 66–68.

40. Quoted in Branscombe, *W. A. Mozart, Die Zauberflöte*, 92. Testimony of Ignaz Castelli. The original German reads: "Es ging zu jener Zeit im Publicum das Gerücht: Ein Geistlicher, ein Freund Schikaneders, verfasse ihm die Stücke, die er dann unter seinem Namen erscheinen lasse." I. F. Castelli, *Memoiren meines Lebens* (1861). Erster Band, 233. British Library 10707.bbb.43. Castelli was a writer, but for a time he deputized as a violinist at the Theater auf der Wieden, Vienna (see Ignaz Franz Castelli, *Moderne Klassiker. Deutsche Literaturgeschichte der neueren Zeit in Biographien, Kritiken und Proben*. Bd. XXVII. [Ernst Balde, Cassel, 1854], 7–8. British Library 816.a.6).

41. See Schuler, "Das 'Zauberflöte'-Ensemble des Jahres 1791: Biographische Miszellen," 119–20. See also Peter Clive, *Mozart and His Circle. A Biographical Dictionary* (London, 1993), 61 and 172.

42. See H. C. Robbins Landon, *Mozart and the Masons,* 2nd ed. (1991), 66, no. 26. He may also be present, with Mozart, in a painting of a Viennese Lodge (32–33 and 46–48), though the identification is not definitive.

43. See Schuler, "Das 'Zauberflöte'-Ensemble des Jahres 1791: Biographische Miszellen," 118.

44. *Salzburgisches Theater-Journal von 1786 den 1. Oktober bis 1787 den 20. Hornung,* von Johann Georg Karl Giesecke, aus Augsburg, Mitglied der hiesigen Schauspielergesellschaft (Salzburg, 1787), folios a4-a5. Museum Carolino Augusteum, Salzburg, 19054/1. See also n47.

45. It was given again on October 15th the following year at the coronation festivities of Leopold II in Frankfurt. It was a day of competing events. Mozart was in town, giving a morning concert which was brought to an end prematurely (after three hours) because "everyone was dying to go and eat" (chacun soupiroit apres le diné [*sic*]). *Aus dem Reisetagebuch des Grafen Ludwig von Bentheim-Steinfurt*, Frankfurt, 15. Oktober 1790. *Dokumente*, 330. In Mozart's own words: "My concert today was at 11 o'clock; it brought me much honor but very little money. Unfortunately a prince was giving a big lunch and there was a grand manouevre by the Hessian troops,—every day there've been obstacles here." (heut 11 Uhr war meine Academie, welche von Seiten der Ehre herrlich, aber in Betreff des Geldes mager ausgefallen ist.—Es war zum Unglück ein gross Dejeuné bei einem Fürsten und grosses Manoever von den Hessischen Truppen,—so war aber alle Tage meines Hierseyns immer Verhinderung). Letter to his wife (15th October 1790), *Briefe*, IV, 118. The *Oberon* performance was evidently not even worth a mention.

46. Egon Komorzynski, *Emanuel Schikaneder. Ein Beitrag zur Geschichte des deutschen Theaters*. 2. Auflage (Wien, 1956), 89–90.

47. Ibid., 92. Komorzynski's account of early ballooning history, highlighting Goethe's enthusiasm for the novelty, makes fascinating reading (pp. 83–86). *Der Luftballon* was written for the Augsburg flight of 24th August 1786, but the opportunist Schikaneder suffered a misfortune, for the balloon (and consequently his opera) remained grounded by bad weather. Balloons were a topical obsession. The *Regensburgisches Diarium* (Num. VII, Dienstags, den 17 Febr. 1784, 53, Staatliche Bibliothek Regensburg, 99 ZM Rat. civ. 439 1784) reported a successful flight in Regensburg on 12th February 1784 in front of more than 5,000 spectators (not mentioned, incidentally, by Komorzynski). A Versailles flight of 19th September 1783 (Komorzynski gives 27th August) had been watched by 130,000, among them the king and royal family (see Num. III, 20th January 1784, 23). The extent of public interest is reflected in the weekly flow of advertisements for descriptions and illustrations of balloon flights that appeared in the *Regensburgisches Diarium* between 13th January and 2nd March 1784. Giesecke might have been in Regensburg at this time, since his *Regensburgisches Theater-Journal von 1784–1786* opens with a report of the departure of the deutsche Nationalschaubühne at the end of February 1784 (p. 5). However, the first clear confirmation of his presence in Regensburg comes with his appearance in a play on 26th May 1784 (p. 7). There is a reference to an air balloon in his *Oberon* libretto, "so erscheint ein Luftballon" (so an air balloon appears)—Act II, No. 15 Die Oper [O] 189; Götz [G] 86.

48. Christoph Martin Wieland, *Lulu oder die Zauberflöte. Dschinnistan*, Dritter Band (Winterthur, 1789), 292–351. British Library 12410.d.9.

49. *Oberon,* (Frankfurt and Leipzig, 1780; British Library 11526.dd.30); *Neue und verbesserte Ausgabe* (Leipzig, 1789; British Library 11517.aa.52); *Die Oper*, ed. Christoph-Hellmut Mahling and Joachim Veit (München, 1993).

Chapter Seven

Mozart's Sketches
and Working Methods

ALTERATIONS

It remains to be discovered whether—and, if so, at what stage in his work on the opera—Mozart came under pressure to accept changes to the libretto. Alan Tyson's paper studies, published in *Mozart, Studies of the Autograph Scores* (1987), have led him to suggest that Mozart himself may have made musical changes.

> . . . it seems likely that Mozart was already revising the first number of *Die Zauberflöte* by the second half of June.[1]

Later he writes:

> It is well known that Mozart had virtually completed *Die Zauberflöte* by July 1791 and that he then went on to write *La clemenza di Tito*, finishing that in Prague, where it was performed on 6 September; then he returned to Vienna, wrote the overture and the Priests' March for *Die Zauberflöte* by 28 September, and conducted its premiere two days later. What paper-studies can show us is that three second-act numbers were also written—or perhaps rewritten?—after Prague: the terzetto of the three boys, "Seid uns zum zweiten Mal willkommen," Pamina's famous G-minor aria, and the B-flat terzetto "Soll ich dich, Teurer, nicht mehr sehn?"[2]

The report that Schikaneder forced Mozart to rewrite the "Bei Männern" Duet no fewer than five times has already been mentioned under the discussion of that number (Act I, No. 7) on p. 13. Was Schikaneder so brazen as to instruct Mozart in the art of composition? Is it not more likely to have been alterations to the libretto that caused the trouble? Mozart was by no means immune to outside interference or pressure. In his discussion "On the Composition of Mozart's *Così fan tutte*" (see *Mozart, Studies of the Autograph Scores* (1987), 177–221) Tyson has written:

> . . . a deletion that Mozart made contentedly in a score is unlikely to be distinguishable from one to which he assented reluctantly. (p. 205)

and

> . . . there can be little doubt that Mozart himself collaborated in cutting certain passages in the opera and helped to repair some of the jagged edges. But the reasons that led to the cuts, and the frame of mind in which he made them, must remain matters for speculation. (p. 210)

To digress for a moment, it would surely have astonished Mozart to know that some sixteen years after he was weighing up these matters, Da Ponte, the librettist of *Così*, was measuring out tea and tobacco in a New York store.

> So I became a grocer. Anyone with a little imagination may think how I laughed at myself every time my poetic hand was obliged to weigh out two ounces of tea or measure half a yard of "pigtail" (tobacco) for a cobbler or carter, or pour him out a morning dram [which was not, however, the drama of the *Cosa Rara* nor of *The Marriage of Figaro*] for three cents. Such is the way of the world![3]

> (The pun on "dram"/"drama" appears only in the original Italian version (see below), but it has been added here in square brackets.)

> Divenni dunque droghiero; e pensi chi ha fior di senno com'io ridea di me stesso tutte le volte che la mia poetica mano era obbligato a pesare due oncie di te, o misurar *mezzo braccio* di *codino di porco* a un ciabattino, o ad un carretiere, o a versagli per tre centesimi, *a morning dram*, che non era però nè il dramma dalla cosa rara, nè delle nozze di Figaro. Così va il mondo.[4]

Meanwhile, Giesecke was cutting rock samples in Greenland!

If we accept in principle that changes were in some instances imposed on Mozart for reasons not necessarily of his own making, then the first-edition text of *The Magic Flute* may indeed be, as Gottfried Weber observes, "in accordance with Mozart's own wishes" (der Absicht Mozarts selbst entsprechend)—see photo 2 and p. 6.

We have Mozart's own word that he worked on his music in his head before writing it down. As he informed his father in a letter of 30th December 1780:

> . . . I must write like crazy—everything is already composed—but not yet written down.

. . . ich muss über hals und kopf schreiben—komponirt ist schon alles—aber geschrieben noch nicht.[5]

Much depends on the timing of possible alterations. It is a part of Mozart legend, though now discredited, that he wrote his music straight out of his head, finished and perfected. But the existence of sketches for the entire opera was reported in the *AMZ* obituary of Benedikt Schack (1758–1826), another participant in the first performance.

> Tamino was written for him; he could specify how and on what occasion, at what time, in what situation every number of *The Magic Flute* was sketched, changed, and finally completed.

> Für ihn ward Tamino geschrieben, er konnte angeben, wie und auf welche Veranlassung, zu welcher Zeit, in welcher Lage jedes Stück der *Zauberflöte* entworfen, geändert, endlich ausgeführt worden.[6]

Schack, the first Tamino, was a composer in his own right, whose works were performed by Schikaneder's company. Again we have to remind ourselves of the length of time that elapsed between the composition of *The Magic Flute* and reported testimony, in this case thirty-five years. Ten months before his death on 10th December 1826, Constanze wrote to Schack, with a supporting note from Nissen, whose biography of Mozart was in course of preparation, requesting that he set down all that he remembered of Mozart. There can be no doubt that she regarded him as a reliable witness.

> I can think of no one at all who was so intimate and who lived through so much with him, no one who knew him better or to whom he was more devoted, than you, and particularly in the most important, last years right up to his death and during the period, especially, that he lived in Vienna. . . .

> Ich wüsste durchaus Niemanden, der in einer solchen Vertraulichkeit und so viel mit ihm gelebt hat, Niemanden, der ihn mehr gekannt oder dem er sich mehr hingegeben hätte, als Sie, und das namentlich in seinen wichtigsten letzten Jahren bis an seinen Tod, und während des Aufenthalts just in Wien. . . .

Later in the letter she reiterates:

> Mozart seems to have been on *intimate* terms with absolutely no one to such a degree as with you.

> Mit gar Niemanden scheint M. in solchem Grade, wie mit Ihnen, *intim* gewesen zu seyn.[7]

Referring to this request for information, Schack's obituary notice offers the explanation that it was refused on the grounds that no good was done by stirring up the old stories.

An interesting theory, rarely considered, is the possibility that Mozart may sometimes have used a slate or wax writing tablet to note down his musical ideas.

> Mr. Haderlein [. . .] 78 years old, was Mozart's barber [. . .]. Mr. Haderlein related the following to me, by the way: [. . .] As I was turning from the Kärntnerstrasse into the Himmelpfortgasse one day in order to be of service to M., he came by on horseback, stopped, and, riding forward a few paces, took out a tablet and wrote down some music. I spoke to him again, asking whether I should come now and he answered in the affirmative.

> Herr Haderlein [. . .] 78 J. alt, war Friseur Mozarts [. . .]. H. Haderlein erzählte mir übrigens: [. . .] Als ich eines Tages eben von der Kärntnerstrasse in die Himmelpfortgasse einbog um M. bedienen zu wollen, kam er zu Pferde daher, hielt still, u: nahm als er einige Schritte weiterritt eine Tafel heraus u schrieb Noten auf ich sprach ihn wieder, ob ich itzt kommen dürfe u. er bejahte es.[8]

Haderlein's testimony was written down by Joseph Hüttenbrenner (1796–1882), brother of the composer Anselm (1794–1868). Pfannhauser, who reported the story, was able to inspect the autograph, still in the Hüttenbrenner family, in 1954 (see *Mozart-Jahrbuch* 1971/1972, 283). In quoting the above in *Mozarts Schaffensweise* (1992), Ulrich Konrad insists that he has not abandoned his "skeptical attitude toward anecdotes" (skeptische Haltung gegenüber Anekdoten). But since a single report that Mozart used a writing tablet is hardly the kind of observation an ordinary person would make in order to give himself an air of importance, he concludes that there is no reason to reject it.

FREDRIK SAMUEL SILVERSTOLPE

The surviving *Magic Flute* sketches are described and reproduced in the NMA.[9] Of special interest are those acquired by Fredrik Samuel Silverstolpe from Constanze, and brought by him to his native Sweden. The warmth of friendship he enjoyed with the Nissens shines through in a letter from Constanze of 21st January 1800.

> I am holding a surprise birthday party for Nissen tomorrow at my house, at which the presence of Herr von Silberstolbe would give me and Nissen the greatest pleasure. I therefore take the liberty of inviting you to eat with us tomor-

Photo 1. Title page of first full-score edition (Bonn: N. Simrock, 1814). From the Music Collection of Senate House Library, University of London.

des National-Reichthums stehend, doch, als Ableiter gefährlicher Conspirationen und Factionen, dem Staatsmanne, der sie wol selbst, des guten Tons wegen, hin und wieder besucht, eher willkommen, als verhasst seyn müssen.

NACHRICHTEN.

Frankfurt a. Mayn. Ende August. Der Bass-sänger, Hr. Häser, von königl. württemb. Hof-theater, hat hier mehrere Gastrollen gegeben; den Joh. Krebs in *Schwestern von Prag*, den Masseru im *Opferfest*, den Herzog in *Camilla*, den Pistofolus in der *Müllerin* etc. Die erste dieser Rollen wiederholte er auf vieles Verlangen und mit unmässigem Beyfall — hauptsächlich wol darum, weil er als Frauenzimmer sehr gut aussahe, und im Falset eine grosse, lange Bravourario mit vielen Rouladen, Trillern u. dergl., gleich einer vermals imponirenden *prima Donna*, wirklich zum Verwundern absang. Variationen von eigener Composition, die er einlegte, und die über ein ungünstiges Thema nicht eben viel aussagten, wurden ruhiger aufgenommen. Compositionen dieser Art taugen auch wol mehr für Privatübung und Unterhaltung gesellschaftlicher Zirkel, als für die Bühne und die Begleitung eines vollen Orchesters. Hrn. Häsers Stimme fand man allerdings angenehm, biegsam und ausgebildet, doch weder an Stärke, noch an Tiefe ausgezeichnet; sein Vortrag und sein Spiel wurden mit vielem Beyfall aufgenommen.

RECENSIONEN.

Il flauto magico, Dramma per musica del Signor *W. A. Mozart* — Die *Zauberflöte*, grosse Oper in zwey Acten von *W. A. Mozart*. Bonn, bey Simrock. (Pr. 48 Franken.)

Es ist doch wahrlich ein recht bündiger Beweis von uneigennützigem Kunstsinn, wenn ein Verleger, zumal in den gegenwärtigen, noch so

ehernen, dem Kunsthandel noch so wenig günstigen Zeiten, es unternimmt, die Partitur eines Werkes herauszugeben, welches zwar allgemein beliebt, aber auch eben darum schon so allgemein verbreitet ist, dass er unmöglich auf zahlreichen Absatz solches kostbaren Verlagsartikels rechnen konnte. Hr. Simrock, der durch dies Unternehmen ein würdiges Seitenstück zu seiner höchst correcten, vollständigen Ausgabe aller haydnschen Symphonien in ausgesetzten Stimmen liefert, kann dabey, nächst einigem Absatz an Bühnen des Auslandes, hauptsächlich nur auf diejenigen Verehrer der mozartschen Muse gerechnet haben, die, etwa angelockt durch die Wohlfeilheit des Ladenpreises, sich diese Partitur zum Selbststudium anschaffen möchten. In der That ist auch der Preis von zwey Carolin für ein Werk von 563 Folioseiten jetziger Zeit gewiss äusserst mässig. Stich und Papier sind schön; und was die Correctheit angeht, so hat Ref., bey aufmerksamster Durchlesung der ganzen Partitur, nur einen einzigen Stichfehler gefunden, der noch dazu zu unbedeutend ist, um nur erwähnt zu werden. *)

Der deutsche Text ist an manchen Stellen nicht ganz der, auf den meisten deutschen Bühnen eingeführte; die Varianten sind aber unbedeutend, und weder schlimmer, noch besser, als die *vulgata*. Auf jeden Fall ist das Ganze der Absicht Mozarts selbst entsprechend, da Hrn. Simrocks Ausgabe, nach dessen Versicherung, von einer handschriftlichen Originalpartitur genommen ist, welche der vorige Kurfürst von Cölln, Max Frans von Oesterreich, von Mozart selbst erhalten hatte.

Auch der beygefügte italienische Text schliesst sich der Musik überall gut an, und ist an sich selbst grösstentheils wohlgerathen, auch echt italienisch. Als Probe mag Monostatos' Liedchen hier stehen:

Regna Amore in ogni loco,
Scherza, gioca, frulla ognor:
Solo a me unga un bel foco,
Perchè bruno ho un pò il color.
Ampodno nel pur fagello,
Mi fe il cerebro bolly;
Sempre star sessa una bella
Sarìa cosa da morir!

Or che almen la sorte è buona
Profittarne anch' io potro.
Santa Luna! mi perdona!
Me una Bianca innamoro.
Bianca, affè! Bia con tua pace!
La vorrei pur carezzar.
Luna mia, se ti dispiace —
Serra gli occhj, o non guardar!

Gottfried Weber.

*) Anm. Das wahrhaft Verdienstliche dieser Ausgabe, so wie manches Ähnliches Unternehmen des Hrn. Simrock, ist zwar schon in einem frühern Aufsatze dieser Blätter anerkannt und auseinander gesetzt worden, ist aber auch von einer Art, wie es dieser Bestätigung zu sehr werth war, als dass wir derselben den Platz versagen könnten.   d. Redact.

Photo 2. Review of first edition, published in Leipzig in the Allgemeine Musikalische Zeitung, 13th September 1815, Jahrgang XVII, columns 625–27. From the Music Collection of Senate House Library, University of London.

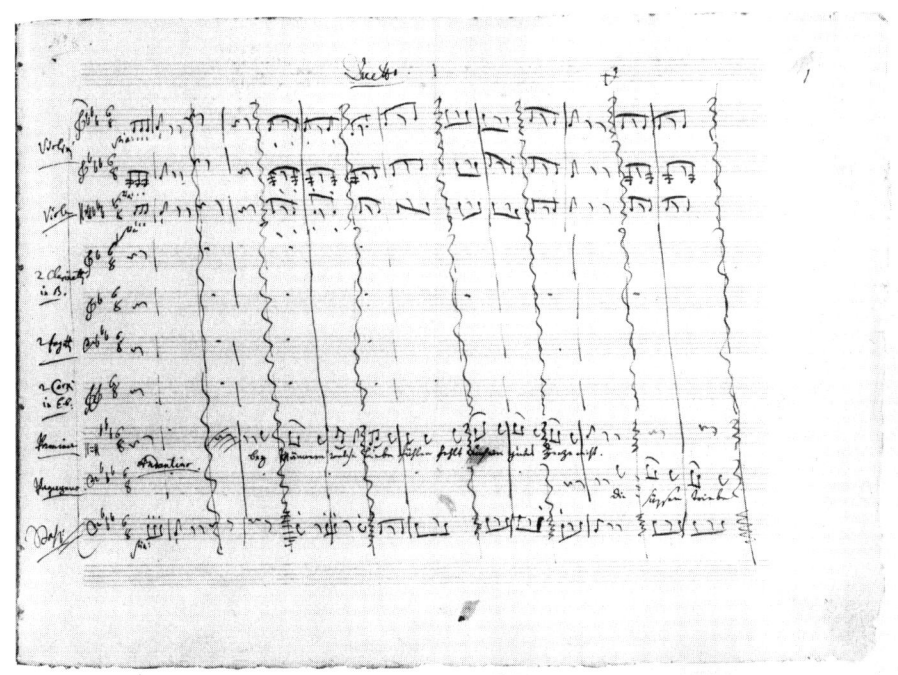

Photo 3.   Duet "Bei Männern," Act I. No. 7, Bars 1–7 and 43–49, showing re-barring in Mozart's autograph. Staatsbibliothek zu Berlin—Preussischer Kulturbesitz, Musikabteilung mit Mendelssohn-Archiv. Facsimile edition by Bärenreiter. From the Music Collection of Senate House Library, University of London.

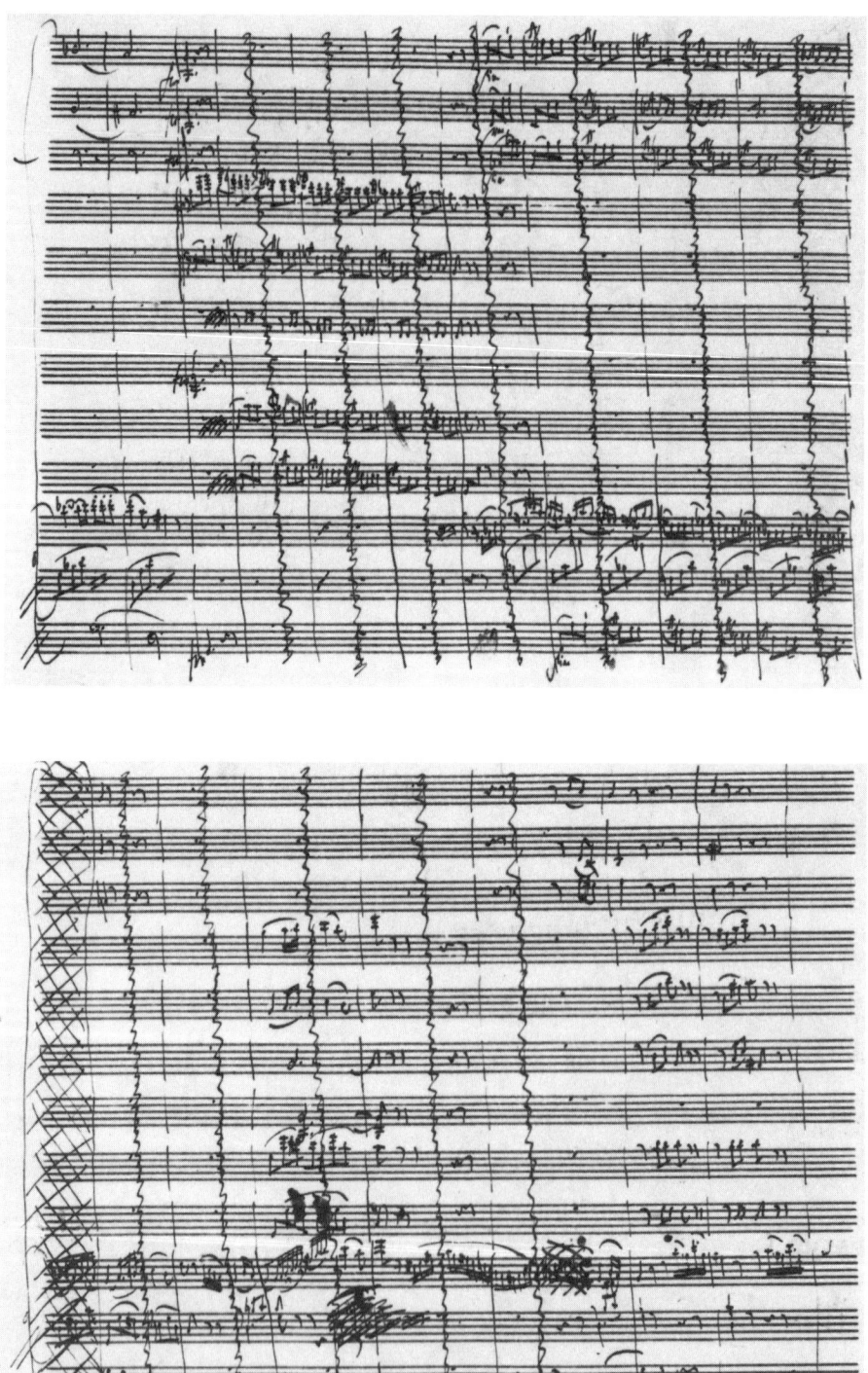

Photo 4. Second movement of Piano Concerto in F K459, Bars 64–80, showing re-barring in Mozart's autograph. Staatsbibliothek zu Berlin—Preussischer Kulturbesitz, Musikabteilung mit Mendelssohn-Archiv.

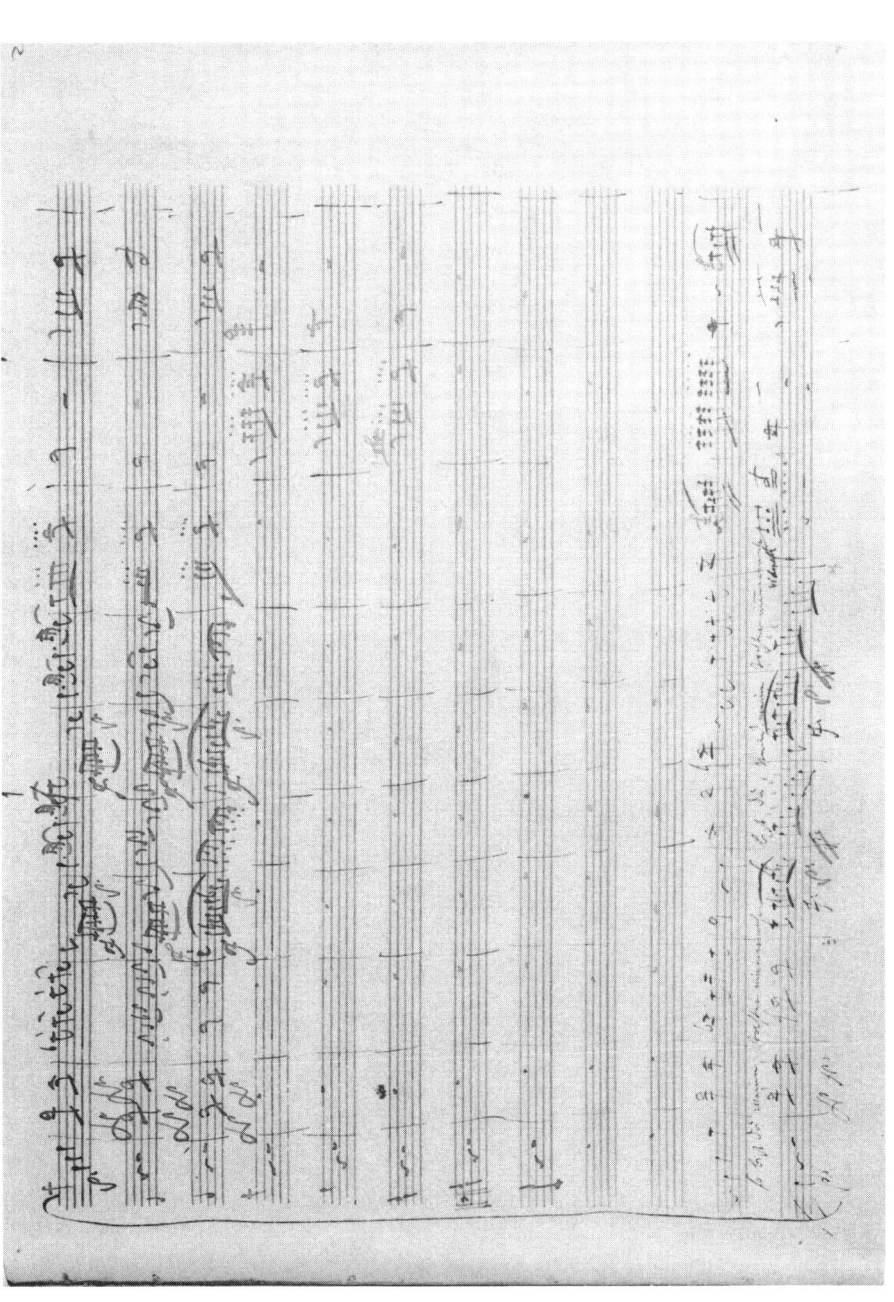

Photo 5. Aria "Der Hölle Rache," Act II, No. 14, Bars 17–26. Mozart's autograph. Staatsbibliothek zu Berlin—Preussischer Kulturbesitz, Musikabteilung mit Mendelssohn-Archiv. Facsimile edition by Bärenreiter. From the Music Collection of Senate House Library, University of London.

Photo 6. 2nd Act Finale. No. 21, Scene 28, Bars 311–28. Mozart's autograph. Staatsbibliothek zu Berlin—Preussischer Kulturbesitz, Musikabteilung mit Mendelssohn-Archiv. Facsimile edition by Bärenreiter. From the Music Collection of Senate House Library, University of London.

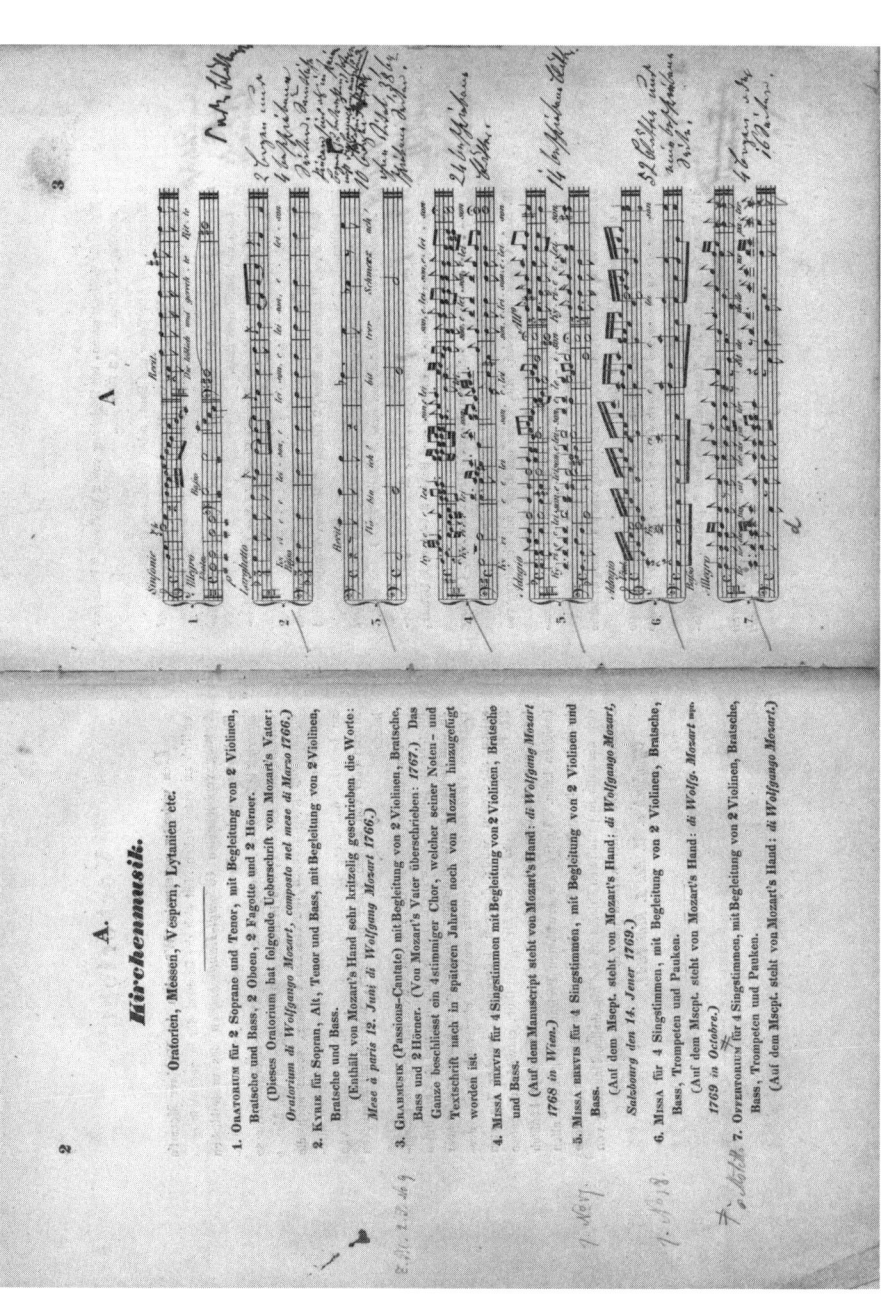

Photo 7. Thematisches Verzeichniss derjenigen Original-Handschriften von W. A. Mozart, welche Hofrath André in Offenbach besitzt (1841). Copy owned by Heinrich Henkel (?). Universitätsbibliothek, Frankfurt am Main Mus. Hs. 778/8.

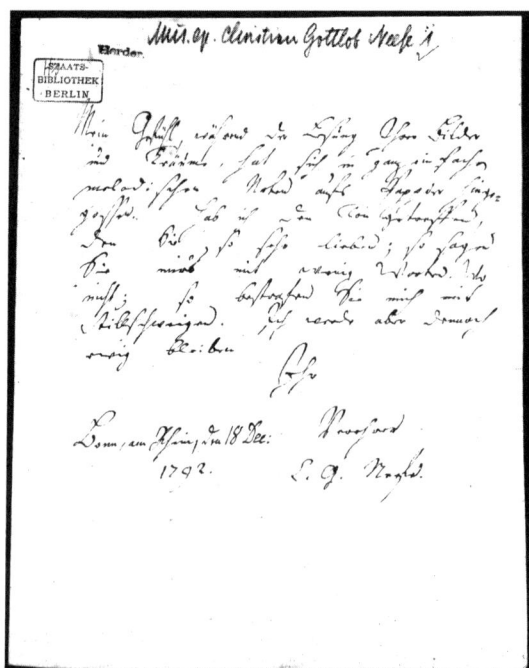

Photo 8a. (top) Tamino's Aria, Act I, No. 3, Bars 1–18. Wienbibliothek im Rathaus MH 10632. (bottom) Autograph letter by C. G. Neefe (18th December 1792). Staatsbibliothek zu Berlin— Preussischer Kulturbesitz, Musikabteilung mit Mendelssohn-Archiv Mus.ep. Chr. G. Neefe 1.

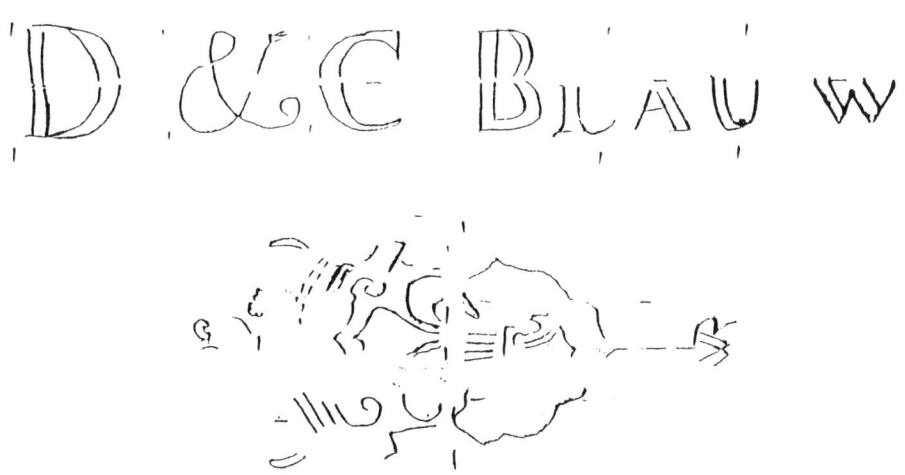

Photo 8b.   D&C Blauw watermark pp. 1–4 and 9–12. Wienbibliothek im Rathaus MH 10632. Tracing by Dr. Erich Duda.

Calender à 2 Mk., und in Seide 3 Mk. Der
Offenbacher Calender à 1 Mk., und in Seide
1 Mk. 8 ß. Der Hamburger Staats-Calen-
der à 12 ß., Taschen-Calender mit Kupfern
und Anekdoten, im Futeral à 8 ß., und in
Seide 1 Mk. Der neue französische Calender
à 4 ß. Gesellschaftliches Liederbuch von 250
Lieder à 1 Mk. 8 ß. Classen-Lottery-Spiel
à 1 Mk. Fragen und Antworten im Futeral
à 12 ß. Illuminirtes Gänsespiel auf einem
Bogen à 2 ß. A B C Spiel à 6 ß. dito mit
Bilder à 8 ß. Fiebeln mit illuminirten Bil-
dern à 8 ß., auch zu 1 Mk. 8 ß. Weihnachts-
Geschenke à 1 Mk. Anekdoten à 4 ß. 68
englische Tänze à 12 ß. dito von 36 Stück
à 6 ß. Das Bildnis des seel. Hrn. Roose à
12 ß. Von allen möglichen Sorten Neujahrs-
wünschen, als: seidne Bänder, gestickte pot
de pouri-Küssen Wünsche mit Noten auf Atlas,
zu verschiedenen Preisen. Wie auch Bogen-
wünsche à 2 ß. Das à caira auf Noten à 4 ß.

Bey Joh. Hinr. von Horn, wohnhaft
bey den Mühren nahe am Steckelhörn, steht zum
Verkauf: Ein Claviecin d'amur, à 12 Rthlr.
Eine schöne Flöte à 4 Rthlr. Zwey Violinen à
4 Rthlr. und 2 Rthlr. Ferner sind bey mir
zu haben: schöne Farben-Kästchens, jedes
mit 24 Gläser und Pinseln. Das Kästchen kostet
4 Mk. 8 ß.

Musikalische Anzeige.

Aus der neuesten Oper, die Zauberflöte,
sind zu haben: 1) Das schöne Duett: Der
Liebe holdes Glück empfinden, 2c. 2)
Das comische Duett zwischen Papageno
und Papagena. 3) Die comische Arie: Ein
Mädchen oder Weibchen. 4) Die beliebte
Arie: In diesen heiligen Hallen 2c. Alle
ganz nach der hiesigen Vorstellung und dem
Texte; sind bey Hermann am Fischmarkt und
an allen gewöhnlichen Orten für 8 ß. zu haben.

Bekanntmachung.

Da der Bau an meiner Eisgrube, welcher
bisher verhindert, meinen resp. Gönnern und
Freunden mit Eis aufzuwarten, vollendet ist,
und ich bereits mit einem großen Vorrath Eis

verseben bin, so kann ich einem jeden damit
nach Verlangen prompt und solide bedienen.
Ich bitte um geneigten Zuspruch.
                    Joh. Simon Behn,
                    Conditor wohnhaft hinter
                                St. Petri.

Schauspiele.

Heute: Der Eßighändler.
Donnerstag: Edelsinn und Armuth.
Freytag: Der gutherzige Alte, und das
Portrait der Mutter.
Am Sonntage, als den 22sten dieses, ist
musikalische Akademie.

Angekommene Fremde.
Den 13 Dec.

Der Herr Encke, ein Kaufmann, kommt
von Gera, und der Herr Professor Voigt,
kommt von Lübeck, logiren im Kramer-Amts-
hause.
Der Herr Landherr von Schulte, kommt
von Harburg, logirt in der Stadt London.
Der Herr Hofrath Sonnenbeck, kommt
aus Schweden, wußte kein Logis.

Den 15 dito.

Der Herr Cammerjunker Rose, kommt aus
dem Holsteinischen, logirt im Adler.
Die Herren Gebrüder Coulet, Kaufleute,
kommen aus der Schweiz, und der Herr
Meillan, ein Kaufmann, kommt aus Spa-
nien, logiren auf Kayserhof.

Den 16 dito.

Der Herr Cammerherr von Schildten,
kommt von Itzehoe, logirt in der Stadt
London.
Der Herr Cammerherr von Ahlefeldt, kommt
aus dem Holsteinischen, logirt in der Stadt
Copenhagen.

Verbesserung.

Im 99sten Stück, pag. 811, Zeile 18 von
unten, bey Frau Faber, geb. Volckmann,
füge man hinzu mß 10000.

In vorigen Stücke pag. 823 unter den Ar-
tikel von Vormundschafts-Sachen lese man:
Joh. Herm. Reimers Sohn erster Ehe, statt
des verstorbenen Joh. Herm. Reimers Sohn
erster Ehe.

Photo 9. Announcement of *Magic Flute* arias and duets for sale in connection with the first Hamburg production. Privilegirte Wöchentliche gemeinnützige Nachrichten von und für Hamburg. 101. Stück. Mittewochen, den 18 December 1793. Staatsarchiv, Hamburg, Z900 704.

Photo 10. Pamina kneeling before Sarastro in the 1st Act Finale, No. 8, Scene 18. Copper engraving (undated), J. C. Zimmer, Hamburg. Universität Hamburg (Zentrum für Theaterforschung/ Hamburger Theatersammlung).

VORWORT.

Die erste Ausgabe der Partitur von Mozarts Zauberflöte wurde nach einer Abschrift gemacht, welche der Verleger von Mozarts Wittwe im Jahr 1792 erworben hatte. Der gegenwärtigen neuen Ausgabe liegt eine genaue Revision nach Mozarts Originalmanuscript zu Grunde, durch welche einzelne Fehler verbessert und namentlich die Vortragsbezeichnungen genauer gegeben werden konnten. Alle Abweichungen der jetzigen von der früheren Ausgabe sind daher auf die Gewähr des Mozart'schen Autographs zurückzuführen, von welchem mit Absicht nur an einer Stelle abgewichen ist. Im Ritornell des Duetts No. 7 sind Takt 2 und 3 die Accorde

Clarini

Corni

von Mozart nicht eingetragen, als er seiner Gewohnheit gemäss, nachdem die Singstimmen, Bass und erste Violine ausgeschrieben waren, die übrigen Stimmen eintrug. Sie können nicht fehlen und stehen auch in der obenerwähnten Abschrift. Das, bei Mozart fast unerhörte, Versehen erklärt sich wohl daraus, dass er anfangs das ganze Duett mit anderer Takteintheilung

Violini

Pamina — Bei Männern welche Liebe fühlen, fehlt auch ein gutes

Bassi.

bis zu Ende durchgeschrieben hatte, so dass der Schluss um drei Achtel wie folgt verlängert war

Viol. 1.

Bassi.

Beim Durchgehen änderte Mozart den Rhythmus, machte die ersten drei Achtel zum Auftakt, strich drei Achtel vom Schluss, und schob die richtigen Taktstriche ein, indem er die alten sämmtlich ausstrich. Bei dieser Arbeit scheint er jene Accorde aus den Gedanken verloren zu haben.

Das Originalmanuscript zeigt ausser in dem angeführten Duett noch an einigen Stellen Veränderungen, welche Mozart während der Ausarbeitung vornahm. Sie betreffen meistens die Instrumentation und sind von keiner grossen Bedeutung, indessen gewähren auch kleine Besserungen des Meisters, zum Theil grade weil sie so klein sind, ein eigenthümliches Interesse, und so wird die Mittheilung derselben neben der vollständigen Partitur erwünscht sein.

In der Ouverture war S. 8 nach Takt 7 ursprünglich folgender Gang für die Clarinette

Viol. 1?

Clarin:

Bassi.

den Mozart bei der Instrumentirung gestrichen hat, dagegen war der Abschluss des ersten Theils anfangs um einen Takt (S. 10 T. 5) verkürzt gewesen.

In der Introduction No. 1 hat Mozart von Anfang her Trompeten und Pauken angewendet, wie folgt:

Clarini in C.

Timp: in C.G

Dies alles ist dann sorgfältig von ihm ausgestrichen worden; dagegen findet sich ein Beiblatt, auf welchem zu S. 22, Syst. 2, Takt 2 Trompeten und Pauken geschrieben sind

Clarini in Es.

Timp: Es 3.

Diese Stimmen sind nicht durchgestrichen, und es ist daher wohl anzunehmen, dass Mozart wirklich den Triumphgesang der drei Damen in solcher Weise auszeichnen wollte.

Am Schlusse der Introduction hatte Mozart denselben eine grosse Cadenz vergünstigt, welche S. 34, Syst. 1, T. 3 einsetzte. (Siehe folgende Seite Anl. A.) So ist sie von Al. Fuchs nach einer alten Abschrift bekannt gemacht (Allg. Wien. Mus. Zeit. 1841 No. 58), im Original ist bis * geschrieben (aber ohne Vervollständigung der Instrumentation) und durchgestrichen, dann fehlt ein Blatt, und das Ende von ⊕ an steht auf der nächsten Seite durchgestrichen. Die beiden Takte, welche jetzt die Veränderung herstellen S. 34 Syst. 1 T. 4 und 5 sind später von Mozart hinzugesetzt. Da übrigens die fünf Takte von * bis ⊕ kein Blatt füllen, so bleibt es immer noch fraglich, ob die Cadenz so wie sie jetzt vorliegt, ganz vollständig ist.

Im ersten Finale S. 70, Syst. 2, T. 1 war zuerst die Flöte angewendet

Flauto

dann aber, ohne fortzufahren, durchgestrichen; ebendort S. 81, Syst. 2, T. 6 ging die erste Violine mit der Singstimme

Viol. 1.

ist aber auch, aus leicht begreiflicher Ursache, getilgt.

In der Arie No. 14 lautete S. 122, Syst. 2, T. 3 und Syst. 3 T. 6 die Violoncellstimme

Cello

Im Terzett No. 19 hatte statt der charakteristischen Figur der Bratsche, Violoncell und Fagott die erste Violine

Viol. 1

aber nur einen Takt lang, der dann corrigirt worden war.

Im zweiten Finale S. 156 Syst. 2 T. 2 waren die nachschlagenden Accorde der Flöten und Clarinetten zuerst den Saiteninstrumenten zuertheilt

Violini

Viola

und ebendaselbst S. 177 Syst. 2 T. 3 lautete die Stimme der zweiten Violine und Bratsche anfänglich

Viol. 2.

Viola.

Der Schikaneder'sche Text, welcher in der ersten Ausgabe mancherlei Veränderungen erfahren hatte, ist jetzt in seiner ursprünglichen Gestalt wieder gegeben worden.

Bonn, December 1862.   Otto Jahn.

Photo 11. Preface to revised Simrock full score, ed. Otto Jahn (Bonn, 1862).

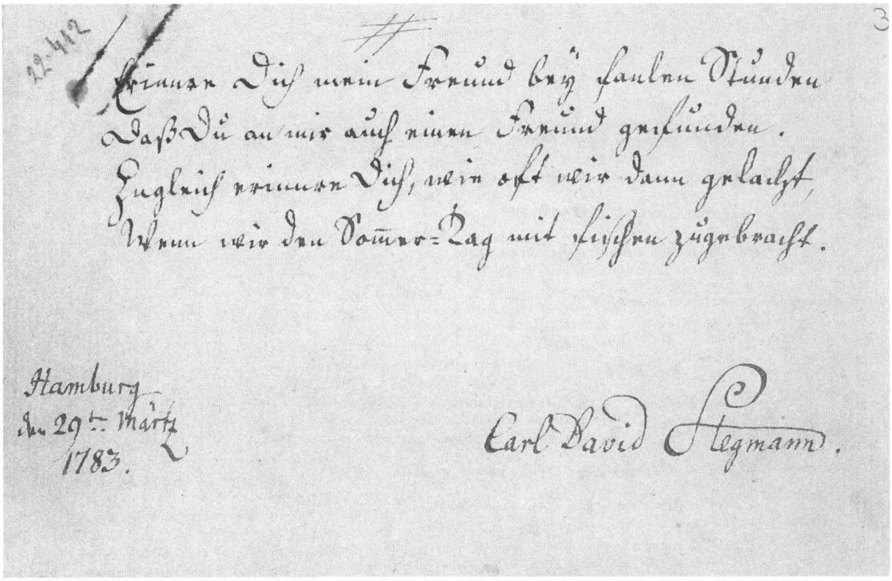

Erinnre Dich mein Freund bey faulen Stunden
Daß Du an mir auch einen Freund gefunden.
Zugleich erinnre Dich, wie oft wir dann gelacht,
Wenn wir den Sonne-Tag mit Fischen zugebracht.

Hamburg
den 29ten März
1783.

Carl David Stegmann.

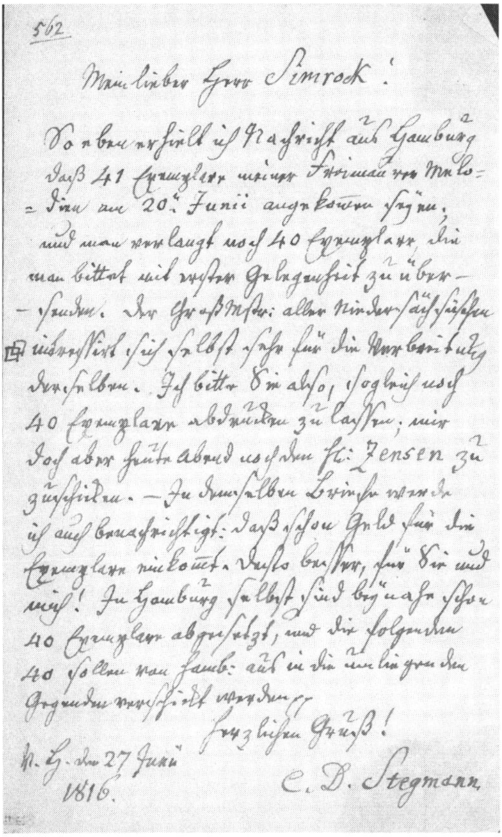

Mein lieber Herr Simrock!

Vorhin erhielt ich Nachricht aus Hamburg daß 41 Exemplare meiner Freimaurer Melodien am 20. Junii angekommen seyen, und man verlangt noch 40 Exemplare, die man bittet mit erster Gelegenheit zu übersenden. Der Großmeister aller Niedersächsischen interessirt sich selbst sehr für die Verbreitung derselben. Ich bitte Sie also, sogleich noch 40 Exemplare abdrucken zu lassen; mir doch aber heute Abend noch den Hr: Jensen zu zuschicken. — In demselben Briefe werde ich auch benachrichtigt: daß schon Geld für die Exemplare einkommt. Desto besser, für Sie und mich! In Hamburg selbst sind beynahe schon 40 Exemplare abgesetzt, und die folgenden 40 sollen von Hamb: aus in die umliegenden Gegenden verschickt werden.

Herzlichen Gruß!

B. G. den 27 Junii
1816.

C. D. Stegmann

Photo 12. Two autograph letters by Carl David Stegmann: (top) 29th March 1783, Staats- und Universitätsbibliothek Hamburg Carl von Ossietzky, LA: Stegmann, Carl David: 1–3; (bottom) 27th June 1816, Stadtarchiv, Bonn, Musikverlag Simrock SN157, Nr. 79.

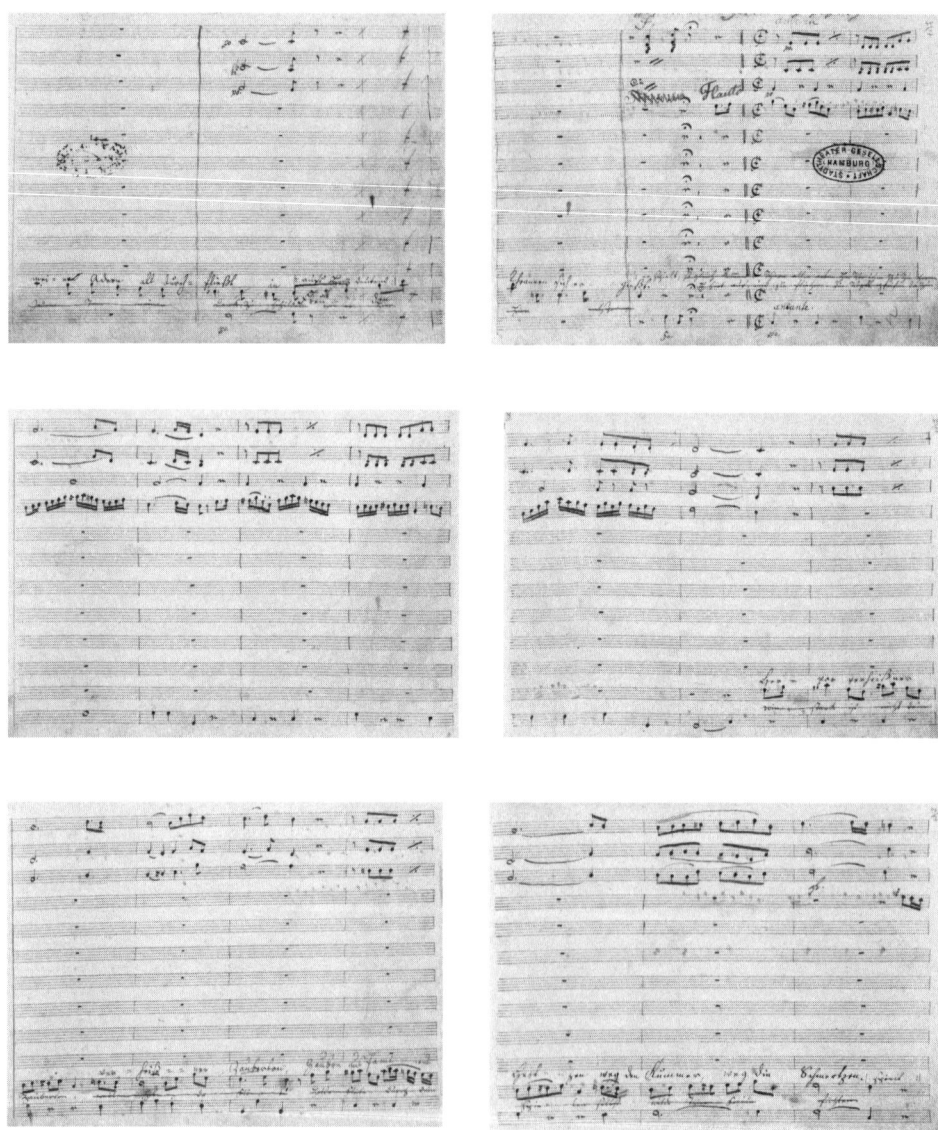

Photo 13.   1st Act Finale, No. 8, Scene 15, Bars 156–75. Simrock manuscript full score from the archive of the Stadttheater, Hamburg. Staats- und Universitätsbibliothek Hamburg Carl von Ossietzky, ND VII 256, vol. 2, fol. 43v–46r.

Photo 14. 1st Act Finale, No. 8, Scene 15, Bars 149–59. Bass part from the orchestral material in the archive of the Stadttheater, Hamburg. Staats- und Universitätsbibliothek Hamburg Carl von Ossietzky, ND VII 256, part book no. 13.

Photo 15. End of *Terzetto*, Act I, No. 6, and beginning of Duet, Act I, No. 7. Simrock manuscript full score from the archive of the Stadttheater, Hamburg. Staats- und Universitätsbibliothek Hamburg Carl von Ossietzky, ND VII 256, vol. 2, fol. 8v–10r.

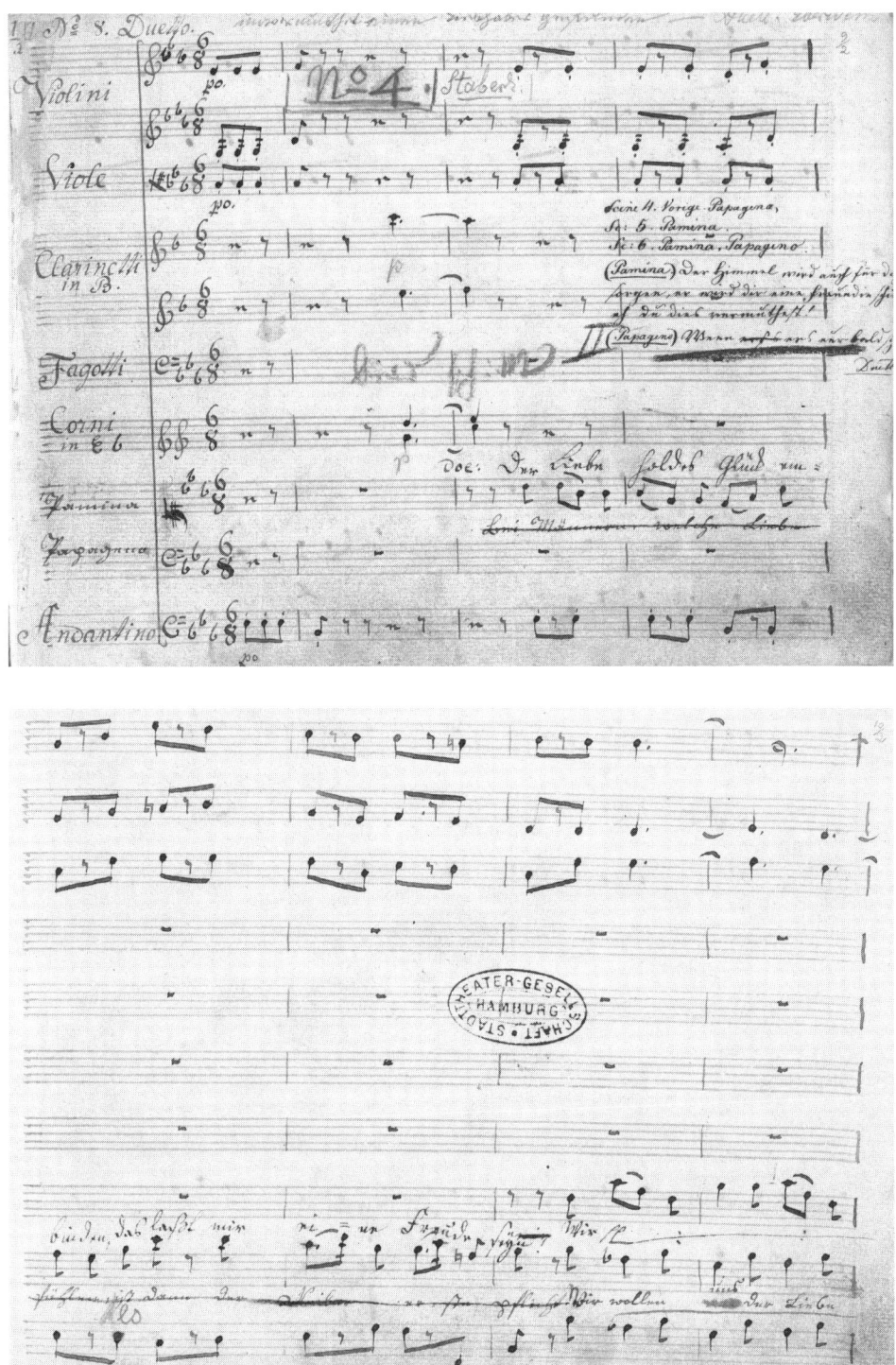

Photo 15. *(Continued)*

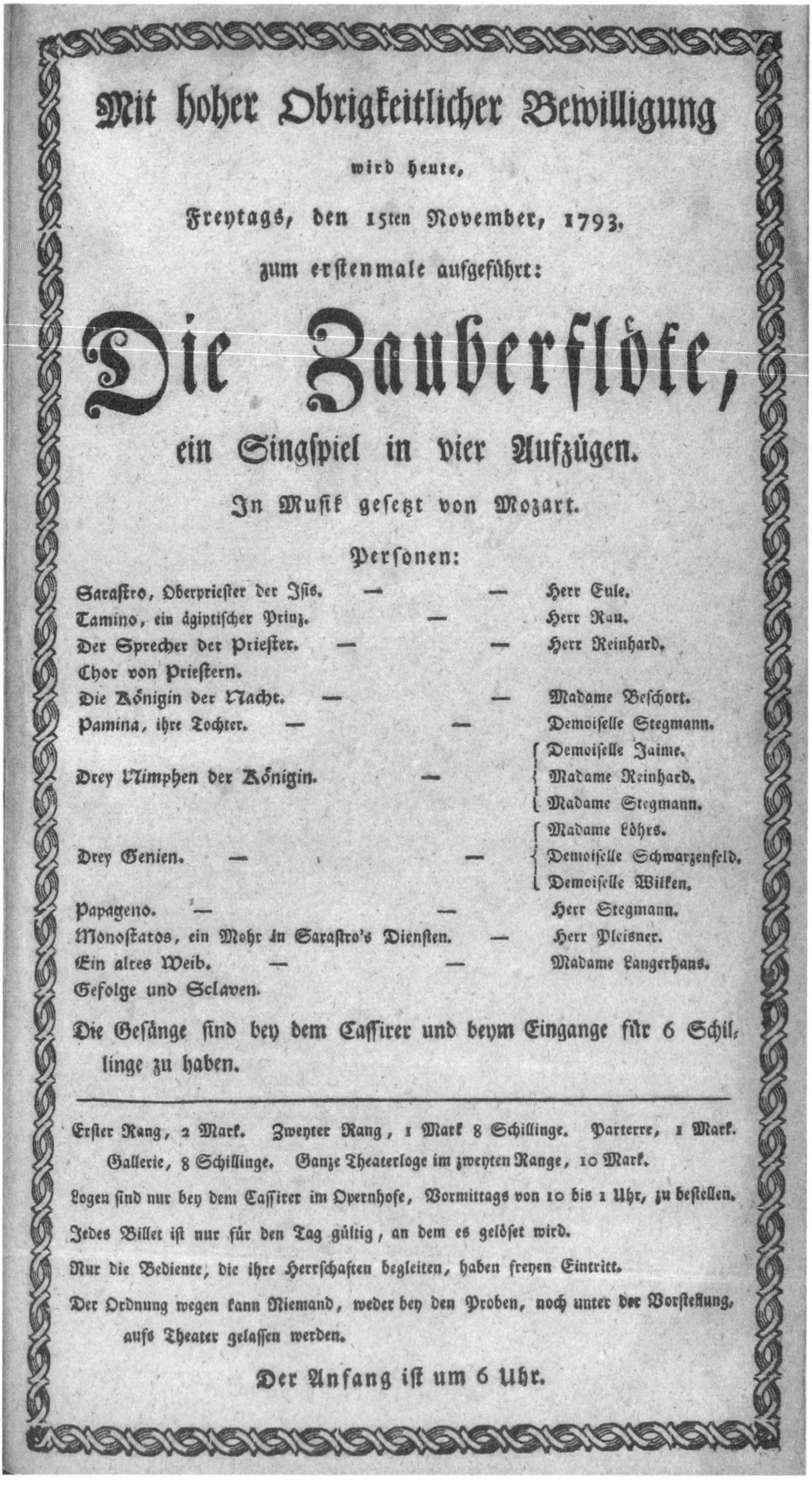

Mit hoher Obrigkeitlicher Bewilligung

wird heute,

Freytags, den 15ten November, 1793,

zum erstenmale aufgeführt:

Die Zauberflöte,

ein Singspiel in vier Aufzügen.

In Musik gesezt von Mozart.

Personen:

Sarastro, Oberpriester der Isis. — —	Herr Eule.
Tamino, ein ägiptischer Prinz. —	Herr Rau.
Der Sprecher der Priester. — —	Herr Reinhard.
Chor von Priestern.	
Die Königin der Nacht. — —	Madame Beschort.
Pamina, ihre Tochter. — —	Demoiselle Stegmann.
Drey Nimphen der Königin. —	{ Demoiselle Jaime. { Madame Reinhard. { Madame Stegmann.
Drey Genien. — —	{ Madame Löhrs. { Demoiselle Schwarzenfeld. { Demoiselle Wilken.
Papageno. — —	Herr Stegmann.
Monostatos, ein Mohr in Sarastro's Diensten. —	Herr Pleisner.
Ein altes Weib. — —	Madame Langerhaus.
Gefolge und Sclaven.	

Die Gesänge sind bey dem Cassirer und beym Eingange für 6 Schillinge zu haben.

Erster Rang, 2 Mark.   Zweyter Rang, 1 Mark 8 Schillinge.   Parterre, 1 Mark. Gallerie, 8 Schillinge.   Ganze Theaterloge im zweyten Range, 10 Mark.

Logen sind nur bey dem Cassirer im Opernhofe, Vormittags von 10 bis 1 Uhr, zu bestellen.

Jedes Billet ist nur für den Tag gültig, an dem es gelöset wird.

Nur die Bediente, die ihre Herrschaften begleiten, haben freyen Eintritt.

Der Ordnung wegen kann Niemand, weder bey den Proben, noch unter der Vorstellung, aufs Theater gelassen werden.

Der Anfang ist um 6 Uhr.

Photo 16.   Theatre bill for first Hamburg *Magic Flute* production, 15th November 1793. Universität Hamburg (Zentrum für Theaterforschung/Hamburger Theatersammlung).

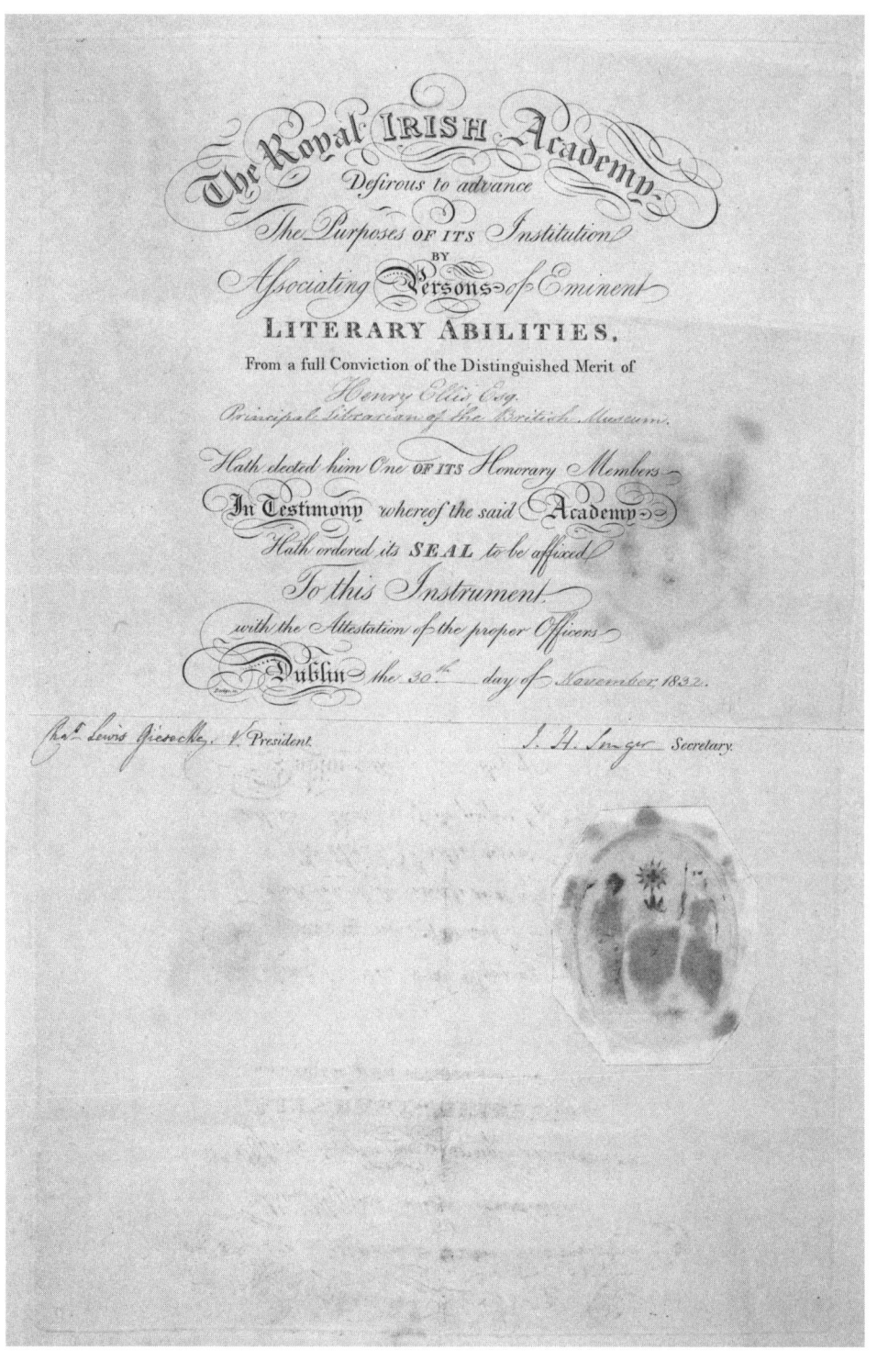

The Royal Irish Academy

Desirous to advance

The Purposes OF ITS Institution

BY

Associating Persons of Eminent

LITERARY ABILITIES,

From a full Conviction of the Distinguished Merit of

Henry Ellis Esq.
Principal Librarian of the British Museum.

Hath elected him One OF ITS Honorary Members

In Testimony whereof the said Academy

Hath ordered its SEAL to be affixed

To this Instrument

with the Attestation of the proper Officers

Dublin the 30th day of November 1832.

Chas. Lewis Giesecke, V. President.

J. H. Singer, Secretary.

Photo 17. Document signed by Giesecke on 30th November 1832 in his capacity as vice president of the Royal Irish Academy. © British Library Board. All Rights Reserved. Add. 36658 f.13.

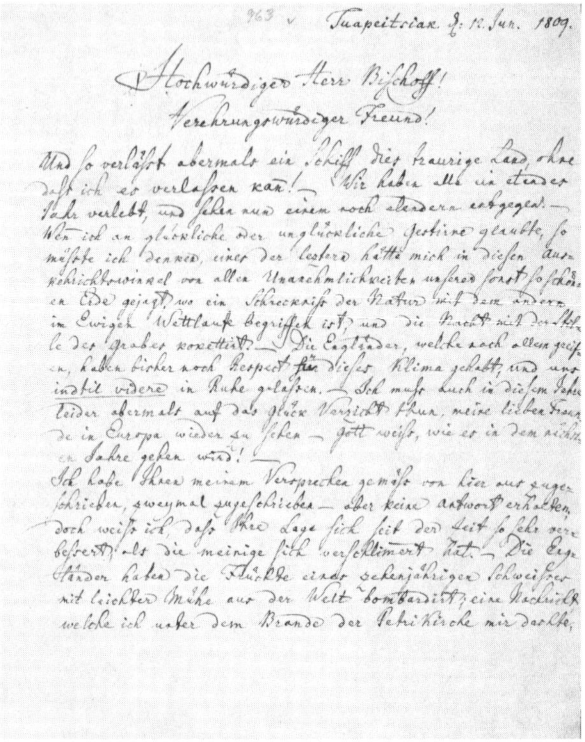

Photo 18.   Karl Ludwig Giesecke. Letter to Friederich Münter, dated 12th June 1809. Royal Library, Copenhagen. Manuscript Dept., NkS.1698, fol. VI.4, no. 963.

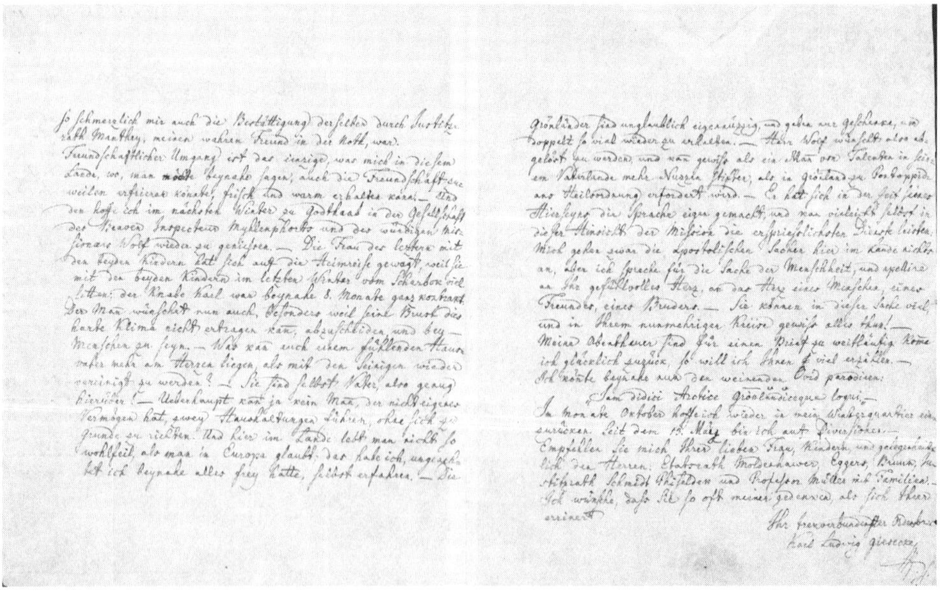

row, and count on you all the more because *after dinner there will be some wind music by* [for?] *my husband* which Herr von Silberstolbe will certainly never have heard before, and which will last no more than an hour at the most.

Ich habe morgen eine kleine Uberraschung [*sic*] bei mir wegen Nissens Geburztage, wobei mir und Nissen gewiss nichts angenehmer seyn könnte, als Herren von Silberstolbe zu sehen. Ich nehme mir daher die Freyheit Ihnen auf morgen zum Essen zu bitten, und zähle um so mehr darauf, weil *Nach Tisch von meinem Manne eine Harmoni musique* seyn wird, die Herr von Silberstolbe gewiss nie gehört haben, und die auch nicht länger, als höchstens eine Stunde dauern darf.[10]

Silverstolpe has left an account, written in 1800 or 1801, of Constanze's heritage of Mozart manuscripts, which he was able to inspect just before her substantial sales to the publisher André.

. . . a countless number of pure rough drafts were kept there, never completed and never used by the greatest genius of art. . . . The first side showed the instruments and theme: then followed a large number of bar-lines, but the bars were empty until a modulation, often very remote from the main key, was announced like a beacon in all parts. This created an effect, leaping out from the whole orchestra. Sometimes a particular instrument seems to have been allotted a solo. At times a harmonic imitation was indicated, just by a single note in each of the imitative parts. But nine-tenths of the whole consisted simply of empty spaces. What an amazing sight!—all this remained a secret in the mind of its creator, snatched from the world by his early death. But by what name shall we call this speed of creation? What a lofty turn of mind for a man who has no time to scratch down the notes, but must content himself with counting the bars, measuring out the rhythm and securing the symmetry, leaving it to the memory to recall the varied undulations of the vocal line, the melodic figuration and everything that was prompted by the original heat of creation!

. . . der förvarades en otalig mängd af blotta utkast, som aldrig vunno fulländning, aldrig begagnades af konstens första snille. . . . Den första sidan tillkännagaf instrumenterne och themat: derpå följde en mängd af taktstrek, men takterna tomma, ända till dess en modulation, ofta rätt aflägsen från hufvudtonen, blef såsom ljuspunkt tillkännagifven uti alla stämmorna. Det var då ett effektdrag,— störtande ur hela orchestern. Ibland syntes något särskildt instrument hafva fått sig ett Solo tilldeladt. Stundom angafs en harmonisk imitation, genom en enda not i hvarje af de härmande stämmorna. Men nio tiondedelar af det hela visade endast tomheter. Hvilken påkostande syn!—allt detta förblef hemligheter innom författarens hjärna, ryckta från verlden genom hans tidiga död. Men hvad namn skall man gifva åt denna snabbhet uti alstring? hvilken tankeflykt hos en man, som icke har tid att upprista teknen, åtnjöjande sig med att räkna takterne, att afväga rhytmen och försäkra sig om symmetrien, och öfverlämnande åt minnet att återfinna sångens mångfaldiga vändningar, melodiens figurer och allt hvad den första uppfinningsvärman förmått ingifva![11]

The Magic Flute sketches are fortunately a little more complete, though they offer neither confirmation nor denial of major libretto changes.[12] Reproductions and transcriptions are given in the NMA *Zauberflöte* volume II:5/xix (1970), 372–79. The recitative between the Priest and Tamino in the 1st Act Finale was sketched without word underlay, with the single exception of the Priest's dramatic "zurück." Clearly a recitative is not composed without words, but as the first edition and autograph text scarcely differ at this point there is no way to establish which one lay on Mozart's desk. The only passage with full text comes from the 2nd Act Finale, covering the final "Papageno/ Papagena" of their duet, scene 29, and the opening "Nur stille! stille! bald dringen wir in Tempel ein" of scene 30 (Monostatos, Queen of Night, and the Three Ladies). This is again, tantalizingly, a passage without text differences between first edition and autograph. On the one hand stands a complete absence of sketches showing an early version of the text; on the other stands the testimony of those close to Mozart at the time, albeit delivered years after the event, pointing to alterations and the involvement of more than one author. If, however, Mozart had sketched the opera from an early text in the manner described by Silverstolpe ("But ninetenths of the whole consisted simply of empty spaces") it would have been of little interest at the time. This is confirmed in a letter from Constanze to Breitkopf und Härtel of 1st March 1800 in which she explains that among Mozart's musical fragments

there were many more of them which have been destroyed because they were totally unusable.

es waren ihrer noch viele, die ihrer gänzlichen Unbrauchbarkeit wegen vernichtet worden sind.[13]

In these circumstances his original version will never be found, nor was it perhaps ever anything but an embryo, with every detail already in place in its creator's mind. There appear to be parallels here with sketches for *Così fan tutte*. Alan Tyson has written:

Two leaves are also known that contain *sketches* for parts of the opera, both for sections of the Act II finale. As is often the case, the sketches—in a hard-to-read "private" style of writing—were entered on the backs of autograph score fragments (drafts), and there is good reason to suppose that this is why they were preserved: such leaves were saved from destruction because of the draft score in "public" writing, not for the sake of the sketches.[14]

If Mozart's *Magic Flute* sketches have been lost, by what possible means might a complete, original version have survived, to reappear in the first edition?

FRANZ XAVER SÜSSMAYR

The short score that, according to Seyfried, Mozart left behind for rehearsals during his absence in Prague had previously been given to Mozart's pupil Franz Xaver Süssmayr to be copied. We learn from Mozart's own letters that he worked on *The Magic Flute* in Vienna in June and July 1791 while Constanze, who was pregnant at the time, rested at the nearby spa of Baden.[15] She was later joined by Süssmayr, who started his copying task even while Mozart was still working on the opera. Suspicions about an illicit relationship need not concern us here. He was certainly on good terms with both the Mozarts, as, indeed, was Schikaneder.

> To Constanze, 7th June 1791
> Yesterday I had lunch at the Hungarian Crown with Süssmayr because I had to be in town at 1 o'clock . . . today I shall eat with Schikaneder, as you know anyhow, because you were invited too.

> Gestern speisste ich mit Süssmaiern bey der ungarischen Krone zu Mittag weil ich mich um 1 Uhr in der Stadt zu thun hatte . . . heute weisst Du ohnehin dass ich bey Schicaneder [*sic*] esse, weil Du auch darzu eingeladen warst.

Later, after Süssmayr had arrived in Baden, Mozart wrote, in an undated letter:

> My greetings to Snai . . . tell him to work hard at the writing so that I get my things back.

> Grüsse mir den Snai . . . er soll fleissig schreiben dass ich meine Sachen bekomme.

The use of a nickname is characteristic. The next letter reveals something of Mozart's working methods.

> 2nd July 1791
> Please tell that fellow Süssmayr to send me my short score of the 1st Act, from the Introduction through to the *Finale*, so that I can do the scoring. It would be good if he could put it together today, so that it goes off with the first coach in the morning, then I would have it by midday.

> Ich bitte dich sage dem Süssmayer dem Dalketen buben, er soll mir vom ersten Ackt, von der Introdution an bis zum *Finale*, meine Spart schicken, damit ich

instrumentiren kann. gut wäre es, wenn ers heute noch zusammen machte, damit
es mit dem ersten Wagen morgen früh abgehet, so bekomme ich es doch gleich
zu Mittag.

One has to admire the efficiency of the Viennese postal service, for the
following day he was able to acknowledge receipt of the Finale, as well as
articles of a more domestic nature.

> 3rd July 1791
> . . . my thanks for the Finale and the clothes. . . . I hope Süssmayr will not
> forget what I laid out for him, also to write immediately—I am also hoping to
> receive the parts of my score today, as I asked.

> . . . ich danke für das überschickte finale und kleider. . . . Ich hoffe Süssmayer
> wird nicht vergessen dass [*sic*] was ich ihm herausgelegt, auch gleich zu sch-
> reiben—auch hoffe ich mir heute die Stücke von meiner Partitur/so ich verlan-
> get/zu erhalten.

"To write immediately" (gleich zu schreiben) would imply "to do his copying work quickly" (see the undated letter above, "er soll fleissig schreiben").
Finally, on 5th July Mozart urged:

> Süssmayr must send me Nos. 4 and 5 of my manuscript—and everything else
> that I asked. . . .

> Süssmayer soll mir doch No:° 4 und 5 von meiner schrift schicken—auch was
> ich sonst begehrt habe. . . .

If Mozart was so keen to work on the orchestration of Act I it might have
been because he had by this time almost completed the short score of Act II.[16]
Süssmayr seems to have started his work with the 1st Act Finale. Nos. 4 and
5 are, in Mozart's autograph numbering, Tamino's Aria ("Dies Bildnis"), and
the entry of the Queen of Night ("O zittre nicht"). What is the meaning of the
cryptic instruction "I hope Süssmayr will not forget what I laid out for him"?
Did Mozart plan to orchestrate first the long and complex Finale before turning
to the shorter and less thickly scored arias?[17] Or was it Süssmayr's choice to
work in this way? After all, when Mozart asks for his short score of the 1st Act
"from the Introduction through to the *Finale*. . . . It would be good if he could
put it together today," he was expecting the whole of Act I immediately.

The suggestion has been made by Karl-Heinz Köhler that Süssmayr's
task was not to copy the score but to prepare vocal and instrumental parts. It
would be interesting to know whether, in the days of laborious hand-copying,
singers would have expected to receive a complete vocal score or were ac-

customed to something more sparse. A vocal score made before Mozart had completed the orchestration would be nothing if not sparse.

> a) He [Mozart] pressed the manuscript into the hand of his pupil Süssmayr, probably with an instruction to copy out the vocal and orchestral parts from it in preparation for rehearsals, as far as was possible at that time.

> b) Even as Mozart was composing the new opera his pupil Süssmayr had to copy out some of the vocal parts from the score and deliver them to the soloists so that they could start work.

> a) Dem Schüler Süssmayr drückte er das Geschriebene in die Hand, wohl mit dem Auftrag, Gesangs- und Orchesterstimmen zur Vorbereitung der Probenarbeit herauszuschreiben, soweit das schon möglich war.

> b) Noch während Mozart an der neuen Oper komponierte, musste sein Studiosus Süssmayr einige der Gesangsstimmen aus der Partitur herausschreiben und den Solisten zuleiten, damit diese mit der Arbeit beginnen konnten.[18]

Common sense dictates that singers who have to learn and memorize a new opera have a more urgent need than orchestral players for access to the musical material. Historical confirmation is provided by John Spitzer and Neal Zaslaw.

> Almost every eighteenth-century author who presumed to give advice to ripienists says that an orchestra musician needs to be a good sightreader. Most orchestras did not permit players to take their parts home to practice, and musicians seem to have considered it inappropriate to practice orchestra music. Therefore an orchestra violinist, as Koch explains, "must perform his part either entirely *prima vista* or at best with one or two rehearsals, where he has no opportunity to practice difficult spots" [Koch, *Musikalisches Lexikon* (Frankfurt-am-Main: Hermann, 1802), 1263–64].[19]

By composing the two purely orchestral numbers, the *Overture* and *Priests' March*, only two days before the first performance, Mozart showed confidence in the orchestra's ability to play even the technically and musically demanding *Overture* with very little preparation. It seems to have been Mozart's practice to use a copy, rather than his autograph score, for rehearsal and performance in the theatre. With regard to *Le Nozze di Figaro* Alan Tyson explains the discrepancies between surviving theatre copies and Mozart's autograph with attractive logic:

> . . . [having] entered several changes in the *Hoftheater Abschrift* and in the performance parts . . . there is no likelihood that at the rehearsal Mozart would

have said: "Before I make any changes I must go back to my apartment and get my autograph and make the changes first in that."[20]

One cannot doubt the need for a second full score in preparing the opera for performance, and until evidence to the contrary is produced, one may reasonably assume that Süssmayr was engaged in making it.

Mozart seems, in the coming months, to have entrusted Süssmayr with awesome responsibilities—not only (supposedly) the writing of the recitatives for *La clemenza di Tito*, but the completion of the Requiem. What special instructions did he issue for the copying of *The Magic Flute*? Were they connected with libretto changes? Süssmayr's copy has disappeared. It is not to be found among the collection of his manuscripts in the British Library, nor is it among his opera manuscripts in the Esterházy Library, now housed in the National Library, Budapest. It is a prime document, dating as it does from the time of composition of *The Magic Flute*—the earliest copy, and Mozart's personal copy. Any text deviations deriving from it must have originated in a formative period in the composition of the opera. The difficulty lies in attempting to explain why they were not already entered in Mozart's short score ("Spart"), which survives today, with the addition of the completed orchestration, as the *Zauberflöte* autograph. The fact that there is no sign of them in the text underlay weighs heavily against the hypothesis that the first-edition text was copied by Süssmayr from this manuscript. The possibility that the word underlay may not have been made clear in every detail has already been proposed (see p. 112, discussion of example 30). Both libretto and music were, after all, still in the draft stage. Was Mozart waiting for expected last-minute alterations before underlaying the libretto in his score? But that would be untenable in the case of the Act I, No. 7 Duet, "Bei Männern," where the original barring, before alteration, matches the words of the final version, not those of the first-edition text. These are troubling questions that ought not to be avoided in a discussion of the authenticity of the first-edition text. Until an answer is found I am mindful of the words of the theoretical physicist and Nobel laureate Richard Feynman, making the case for

a kind of utter honesty—a kind of leaning over backwards. For example, if you're doing an experiment, you should report everything that you think might make it invalid—not only what you think is right about it. . . . Details that could throw doubt on your interpretation must be given, if you know them. You must do the best you can—if you know anything at all wrong—to explain it. If you make a theory, for example, and advertise it, or put it out, then you must also put down all the facts that disagree with it, as well as those that agree with it. . . . In summary the idea is to try to give *all* of the information to help others to judge the value of your contribution; not just the information that leads to judgement in one particular direction or another.[21]

NOTES

1. Alan Tyson, "New Dating Methods: Watermarks and Paper-Studies," in *Mozart, Studies of the Autograph Scores* (Cambridge, MA: Harvard University Press, 1987), 21.

2. Alan Tyson, "Redating Mozart: Some Stylistic and Biographical Implications," in *Mozart, Studies of the Autograph Scores* (Cambridge, MA: Harvard University Press, 1987), 35.

3. Lorenzo da Ponte, *Memoirs of Lorenzo da Ponte*, trans. L. A. Sheppard (1929), 310 (British Library 12211.ss.2/1).

4. Lorenzo da Ponte, *Memorie di Lorenzo da Ponte*. II Volume, Parte II (Nuova-Jorca, 1829, 30), 7. British Library 1448.a.12.

5. The meaning of this statement is discussed in Ulrich Konrad, *Mozarts Schaffensweise. Studien zu den Werkautographen, Skizzen und Entwürfen* (Göttingen, 1992), 73.

6. Benedikt Schack's obituary (1827). *AMZ*. 25th July 1827. Jahrgang XXIX. Column 519. Quoted in *Dokumente*, 459.

7. 16th February 1826. *Briefe* IV, 476 and 478.

8. K. Pfannhauser, "Epilegomena Mozartiana." *Mozart-Jahrbuch* 1971/72, 284–85. Quoted by Ulrich Konrad in *Mozarts Schaffensweise. Studien zu den Werkautographen, Skizzen und Entwürfen* (Göttingen, 1992), 101–102.

9. NMA II:5/xix, ed. Gernot Gruber, 1970.

10. *Briefe* IV, 308.

11. Fr. S. Silfverstolpe, *Några Återblickar* (Stockholm, 1841), 26–27. Kongl. Musikaliska Akademiens Bibliotek, Stockholm, C351. See also C.-G. Stellan Mörner, *Festschrift Alfred Orel*, ed. Hellmut Federhofer (1960), 115; and M. Heinz Gärtner, *Mozarts Requiem und die Geschäfte der Constanze* (1986), 107.

12. Siverstolpe's sketches, which are now in the University Library, Uppsala, Sweden, are the subject of an article by Richard Engländer in *The Musical Quarterly* (Jg. 27) of 1941, p. 343. See also *Die Musik* XIV (1914), Beilage, 48f.; and Richard Engländer, *Die Mozart-Skizzen der Universitätsbibliothek Uppsala. Svensk Tidskrift för Musikforskning* (Stockholm, 1955), 96.

13. *Briefe* IV, 324. See also Alan Tyson, "The Mozart Fragments in the Mozarteum, Salzburg: A Preliminary Study of Their Chronology and Their Significance," in *Mozart. Studies of the Autograph Scores* (Cambridge, MA: Harvard University Press, 1987), 126.

14. Alan Tyson, "On the Composition of Mozart's *Così fan tutte*," in *Mozart. Studies of the Autograph Scores* (Cambridge, MA: Harvard University Press, 1987), 191.

15. Baden retains considerable architectural charm and atmosphere today. For a discussion of the probable lodgings used by Constanze and Mozart on their visits in

1791, see Paul Tausig, "Mozarts Beziehungen zu Baden." *Sonderabdruck aus Nr. 55–57 der Badener Zeitung* (1914), 9–15. Stadtarchiv Baden bei Wien [Abth.MBNr.16], Städtische Sammlungen Archiv/Rollettmuseum der Stadtgemeinde Baden.

16. Seyfried reported in his letter to Treitschke (see pp. 121–23) that Mozart had only the short score ready by the time he left for Prague (the last week of August). This is surprising in view of Mozart's eagerness to start work on the orchestration in early July. In his own thematic catalog (*Verzeichnüss aller meiner Werke*) Mozart dates both *Die Zauberflöte* and *La Clemenza di Tito* "im Jullius," with an additional entry on 28th September "zur Oper. *die Zauberflöte*—einen PriesterMarsch und die Ouverture." Alan Tyson's paper studies point to still further work on the opera in September after Mozart's return from Prague (see p. 143).

17. In his study of the paper types used in *Così fan tutte* Alan Tyson concludes: "It appears, then, that as a matter of deliberate policy Mozart first tackled the ensembles in the first act and left the solo numbers until later. It has been possible to detect him doing the same thing elsewhere as well, for example, in *La clemenza di Tito*." Tyson, *Mozart: Studies of the Autograph Scores*, 182.

18. Karl-Heinz Köhler, *Das Zauberflötenwunder: eine Odyssee durch zwei Jahrhunderte* (Weimar and Jena: Wartburg Verlag, 1996), 24, 30.

19. John Spitzer and Neal Zaslaw, *The Birth of the Orchestra* (Oxford: Oxford University Press, 2004), 384–85.

20. Tyson, *Mozart. Studies of the Autograph Scores*, 307.

21. Richard P. Feynman, *"Surely You're Joking, Mr. Feynman!" Adventures of a Curious Character as Told to Ralph Leighton*, ed. Edward Hutchings (London: Vintage, 1992), 341.

Chapter Eight

Conclusion

When the Elector of Cologne placed his order with Constanze, she was able to satisfy his requirements. Her copyist did not work from Mozart's autograph, which she later claimed to have been retained by Schikaneder. The nearest and most reliable alternative would certainly have been Süssmayr's copy; near because it belonged to her late husband and might therefore have been in the house when he died, reliable because it was made not only to his exact instructions but under her very eye.

The weight of three independent documents provides evidence that the Simrock first full-score edition is based on a source that originated from either Mozart or Constanze. They are:

1. Gottfried Weber's review in the *AMZ* of 13th September 1815. The review reports Simrock's assurance that the source of the new edition is the former Elector of Cologne's manuscript, obtained "from Mozart himself."
2. Constanze's letter of 28th December 1791 to Simonetti, the elector's leading tenor. She indicates her willingness to have a copy of *The Magic Flute* made for him, speedily, and at a price of 100 ducats.
3. Otto Jahn's preface to the Simrock revised full score of 1862. He corroborates that the copy supplied by Constanze in 1792 was the source of the Simrock first full-score edition.

It is Simrock's reported claim linking his edition directly with Mozart that demands our attention. Unfortunately he left no surviving evidence beyond the inspirational quality of the word-music relationship. From the facts known to us it is possible, however, to project a plausible scenario. Constanze, it is sometimes argued, sought to take advantage of the remarkable similarity between Süssmayr's and Mozart's handwriting by attempting to pass off the entire score of the Requiem as the work of Mozart so that she could claim payment in full. It was at almost the same time that she offered to provide a score of *The Magic Flute* for the court of the Elector of Cologne. It seems that for her asking price of 100 ducats the elector had every right to expect Mozart's original manuscript. Lacking the autograph, might she not therefore have been tempted to send a manuscript copy of *The Magic Flute* in Süssmayr's handwriting? The reward for the deception would have been twofold—she would be able to insist on payment of the full 100 ducats she had asked, and she would save the cost to herself of having the opera copied. The elector may thus have been led to believe that his *Magic Flute* score was none other than Mozart's autograph. This would have been Simrock's understanding, too, though Jahn, familiar with the authentic autograph, was not so persuaded in 1862.

The similarity between Süssmayr's and Mozart's handwriting has been the cause of much confusion. As recently as 1980 Alan Tyson discovered an original Mozart manuscript (three leaves from the Rondo for Piano and Orchestra K386) in the British Library, lying cataloged under Süssmayr's name.[1] The volume (Add. MS 32181) containing the Mozart autograph pages (fols. 250–52 with a blank leaf fol. 253) formed part of a collection of manuscripts purchased from the Leipzig firm of List and Francke in 1884 and said to have been owned by Johann Nepomuk Hummel. Likewise the manuscript score of the Rondo from Mozart's D-major Horn Concerto, accepted even by Jahn as Mozart's autograph,[2] turns out to be in Süssmayr's hand.[3] The difficulty of distinguishing between Süssmayr's and Mozart's handwriting is further complicated by Süssmayr's forgery of Mozart's signature on the score of the Requiem.[4] But this is hardly a serious attempt at deception, since he dated it 1792. He later wrote to Breitkopf und Härtel:

> I owe too much to the teaching of this great man to remain silent and permit a composition which is for the most part my work to be passed off as his, because I am firmly convinced that my work is unworthy of his great name.

> Ich habe den Lehren dieses grossen Mannes zu viel zu danken, als dass ich stillschweigend erlauben könnte, dass ein Werk, dessen grösster Theil meine Arbeit ist, für das seinige ausgegeben wird, weil ich fest überzeugt bin, dass meine Arbeit dieses grossen Namens unwürdig ist.[5]

If Constanze sought to extract the maximum financial gain from her late husband's last works, it was out of necessity rather than greed. Many friends rallied to her side, including even Schikaneder.

Everyone tries to outdo the other in endeavoring to repair Mozart's widow's loss in some way and to comfort her. . . . Herr Schikaneder arranged the exequies for the deceased, during which the Requiem which he had composed in his final illness was played. In the next few days Herr *Schikaneder* will be giving a benefit performance of *The Magic Flute* for the widow.

Alles wetteifert um Mozarts hinterlassene Wittwe, ihren Verlust einigermassen zu ersetzen, und sie zu trösten. . . . Herr Schikaneder hat für den verstorbenen die Exequien halten lassen, wobey das Requiem welches er in seiner letzten Krankheit komponirt hatte, exequirt wurde. Zum besten der Wittwe wird Herr *Schikaneder* dieser Tage eine Vorstellung der Zauberflötte [*sic*] geben.[6]

The only part of the Requiem fully scored by Mozart and ready for performance when he died was the *Requiem aeternam*.[7] Since the performance at Mozart's exequies must necessarily have been but a fragment of the whole, Constanze might have expected problems in attempting subsequently to pass off Süssmayr's completion as the work of her late husband. By comparison, an opportunity to sell Süssmayr's *Magic Flute* copy as a Mozart autograph to the Elector of Cologne would surely have appeared attractively straightforward.

The report in the *AMZ* of 13th September 1815 declaring that the elector obtained his score "from Mozart himself" is inconsistent with the statement published seventeen years earlier, on 7th November 1798, in the same journal (see pp. 60–61 and 68n45) that the opera's fame spread rapidly "even though not a single person had received a score from Mozart." This statement ought to have alerted the former elector (who had been deposed by Napoleon in 1794) and Simrock to the possibility of dishonest dealings on Constanze's part, but their reactions, if any, are not recorded. Sixteen more years were to pass before the elector's manuscript was published and thus given the seal of authenticity by Simrock. Simrock's use of the first-edition text lasted from 1814 until and including publication of his vocal score of c.1830, which may have been prepared at about the same time as André's 1829 score of the Overture showing Mozart's compositional method. One may surmise that André's publication, giving proof that Mozart's original autograph was in his possession, put a stop to further Simrock editions based on the first-edition text.

If Jahn had access to the manuscript source of the first edition in preparing the revised Simrock score of 1862, it would seem worthwhile to look for it in the Simrock Archive. During the DDR years the archive was declared lost in the war. However, documents from file Börsenverein 12 2 56 in the former Leipziger Staatsarchiv (now the Sächsisches Staatsarchiv) indicate that in 1962, one hundred years after Jahn's researches, the archive was still in existence. In 1929 Simrock had been bought by the publisher Benjamin, whose business was appropriated by the Nazis in 1938 under anti-Jewish laws and given to the firm of Sikorski. The liquidation of Sikorski and its assets was discussed in 1962 by a Leipzig cultural board with representatives from the town, music publishers, and the university library.

> Concerning the liquidation of the music publisher Sikorski. . . . The Ministry of Culture has recommended that, of the 2,000 packets whose contents have not yet been examined, the older holdings should be handed over to the Deutsche Staatsbibliothek and the post-1912 holdings to the Deutsche Bücherei and worthless material disposed of. It is not known whether the 2,000 packets contain worthless popular hits or possibly also archive material or perhaps even original manuscripts and letters of famous composers. . . . Since the work of examining the 2,000 packets and registering the holdings will be difficult and lengthy (3 men working for about 2 years at an estimate) . . . an attempt should first be made to sell the holdings, with the agreement of the Department of State Property, to the Deutsche Staatsbibliothek. . . . Should the Deutsche Staatsbibliothek decline, the Deutscher Verlag für Musik will gradually take over the holdings. . . . Archive material, valuable manuscripts, letters etc. are to be preserved./ 23rd August 1962 / Dr. FR/L

> Betr. Liquidierung des Musikverlages Sikorski. . . . Das Ministerium für Kultur hat empfohlen, von den noch vorhandenen 2.000 Paketen, deren Inhalt noch nicht gesichtet worden ist, die älteren Bestände der Deutschen Staatsbibliothek und die Bestände aus der Zeit nach 1912 der Deutschen Bücherei zu übergeben und das Wertlose zu makulieren. Unbekannt ist, ob die 2.000 Pakete wertlose Schlagernoten oder evtl. auch Archivmaterial oder vielleicht auch Originalmanuskripte und Briefe berühmter Komponisten enthalten. . . . Da die Sichtung der 2.000 Pakete und die Bestandsaufnahme eine schwierige und langwierige Arbeit darstellt (schätzungsweise 3 Mann etwa 2 Jahre) . . . soll zunächst versucht werden, die Bestände mit Zustimmung der Abteilung Staatliches Eigentum an die Deutsche Staatsbibliothek zu verkaufen. . . . Sollte die Deutsche Staatsbibliothek ablehnen, wird der Deutsche Verlag für Musik nach und nach die Bestandsaufnahme vornehmen . . . . Das Archivmaterial, wertvolle Handschriften, Briefe usw. sollen aufgehoben werden./23 August 1962/Dr. FR/L

The outcome was that the printed editions of the Simrock Archive were accepted by the Deutsche Staatsbibliothek, East Berlin, while the archival holdings remained in Leipzig, to be housed in the Staatsarchiv (then Landesarchiv) under the administrative responsibility of the Deutscher Verlag. In a letter dated 28th January 1963 the Deutscher Verlag referred to "valuable archive material" (wertvolles Archivmaterial) in the packets delivered to the Staatsarchiv on 24th October 1962 (nos. 1814–1850). The material evidently included manuscripts, for four years later, on 9th November 1966, the Deutscher Verlag forwarded a card index for the manuscripts contained in packets 1821–1841.

In 1976 the Staatsarchiv assumed control of the complete Deutscher Verlag archive.

—Director—
VEB Deutscher Verlag für Musik . . .

11.8.1976

Execution of New Legal Instructions Concerning the Organization of State Archives

. . . the Staatsarchiv is now the proper, conclusive authority for the archive of your publishing firm. It follows from this that
—the archive property is to be transferred to the Staatsarchiv . . .
—after the transfer the Staatsarchiv as decreed will look after the business of archival tasks, including those that guarantee order and security as well as availability . . . and thus also the interests of your publishing house.

—Direktor—
VEB Deutscher Verlag für Musik . . .

11.8.1976

Durchführung der neuen Rechtsv-orschriften [*sic*] über das staatliche Archivwesen

. . . ist das Staatsarchiv Leipzig jetzt das zuständige Endarchiv für Ihren Verlag. Daraus ergibt sich, dass
—das Archivgut im Sinne der VO . . . an das Staatsarchiv abzugeben ist . . .
—nach der Übernahme das Staatsarchiv die archivarischen Aufgaben, auch die der Ordnung und Sicherheit sowie der Benutzbarkeit . . . gewährleisten und dabei auch die Belange Ihres Verlages wahren wird.

No explanation for the disappearance of the substantial part of the Simrock Archive from the Leipziger Staatsarchiv (now the Sächsisches Staatsarchiv, Leipzig) has been forthcoming. The Deutsche Staatsbibliothek, Berlin, which had accepted the printed editions, returned them to the legal owners, the firm of Benjamin, Hamburg, in 1993. At that time the Staatsbibliothek zu Berlin (as it has been called since German reunification) was able to confirm to the present writer, in a letter dated 9th June 1993, that the Simrock Archive was for the most part in Leipzig, with only a relatively small part, containing mainly printed material, in Berlin. Its total size in 1962 has already been indicated in the document dated 23rd August 1962 in the Staatsarchiv's own file Börsenverein 12 2 56.

During the twelve years between 1990 and 2002, some 170 letters from Brahms to Simrock, of unattributed provenance but presumably once in the Simrock Archive, were sold at Sotheby's in London. This substantial collection did not attract the attention it deserves because it was sold at half-yearly intervals in small groups of six to eight at a time. A further eight went under the hammer on 1st December 2005 and five more on 19th May 2006. In 1992 about seventy letters to Simrock from Joachim, von Bülow, and leading music publishers were sold, as well as papers documenting the division and sale of the Simrock *Nachlass* in the years 1929–1933, amounting to several hundred pages (see Sotheby's sale catalog 4th December 1992, Lots 449 and 450). The catalog entry for Lot 450 continues: "The various sales were not on the whole successful and most of the important manuscripts which were apparently offered for sale publicly were unsold. There is information here about what happened to the unsold manuscripts after the sales and details of important autographs which were never offered for sale." I am grateful to Richard Macnutt for alerting me to these Sotheby's catalog entries. On 2nd August 1994 a request for access to this material for the purposes of research was made to the purchaser(s) via Sotheby's, but it drew no response.

In late 2001 ownership of the Simrock Archive passed to Boosey & Hawkes, which was itself shortly to acquire new owners. Following a period of uncertainty it was reassuring to hear from the new London management, in a letter to the present writer of 22nd October 2003, that the company was mindful of the historical and cultural importance of all its archives and was committed to preserving them and making them available, so far as they were reasonably able, to scholars and researchers. A year later the commitment was diluted, with the Director of Business Affairs asserting in a telephone conversation on 20th October 2004 that, owing to other priorities, nothing was likely to be done in the foreseeable future.

Should the Leipzig portion of the archive ever be recovered it might be possible to delve deeper into the history and authenticity of the text used in early Hamburg performances of *Die Zauberflöte* and in the Simrock first full-score edition. The discovery of Constanze's score, last examined by Otto Jahn in 1862, would be the greatest prize, but, failing that, correspondence relating to it could help establish whether she did indeed claim to have sent the Mozart autograph to Bonn. In that event, with the autograph unavailable to her at the time, the Süssmayr copy would seem the most likely source for the text. This could be readily confirmed by comparing the handwriting with the many Süssmayr autographs in the National Library, Budapest (Országos Széchényi Könyvtár), and in the British Library, London.

The 1814 first full-score edition carries a text that originated, in any event, no later than 1792, when it reached the Elector of Cologne. There is nothing to prove or disprove an even earlier origin. Coming from Mozart's widow its connection with the Mozart household is established. If this text lay on

Mozart's desk as he worked on the opera during the summer of 1791, then Simrock published the original libretto of *The Magic Flute*, and the first-edition score assumes a place of unique importance alongside the autograph.

The failure of both nineteenth- and twentieth-century scholarship to grasp the significance of the first edition is regrettable. Its source has remained disguised behind a relatively late publication date and the rare beauty of its word-music relationship gone unrecognized for nearly two centuries. One may hope that future discoveries will not only close the remaining gaps in the history of the first edition but broaden our knowledge of the original textual inspiration for the music of *The Magic Flute*.

NOTES

1. See Alan Tyson, *Mozart. Studies of the Autograph Scores* (Cambridge, MA: Harvard University Press, 1987), chap. 17.

2. Otto Jahn, *W. A. Mozart* (Leipzig, 1858), vol. III, 294 n44.

3. See Tyson, *Mozart. Studies of the Autograph Scores*, chap. 16.

4. For facsimiles see H. C. Robbins Landon, *1791. Mozart's Last Year* (1988), 163; and Dalchow, Duda and Kerner, *Mozarts Tod* (Pähl, 1971), 87 and Anhang.

5. *Dokumente*. Joseph Heinz Eibl, Addenda und Corrigenda (1978), 89. Letter from Franz Xaver Süssmayr to Breitkopf & Härtel, 8th February 1800.

6. *Dokumente*, 374. Aus der handschriftlichen Wiener Zeitung *"Der heimliche Botschafter,"* 16th December 1791.

7. See H. C. Robbins Landon, *1791. Mozart's Last Year* (1988), 150; and Christoph Wolff, *Mozart's Requiem* (Oxford, 1994), 4, originally published in German as *Mozarts Requiem: Geschichte-Musik-Dokumente-Partitur des Fragments* (Deutscher Taschenbuch Verlag GmbH & Co. KG, München, and Bärenreiter-Verlag Karl Vötterle GmbH & Co. KG, Kassel, 1991).

The Character and Career of Karl Ludwig Giesecke (1761–1833)

Foreword by Stephen Moorbath, F.R.S., Professor
Emeritus of Earth Sciences, Oxford University

If conclusive evidence should ever come to light that Giesecke was full- or part-author of the libretto of *The Magic Flute*, then Mozart can claim to have had two truly remarkable and outstanding men as librettists for his four most renowned operas. The other was, of course, Lorenzo da Ponte. We must admit at the outset that Giesecke's reported claim for the authorship of the libretto is circumstantial. But he was in the right place at the right time, had close contact with all the right people, and had ample literary expertise and theatrical experience to produce the text of what became, in Mozart's hands, one of the world's truly great operatic masterpieces.

For the time being, one may speculate on the evidently symbiotic relationship between Schikaneder and Giesecke throughout the 1790s and, from the limited evidence, reach one's own conclusions. What is unacceptable, however, is for some musicologists, for reasons of furthering their own agenda or out of plain ignorance, to indulge in a totally unjustified character assassination of Giesecke (e.g., E. Komorzynski, 1956). In this book Michael Freyhan presents a balanced and accurate picture of Giesecke's many-sided personality and diverse achievements as well as documenting some of the actual evidence at the heart of the libretto controversy. In addition, this appendix contains a report on Giesecke's activities in the early decades of the nineteenth century, long after he had left his theatrical life in Vienna.

I became interested in the Giesecke controversy many years ago because Mozart has always been my closest and most constant musical companion while, as a professional geologist, I have taken part in numerous geological expeditions to West Greenland over the past fifty years. Here, I had the opportunity of visiting some of the same localities Giesecke did during his monumental, pioneering voyages of discovery in the years 1806–1813. It is difficult nowadays, in visiting these localities in the relative comfort provided by modern aids to arctic exploration and geological fieldwork, to imagine Giesecke's physical hardships and emotional trials and tribulations as he traveled for seven years with his faithful Eskimos (nowadays called Inuit or Greenlanders) in small, open native boats through tempestuous weather, rough seas, and wild scenery, to amass the large collection of specimens that later enriched the mineral and rock cabinets of scientific museums and imperial collections throughout Europe. (For readers' information, rocks are fine- to coarse-grained assemblages usually composed of several different types of crystalline chemical compounds called minerals. But minerals can also occur on their own, often in aggregates of large, individual crystals, and these are what Giesecke concentrated on.)

Regretfully, there is no mention in Giesecke's personal and scientific diary of the years 1806–1813 of his former theatrical activities in Vienna before 1801. There was probably nobody in Greenland with whom he could discuss his former life, and the diary was hardly an appropriate place to do so. Nor is his correspondence any more informative in this respect. One may wonder whether during all that traveling in fantastical surroundings, Giesecke recalled tunes from *The Magic Flute*, to which he may well have contributed at least part of the text and in which he participated (as First Slave) in the first performance.

Giesecke was not yet a modern type of scientist, because he concentrated mainly on describing, classifying, categorizing, and collecting minerals and rocks, in the same way that biologists had long been doing for animals and plants. His later years coincided with the time when the fundamental principles of the new science of geology were being placed on a firm footing, and when minerals and rocks became an end to understanding the origin, age, evolution, and structure of the earth, rather than an end in themselves. Nonetheless, there is ample evidence that Giesecke kept fully abreast of these early scientific developments. In addition, Giesecke had a close knowledge of all aspects of the natural and political history of Greenland, as well as the culture, customs, and language of the natives. This is evident from his eloquent, detailed, and highly recommendable article "Description of Greenland" in the *Edinburgh Encyclopaedia* of 1816. Much of the article held true for some 150 years, after which the disruptive effects of modern European culture became overwhelming. Giesecke's description in the 1816 article of the distinctly unhygienic customs of the natives in the preparation and presentation of food would grace any comic opera libretto of 1790s Vienna! But there was at all times great mutual fondness between Giesecke and the Inuit.

Any convincing solution to the libretto problem clearly depends on the discovery of additional documentary evidence from Giesecke's Vienna years. In his perceptive and moving book *Mozart and his Operas* (Penguin Books,

2007), David Cairns states in a short footnote (p. 205) that Giesecke's claim to be the author of the libretto of *The Magic Flute* is now generally discredited. I think this statement is too simplistic and could well inhibit future research. A more realistic appreciation of Giesecke's impressive personality as well as his extraordinarily productive bimodal literary and scientific career may encourage musicologists not to drop the issue just yet.

My own admittedly subjective interpretation is that the claim about authorship of the libretto that Giesecke made privately to his old and new friends in Vienna in 1818 is probably close to the truth. By this time, twenty-seven years had elapsed since production of *The Magic Flute*. Giesecke was beginning to be honored and feted throughout Europe for his scientific work and was already ensconced in Dublin as professor of mineralogy. He was a man of immense integrity and modesty, and he had no need to acquire an additional reputation at that stage for his former artistic work. In any case, it seems that the libretto of *The Magic Flute* was not then regarded as a work of the first order, especially when compared to Mozart's immortal music. One cannot doubt that Schikaneder contributed in some way to the final libretto, perhaps as chairman of the company's "libretto committee," but the realization right from the beginning that *The Magic Flute* was the star turn of the company's output may have made him less willing to share the honors. But this is pure speculation, and far more objective evidence is required.

In conclusion, I quote the inscription on Giesecke's memorial plaque in St. George's Church, Dublin:

> To the memory of CHARLES L METZLER GIESECKE
> Knight Commander of the Royal Danish Order of Danebrog
> FRSE & GSL VPRIA HMRDS MWS MMBSLM RDAS
> Member of the Royal Societies of Copenhagen Upsala St. Petersburg Dresden Munich Jena Wetterau
>
> Who devoted thirty-six years to the sciences of mineralogy and geology in the pursuit of which he traversed a great part of Europe and passed seven years in Greenland amidst unnumbered obstacles & privations with an ardour unabated by the severity of inhospitable clime. He was distinguished by the favour of many of the crowned heads of Europe and was for nineteen years professor of mineralogy in the Royal Dublin Society
>
> He was beloved as a friend and sought as a companion by all who knew him.
> BORN AT AUGSBURG: APRIL 6th 1761
> DIED AT DUBLIN: MARCH 4th 1833

Stephen Moorbath

* * *

Giesecke's apparent claim to have been the librettist of *The Magic Flute* calls for a balanced investigation of his character and career. A man of many parts, he devoted himself primarily to the study of science, especially mineralogy. His standing among his contemporaries was high. He was one of the earliest European explorers of Greenland, and his own diary entries and articles make fascinating reading, even for the nonscientist. Edward Dent alone, it seems, among musicologists, has taken an interest in Giesecke's achievements in this field (see Edward J. Dent, *Mozart's Operas: A Critical Study* (1913), 345–59). If Giesecke was indeed responsible, at least in part, for *The Magic Flute* libretto, whose profundities lie, like an iceberg, seven-eighths below the surface, his outstanding human qualities come as no surprise.

His article on Greenland in the *Edinburgh Encyclopaedia* of 1816 is remarkable for its depth and breadth of knowledge. It was also published separately in the same year under the title *Description of Greenland*; there is a copy in the British Library (B.471.[18.]) with a dedication in his own hand. His survey ranges through the history and language of the Eskimos, their customs, their dress; the mineralogy, botany, and zoology of Greenland; and life in its surrounding seas, including whales, fishes, and shells. Although written as a scientific tract, it is Giesecke's humanity that shines through, especially in his description of the harsh living conditions of the Greenlanders. His sympathetic understanding appears to have won their hearts. This emerges in a letter written on 8th December 1817 announcing the imminent publication of Giesecke's three-volume account of his researches in Greenland during the seven years between 1806 and 1813.[1] It was signed F.B. and sent from Copenhagen to the editors of the *Bibliothèque Universelle*, Geneva, who published an extract from it the following year. The letter makes a significant contribution to our assessment of Giesecke's character and credibility. It states:

> This journey, already extremely interesting on account of the observations one finds gathered together, becomes even more so when one knows the character of the author, who, equipped with a great fund of knowledge, is animated by the most ardent love of truth. Imprisoned for a considerable portion of his life by the consequences of the war on land and sea in the frightful country from which he has returned, he endured privations there but was able to turn the very misfortune of his situation to the profit of science. He has remained sincerely attached to these poor Greenlanders, who still write him letters full of affection.

> Ce voyage, déjà fort intéressant par les observations qu'on y trouve rassemblées, le devient encore davantage lorsqu'on connoît le caractère de l'auteur, qui, muni d'un grand fonds de connoissances, est animé de l'amour le plus ardent pour la

vérité. Emprisonné par les conséquences de la guerre de terre et de mer, pendant une portion considérable de sa vie, dans l'affreux pays dont il est revenu, il y a vécu de privations, et il a su faire tourner au profit de la science le malheur même de sa situation. Il est demeuré sincèrement attaché à ces pauvres Groënlandais, qui lui écrivent encore des lettres pleines d'affection.[2]

An article published in 1819 in the journal *Annalen der Physik* drew attention to the letter, identifying the initials F.B. as belonging to the writer Friederike Brunn. This article, predating Cornet's book by thirty years, provides contemporary confirmation of the welcome that awaited Giesecke on his return to Vienna. Though his earlier collaboration with Schikaneder is given no more than a passing mention (which is hardly surprising in a scientific periodical), one detects, beneath the dry, factual tone of the account, the respect his scientific work and his fortitude had earned him.

Herr Karl Ludwig Metzler-Giesecke, born in Augsburg, studied in Göttingen and then lived in Vienna for 13 years. He had an admirable reputation here with the general public as a gifted actor at the Theater an der Wien (for which he wrote some plays and was adviser and practical assistant to its director, Schikaneder), and with science-lovers as a zealous mineralogist . . . in April 1806 he embarked under the sponsorship of the Danish government . . . and landed on 31st May at *Frederikshaab* in Greenland. Prevented from returning by the war at sea which broke out soon afterwards, he remained in this inhospitable land for 7 years and 4 months, till 16th August 1813, under difficulties and privations of all kinds; he spent three winters in *Godthaab* at latitude 65°, 3 more winters in *Gothaven* on Disko Island at latitude 70°, and one winter in *Uppernak* at latitude 73°, and he traveled the whole coast of Greenland, from the southernmost point *Cape Farewell* at latitude 59½° right up to the northernmost boundary, the *ice cliff Vierwohl* at latitude 78°. At the end of the fourth year he sent his collected natural history specimens to Denmark, but the ship was captured by an English privateer and the cargo sold in London and Edinburgh. . . . He therefore had to start collecting all over again, and that took him another 3 years and 8 months. . . .

He is on the point of publishing his Description of this Journey, which should appear simultaneously in English and German in 3 quarto volumes, with about 50 engravings. It is his intention to proceed by subscription so as to be covered in this enterprise. So far as I know, the terms of the subscription have not yet been announced, but the printing of the first volume is supposed to be almost complete.

In 1808 Herr Giesecke had been commissioned in Greenland by the Imperial Royal Natural History Collection in Vienna, through its energetic Director, Herr von Schreiber, to supply specimens for this collection, and had agreed to carry out the task. Only last year was it possible for him to assemble the collected treasures in one place and sort them out. He then brought them in person to

Vienna, in order to lay them as a gift at the feet of the emperor as a small sign of his attachment and gratitude; a gift worth at least 7,000 florins, and which now constitutes one of the finest adornments of the Imperial Royal Natural History Collection in Vienna, which, under the direction of Herr von Schreiber, must have become one of the best in Europe, not simply through its riches but also through its purely scientific exhibits and tasteful arrangement.

Herr Karl Ludwig Metzler-Giesecke, geboren zu Augsburg, hat in Göttingen studirt, und dann 13 Jahre lang in Wien gelebt. Dem Publikum war er hier als talentvoller Schauspieler bei dem Theater an der Wien, (für das er einige Schauspiele schrieb, und dessen Direktor Schikaneder er mit Rath und That beistand), und den Freunden der Wissenschaften als eifriger Mineralog rühmlich bekannt . . . im April 1806 schiffte er sich mit Unterstützung der Dänischen Regierung ein . . . und landete am 31. Mai zu *Frederikshaab* in Grönland. Durch den Seekrieg, der bald darauf ausbrach, an der Rückkehr verhindert, verweilte er in diesem unwirthbarem Lande 7 Jahr und 4 Monate, bis zum 16 August 1813, unter Beschwerlichkeiten und Entbehrungen aller Art; drei Winter brachte er zu *Godthaab* in 65° Breite, 3 andere Winter zu *Gothaven* auf der Insel Disko, in 70° Breite, und einen Winter zu *Uppernak*, in 73° Breite, zu, und er hat die ganze Küste Grönlands, vom südlichsten Punkte *Cap Farewell* 59½° Br. bis zur nördlichsten Grenze, dem *Eisblink Vierwohl*, im 78° Breite bereist. Am Ende des vierten Jahrs sendete er seine eingesammelten Naturalien nach Dänemark, das Schiff wurde aber von einem englischen Kaper genommen und die Ladung in London und Edinburg verkauft. . . . Er musste daher mit Sammeln von vorn anfangen, und dazu verwendete er noch 3 Jahr und 8 Monate. . . .

Im Begriff, die *Beschreibung dieser Reise* herauszugeben, welche in 3 Quartbänden mit ungefähr 50 Kupfertafeln englisch und deutsch zugleich erscheinen soll, wollte er damals den Weg der Subscription einschlagen, um bei dem Unternehmen gedeckt zu seyn; die Bedingungen der Subscription sind zwar, so viel ich weiss, noch nicht bekannt gemacht worden, es soll aber der Druck des ersten Bandes bereits vollendet seyn.

Hr. Giesecke hatte im J. 1808 von dem Kaiserl. Königl. Naturalienkabinet zu Wien, durch den thätigen Direktor desselben, Hrn. von Schreibers Aufträge zu Sammlungen für dieses Kabinet nach Grönland erhalten und sie auszurichten übernommen. Erst im vorigen Jahre wurde es ihm möglich, die gesammelten Schätze auf einen Punkt zusammen zu bringen und zu sondern. Er überbrachte sie dann in Person nach Wien, um sie als Geschenk dem Kaiser als ein schwaches Zeichen seiner Anhänglichkeit und Dankbarkeit zu Füssen zu legen; ein Geschenk, dessen Werth auf wenigstens 7000 Gulden geschätzt wurde, und das jetzt eine der vorzüglichsten Zierden des Kais. Königl. Naturalienkabinets in Wien ausmacht, welches unter der Direktion des Hrn. von Schreibers nicht blos durch Reichthum, sondern auch durch rein-wissenschaftliche Ausstellung und geschmackvolle Anordnung eins der ersten in Europa geworden seyn soll.[3]

A footnote on page 181 of the article quotes from the *Hamburger Correspondent* of 31st May 1819.

The famous mineralogist Giesecke, born in Augsburg, whose real name was Metzler, recently left his German fatherland again to make the return journey from Vienna to Dublin. The fate of this man is really singular. At first he was a student of law, then actor, writer, scholar of private means, mineralogist who lived for a long time in Iceland (Greenland), professor, member of leading learned societies etc. He is a very capable man.

Der berühmte Mineralog Giesecke, nach seinem wahren Familiennamen Metzler, ein geborner Augsburger hat vor Kurzem sein deutsches Vaterland wieder verlassen und seine Rückreise von Wien nach Dublin angetreten. Das Schicksal dieses Mannes ist wirklich sonderbar. Anfangs war er Jurist, dann Schauspieler, Dichter, privatisirender Gelehrter, Mineralog, der sich lange in Island (Grönland) aufhielt, Professor, Mitglied der ersten Gelehrten Gesellschaften etc. Er ist ein sehr vermögender Mann.

Giesecke's personal travel diary was first published in Copenhagen in 1878 by F. Johnstrup under the title *Gieseckes Mineralogiske Rejse I Grønland* (British Library 7106.g.19.). A second edition, entitled *Meddelelser om Grønland* (National Library of Ireland 549 G2), was published in 1910, with an elaborate preface by K. J. V. Steenstrup giving a full biography of Giesecke showing that Giesecke and Metzler were one and the same person. No one knows why Giesecke used his chosen name in preference to his real name, Johann Georg Metzler, but he did so from at least as early as the age of twenty.[5] Steenstrup points out on page I of his preface that the editorial cuts and amendments of the first edition have been replaced by Giesecke's full, verbatim text. For this reason all the quotations and page numbers given below are taken from the Steenstrup edition, including idiosyncrasies and inconsistencies of spelling.

The diary is predominantly scientific in content, but an impressive picture of Giesecke the man emerges, despite the restrained manner of its reporting which allows only rare glimpses of his personal feelings. It reveals how, year by year, circumstances conspired to keep Giesecke in Greenland for much longer than he had originally intended. Let us start with the loss of his collections, which were dispatched earlier, it appears, than the report in *Annalen der Physik* indicated.

1808

On Sunday 15th May

Inspector MOTZFELDT received a letter, via an English whaling captain, from Captain JEPSEN, dated London 15th February 1808, from which we learned of the loss of five Danish merchant vessels, which was doubly painful for me since with them were lost the collections which I had made with much trouble over the last two years or more.

Sonntags d: 15. May/ Erhielt Herr Inspekteur MOTZFELDT durch einen Englischen Wallfischfängerkapitän einen Brief von Kapitan [*sic*] JEPSEN aus London vom 15. Febr. 1808 datirt, wodurch wir Nachricht von dem Verluste 5. Dänischer Handelsschiffe erhielten, welches mich doppelt schmerzte, da ich mit denselben meiner diese 2. Jahre über mit vieler Mühe gemachten Samlungen verlustig wurde. (p. 114)

Two months later he reported his decision to make good the loss.

Thursday 14th July
     . . . and so I resolved to spend one more year in Greenland and examine and collect as much as possible, since the bitter fruits of my applied labors up to now have for the most part fallen into the hands of the English.

Donnerstags. d: 14. Julius / . . . so beschloss ich, noch ein Jahr in Grönland zuzubringen, und noch so viel möglich zu untersuchen und einzusammeln, da die sauren Früchte meiner bisher angewandten Mühe grösstentheils in Englische Hände gefallen sind. (p. 134)

But the next year brought further bad news from Europe and still no prospect of an early return.

1809

Sunday 28th May
     . . . Against all expectation postal kayaks arrived from Fiskenæs at 9 p.m. . . . bringing letters from Europe. . . . For me the loss of all my painstaking collections and natural history work, which were destroyed by fire in the burning of the St. Peter's priests' house, was, if not unexpected, painful indeed; on top of that came confirmation of the loss of all my two-year collecting of natural specimens in Greenland, which fell into the enemy's hands. I immediately decided, without heed to all the unfavorable prospects, to remain in the country one more year, in order in some measure to repair the gaps by collecting anew, since it seemed to me on the whole inadvisable to entrust myself or the remainder of my collection to such a precarious sea journey.

Sonntags, den 28 May / . . . Abends um 9 Uhr kamen wider alles Erwarten Postkajakken von Fiskenæs . . . und brachten zugleich die Briefe aus Europa mit. . . . Mir war der Verlust aller meiner mühsamen Samlungen und naturhistorischen Arbeiten, welche bey dem Brande des Petri Priesterhauses ein Raub der Flammen wurden, zwar nicht unerwartet, aber doch schmerzlich; wozu noch die Bestättigung des Verlustes aller meiner durch zwey Jahre in Grönland gesammelten Naturprodukte kam, welche in die Hände des Feindes fielen. Ich war sogleich entschlossen, aller ungünstigen Aussichten ungeachtet, noch ein Jahr im Lande zu verbleiben, um die Lücken doch einigermassen wieder durch neues Einsammeln zu ergänzen, da es mir überhaupt nicht rathsam schien, mich selbst oder den Rest meiner gemachten Sammlung einer so unsichern Seereise anzuvertrauen. (pp. 197–98)

Two weeks later he wrote, in a private letter to Friederich Münter (see photo 18):

Tuapeitsiak. 12th June 1809
Right Reverend Bishop!
Venerable friend!

And so once again a ship leaves this dismal land without my being able to leave!—We have all spent a miserable year, and face the prospect of an even more miserable one.—If I believed in lucky and unlucky stars I would imagine that one of the latter had driven me into this scrap heap of all the unpleasant things of this otherwise so beautiful earth, where one horror of nature is engaged in an eternal race with another, and night flirts with the silence of the grave. . . . This year, too, I must unfortunately once more abandon all hope of seeing my dear friends in Europe again—God knows how things will go next year!— . . . . With little trouble the English have pounded off the face of this earth the fruits of ten years' sweated labor; I had suspected this news with the burning of St. Peter's, but confirmation through the King's Counsel Manthey, my true friend in need, was painful indeed. Contact with friends is the only thing that can keep me alive and warm in this land where, one might almost say, even friendship could sometimes freeze up. . . .

Your most loyal brother of the Order
Karl Ludwig Giesecke

Tuapeitsiak d: 12. Jun. 1809. Hochwürdiger Herr Bischoff! Verehrungswürdiger Freund! Und so verlässt abermals ein Schiff dies traurige Land, ohne dass ich es verlassen kan̄!—Wir haben alle ein elendes Jahr verlebt, und sehen nun einem noch elendern entgegen.—Wen̄ ich an glückliche oder unglückliche Gestirne glaubte, so müsste ich denken, einer der letztern hätte mich in diesen Auskehrichtswinkel von allen Unanehmlichkeiten unserer sonst so schönen Erde gejagt, wo ein Schreckniss der Natur mit dem andern im Ewigen Wettlaufe begriffen ist, und die Nacht mit der Stille des Grabes kokettirt. . . . . Ich muss auch in diesem Jahre leider abermals auf das Glück Verzicht thun, meine lieben Freunde in Europa wieder zu sehen—Gott weiss, wie es in dem nächsten Jahre gehen wird!—. . . . Die Engländer haben die Früchte eines zehenjährigen [*sic*] Schweisses mit leichter Mühe aus der Welt bombardirt; eine Nachricht, welche ich unter dem Brande der Petrikirche mir dachte, so schmerzlich mir auch die Bestättigung derselben durch Justitzrath Manthey, meinen wahren Freund in der Noth, war. Freundschaftlicher Umgang ist das einzige, was mich in diesem Lande, wo, man möchte beynahe sagen, auch die Freundschaft zuweilen

erfrieren könnte, frisch und warm erhalten kann. . . . Ihr treuverbundenster Or-
densbru Karl Ludwig Giesecke.[5]

The weather, too, may have contributed to Giesecke's depressive mood, for
he reported in his diary:

On Monday 12th June
  the weather was exceptionally stormy.
On Tuesday 13th June
  the gale brought my tent down around my head twice in one night, forcing me
to take refuge in a more strongly built Greenland tent. . . .

Montags, den 12 Junius / war die Witterung ausserordentlich stürmisch.
  Dienstags, den 13 Junius / Warf der Sturmwind mir das Zelt in einer Nacht
zweymal über dem Kopf zusammen, wesswegen ich mich genöthigt sah, unter
ein stärker gebauetes, grönländisches Zelt zu flüchten. . . . (p. 201)

Here the place name is spelled *Tuapatsiait*. At the age of forty-eight, Giesecke probably felt that such adventures had outlived their excitement.
  The summer of 1810 was a time of renewed hope.

1810

Tuesday 31st July
  . . . On the friendly invitation of Inspector MOTZFELDT I resolved to use
the good opportunity to travel with him to Godhavn, because I had reason to
suspect that I might be able to return to Europe from North Greenland perhaps
this autumn or in any case in the spring.

Dienstags, den 31 Julius / . . . Ich beschloss, auf die freundschaftliche Einladung des Herrn Inspekteurs MOTZFELDT, die gute Gelegenheit zu benüzzen,
und mit ihm nach Godhavn abzureisen, weil ich nicht ohne Grund vermuthen
konnte, von Nordgrönland aus vieleicht noch in diesem Herbste, oder doch im
Frühjahre nach Europa zurückgehen zu können. (p. 280)

But two and a half weeks later the dangers of travel in this inhospitable part
of the world nearly cost Giesecke his life.

Friday 17th August
  . . . A huge wave, which broke in from the windward side, would almost have
swept me overboard had not at the same moment another crashed in from the
leeward side, throwing me back down into the boat. Soaked through, I thanked
God—and crept into the cabin.

Freytags, den 17 August / . . . Eine schwere Welle, welche von der Luvartseite hereinbrach, hätte mich beynahe über Bord genommen, wenn nicht im nemlichen Augenblik eine andere von der Leeseite hereingestürzt wäre, welche mich wieder unter die Jolle gleichsam zurückwarf. Ganz durchnässt dankte ich Gott, und—kroch in die Kajüte. (p. 286)

His problems included shortage of food and supplies.

On Sunday 25th November
   Messrs. RASMUSSEN and BRANDT arrived here safely with some provisions after a difficult journey. The faces of the colonists and Greenlanders, which had become badly wrinkled, gradually smoothed out again.—It is really hard, with the catch having entirely failed everywhere this year, to struggle through on half rations, which have for some time been apportioned to all without exception.—One feels these wants even more because of the lack of fuel. . . .

Sonntags, den 25 November / kamen die Herrn RASMUSSEN und BRANDT nach einer beschwerlicher Reise glücklich mit einigen Erfrischungen hier an. Die Angesichten der Kolonisten und Grönländer, welche sich bisher in schlimme Falten gezogen hatten, glätteten sich allmählich wieder aus.—Es ist wirklich hart, bey dem dieses Jahr an allen Orten durchaus fehlschlagenden Fang mit halber Kost sich durchzuschlagen, welche allen ohne Ausnahme seit einiger Zeit zugemessen wurde.—Der Mangel an Brennmaterial macht diese Entbehrungen noch fühlbarer. . . . (p. 296)

In the year of his fiftieth birthday he once again survived a life-threatening incident, and there was still no early prospect of returning home.

1811

Thursday 30th May
   . . . in the middle of our journey . . . we came to a double, open channel in the ice. . . . But when I made my jump the ice, which was unfortunately already fractured from underneath at this point, gave way with me on it, plunging me into the sea. However when I came up I held on tightly to the firm ice on the opposite side and with some difficulty swung myself back onto the dry.

Donnerstags, den 30 May / . . . auf der Mitte des Wegs . . . kamen wir an eine doppelte, offene Eisrinne. . . . Als ich aber meinen Sprung machte, brach das Eis, welches zum Unglück an dieser Stelle von unten zu schon durchfressen war, mit mir ein, und ich plumpte in die See. Doch hielt ich beym Heraufkommen am gegenüberstehenden festen Eise fest, und schwang mich mit einiger Mühe wieder auf das Trockene. (p. 328)

Sunday 21st July
 . . . On my arrival here I received the (for me) unpleasant news that Captain
LAURITZ MATHIESEN . . . sailed for Europe a couple of days ago. . . . I see
myself compelled to hold out for another year.—

Sonntags, den 21 Julius / . . . Ich erhielt hier bey meiner Ankunft die für mich
unangenehme Nachricht, dass der Kapitän LAURITZ MATHIESEN . . . vor ein
Paar Tagen nach Europa abgesegelt sey . . . Ich sehe mich also nothgedrungen,
noch ein Jahr auszuharren.— (pp. 360–61)

The sense of isolation from Europe is evident in an entry early the following year. From the surrounding dates it is clear that Friday falls on 13th; the
misdating is probably error rather than superstition on Giesecke's part, since
Friday 13th occurs elsewhere in his diary.

1812

On Friday 12th [13th] March
 15 European men and two women were gathered at the home of the Inspector
in Godhavn. . . . It is something rare in this country to be able to enjoy social
life in such numbers!—

Freytags, den 12 [13] März / waren zu Godhavn bey dem Herrn Inspecteur 15
Europäische Männer und zwey Frauen versammelt. . . . Es ist etwas seltenes hier
im Lande in so zahlreicher Menge sich des gesellschaftlichen Lebens freuen zu
können!— (p. 394)

In that year, 1812, it was still the progress of the war that obstructed Giesecke's return.

Monday 13th April
 . . . At 5.0 o'clock the English ship "True Love," commanded by Captain
WATSON, came quite close to land. . . . He hove to outside Godhavn and raised
his flag to indicate that we should receive a letter . . . he also sent us a present
of potatoes and onions, some newspapers and a note in which he informed us
that the war between England and Denmark was up to now still in progress,
against the will and wishes of the English nation, news which depressed us all
very much.

Montags, den 13 April / . . . Um 5 Uhr kam das englische Schiff "True Love,"
geführt von Kapitän WATSON, dem Lande ziemlich nahe . . . . Er legte unter
Godhavn bey, und zog die Flagge auf, um uns einen Brief erhalten zu machen.
. . . Auch sandte er uns eine Verehrung von Kartoffeln und Zwiebeln, einige

Zeitungen, und ein Billet, in welchem er uns meldete, dass der Krieg zwischen England und Dännemark gegen den Wunsch und Willen der Englischen Nation bisher noch fortdauere; eine Nachricht, welche uns alle sehr niederschlug. (p. 396)

Thursday 16th April

. . . Two English ships approached land. . . . From one of them, Captain LAWSON, we received written news that one or two supply ships would once again visit or call in on Greenland this year at the expense of the English government, and that no Danish ship would come.

Donnerstags, den 16 April / . . . . Zwey Englische Schiffe näherten sich dem Lande. . . . Von einem derselben, Kapitän LAWSON erhielten wir die schriftliche Nachricht, dass Grönland dieses Jahr abermals von einem oder zweyen auf Kosten der Englischen Regierung mit Proviant versehenen Schiffen besucht, oder heimgesucht werden würde, und dass kein Dänisches Schiff kommen werde. (p. 397)

Nevertheless, two Danish vessels seem to have got through, but the news reached Giesecke too late.

Friday 14th August

. . . At 11 o'clock in the evening express kayaks arrived here with letters from South Greenland. From them we received news that Captain ERKEN arrived in Holsteinsburg with the ship Jupiter on 13th June and departed again on 4th August!!

Freytags, den 14 August / . . . Abends um 11 Uhr kamen Kajaksexpressen mit Briefen aus Südgrönland hier an. Durch sie erhielten wir die Nachricht, dass Kapitän ERKEN den 13 Junius mit dem Schiffe Jupiter zu Holsteinsburg angekommen und, den 4den [*sic*] August wieder abgereist sey!! (p. 413)

Friday 16th October

. . . This gave us the opportunity to receive the news so longingly awaited from South Greenland of Captain Mathiesen's arrival there. The letters that followed with it stifled the last, weak, still glowing embers of hope for help from Europe, and the prospect of a long, needy winter, bare of so many necessities of life, made us very depressed. My ardent desire to return to Europe this year had, this time too, to remain unfulfilled, since I received the letter from the Royal High Greenland Board of Trade dated 15th May 1812 only after the departure of the ship from Greenland, and a journey from here to Godthaab, a distance of 120 miles, was altogether out of the question on account of the impenetrable mass of ice.

Freytags, den 16 Oktober/ . . . Wir erhielten mit dieser Gelegenheit die so sehnsuchtsvoll erwartete Nachrichten aus Südgrönland von MATHIESENS Ankunft daselbst. Die mitfolgenden Briefe erstickten den lezten schwachen noch in der Asche glimmenden Funken von Hoffnung auf Hülfe von Europa, und die Aussicht auf einen langen dürftigen Winter, entblösst von so manchen Bedürfnissen des Lebens machte uns sehr niedergeschlagen. Mein sehnlicher Wunsch in diesem Jahre nach Europa zurückzukehren, musste also auch diesmal unerfüllt bleiben, da ich das Schreiben von der Hohen Königl. grönländischen Handelsdirection datirt vom 15ten May 1812 erst nach Abreise der Schiffe von Grönland erhielt, und überhaupt eine Reise von hier nach Godthaab einen Weg von 120 Meilen, des undurchdringlichen, grossen Eises wegen unmöglich war. (p. 433)

In 1813 he was at last able to depart. Only in the final pages of his diary does he give full expression to his feelings.

1813

Sunday 8th August
   . . . At 9 o'clock in the evening Captain Lindberg returned from Omenak after a 4-week journey. The same evening I informed him in writing of my decision to leave Greenland on the brig "Hvalfisken," and in the same letter requested the favor, as it was still such an opportune time of year, of passing by the colony of Holsteinsburg on the homeward journey, where all the natural history specimens I had collected in southern Greenland, some books, bedclothes and other possessions of mine stood packed and ready to be loaded. I had also previously written to Mr. GRÖNWALD, a tradesman in Holsteinsburg, asking him to come out in a sloop to meet the ship when it approached. To this written request of mine

Monday 9th August
   Captain LINDBERG answered in a rather laconic letter, that he could in no circumstances do this. This disobliging behavior, for which I am at a loss to account, puts me in the disagreeable position of not being able, as I would have wished, to deliver the enclosures which belong with my diary entries on South Greenland together with the diary; what is more I cannot in the present circumstances determine when this will happen. . . .

Monday 16th August
   . . . It was by no means easy to leave a land which had given me friendly shelter for so many years, to part from friends and acquaintances with whom I had shared fraternally many a bitter hour, many a gloomy prospect.—My grateful heart will also never forget the happy hours which their shared acquaintance granted me. . . . My thanks to all the working people who were of service to

me!—My thanks to all the noble people of the nation who were agreeable companions to me on my often gruelling land and sea journeys and jointly endured the daily hardships of the climate with me. I will see them no more!—We left Godhavn at 2 a.m. . . .

Saturday 22nd August
. . . At 4 p.m. we had the coast of Holsteinsburg 2 miles to windward of us. Anyone who has made such journeys will feel how painful it was for me to be so close to the land and nevertheless have to leave behind my collections preserved there, the fruits of so much painful effort, uncertain whether, under present circumstances, such a good opportunity to fetch these collections and put them to good purpose will be encountered so soon. But an unfavorable star, which shone so darkly for me over the last few years, even on this journey, where I least expected it, refused to give a friendly light . . . .

Wednesday 8th September
In the night of 6th to 7th my boxes of Greenland plants, which I had painstakingly collected and looked after for 7 years, were badly damaged by the crashing of the sea. . . .

Tuesday 14th September
We had one of the severest storms of the whole journey, coming from the northwest, with a terrible sea running and heavy thunder showers. . . . We got several waves crashing over the ship and, in the afternoon, a heavy sea in the cabin.

Sunday 19th September
After lengthy to-ing and fro-ing for five days we anchored safely at the roadstead of Leith at 1 o'clock this morning.

Sonntags, den 8 August / . . . Abends 9 Uhr kam Kapitän LINDBERG nach einer 4 wöchentlichen Reise von Omenak zurück. Ich berichtete ihm noch den nemlichen Abend schriftlich meinen Entschluss, mit der Brigg Hvalfisken Grönland zu verlassen, und ersuchte ihn im nemlichen Briefe um die Gefälligkeit, da es noch so zeitig im Jahre war, auf der Heimreise die Kolonie Holsteinsburg anzulaufen, woselbst alle meine im südlichen Grönland gesammelte Naturalien, einige Bücher, Bettzeug und andre mir gehörige Sachen eingepackt und zum Empfange bereit standen. Ich hatte auch vorläufig Herrn GRÖNWALD, Kaufmann zu Holsteinsburg, schriftl. ersucht, bey des Schiffes Annäherung mit einer Schaluppe entgegen zu kommen.—Auf dieses mein schriftliches Ansuchen antwortete

Montags, den 9 August / Kapitän LINDBERG in einem ziemlich laconischen Briefe, dass er dieses keineswegs thun könnte. Dieses ungefällige Betragen, dessen Grund ich mir schlechterdings nicht erklären kann, sezzt mich in die unangenehme Lage, dass ich nicht, wie ich es gewünscht hätte, im Stande bin, die Belege zu meinen im Tagebuche ertheilten Nachrichten über Südgrönland sogleich mit dem Tagebuche abzuliefern; so wie ich auch unter den jezigen Umständen nicht bestimmen kann, wann dieses geschehen wird. . . .

Montags, den 16 August / . . . Es fiel mir wirklich schwer, ein Land zu verlassen, welches mich durch so viele Jahre freundlich beherbergt hatte; mich von Freunden und Bekannten zu trennen, mit welchen ich in den letzten Jahren manche bittre Stunde, manche trübe Aussicht brüderlich getheilt hatte.—Auch die frohen Stunden, welche mir ihr theilnehmender Umgang gewährte, wird mein dankbares Herz nie vergessen. . . . Dank allen den Arbeitsleuten, welche mir zu Dienste waren!—Dank allen den Edeln der Nation, welche mir gefällige Gefährten auf meinen oft sauren Land und Seereisen waren und täglich vereint mit mir die Beschwerden des Climas duldeten. Ich sehe sie nicht wieder!—Um 2 Uhr Morgens verliessen wir Godhavn. . . .

Sonnabends, den 22 August / . . . Nachmittags vier Uhr hatten wir das feste Land von Holsteinsburg 2 Meilen in Luvart von uns. Wer solche Reisen gemacht hat, kann fühlen, wie schmerzlich es für mich seyn musste, so nahe dem Lande zu seyn und doch meine dorten verwahrten Samlungen, die Früchte so mancher sauern Anstrengung, zurückelassen zu müssen; ungewiss, ob unter dermaligen Umständen sobald sich eine so gute Gelegenheit treffen möchte, diese Samlungen abzuholen, und zweckmässig zu verwenden. Allein ein ungünstiger Stern, welcher seit einigen Jahren so düster für mich schien, wollte auch bey dieser Reise, wo ich es am wenigsten vermuthete, nicht freundlich glänzen. . . .

Mittwochs, den 8 September / In der Nacht vom 6 zum 7ten wurden meine Kassen mit Grönländischen Pflanzen, welche ich in 7 Jahren mühsam gesammelt und gepflegt hatte, von den Seestürzungen sehr beschädigt. . . .

Dienstags, den 14 September / Wir hatten einen der schwersten Stürme auf der ganzen Reise, und zwar aus Nordwest, mit grässlichem Seegang und heftigem Gewitterregen. . . . Wir kriegten mehrere Stürzungen über das Schiff und Nachmittags eine schwere See in die Kajüte.

Sonntags, den 19 September / Nach langem Hin- und Herkreuzen durch fünf Tage kamen wir heute Morgens 1 Uhr glücklich auf der Rheede bei Leith vor Anker. (pp. 471–78)

The "unfavorable star" was not entirely without mercy, however, for the samples collected by Giesecke during his first two years in Greenland, and captured at sea by the English, fell into the hands of the English mineralogist

Thomas Allan. In a paper read at a meeting of the Royal Society of Edinburgh on 20th April 1812 and published in *Annals of Philosophy* (February 1813), Allan correctly identified the owner of the collection.

> . . . the collector is a German mineralogist of high repute, of the name of Gie-seké. Having heard of the fate of his minerals, soon after they were captured, with an enthusiasm much to be admired, being still in Greenland, I am informed he immediately employed himself in repairing the loss by forming another collection. The return of Mr. Gieseké to Europe is expected next spring; and as we have reason to hope that he will arrive at the port of Leith, we may be able to obtain farther [*sic*] elucidation on several interesting points. . . .[6]

In March 1813 Giesecke was mentioned again in *Annals of Philosophy*: "He has long been well known on the Continent as a dealer in minerals, adding to unbounded zeal a great knowledge of mineralogy" (p. 218).

After Giesecke's arrival Allan seems to have lost no time in making contact with him. In a letter to the editor of *Annals of Philosophy* dated 12th October 1813, Allan wrote:

> . . . I have now the pleasure to announce to you the safe arrival of Mr. Geisecké [*sic*], after a residence of seven years and a half in Greenland. . . . Mr. Geisecké is possessed of a great deal of interesting intelligence, not only with regard to the mineralogy and geology, but also the zoology and botany, of the country: the former were his principal objects; and from his accurate knowledge of every part of the science, we have reason to expect a great deal of most useful and interesting information, as he is about to publish an account of his travels in Greenland.

There follows a scientific report, and the letter continues:

> Your readers will probably be anxious to know the kind of country Mr. Geisecké met with in Greenland. So far as he saw, the continent was entirely primitive, excepting the peninsula of Norsoak, in 71°. . . .

> The difficulties Mr. G. had to contend with were innumerable, and the dangers continual. He frequently had to walk 30 or 40 miles, carrying on his shoulders the fruits of his labour; and in going from one island to another, he had nothing to convey him but the miserable seal-skin boats of the country, and these always managed by women.[7]

Five days later Allan supported Giesecke's application for a professorship in Dublin.

Edinburgh, October 17, 1813 . . .

Sir,
    I have the pleasure to inclose [*sic*] a letter from Mr. Charles Ludovic Metzler
Giesecké, offering himself as a candidate for the Professorship of Mineralogy,
at present vacant in the Dublin Society. . . . This gentleman arrived lately from
Greenland, and has lived about three weeks in my house, where I have had suf-
ficient opportunity of observing his perfect capacity as a Mineralogist, and his
thorough knowledge of the detail, which constitutes what may be called, in that
department, a man of science.[8]

His application having succeeded, his career and activities in Dublin may
be followed in the pages of *The Proceedings of the Dublin Society* (from
1820 the Royal Dublin Society). He cataloged and rearranged the Society's
collections, adding specimens from his own Greenland collection. These
included, besides more than four hundred minerals, "quadrupeds and fishes,
birds, insects and shells, dresses, models and other curiosities" (vol. 52
[1815–16], 212). Happily the portion of the collection relating to southern
Greenland, which he was obliged to leave behind at Holsteinsburg, arrived
safely in Copenhagen (213). On 4th July 1816 he sought permission to give
public lectures (220), and was subsequently elected an Honorary Member of
the Society (238), followed in 1817 by the award of its gold medal (vol. 53
[1816–17], 235, 254–55). In a letter sent from Vienna on 22nd February 1819
Giesecke reported that he had made good contacts for the Society and its museum and that he would be leaving for London via Italy in three days' time
(vol. 55 [1818–19], 99–100). It was, of course, during this visit to Vienna that
he met Cornet, who subsequently reported Giesecke's claim to authorship of
The Magic Flute libretto.
    In the National Library of Ireland there are two personal albums (MS 3533
and 3534) belonging to Giesecke, containing inscriptions, poems, and pictures contributed by acquaintances and friends. The format and chronology
is haphazard, but they have been put into order in an unpublished typescript
by Gilbert Waterhouse, which, as announced in *Proceedings of the Royal
Irish Academy*, 21st July 1970, is deposited in the library of the Royal Irish
Academy (4.A.52).

SIR CHARLES GIESECKE'S AUTOGRAPH ALBUMS, by G. Waterhouse.
. . . In *Proceedings of the Royal Irish Academy*, Vol. 43 C9, 1936, [pp. 291–306]
I published a summary of the contents of these albums and I have now deposited in the library of the Academy a complete transcript of all the entries, both
important and trivial, rearranged in chronological order. A running commentary
fills in the background and provides the foundation for a full biography of this
remarkable man. . . . In the paper quoted above . . . I expressed my belief in
the existence of another album . . . which must have covered his career as an

actor from 1783 to 1800. This conjecture has recently been confirmed (1969) by Professor G. Raddatz (Berlin-Friedenau) and Herr Gerd Ibler (Augsburg), who have both been kind enough to inform me that they have found, in the municipal archives of Vienna, a record of proceedings against Giesecke for non-payment of rent. The albums show that Giesecke left Schikaneder's company in August 1800 but it now appears that he left clandestinely, and in 1801, a full year later, distraint was levied on such effects as he had left behind. Professor Raddatz found a catalogue of the books and papers sold, among them: "Ein Stammbuch mit einigen Gemälden . . ." [an album with some pictures]. The search for this third album . . . can now begin. . . . The frequent interruptions in the sequence of entries in the albums, some for years together, will no doubt be made good by the missing volume, if it is ever found. It will probably contain the autographs of Mozart, Schikaneder, and other celebrities.[9]

Waterhouse's 1936 article, to which he refers above, provides an admirable analysis of the two available albums and includes selections from the entries. Pointing out that their numbering, 3 and 5, is not in Giesecke's hand, he doubts the existence of numbers 1 and 2, on the grounds that numbers 3 and 5 both start as early as 1781, when Giesecke was only twenty. However, a Dublin sale catalog of Giesecke's effects in the library of the Royal Irish Academy (C/19/3/A), dated 1834, shows that there were five volumes put up for sale after Giesecke's death (pp. 72–73), including two together in one case. According to the catalog, one of them contained Haydn's signature, but there is no mention of Mozart or Schikaneder. Schikaneder's niece Nanette, however, makes an appearance in album 3 with a short couplet dated 13th November 1800: "The moment of meeting is worth the anxious hours of separation" (Der Augenblick des wiederschauns [?wiedersehens] / lont der trennung bange stunden).[10] She is reputed to have sung First Boy in the premiere of *The Magic Flute*. (Giesecke was First Slave.)

The two surviving albums bear ample testimony to Giesecke's continuing involvement in Freemasonry, with Masonic symbols scattered among the signatories and adorning his own signature. The daughter of Giesecke's executor, who was only nine years old when Giesecke died, later recalled seeing "albums full of quotations and little pictures stuck in, not of any interest. Most of them have been given away."[11]

The album sold in Vienna appears to bring the number of Giesecke's recorded albums to six. In a letter to Gilbert Waterhouse dated 2nd September 1968 (Institute of Germanic and Romance Studies, London University, IGS/Archives/GWA box 113) Professor G. Raddatz indicates that documents relating to proceedings against Giesecke are to be found in the Wiener Magistratsarchiv (Rathaus), Alte Zivil-Justiz, Fasz. 7, 1308/1801 (the correct reference today is Wiener Stadt- und Landesarchiv, Magistratisches Zivilgericht,

Fasz. 7, 1308/1801). Document no. 4295, headed 25th February 1802 and dated 4th March 1802 at the bottom, reveals agreement between the parties that three-quarters of a year's rent was owing.

Herr D. Sprieger, the trustee appointed for the defendant in his absence, considered a debt of only three-quarters of a year's rent, rather than the full year claimed, to be correct, with which the plaintiff declared himself satisfied[.]

Verdict

In the case of the plaintiff Johann Arnhold, roof tiler by profession, represented by Herr D. Montibeller, against the defendant Karl Ludwig Metzler also known as Giesecke, and in view of his unknown whereabouts represented in his absence by an appointed trustee, Herr D. Sprieger, with regard to a writ of collateral offered by the former, in pursuance of the contract of assets enacted on 4th August 1800 for a whole year's rent from St. George's Day [23rd April] 1801 to the same in 1802, besides defendant's deposit, the verbal settlement agreed between the plaintiff in person and the latter Herr D. Sprieger on 23rd of this month is recognized by the magistrate etc. as conclusive.

Der für den Geklagten zum Kurator abs: aufgestellte Herr D. Sprieger hielt an der angesprochenen Schuld als ganzjährige Zinns [sic] blos 3 Vierteljahre für richtig, womit sich der Kläger zufrieden erklärte[.]

Urtheil

Von dem Maggistrato etc wird in der Rechtssache des durch Hrrn D. Montibeller vertretenen Johann Arnhold berufl. Ziegle[el]decker Klägers, wider den Karl Ludwig Metzler, sonst auch Giesecke genannt u respekt wegen dessen unbekannten Aufenthalt den ihm zum Kurator abs: aufgestellten Herrn D. Sprieger Geklagten, wegen von ersterem gebothener Absicherungsauflage in folge Bestandkontraktes atto 4. Augst. $\overline{8}$00. eines ganz Jährigen Zinnses [sic] von Georgi $\overline{8}$01. bis dahin $\overline{8}$02. nebst Ansatz des Geklagten, über das mit Kläger persönnlich [sic] und dem Herrn D. Sprieger unteren 23. d. M. geschlichtene mündliche Verfahren zu Recht erkannt.

I am grateful to Werner Kilian for help in clarifying the language and content of this document. By mutual consent the plaintiff's original rent claim of 130 gulden was reduced to 97 gulden, representing three-quarters of a year. It seems that, whatever may have transpired in his absence, Giesecke left Vienna not clandestinely but with due contractual arrangements in place for the storage of his possessions, and thus probably with the intention of returning.

The "album with some pictures" is number 31 in the catalog of books. It was sold for 4 Gulden 4 Kreuzer, a little less than the price of a box in Vienna's Burgtheater (see H. C. Robbins Landon, *1791: Mozart's Last Year* (1988), 6) though more than four times the estimate price of 1 Gulden ("1 fl."). Was Waterhouse perhaps right in surmising that it contained "the autographs of Mozart, Schikaneder, and other celebrities"?

The catalog of books is dated 13th May 1802 and contains 242 titles. It is headed "<u>Catalog</u> and valuation of the books of Herr Karl Gieseke, member of the imperial royal (by appointment) Theater an der Wien" (<u>Verzeichniss</u>. und Schätzung der Bücher des Hrn. Karl Gieseke Mitglied des k.k. priv: Theaters an der Wien). The subjects reflect Giesecke's broad cultural interests, encompassing mineralogy, the natural world, science, mathematics, philosophy, history, law, travel, and both classical and modern literature. He evidently read German, French, Spanish, Italian, and Latin, and there are also dictionaries and language tutors for English, Greek, Czech, and Turkish. The censor removed some twenty books, including such provocative and subversive titles as *Mannes und sein Guckkasten* (Mannes and his peep-show), *Les confidences d'une jolie femme* (The secrets of a pretty woman), a thriller entitled *Geist der Hölle* (Ghost of Hell), *Les plaisirs de l'amour* (The pleasures of love), *De l'esprit* (Of the intellect), *Eine Anzahl verschiedener Freymaurer Schriften* (A number of different Masonic writings), and two books on Kaiser Heinrich IV. Giesecke's scientific collections, clothes, and furniture were also sold. According to a valuation dated 10th April 1802, considerable quantities of mineralogical samples of different sizes were included in the sale (six hundred small samples, one thousand medium, and four thousand large), as well as a large magnet. The minerals were valued at 460 gulden, the books raised 161 gulden, and his personal effects 222 gulden. This gives a total of 843 gulden, from which there would have been no difficulty in paying his rent arrears of 97 gulden. One may conclude that Giesecke was solvent.

His movements after leaving Vienna are recorded in detail in Waterhouse's chronological typescript of his albums, as well as in K. J. V. Steenstrup's preface to *Meddelelser om Grønland*, X. Giesecke went to Germany and was constantly on the move, almost certainly pursuing the geological interests that were the new focus of his life. In the end he forfeited his Viennese possessions, but not, it seems, his collecting zeal. The 1834 Dublin catalog of his estate mentioned above (p. 181) shows that at his death he owned 1325 books. They are indexed in twelve subject categories: "English Miscellanies / Voyages and travels / Auctores Classici Gr. et Lat. et Lat. Misc. / Mineralogy, Geology, &c. French and English / Irish History / Divinity / Foreign Literature / Italian, Spanish, and Portuguese / German / Danish, Swedish, and Dutch / Various Languages / Maps, Charts, Sheet Prints, Copper Plates, Autographs, &c." The sale was due to commence in Dublin on May 14th 1834 and was expected to take several days. A week later his "valuable minerals, petrifactions, Greenland curiosities, splendid diamond snuff box, gold watches, jewellery, optical and other instruments, articles of vertu, cabinets

&c. &c. including several rare minerals, hitherto only found in Greenland, Giesekite, Cryolite, Sodalite, Eudyalite, Allanite, and some beautiful varieties of felspar, &c. &c." came under the hammer. Once again an auction lasting some days was anticipated. Just two weeks after Giesecke's death the auctioneer Charles Sharpe preannounced for "the Months of April and May" the sale of his "valuable collection of German literature, English Books, choice Minerals and rare Museum Curiosities, &c." in a classified advertisement appearing in Dublin's *Freeman's Journal and Daily Commercial Advertiser.*[12] A similar advertisement appeared in the same journal on 20th November 1833.[13] This time the auctioning of his "Library" was separated from that of his "Minerals, Shells, Precious Stones, Diamond Snuff Box, &c." Were unexpected cataloging difficulties the cause of the year's delay in bringing Giesecke's substantial effects to auction, or was there some other reason?

But let us return to the date of Giesecke's departure from Vienna following his visit in 1819. According to his letter of 22nd February printed in *The Proceedings of the Dublin Society* (to which reference was made on p. 180), this was to have been in three days. However, the attentive reader will recall the quotation from the *Hamburger Correspondent* of 31st May 1819 (pp. 168–69), reporting that Giesecke had just left Vienna. In a further article, *Goethe, Giesecke, Schikaneder and "Die Zauberflöte,"*[14] Waterhouse confirms Giesecke's presence in Vienna by means of entries from the albums, four in March and five in May 1819, the last on 24th May. A Munich entry, dated 14th June 1819 and signed Fred. Schlichtegroll, is the first indication that Giesecke had finally left.[15] It had been a long three days. If this was the Friedrich Schlichtegroll (1765–1822) who published the first Mozart biography in 1793 (*"Johannes Chrysostomus Wolfgang Gottlieb Mozart," Nekrolog auf das Jahr 1791* [Gotha, 1793]), one is entitled to wonder whether he had been able to call on Giesecke's memories of Mozart at that time. Significantly, perhaps, this volume is listed in the sale catalog of Giesecke's effects (p. 54).

The Goethe-Giesecke connection was first investigated by Waterhouse in 1933 in an article entitled "Goethe, Giesecke and Dublin" published in *Proceedings of the Royal Irish Academy.*[16] He returned to the subject in a paper read at a meeting of the Academy on 26th June 1944.[17] It was Goethe's scientific interest that instigated the correspondence. Giesecke sent him mineral samples, including some from Greenland, and barometer readings taken in Ireland. There is no hint that Giesecke ever knew of Goethe's interest in *The Magic Flute* and his unfinished sequel to the opera; nor, on the other hand, was Goethe apparently aware of Giesecke's participation in the first performance, let alone his claim to have contributed to the writing of the libretto. The two men do not appear to have met, but in 1819 Goethe arranged for Giesecke to be honored with a diploma of the Jena Mineralogical Society[18] and Giesecke reciprocated in 1825 with an honorary membership for Goethe (received by him in 1826) in the Royal Irish Academy.[19]

In addition to Giesecke's two personal albums, the National Library of Ireland possesses a remarkable manuscript catalog of minerals that he made in 1801 (MS 262), numbering no less than 4,896 items, each individually described. Another hardly less substantial volume carefully lists the recipients (both individuals and museums) of items from his collection of Greenland minerals (MS 263). The library also possesses two manuscripts of Giesecke's travel diary in Greenland (Bericht einer Mineralogischen Reise auf Grönland. In Form eines Tagebuches), one in his own hand (1806–9 [MS264], 1810–13 [MS 265]), the other a copy (1806–13 [MS266]). But it seems that Giesecke himself wrote out his whole diary a second time, for there is another autograph copy in Copenhagen. Comparing the Dublin with the Copenhagen autograph, Steenstrup proposes that Giesecke wrote

> one for himself and one for the Royal Greenland Trade Commission, and since a number of observations and corrections which appear in the margin in the Dublin copy are to be found in the text of the Copenhagen manuscript, it is therefore established that the latter is the real fair copy.

> eins für sich selbst uns [*sic*] eins für den Königl. Grönländischen Handel, und da mehrere Bemerkungen und Berichtigungen, die in dem Dubliner Exemplare am Rande angeführt sind, in dem Kopenhagener Manuscript sich im Texte finden, so ist damit festgestellt, dass letzteres die eigentliche Reinschrift ist.[20]

When Giesecke died, on 5th March 1833, the Royal Dublin Society announced

> the lamented death of their highly talented and esteemed Professor of Mineralogy and Keeper of the Museum, Sir Charles Giesecké, which melancholy event took place in the afternoon of Tuesday last, very suddenly,
>
> RESOLVED
>
> That the Society do express, by placing the same on the Minutes of their Proceedings, their sincere sorrow at the loss they have sustained, and the high sense they entertain of the long-tried talents, as a Scientific Professor, and the amiable manners and character, of the late Sir Charles Giesecké.
>
> RESOLVED
>
> That as a mark of respect to the memory of Sir Charles Giesecké, the Museum be closed for one fortnight.
>
> RESOLVED
>
> That it be referred to the Committees of the Museum and of Mineralogy, to adopt, at their Meeting tomorrow, any other measure that may be deemed expedient for further marking the feelings of the Society at large.[21]

The following year George Bellas Greenough, president of the Geological Society of London, paid tribute to him at the Anniversary Meeting of the Society held on 21st February 1834.

> Sir Charles Gieseckè was born at Augsburg in 1761 . . . after various changes of occupation and a life of some adventure . . . he entered into the service of Denmark and repaired to Greenland, leaving at Copenhagen a valuable collection of books and minerals, which were destroyed during the bombardment of that city. In Greenland he formed acquisitions of great interest in various departments of natural history, but foreseeing the probability of their capture on the passage to Europe, he with great resolution and perseverance went a second time over the ground he had examined, and remained in that desolate region till his object was accomplished. In the mean time the vessel which contained his first treasures was taken, and the cargo sold by auction at Leith. . . . Mr. Allan purchased nearly the whole collection, which upon examination proved to contain a great number of new and rare substances of the highest mineralogical interest . . . and all in such abundance that most of the cabinets of England . . . were supplied from this source. Mr. Gieseckè himself accidentally arrived at Leith in 1813, not long after Mr. Allan had published an account of his purchases, and with great generosity contributed to the improved catalogues and descriptions of specimens which subsequently appeared. He was soon after appointed Professor of Mineralogy to the Royal Dublin Society. . . . Sir Charles Gieseckè meditated, after his return from Greenland, an extensive work upon that country; he published a brief account of it in Dr. Brewster's Encyclopedia, but the larger work was deferred till the voyages of Ross and Parry had deprived the subject of the interest of novelty.[22]

A lengthy "Biographical Sketch," divided into two parts, appeared, unsigned, in the *Dublin University Magazine* of February and March 1834.[23] Though it focuses on Giesecke's scientific achievements, it also fills in many interesting (if unsubstantiated) details of his earlier life. One may expect an obituary published in the university magazine of a deceased person's home city to be based on accurate sources of information. However, it is certainly incorrect in its assertion (on p. 161) that Giesecke was the surname "of his mother's family," and that he adopted it in order to escape financial embarrassment resulting from theatrical failures. Steenstrup shows on pp. II–V of his preface (see n4) that Giesecke's mother was married under the name Sibylla Magdalena Götz, and that in 1781, at the age of twenty, Giesecke already signed his name "Carolus Ludovicus Metzler cognomine Giesecke" (see album 3, National Library of Ireland MS 3534, p. 3). Perhaps "his mother's family" means his maternal grandmother's maiden name—but that is stretching the imagination.

Giesecke is credited with considerable musical talent.

His love of music was so strong as to amount to a ruling passion; and though he
never attained to any particular eminence as a performer, his compositions were
much admired. Whilst attached to the stage, he was concerned in the composition of two operas, the musical departments of which were especially allotted to
him. Little is, however, known in this country respecting his productions in this
peculiarly captivating path of literature, into which youthful talent is so often
seduced; even the names of the operas are unknown.[24]

This is a little thin on hard facts and should probably not be taken at face
value. One has the impression that the writer himself feels on shaky ground.
If there is no direct reference to *The Magic Flute* perhaps Giesecke's own
modesty is to blame; those who knew him made a point of mentioning this
trait in his character.

"He is an interesting and unassuming man" (Er ist ein interessanter und an-
spruchsloser Mann). Probst (Provost) Frederik Schmidt.

"He was a singular man, very shy I fancy." Miss Hutton (daughter of Giesecke's
executor).[25]

A further unsigned article in the *Dublin University Magazine* (May 1836),
entitled "Extracts from a Journal (German MS.) Kept in Greenland, by the
Late Sir Charles Lewis Giesecké,"[26] quotes from a letter Giesecke wrote to the
King of Denmark shortly after his arrival in Greenland in 1806.

From my twentieth year, I sought my fortune in the wide world. I was sometime
poet to the theatre; sometime a private secretary; sometime a teacher of mineralogy, and I also dealt in minerals. (p. 497)

With this one short paragraph Giesecke dismisses his early life. The purpose
of the letter was to request financial assistance for his sister in the event of
his death.

Giesecke's journey to Greenland was hardly undertaken for financial reward. Also quoted in the above article is a letter, written before his departure
"To the Company of Directors of the Royal Greenland Board of Trade," in
which Giesecke explains his purpose.

It was only in consequence of the proposal of the Company of Directors that I
expressed my readiness to make this journey, and if they had not made such a
proposal, I should not have intimated such a wish *to them*.

Besides I did not presume to demand a salary or honorarium, as it is called; I made no request, except that I might be allowed such small sum for the equipment as is absolutely necessary in consideration of the climate of Greenland. . . . I now request the Royal Company to procure for me the permission of his Majesty to make a voyage to Greenland, which I will perform without any supply from the royal purse, and to which I feel that my honour and the relation in which I stand to the scientific world, both here and abroad, alike urge me, having been amply supplied with books and other help for the undertaking. C. L. Giesecké. (p. 496)

In this connection it is interesting to note that, on his return from Greenland, he wrote to Friederich Münter:

I have taken this opportunity of sending my diary, containing more than 1,200 pages in quarto, to the Directors. I hope I have done everything that a man working alone <u>without </u>assistance can do—and in this conviction I find my reward.—It seems, by the way, as if I have been somewhat forgotten in Copenhagen.

Mein Tagebuch, welches über 1200 Seiten in 4 beträgt, habe ich mit dieser Gelegenheit an die Direction gesandt; ich hoffe alles gethan zu haben, was ein einzelner Mensch <u>ohne</u> Beyhülfe thun kann—und in dieser Ueberzeugung finde ich meine Belohnung.—Es scheint übrigens, als ob man mich hie und da in Kopenhagen vergessen hätte.[27]

Recalling that Giesecke was "intimately known to many of the readers of our Magazine" (p. 495) the unknown writer of the *Dublin University Magazine* article describes him as

a man whom to know—was to like. His career in life was a very uncommon one. Few men with whom we have been acquainted, or of whom we have read, had seen more of the world, or had so acute perception or so quick observation both of men and things. (p. 495)

adding, in a perceptive touch of his own,

His personal fatigues, inconveniences, and dangers are so slightly touched on in his diary, that it is only the experienced traveller who can discover, through the veil which he has cast over his relations, his frequent distressing anxiety of mind, the alarming dangers to which he was so often exposed, and the excessive and overpowering fatigue to which he was subjected. (p. 496)

Steenstrup observes in his preface:

When one reads the diary one gets a secure feeling that one can totally rely on his entire account. . . .

Wenn man das Tagebuch liest, hat man ein sicheres Gefühl davon, dass man
sich vollständig auf alle seine Angaben verlassen kann. . . .

As has already been suggested on p. 128, Giesecke may never have pressed
his claim to authorship of *The Magic Flute* libretto because he recognized,
in all honesty, that Schikaneder had altered a significant proportion of his
original text. The Simrock first-edition full score first appeared in Bonn just
as Giesecke was settling into his new professorial career in Dublin. It was
reprinted c.1820, and at the same time Simrock produced a vocal score, followed c.1830 by yet another vocal score. The undated Cranz vocal score and
Nestler libretto, both published in Hamburg with first-edition text, must also
have appeared within his lifetime. However, it remains a matter for speculation whether anybody ever drew Giesecke's attention to them. Not one of
these six publications is listed in the sale catalog of his effects.

Some of the information in the *Dublin University Magazine* is repeated in
an article on Giesecke in *The Imperial Dictionary of Universal Biography*,
edited by John Francis Waller.[28] Waller graduated from Trinity College,
Dublin, in 1831, at the age of twenty-one. Giesecke died two years later, but
it is not known whether they ever met. However, in March 1874 the *Dublin
University Magazine* (no. CCCCXCV, vol. LXXXIII) featured Waller in its
Portrait Gallery series. On page 313 readers learn that Waller contributed
regularly to the magazine from as early as its third volume, eventually becoming editor. The unsigned "Biographical Sketch" of Giesecke, mentioned
above, was published in volume 3 of the *Dublin University Magazine*. It
could therefore, in theory at least, have been Waller's work, or, if not, it was
the work of a colleague.

Nearly half a century after his death, Giesecke's achievements continued
to be recognized. A book published in London in 1877 by Hinrich Johannes
Rink (ed. Dr. Robert Brown) entitled *Danish Greenland* (British Library
10460, cc. 14) described him as "[t]he renowned traveller, Charles Giesecke,
to whose explorations early in this century the greater part of our information about the Greenland minerals is due . . ." (p. 382). In 1878 came the
publication of his diaries. An assessment of them in *Jahresbericht der Geographischen Gesellschaft in München für 1877–1879* concluded that they bore
witness to his exceptional qualities as a scientist.

His prominent position in the science of mineralogy is recognized by experts.
But only through his diary, which shows his leading place among polar explorers, can one get to know the whole extent of his research work. No naturalist
before him had thoroughly investigated any genuine polar area and no traveler
had drawn up such a complete report and such faithful and at the same time
artistic descriptions of the natural phenomena and people of these regions. In

the history of geography Giesecke ranks immediately next to Reinhold Forster, who became similarly a pioneer of knowledge of natural conditions in the south polar regions as did Giesecke of that in the north. . . . In his last, peaceful two decades he was awarded a rich measure of worldly honours, such as the title Sir, the Knighthood of the Order of Danebrog, amongst others. The English knew him as Sir Charles Lewis Giesecke.

Seine hervorragende Stellung in der Wissenschaft der Mineralogie wird von den Fachmännern anerkannt. Aber die ganze Ausdehnung seiner Forscherarbeit hat erst sein Tagebuch kennen gelernt, welches ihm eine erste Stelle unter den Polarforschern anweist. Kein Naturforscher hatte vor ihm ein ächtes Polargebiet genau durchforscht und kein Reisender hatte von den Naturerscheinungen und den Menschen in diesen Regionen so vollständigen Bericht und so treue und zugleich künstlerische Schilderungen entworfen. Giesecke reiht sich in der Geschichte der Erdkunde unmittelbar an Reinhold Forster an, welcher ähnlich bahnbrechend für die Kenntnis der südpolaren Naturverhältnisse geworden ist wie jener für die der nordpolaren. . . . In seinen letzten ruhigen zwei Jahrzehnten war ihm noch ein reiches Mass weltlicher Ehren, wie der Sir Titel, das Kommandeurkreuz des Danebrog u. a. zugemessen worden. Die Engländer kannten ihn als Sir Charles Lewis Giesecke.[29]

It seems that the title Sir reflected his Danish knighthood and was not an honor conferred by the English monarchy. An assessment of his achievements and status in Ireland may be found in *The Royal Dublin Society, 1731–1981* (Dublin, 1981).[30] It is pointed out that in 1826 Giesecke was asked "to collect specimens of native insects and birds" (p. 153), an unusual assignment for a professor of mineralogy. In the same year, at the age of "at least sixty-five years," he made "a pedestrian excursion over the mountains to the most western point . . . called Achill Head, a distance of ten miles" (p. 159). And back in the lecture hall "'small but distinct specimens of European minerals were given gratis' to serious followers of the course" (p. 162). It is hard to escape the conclusion that he had an unquenchable enthusiasm for science, and for life.

Whatever the truth about Giesecke's part in the writing of *The Magic Flute* libretto, it is hoped that this account of his activities and achievements will serve to redress the impression given by so many commentators that he was a man of little stature. On the contrary, he appears to have possessed outstanding character and breadth of interests. He himself wrote:

. . . I am altogether very adaptable, and will act in a comedy tomorrow with as much gusto as I put to sea the day after. And so I can never say: I wouldn't have expected that.

. . . ich bin überall gleich eingewöhnt, und spiele mit eben dem Gusto morgen Komödie, mit welchem ich übermorgen zur See gehe. Daher kann ich auch nie sagen: das hätte ich nicht erwartet.[31]

But death came with unexpected suddenness.

SIR CHARLES GIESECKE—This distinguished man died, suddenly, on the 5th instant, at the residence of a particular friend, in Rutland-square [*sic*], in Dublin. His health had been for some time declining. A few moments before his death he was engaged, in the highest spirits, in animated conversation.[32]

In this final, inspired passage from Giesecke's diary one may savor his gift for "faithful and at the same time artistic descriptions." He was surely one of the most remarkable men of Mozart's acquaintance.

1810

1st June . . . This same evening I went to the awesomely beautiful ice cliff (Sermersoak in the Greenlanders' language), which is surrounded by a lake and is about 80 feet high at its lowest points.—Its outer edge is split from top to bottom into wedge-shaped, pointed prisms, some of them needle-sharp.—Its surface rises and falls in large, often undulating shapes.—One shudders at the first sight of it; the scenery all around is completely barren, which put me in a melancholy mood; I seemed to have been transported into another world. It was midnight—I rested alone in this sad region where no European had probably set foot before. And in a short while I experienced a revitalising, great spectacle in this wilderness, the sunrise behind this colossal mirror of ice, which took up the sun's blood-red rays over its entire, immeasurable surface and returned it with a million reflections. In an instant the ice cliff was transformed into a sea of fire, and an indescribable feeling seized me and made me forget all the hardships I had endured today.—

1. Juni . . . Ich gieng noch diesen Abend bis an den fürchterlich schönen Eis-blink, (grönländisch Sermersoak) welcher mit einem See umgeben, und an den niedrigsten Stellen gegen 80 Fuss hoch ist.—Sein äusserster Rand ist von oben bis unten in keilförmig zugespizte Prismen zerspalten, welche zuweilen beynahe piramidalisch zugespizt sind.—Seine Oberfläche hat grosse oft wellenförmige Erhöhungen und Vertiefungen.—Der erste Anblick ist schauderlich; die rund umher ganz ausgestorbene Natur sezte mich in eine wehmüthige Stimmung; mir schien es, als ob ich in eine andere Welt versezzt wäre. Es war Mitternacht—ich ruhte einsam in dieser traurigen Gegend aus, welche wohl vor mir noch kein Europäer betreten hatte. Und bald genoss ich ein erquickendes

grosses Schauspiel in dieser Wüste, das Aufsteigen der Sonne hinter diesem kolossalischen Eisspiegel, welcher über seine ganze, unabsehbare Oberfläche ihre bluthrothe Strahlen aufnahm, und mit millionfachem Wucher wiedergab. Ein Augenblick schuf den Eisblink zum Feuermeere um, und ein unbeschreibliches Gefühl ergriff mich, und machte mich alles diesen Tag ausgestandne Ungemach vergessen.— (pp. 257–58)

NOTES

1. The account never appeared, perhaps because Giesecke was intent on trying to recover the cost by subscription, in order to mitigate the anticipated "Dieberey der Nachdrukker" (robbery by subsequent printers). See letter to Frederikke Brun, 26th November 1817. Royal Library, Copenhagen, Manuscript Dept. NY KGL SAML 1992 4to 169 II. Quoted by K. J. V. Steenstrup in the preface to *Meddelelser om Grønland*. Commmissionen for Ledelsen af de geologiske og geographiske Undersøgelser i Grønland (Copenhagen, 1910), p. XXVII. National Library of Ireland 549 G2.

2. *Bibliothèque Universelle*, Geneva, Tome VII (1818). "Mélanges. Notice sur un voyage en Groenland," 138–39. Complete article pp. 133–39. British Library Science Reference and Information Service (P)Bx80-F(57).

3. *Annalen der Physik*, hrsg. Ludwig Wilhelm Gilbert. Bd. 62. (Bd. 32 Neueste Folge) (Leipzig, 1819), 180–83. Complete article pp. 167–184. British Library P.P. 1487. See also p. 127.

4. Steenstrup, preface to *Meddelelser om Grønland*, pp. II–V. National Library of Ireland 549 G2.

5. Karl Ludwig Giesecke. Letter to Friederich Münter, dated 12th June 1809. Det Kongelige Bibliotek (Royal Library), Copenhagen, Manuscript Dept. Ny kgl. Saml. 1698, fol. VI.4, no. 963. Reproduced in part in Steenstrup's preface to *Meddelelser om Grønland*, pp. XXI–XXII. National Library of Ireland 549 G2.

Even in Greenland Giesecke kept his commitment to Freemasonry alive. On the same day Giesecke wrote another letter conveying similar news and sentiments. It was addressed to an unknown recipient, Chevalier de Co[. . . .] in Augsbu[rg]. There is a photocopy of the letter (original in Albi Rosenthal private collection) in the Institute of Germanic and Romance Studies, London University, IGS/Archives/GWA box 113. Among other letters of Giesecke in the Royal Library, Copenhagen, is one dated 26th November 1817, giving a brief outline of his travels and observations in Greenland (Ny kgl. Saml. 1992 4to 169 II.). It was addressed to Frau Conferenzräthin (Councillor) Brunn, doubtless the Friederike Brunn identified in *Annalen der Physik*, 1819 (see p. 167).

6. Thomas Thomson, ed., *Annals of Philosophy*, Vol. I. (London, February, 1813). Thomas Allan, "Memorandums respecting some Minerals from Greenland," 100. British Library 439. e. 10. [Microfilm PB Mic C5360–5362].

7. Ibid., vol. II (London, November, 1813). Thomas Allan F.R.S.E., "Some Mineralogical Remarks on Greenland," 389–90.

8. *The Proceedings of the Dublin Society*, vol. 50 (1813–14): 35. National Library of Ireland IR 506 R9.

9. *Proceedings of the Royal Irish Academy*, vol. 70, sec. C, no. 1 (1970): 1–2. National Library of Ireland IR 506.

10. Album 3, no. 145. See page 15 of Waterhouse's typescript. Also quoted by E. J. Dent in *Mozart's Operas. A Critical Study* (1913), 350.

11. Steenstrup, preface to *Meddelelser om Grønland*, p. VIII. National Library of Ireland 549 G2. Also quoted in G. Waterhouse, "Sir Charles Giesecke's Autograph Albums". *Proceedings of the Royal Irish Academy*, vol. 43, sec. C, no. 1 (1935–37): 298, National Library of Ireland IR 506. Waterhouse's notes and correspondence relating to his Giesecke researches are in the Institute of Germanic and Romance Studies, London University, IGS/Archives/GWA boxes 111–113.

12. *The Freeman's Journal and Daily Commercial Advertiser*, vol. LXVIII, 19th March 1833, p. 1, col. 2 (British Library Newspaper Library IRL M19970–5 1831–1833); see also online at http://newspapers.bl.uk/blcs (10 August 2009).

13. Ibid., 20th November 1833, p. 1, col. 2.

14. Published in *Hermathena* vol. 95 (1961): 36–52. National Library of Ireland G 8805 h1.

15. Ibid., 49–50.

16. Gilbert Waterhouse, "Goethe, Giesecke and Dublin," *Proceedings of the Royal Irish Academy*, vol. 41, sec. C, no. 9 (1932–34): 210–18. National Library of Ireland IR 506.

17. Ibid., vol. 50, Session 1943–44, 18–22.

18. Ibid., vol. 41, 1932–34, C, 211.

19. Ibid., vol. 41, 1932–34, C, 213–14 and vol. 50, Session 1943–44, "Minutes of Proceedings," 26th June 1944, p. 20.

20. Steenstrup, preface to *Meddelelser om Grønland*, p. XXXII. National Library of Ireland 549 G2.

21. *Proceedings of the Royal Dublin Society*, vol. 69 (1832–33): 117–18.

22. *Proceedings of the Geological Society of London*. November 1833 to June 1838, Vol. II (London, 1838), 45–46. British Library Ac. 3171/4—also T. 1572. (13). The same address was published in *The London and Edinburgh Philosophical Magazine and Journal of Science*, ed. Brewster. vol. 4, June 1834, 445–46. British Library P.P.1433. Third Series, Vol. IV.

23. *Dublin University Magazine*, vol. III (February and March 1834): 161–75 and 296–306, British Library P.P. 6155.

24. *Dublin University Magazine*, vol. III (February 1834): 161, British Library P.P. 6155.

25. Steenstrup, preface to *Meddelelser om Grønland*, pp. XXXI–XXXII. National Library of Ireland 549 G2.

26. "Extracts from a Journal (German MS.) Kept in Greenland, by the Late Sir Charles Lewis Giesecké," *Dublin University Magazine*, vol. VII (May 1836): 494–505, British Library P.P. 6155.

27. Karl Ludwig Giesecke, letter to Friederich Münter sent from Leith on 22nd October 1813 (Royal Library, Copenhagen, Manuscript Dept. NkS.1698, fol. VI.4,

no. 964). For further discussion of Giesecke's financial arrangements with the Greenland Board of Trade, including reproduction in part of the above letter, see pp. XXII–XXIII of Steenstrup's preface to *Meddelelser om Grønland*. National Library of Ireland 549 G2.

28. *The Imperial Dictionary of Universal Biography*, ed. John Francis Waller (London, Glasgow [printed], and Edinburgh, 1857–63), 621–22. British Library 10601.y.2.

29. *Jahresbericht der Geographischen Gesellschaft in München für 1877–1879*. Friedrich Ratzel, "Zur Biographie des Augsburger Grönlandforschers Johann Georg Karl (oder Karl Ludwig) Metzler-Giesecke" (München, 1880), 163–65.

30. James Meenan and Desmond Clarke, eds., *The Royal Dublin Society, 1731–1981* (Dublin, 1981), 153, 158–59, 161–62, 164–65 (British Library X.800/31426).

31. Karl Ludwig Giesecke, letter to Friederich Münter dated 25th May 1807. Royal Library, Copenhagen, Manuscript Dept. NkS.1698, fol. VI.4, no. 962. Reproduced on p. XXI of Steenstrup's preface to *Meddelelser om Grønland*. National Library of Ireland 549 G2.

32. *The Hull Packet and Humber Mercury* (Hull, England), 22nd March 1833, issue 2522, p. 3, col. 4. British Library Newspaper Library EW M42333 1833–1834. See also online at http://newspapers.bl.uk/blcs (10 August 2009).

The Complete First-Edition Libretto, with Autograph Differences and a Literal English Translation

The complete first-edition text is given in the left-hand column, with Mozart's autograph score differences shown on the right. Each column follows the original source exactly; there has been no attempt to iron out inconsistencies or correct possible errors or misprints. In order to draw full attention to the genuine differences between first edition and autograph, minor divergences in spelling and punctuation (Mozart was not pedantic about these matters)[1] are not accorded a special entry in the right-hand column.

The stylistic niceties that separate the first edition from the autograph text arise from the character of the German language. The translation, supplied by the author, is designed to assist the reader toward an appreciation of these linguistic refinements. It keeps as close as possible to the German word order and is not intended as an English version in its own right, still less as a performing version. In the few instances where minute differences in the German have no English equivalents, the same English version is given twice. Punctuation follows the original German, with a minimum of adjustments for the requirements of English style.

While it is hoped that the text comparison will prove of interest, the reader should bear in mind the all-important relationship between words and music that exists in the first edition. The isolated examples in chapter 2 may serve to demonstrate its nature, but the overall impression of unity becomes overwhelming in a reading of the entire score. When placed side by side with Mozart's music this first publication in modern times of the German text of the first edition will enable the reader to judge the strength of this relationship. Occasional allowances need to be made where the music repeats a word or phrase, or where, in the first-edition score, an extra note or group of notes has been added to accommodate an extra syllable. The reader is reminded that the complete Simrock first full-score edition can be seen online at the

Harvard University website in the Digital Scores Collection of the Loeb Music Library (http://pds.harvard.edu:8080/pdx/servlet/pds?id=2573661 [10th August 2008]).

It should be remembered that the first-edition numbering system starts with the Overture (as does Mozart's autograph), the opening scene (Introduction) being No. 2, and so forth, to the 2nd Act Finale, No. 22. Consequently all numbers are higher by one in relation to modern editions. However, modern numbering, in conformity with the NMA, is used in the following libretto comparison, as it is throughout the book.

Selected Simrock page numbers are given in order to assist navigation in particular of the long 1st and 2nd Act Finales.

NOTES

1. Mozart's punctuation in the autograph of *The Magic Flute* is analyzed by Gernot Gruber in an article entitled "Das Autograph der Zauberflöte. Eine stilkritische Interpretation des philologischen Befundes. Erster Teil," *Mozart-Jahrbuch 1967* (Salzburg, 1968), 127–49.

DIE ZAUBERFLÖTE

First Edition. Simrock, Bonn, 1814 [S]   *Differences in Mozart's Autograph*

german

ERSTER AKT (FIRST ACT)
Nr. 1, [S] 30

Tamino
Zu Hülfe! Zu Hülfe! Sonst bin ich
   verlohren!
Der listingen Schlange zum Opfer
   erkohren;
Barmherzige Götter! schon nahet
   sie sich!
Ach! rettet mich! Ach, schützet mich.
3 Damen
Stirb, Ungeheuer! durch uns're Macht!
Triumph! Triumph! sie ist vollbracht,
Die Heldenthat. Er ist befreit
Durch unsers Armes Tapferkeit.
1te Dame
Ein holder Jüngling sanft und schön,
2te Dame
Schön, als ich keinen noch gesehn.   So schön, als ich noch nie gesehn.
3te Dame
Ja, ja, gewiss, zum Malen schön.
3 Damen
Würd' ich mein Herz der Liebe weih'n,
So müsst' es dieser Jüngling seyn.
Lasst uns zu unsrer Fürstin eilen,

english

THE MAGIC FLUTE
ACT I
No. 1, [S] 30

Tamino
Help! Help! Or else I am lost!
Destined to be the victim of the
   cunning serpent;

Merciful gods! It is already
   approaching!
Ah! Save me! Ah, protect me.
3 Ladies
Die, monster! through our power!
Triumph! Triumph! It is done,
The heroic deed. He is freed
By the bravery of our arm.
1st Lady
A noble youth, gentle and handsome,
2nd Lady
Handsome, as I never before have seen.   So handsome as I have never yet
                                             seen.

3rd Lady
Yes, yes, indeed, handsome enough to
   be painted.
3 Ladies
Were I to devote my heart to love,
It would have to be this youth.
Let us hasten to our princess,

german

Ihr diese Nachricht zu ertheilen,
Vielleicht dass dieser schöne Mann
Die vor'ge Ruh ihr geben kann.
1te Dame
So geht und sagt es ihr,
Ich bleib' indessen hier.
2te Dame
Nein, nein, geht ihr nur hin,
Ich bin hier Hüterin,   Ich wache hier für ihn!
3te Dame
Nein, nein, das kann nicht seyn,
Ich hüt' ihn hier allein,   Ich schütze ihn allein
1te Dame
Ich bleibe,
2te Dame
Ich wache,
3te Dame
Ich schütze,
3 Damen
Ich! ich! ich!

Ich sollte fort? Ei, Ei! wie fein!
Sie wären gern bei ihm allein;
Nein, nein! Das kann nicht seyn.
Was wollte ich darum nicht geben,
Könnt' ich mit diesem Jüngling leben!

english

To impart this news to her,
Perhaps this handsome man
Can bring her back her former calm.
1st Lady
So go and tell her,
Meanwhile I'll stay here.
2nd Lady
No, no, you go,
I am the keeper here.   I'll keep watch over him!
3rd Lady
No, no, that cannot be,
I alone will guard him,   I alone will protect him
1st Lady
I'll stay,
2nd Lady
I'll watch,
3rd Lady
I'll protect,
3 Ladies
I! I! I!
I should go? Hey, Hey! That's good!
They want to be alone with him;
No, no! That cannot be.
What wouldn't I give
To be able to live with this youth!

german

Hätt' ich ihn doch so ganz allein!
Doch keine geht; es kann nicht seyn.
Am besten ist es nun, ich geh'.
Du Jüngling schön und liebevoll!
Du trauter Jüngling lebe wohl!
Bis ich dich wiederseh'.

Nr. 2, [S] 56

Papageno
Der Vogelfänger bin ich ja,
Stets lustig, heisa! hopsasa!
Ich Vogelfänger bin bekannt
Bei alt und jung im ganzen Land.
Versteh aufs Locken trefflich mich,   Weis mit dem Locken umzugehn
Und auf das Pfeifen meisterlich!   Und mich aufs Pfeifen zu verstehn
Drum kann ich froh und lustig seyn,
Denn alle Vögel sind ja mein.

Der Vogelfänger bin ich ja,
Stets lustig, heisa! hopsasa!
Ich Vogelfänger bin bekannt
Bei alt und jung im ganzen Land.
Wär doch ein Netz für Mädchen mein   Ein Netz für Mädchen möchte ich
Blitz! dutzendweis fieng ich sie ein!   Ich fing sie dutzendweis für mich,

english

To have him completely to myself!
But no one goes; it cannot be.
It would be for the best if I go.
Thou youth, handsome and loving!
Thou dearest youth, farewell!
Until I see you again.

No. 2, [S] 56

Papageno
The bird-catcher, that's me,
Always merry, heigh-ho! Hop-a-
  doodle-doo!
I, the bird-catcher, am known
To old and young in all the land.
I am an expert at luring them,   I know how to go about luring them
And a master in whistling!   And understand the art of whistling
And so I am happy and merry,
For all birds are mine.

The bird-catcher, that's me,
Always merry, heigh-ho! Hop-a-
    doodle-doo!
The bird-catcher is known
To old and young in all the land.
If only I had a net for maidens,   I'd like to have a net for maidens
Whoopee! I'd catch them in dozens!   I'd catch them for myself in dozens,

german

In Käfigt müssten gros und klein,   Dann sperrte ich sie bey mir ein,
Und alle Mädchen wären mein.

Wenn alle Mädchen wären mein,   *[KEINE DRITTE STROPHE]*
So tauschte ich brav Zucker ein,
Die, welche dann recht zärtlich wär',
Der gäb' ich gleich den Zucker her,
Und küsste sie mich zärtlich, dann
Wär' sie mein Weib, ich wär' ihr
    Mann;
Sie schlief an meiner Seite ein,
Ich wiegte wie ein Kind sie ein.

Nr. 3, [S] 60

Tamino
So reizend hold, so zaubrisch schön,   Dies Bildnis ist bezaubernd schön,
Hab' ich noch nie ein Weib gesehn,   Wie noch kein Auge je gesehn.
Fürwahr, es ist ein Götterbild,   Ich fühl' es, wie dies Götterbild
Wie's meine ganze Seele füllt.   Mein Herz mit neuer Regung füllt.
Zwar mein Gefühl, ich kanns nicht   Dies etwas kann ich zwar nicht
    nennen,   nennen,
Doch ewig wird dies Feuer brennen;   Doch fühl ich's hier wie Feuer
                                              brennen;

Soll die Empfindung Liebe seyn?   Ja, Ja, die Liebe ist's allein.
Ja, ja, die Liebe muss es seyn.   O wenn ich sie nur finden könnte!
O, dass ich doch das Urbild fände!   O wenn sie doch schon vor mir
In seinen [*sic*] Blick verlohren stände!   stände

english

Big and small they'd go into the cage,   Then I'd lock them up at home,
And all maidens would be mine.

If all maidens were mine,   *[NO THIRD VERSE]*
I'd do a deal to get some sugar;
The one who was really tender,
To her would I straightaway give the
    sugar,
And if she then kissed me tenderly
She would be my wife, I would be her
    man;
She would go to sleep at my side,
I would rock her like a child.

No. 3, [S] 60

Tamino
So charmingly lovely, so magically   This portrait is bewitchingly
    beautiful,   beautiful,
I never yet saw such a woman,   Such as no eye has ever seen
                                                 before.

Truly, it is the image of a goddess,   I feel how this goddess
How it fills my whole soul.   Fills my heart with new excitement.
For sure my feeling I can't name,   I can't find a name for this
                                                 something,

But this fire will burn forever;   But I feel it here burning like fire;
Should the feeling be love?
Yes, yes, it must be love.   Yes, yes, it is indeed love.
Oh, if I could only find her in person!   Oh if only I could find her!
Stand, overwhelmed, before her!   Oh if only she already stood before
                                                 me

german

Ich würde—würde—warm und rein . . .
Was würde ich?
Umschlingen sie, voll Entzücken   Ich würde sie voll Entzücken
An diesen heissen Busen drücken,
Und ewig wäre sie dann mein.

Nr. 4, [S] 65

Königinn der Nacht
O zitt're, edler Jüngling! nicht!
Du bist unschuldig, weise, fromm.
Dein offenes Gesicht verkündigt
   meinem Herzen,
Du endigest der bangen Mutter
   Schmerzen.
Zum Leiden bin ich auserkohren:
Ach meine Tochter fehlet mir;
Mit ihr ging all' mein Glück verlohren;

Ein Bösewicht entfloh mit ihr.
Noch seh' ich ihr Zittern,
Mit bangem Erschüttern,
Ihr ängstliches Beben,
Ihr schüchternes Streben.
Ich musste sie mir rauben sehen!
Ach helft, ach helft!
War alles was sie sprach,
Allein vergebens war ihr Flehen,

O zittre nicht, mein lieber Sohn,

Ein Jüngling so wie du, vermag am
   besten
Das tief betrübte Mutterherz zu
   trösten.–

Denn meine Tochter fehlet mir.
Durch sie gieng all mein Glück
   verlohren,

english

I would—would—warm and pure . . .
What would I do?
Embrace her, press her, full of rapture,
Warmly to my bosom,
And she would then be mine forever.

I would press her, full of rapture,

No. 4, [S] 65

Queen of Night
Oh tremble not, noble youth!
You are innocent, wise, devout.
Your honest face proclaims to my
   heart
That you will end the grievings of a
   frightened mother.

Oh tremble not, my dear son,

A youth such as you is best able

To bring comfort to the deeply
   troubled maternal heart.

I am destined for suffering:
Ah, I miss my daughter;
With her vanished all my happiness;

A villain made off with her.
I still see her trembling,
With fearful shock,
Her anxious quaking,
Her timid striving.
I had to see her snatched from me!
Ah help, ah help!
Was all she said;
But in vain was her beseeching,

For I miss my daughter.
Through her vanished all my
  happiness,

german

Denn meine Hülfe war zu schwach.
Du wirst sie zu befreyen gehen,
Du wirst der Tochter Retter seyn!
Und werd' ich dich als Sieger sehen,
So sey sie dann auf ewig dein.

Nr. 5, [S] 73

Papageno
Hm, hm, hm, hm, hm, hm!
Tamino
Du wirst nie mehr zu lügen wagen,
Denn deine Sprache ist dahin.
Papageno
Hm, hm, hm, hm, hm, hm!
Tamino
Ich kann nicht mehr, als dich beklagen,

Weil ich zu schwach zu helfen bin.
1ᵗᵉ Dame
Die Königinn begnadigt dich,
Erlässt die Strafe dir durch mich.
Papageno
Nun plaudert Papageno wieder.
1ᵗᵉ Dame
Ja plaud're, lüge nur nicht wieder.

Der Arme kann von Strafe sagen,
Denn seine Sprache ist dahin!

Ich kann nichts thun als dich
  beklagen,

Entlässt die Strafe dir durch mich.

english

For my help was too weak.
You will go to free her,
You will be my daughter's savior!
And if you return triumphant,
She will be yours forever.

No. 5, [S] 73

Papageno
Hm, hm, hm, hm, hm, hm!
Tamino
You will never dare to lie again,   The poor man knows what
                                                  punishment is,

For your speech is taken away.   For his speech is taken away!
Papageno
Hm, hm, hm, hm, hm, hm!
Tamino
I can do no more than pity you,   I can do nothing but pity you,
Because I am powerless to help.
1st Lady
The Queen pardons you,
Remits your punishment through me.   Releases you from punishment
                                                  through me.

Papageno
Now Papageno talks again.
2nd Lady
Yes, talk, just don't lie again.

german

Papageno
Nie lüg' ich wieder, nein, nein, nein!   Ich lüge nimmermhr Nein, Nein!
3 Damen
Dies Schloss soll deine Warnung seyn.
Papageno
Dies Schloss soll meine Warnung seyn.
Papageno, Tamino, 3 Damen
Bekämen doch die Lügner alle
Ein solches Schloss vor ihren Mund.   Ein solches Schloss vor ihrem Mund

Nie trübten Hass, Verläumdung, Galle,   Statt Hass, Verläumdung schwarzer
                                              Galle

Der Menschheit schönen Bruderbund.   Bestünde Lieb und Bruderbund!
1ᵗᵉ Dame
Hier Prinz, nimm dies Geschenk von   O Prinz! nimm dies Geschenk von
   mir;   mir
Von unsrer Fürstin bring ichs dir.   Dies sendet unsre Fürstin dir.
Die Zauberflöte wird dich schützen,
Und tobt um dich ein Heer von Blitzen. Im grössten Unglück unterstützen
3 Damen
Durch sie kannst du allmächtig   Hiemit kannst du allmächtig
   handeln,   handeln
Nach Willkühr Leidenschaft   Der Menschen Leidenschaft
   verwandeln,   verwandeln
Sie schmilzt zur Freude jedes Leid,   Der Traurige wird freudig seyn
Lehrt Hagestolze Zärtlichkeit.   Den Hagestolz nimmt Liebe ein.
Papageno, Tamino, 3 Damen
O! so eine Flöte ist mehr als Gold und
   Kronen werth,

english

Papageno
I will never lie again, no, no, no!   I will lie no more no, no!
3 Ladies
This lock shall be your warning.
Papageno
This lock shall be my warning.
Papageno, Tamino, 3 Ladies
If all liars got
Such a lock over their mouths   Such a lock over their mouths
Never would hatred, slander, and gall Instead of hatred, slander and black
   darken   gall
The fair brotherhood of mankind.   There would stand love and
                                          brotherhood!

1st Lady
Here prince, take this present from me; Oh prince! take this present from me
I bring it to you from our princess.   Our princess sends it to you.
The magic flute will protect you,
Even though a host of lightning flashes Support you in the greatest
   rage around you.   adversity

3 Ladies
Through it you can deal all-powerfully,

Change passions at will,
It melts to joy every sorrow,
Teaches tenderness to the loveless.
Papageno, Tamino, 3 Ladies
Oh! Such a flute is worth more than
　gold and crowns,

With this you can deal all-
　powerfully
Change human passions,
The sad person will be joyful
Love takes in the loveless.

german

Denn durch sie wird Menschenglück
　und Zufriedenheit vermehrt.
Papageno
Nun ihr schönen Frauenzimmer,
Darf ich – so empfehl' ich mich?
3 Damen
Dich empfehlen kannst du immer,
Doch bestimmt die Fürstinn dich,
Mit dem Prinzen ohn' Verweilen,
Nach Sarastros Burg zu eilen.
Papageno
Dank ergebenst, bleibe hier!
Denn ihr selbst erzähltet mir,
Dass er, o ich bin kein Thor,
Jedem Fremden, den er spähet,
S' Hirn einschlägt, den Hals umdrehet,
Dann ihn wirft den Hunden vor.
3 Damen
Dich schützt der Prinz, trau' ihm allein,
Dafür sollst du sein Diener seyn.
Papageno
Dass doch der Prinz beym Henker
　wäre;
Mein Leben ist mir lieb.
Kömmt nur Gefahr, bei meiner Ehre!
Er trollt ab, wie ein Dieb.

Nein dafür bedank ich mich
Von euch selbsten hörte ich
Dass er wie ein Tigerthier
Sicher liess ohn alle Gnaden
Mich Sarastro rupfen, braten,
Setzte mich den Hunden für.

Dass doch der Prinz beym Teufel
　wäre

Am Ende schleicht bey meiner Ehre
Er vor mir wie ein Dieb.

english

For through it human happiness and
  contentment are increased.

Papageno
Now, you lovely ladies,
If I may—I'll take my leave?

3 Ladies
You can always take your leave,
However the princess commands you
Without delay to hurry with the prince
To Sarastro's castle.

Papageno
Thanks truly, I'll stay here!   No thanks very much
For you told me yourselves   For I heard from you yourselves
That he, oh I'm no fool,   That he is like a tiger
Beats in the brains and wrings the neck Without mercy Sarastro would
                                            certainly
Of every stranger that he spies,   Have me plucked, roasted,
Then throws him to the dogs.   And put out for the dogs.

3 Ladies
The prince will protect you, trust only
  him,
That's why you should be his servant.

Papageno
The prince can go to the hangman;   The prince can go to the devil
My life is dear to me.
Should there be any danger, on my   When it comes to it, on my honor,
  honor!
He would skedaddle like a thief.   He would sneak past me like a thief.

german

1ᵗᵉ Dame
Hier nimm dies Kleinod, es ist dein.

Papageno
Ei! ei! was mag darinnen seyn?

3 Damen
Darinnen hörst du Glöckchen tönen.

Papageno
O lasst doch hören, holde Schönen!   Werd ich sie auch wohl spielen
                                            können?

3 Damen
Du wirst sie hören, ganz gewiss.   O ganz gewiss! Ja Ja gewiss!

Papageno, Tamino, 3 Damen
Silberglöckchen, Zauberflöten,
Sind zu _{eurem} ^{unserm}) Schutz vonnöthen.
Lebet wohl! wir wollen gehn,
Lebet wohl! auf Wiedersehn.

Tamino
Doch schöne Damen, saget mir: Doch schöne Damen saget an

Papageno, Tamino
Wie man die Burg wohl finden kann?

3 Damen
Drey Knäbchen, jung, schön, hold und
    weise,
Umschweben euch auf eurer Reise,
Sie werden eure Führer seyn,
Folgt ihrem Rathe ganz allein.

english

1st Lady
Here take this trinket, it is yours.

Papageno
Hey! Hey! What might be inside it?

3 Ladies
You hear bells ringing inside it.

Papageno
Oh, let's hear them, my lovely   Shall I also be able to play them?
    beauties!

3 Ladies
You will hear them, for sure.   Oh for sure! Yes, yes, certainly!

Papageno, Tamino, 3 Ladies
Silver bells, magic flutes
Are needed for _{your} ^{our}) protection.
Farewell! We must go,
Farewell! Goodbye.

Tamino
But, lovely ladies, tell me: But, lovely ladies, say

Papageno, Tamino
How one can find one's way to the
    castle?

3 Ladies
Three Boys, young, handsome, pure,
    and wise,
Will hover around you on your journey,
They will be your guides,
Only follow their advice.

german

Papageno, Tamino
Drei Knäbchen, jung, schön, hold und
    weise,
Begleiten uns auf unsrer Reise.   Umschweben uns auf unsrer Reise?
3 Damen
Sie werden eure Führer seyn,
Folgt ihrem Rathe ganz allein.
Papageno, Tamino, 3 Damen
So lebet wohl! wir wollen gehn,
Lebt wohl! lebt wohl! auf Wiedersehn.

Nr. 6, [S] 93

Monostatos
Du feines Täubchen, nur herein.
Pamina
O welche Marter, welche Pein!
Monostatos
Verlohren ist dein Leben.
Pamina
Der Tod macht mich nicht beben,
Nur du, o Mutter, dauerst mich;   Nur meine Mutter dauert mich,
Der Schmerz um mich, er tödtet dich.   Sie stirbt vor Gram ganz sicherlich
Monostatos
He! Sklaven! legt ihr Fesseln an,
Mein Hass soll dich verderben.

english

Papageno, Tamino
Three Boys, young, handsome, pure,
    and wise,
Will accompany us on our journey.   Will hover around us on our
                                             journey?

3 Ladies
They will be your guides,
Only follow their advice.
Papageno, Tamino, 3 Ladies
So farewell! we must go,
Farewell! Farewell! Goodbye.

No. 6, [S] 93

Monostatos
You handsome dove, come in here.
Pamina
Oh what torture, what pain!
Monostatos
Your life is lost.
Pamina
Death does not make me tremble,
Only you, oh mother, have my pity;   Only my mother has my pity,
Grief for me will kill you.   She will quite certainly die of
                                               sorrow.

Monostatos
Hey! Slaves! Put fetters on her,
My hatred shall be your ruin.

german

Pamina
O lass' mich lieber sterben,
Weil nichts, Barbar! dich rühren kann.
Monostatos
Nur fort! Lasst mich bei ihr allein.
Papageno
Wo bin ich wohl? wo mag ich seyn?
Aha! da find' ich Leute;
Gewagt! ich geh hinein.
Ein Mädchen, jung und fein,   Schön Mädchen jung und rein
Traun, keine üble Beute.   Viel weisser noch als Kreide . . .
Monostatos, Papageno
Hu! das ist der Teufel sicherlich.
Hab Mitleid! verschone mich!
Hu! Hu! Hu!

Nr. 7, [S] 98

Pamina
Der Liebe holdes Glück empfinden,   Bey Männern welche Liebe fühlen
Kann nur der gute Mann allein.   Fehlt auch ein gutes Herze nicht.
Papageno
Ach, an ein gutes Weib sich binden,   Die süssen Triebe mitzufühlen
Das lasst mir eine Freude seyn!   Ist dann der Weiber erste Pflicht.
Pamina, Papageno
Wir wollen uns der Liebe weihn,   Wir wollen uns der Liebe freun

english

Pamina
Oh let me rather die,
Since nothing, barbarian! can move you.
Monostatos
Off with you! Leave me alone with her.
Papageno
Where am I then? Where might I be?
Aha! I find people here;
I dare! I'll go in.
A girl, young and handsome,   Lovely girl, young and pure,
How's this for a catch.   Much whiter even than chalk . . .
Monostatos, Papageno
Huh! That is undoubtedly the devil.
Have pity! Spare me!
Huh! Huh! Huh!

No. 7, [S] 98

Pamina
Only a good man can feel   With men who feel love
The pure joy of love.   A good heart is not lacking either.
Papageno
Ah, to be tied to a good woman,   To share these sweet impulses
That's what I call joy!   Is then a woman's first duty.
Pamina, Papageno
We want to dedicate ourselves to love,   We want to rejoice in love,

german

Wir leben durch die Lieb' allein.

Pamina
Die Liebe mildert jede Plage,   Die Lieb versüsset jede Plage
Ihr opfert jede Kreatur.
Pamina
Verschönt des Erdenlebens Tage,   Sie würzet unsre Lebenstage
Ist Heil und Seegen der Natur.   Sie wirkt im Kreise der Natur.
Pamina, Papageno
Ihr hoher Zweck zeigt deutlich an,
Nichts edlers sey als Weib und Mann;
Mann und Weib, und Weib und Mann,
Reihen sich den Göttern an.   Reichen an die Gottheit an.

Nr. 8, [S] 102

3 Knaben
Zum Ziele führt dich diese Bahn,
Doch musst du Jüngling männlich
   siegen.
Drum höre unsre Lehre an:
Sey standhaft, duldsam und
   verschwiegen.
Tamino
Ihr holden Kleinen sagt mir an,   Ihr holden Kleinen saget an,
Ob ich Paminen retten kann?
3 Knaben
Dies kund zu thun, steht uns nicht an,

english

We live through love alone.
Pamina
Love softens every torment,   Love sweetens every torment
All creatures sacrifice to it.
Papageno
Enhances the days of earthly life,   It adds spice to our living days
Is the salvation and blessing of nature.   It operates in the circle of nature.
Pamina, Papageno
Its high purpose shows clearly
That there is nothing more noble than
   wife and man;
Man and wife, and wife and man,

Join up with the gods.   Reach up to the deity.

No. 8, [S] 102

3 Boys
This path leads you to your goal,
But, youth, you have to conquer like
     a man,
So listen to our teaching:
Be resolute, patient and silent.
Tamino
You charming little ones, tell me   You charming little ones, tell me
Whether I can rescue Pamina?
3 Boys
It is not for us to give this information,

german

Sey standhaft, duldsam und
     verschwiegen.
Bedenke dies; kurz, sey ein Mann;
Dann Jüngling, wirst du männlich
     siegen.

Tamino   [S] 106
Die Weisheitslehre dieser Knaben
Sey ewig mir ins Herz gegraben.
Wo bin ich nun? was wird mit mir?
Ist dies der Sitz der Götter hier?
Es zeigen die Pforten, es zeigen die   Doch zeigen die Pforten—es zeigen
     Säulen,   die Säulen,
Dass Klugheit und Arbeit und Künste
     hier weilen;
Wo Thätigkeit thronet, und
     Müssiggang weicht,
Erhält seine Herrschaft das Laster
     nicht leicht.
Ich wage mich muthig zur Pforte hinein,
Die Absicht ist edel und lauter und rein.
Erzittre, feiger Bösewicht!
Paminen retten, ist mir Pflicht.

Eine Stimme
Zurück!
Tamino
Zurück! so wag' ich hier mein Glück.
Eine Stimme
Zurück!
Tamino
Auch hier ruft man zurück?

english

Be resolute, patient, and silent.
Remember this; in short, be a man;
Then, youth, you will conquer like a
    man.

Tamino   [S] 106
The wisdom taught by these boys
Be ever engraved in my heart.
Where am I now? What is happening
    to me?
Is this the seat of the gods here?
The gates show, the pillars show   The gates certainly show—the
                                                                pillars show

That prudence and work and skills
    reside here;
Where activity reigns and idleness
    succumbs,
Vice cannot easily hold sway.
I will boldly enter the gate,
The purpose is noble and pure and
    clear.
Tremble, cowardly villain!
To rescue Pamina is my duty.
A Voice
Back!
Tamino
Back! So I'll try my luck here.
A Voice
Back!

Tamino
Here too they call back?

german

Da seh' ich noch eine Thür!
Vielleicht find' ich den Eingang hier.
Priester
Wo willst du kühner Fremdling hin,
Was suchst du hier im Heiligthum?
Tamino
Der Lieb' und Tugend Heiligthum.   Der Lieb und Tugend Eigenthum.
Priester
Die Worte sind von hohem Sinn,
Allein wie willst du diese finden?
Dich leitet Lieb' und Tugend nicht,
Weil Tod und Rache dich entzünden.
Tamino
Nur Rache für den Bösewicht.
Priester
Den wirst du wohl bey uns nicht finden.
Tamino
Sarastro herrscht in diesen Gründen?
Priester
Ja! ja! Sarastro herrschet hier.
Tamino
Doch in dem Weisheitstempel nicht.
Priester
Er herrscht im Weisheitstempel hier.

english

I see yet another door there!
Perhaps I'll find the entrance here.
Priest
Where are you going, bold stranger,
What do you seek here in the
    sanctified place?
Tamino
The sanctified place of love and virtue.   The possession of love and virtue.
Priest
The words are high-minded,

However, how do you intend to find
   these?
It is not love and virtue that lead you,
Because death and revenge inflame you.
Tamino
Only revenge for the villain.
Priest
You surely won't find him among us.
Tamino
Sarastro rules in these grounds?
Priest
Yes! Yes! Sarastro rules here.
Tamino
Not, however, in the temple of wisdom.
Priest
He rules here in the temple of wisdom.

german

Tamino
So ist denn alles Heucheley!
Priester
Willst du schon wieder gehn?
Tamino
Ja, ich will gehn, froh, und frey,
Nie euren Tempel sehn.
Priester
Erklär' dich näher mir,
Dich täuschet ein Betrug.
Tamino
Sarastro wohnet hier?
Dies ist mir schon genug.   Das ist mir schon genug!
Priester
Wenn du dein Leben liebst
So rede: bleibe da!
Sarastro hassest du?
Tamino
Ich hass' ihn ewig, ja!
Priester
So gieb mir deine Gründe an.   Nun gieb mir deine Gründe an!
Tamino
Er ist ein Unmensch, ein Tyrann!

Priester
Ist das, was du gesagt, erwiesen?

english

Tamino
So everything is then hypocrisy!
Priest
Do you already want to leave again?
Tamino
Yes, I want to leave, happy and free,
And never see your temple.
Priest
Explain yourself more closely to me,
You are deluded by a deceit.
Tamino
Sarastro lives here?
This is quite enough for me.   That's quite enough for me!
Priest
If your life is dear to you
Speak, stay there!
You hate Sarastro?
Tamino
I hate him forever, yes!
Priest
So give me your reasons.   Now give me your reasons!
Tamino
He is a monster, a tyrant!
Priest
Is what you said proven?

german

Tamino
Durch ein unglücklich Weib bewiesen,
Die Gram und Jammer niederdrückt.
Priester
Ein Weib hat also dich berückt?
Ein Weib thut wenig, plaudert viel;
Du Jüngling glaubst dem Zungenspiel?
Sarastro handelt stets nach Pflicht,   O legte doch Sarastro dir
Und du kennst seine Absicht nicht.   Die Absicht seiner Handlung für!

Tamino
Die Absicht ist nur allzu klar;
Riss nicht der Räuber ohn' Erbarmen,
Paminen aus der Mutter Armen?
Priester
Ja, Jüngling, was du sagst ist wahr.
Tamino
Wo ist sie, die er uns geraubt?
Man opferte vielleicht sie schon?
Priester
Dir dies zu sagen, theurer Sohn,
Ist jetzund mir noch nicht erlaubt.
Tamino
Erklär' dies Räthsel, täusch' mich nicht.
Priester
Die Zunge bindet Eid und Pflicht.

english

Tamino
Demonstrated by an unhappy woman,
Oppressed by grief and misery.
Priest
So a woman has beguiled you?
A woman does little, talks a lot;
You, youth, believe a wagging tongue?
Sarastro acts only according to duty,   Oh if only Sarastro put before you
And you don't know his purpose.   The purpose behind his actions!
Tamino
The purpose is all too clear to me;
Did not the thief tear Pamina without
   mercy
From her mother's arms?
Priest
Yes, youth, what you say is true.
Tamino
Where is she, whom he robbed
   from us?
Has she perhaps already been
   sacrificed?

Priest
To tell you this, dear son,
Is not yet allowed to me now.
Tamino
Explain this riddle, don't deceive me.
Priest
My tongue is bound by oath and duty.

german

Tamino
Wann also wird die Decke schwinden?
Priester

Sobald dich an der Weisheit Band	Sobald dich führt der Freundschaft Hand
In's Heil geführt der Freundschaft Hand.	Ins Heiligthum zum ewgen Band.

Tamino

O dunkle Nacht! wann wirst du schwinden?	O ew'ge Nacht! wann wirst du schwinden?
Wann wird das Licht mein Auge finden?	

Chor
Bald, Jüngling, oder nie.
Tamino
Bald, sagt ihr, oder nie?
Ihr Unsichtbaren, saget mir,
Lebt denn Pamina noch?
Chor
Pamina lebet noch.
Tamino

Sie lebt? sie lebt? O tausend Dank dafür.	Sie lebt, sie lebt! ich danke euch dafür
O! dass mir doch ein Ton gelänge,	O wenn ich doch im Stande wäre,
Der euch den Dank des Herzens sänge;	Allmächtige, zu eurer Ehre,
Der meine Adern all' durchfliesst,	Mit jedem Tone meinen Dank zu schildern,
In Freudenthränen sich ergiesst.	Wie er hier (*aufs Herz deutend*) hier—entsprang.

english

Tamino
So when will the veil be lifted?

Priest
As soon as the hand of friendship
Has led you on wisdom's bond to
   salvation.

As soon as the hand of friendship
Leads you into the sanctuary to
   eternal bond.

Tamino
Oh dark night! When will you vanish?

Oh eternal night! When will you
   vanish?

When will light reach my eye?
Chorus
Soon, youth, or never.
Tamino
Soon, you say, or never?
You invisible ones, tell me,
Does Pamina then still live?
Chorus
Pamina still lives.
Tamino
She lives? She lives? Oh, a thousand
   thanks for that.

She lives, she lives! I thank you for
   that.

Oh! If only I could find the sound
To sing the thanks in my heart;
Which flows through all my arteries,

If only I were truly able,
Almighty, in your honor,
To describe my thanks with every
   sound that I make,

Pouring forth in tears of joy.

As it here, (*pointing to his heart*)
   here—arose.

german

[S] 121

Wie stark ist nicht dein Zauberton!
Weil holde Flöte durch dein Spielen
Selbst wilde Thiere Freude fühlen.
Doch nur Pamina bleibt davon.
Pamina, höre! höre mich!
Umsonst! Wo? ach wo find' ich dich?
Ha! Das ist Papagenos Ton.
Vielleicht sah er Paminen schon,
Vielleicht eilt sie mit ihm zu mir,
Vielleicht führt mich der Ton zu ihr.

Papageno, Pamina [S] 126–27
Schnelle Füsse, rascher Mut,
Schützt vor Feindes List und Wuth,

Fänden wir Tamino doch,
Sonst erreichen sie uns noch.   Sonst erwischen sie uns noch!
Pamina
Holder Jüngling!
Papageno
Stille, stille! ich kann's besser.
Papageno, Pamina
Ha! nun wird das Herz mir grösser,   Welche Freude ist wohl grösser
Freund Tamino hört uns schon;
Hieher kam der Flötenton!
Welch ein Glück, wenn ich ihn finde,

english

[S] 121

Is not your magic tone strong!
Because, noble flute, through your
    playing
Even wild animals feel joy.
But only Pamina remains absent.
Pamina, hear! hear me!
In vain! Where? ah, where do I find
    you?
Ha! That is Papageno's sound.
Perhaps he already saw Pamina,
Perhaps she is hurrying with him to me,
Perhaps the sound leads me to her.

Papageno, Pamina [S] 126–27
Nimble feet, speedy courage,
Protects from the enemy's cunning
    and rage,
If we could only find Tamino,
Otherwise they will yet reach us.   Otherwise they will yet catch us!
Pamina
Noble youth!
Papageno
Hush, hush! I can do it better.
Papageno, Pamina
Ha! Now my heart is getting bigger   What joy could be greater

Friend Tamino hears us already;
From over there came the sound of the
   flute!
What happiness if I find him,

german

Nur geschwinde, nur geschwinde.
Monostatos
Nur geschwinde, nur geschwinde.
Ha! hab' ich euch noch ertappt?   Ha!—hab ich euch noch erwischt!
Nur herbei mit Stahl und Eisen;
Wart, man wird euch Mores weisen;
Den Monostatos berücken!
Nur herbei mit Band und Stricken!
He! ihr Sklaven kommt herbei!
Papageno, Pamina
Ach! nun ist's mit uns vorbei!
Papageno
Wer viel wagt, gewinnt oft viel,
Komm, du schönes Glockenspiel,
Lass die Glöckchen klingen, klingen,
Dass die Ohren ihnen singen.

Monostatos, Sklaven [S] 133
Das klinget so herrlich, das klinget so
   schön;
Larala, lala laralala la larala.
Nie hab' ich so etwas gehört noch   Nie hab' ich so etwas gehört und
   gesehn,   gesehn!
Larala, lala laralala la larala.
Papageno, Pamina
Könnte jeder brave Mann
Solche Glöckchen finden,
Seine Feinde würden dann

english

Quick, quick.
Monostatos
Quick, quick.
Ha! Did I take you by surprise?   Ha!—I've caught you!
Over here with steel and iron

Just wait, you'll be taught some
   manners;
You dare to trick Monostatos!
Over here with cord and ropes!
Hey! Slaves, come over here!
Papageno, Pamina
Ah! now it's all over with us!
Papageno
He who ventures much, often wins
   much,
Come, lovely bells.
Let the bells ring, ring,
So that all ears are in song.

Monostatos, Slaves [S] 133
That rings so magnificently, that rings
   so beautifully;
Larala, lala laralala la larala.
I never heard or saw anything like it!   I never heard and saw anything like
                                              it!

Larala, lala laralala la larala.
Papageno, Pamina
If every honest man
Could find such bells,
His enemies would then

german

Ohne Mühe schwinden;
Und er lebte ohne sie
In der besten Harmonie.
Ja, sanft mildert Harmonie   Nur der Freundschaft Harmonie
Jegliche Beschwerden,   Mildert die Beschwerden
Schmilzt das Herz zur Sympathie,   Ohne diese Sympathie
Sagt zur Freude: Werde!   Ist kein Glück auf Erden

Chor [S] 136
Es lebe Sarastro! Sarastro lebe!
Papageno
Was soll dies bedeuten? ich zittre, ich
   bebe.
Pamina
O Freund! Nun ist's um uns gethan,
Dies kündigt den Sarastro an.

Papageno
O wär' ich eine Maus,
Wie wollt' ich mich verstecken;
Gehört ich zu den Schnecken,   Wär ich so klein wie Schnecken
Husch, kröch' ich in mein Haus.   So kröch ich in mein Haus!
Mein Kind, was werden wir nun
    sprechen?
Pamina
Die Wahrheit! sey sie auch
    Verbrechen.
Chor
Es lebe Sarastro, Sarastro soll leben!
Er ist es, dem wir uns mit Freuden
    ergeben!

english

Disappear effortlessly;
And he would live without them
In perfect harmony.
Yes, harmony gently smoothes   Only the harmony of friendship
Every trouble,   Softens troubles,
Melts the heart to sympathy,   Without this sympathy
Says to joy: arise!   There is no happiness on earth.

Chorus [S] 136
Long live Sarastro! Sarastro live!
Papageno
What is the meaning of this? I tremble,
    I quake.
Pamina
Oh friend! Now we are done for,
This announces the arrival of Sarastro.
Papageno
Oh were I a mouse,
How I would love to hide;
If I belonged to the snails,   Were I as small as the snails
Shh! I would creep into my house.   Then I would creep into my house!
My child, what are we going to say?
Pamina
The truth, be it even a crime!

Chorus
Long live Sarastro, Sarastro shall live!
He is the one to whom we joyfully
   devote ourselves!

german

Stets mög' er des Lebens als Weiser sich freun.
Er ist unser Abgott, dem alle sich weihn.

Pamina   [S] 144
Herr! ich bin zwar Verbrecherinn!
Ich wollte deiner Macht entfliehn;
Doch ganz gehört die Schuld nicht mir!   Allein die Schuld ist nicht an mir!
Der böse Mohr verlangte Liebe,
Darum, o Herr, entfloh ich ihm.   Darum, o Herr, entfloh ich dir!
Sarastro
Steh auf, erheitre dich, o Liebe!
Denn ohne erst in dich zu dringen,
Weis ich von deinem Herzen mehr,
Es ist für mich von Liebe leer;   Du liebest einen andern sehr
Zur Liebe will ich dich nicht zwingen,
Doch geb' ich dir die Freiheit nicht.
Pamina
Mich rufet ja, die Kindespflicht,
Denn meine Mutter
Sarastro
Steht in meiner Macht;
Du würdest um dein Glück gebracht,
Wenn ich dich ihren Händen liesse.
Pamina
Mir klingt der Mutter Nahmen süsse;
Sie ist es—

english

May he ever enjoy life as a wise man.
He is our idol, to whom all are dedicated.

Pamina [S] 144
My lord! It is true that I have
   transgressed!

I wanted to escape your power;
But the guilt does not rest entirely   But the guilt is not on me!
   with me!
The wicked Moor demanded love,
Hence, my lord, I fled from him.   Hence, my lord, I fled from you!
Sarastro
Arise, be cheerful, my dear!
For without first pressing you,
I know more about your heart,
It is empty of love for me;   You love another very much
I won't force you to love,
On the other hand I won't give you
   your freedom.
Pamina
It is my duty as a child that calls me,
For my mother—
Sarastro
Stands in my power;
It wouldn't make for your happiness
If I released you into her hands.
Pamina
The name of my mother is sweetness
   to my ears;
She is the one—

german

Sarastro
Und ein stolzes Weib.
Ein Mann muss eure Herzen leiten;
Denn ohne ihn pflegt jedes Weib
Aus ihrem Wirkungskreiss zu schreiten.

Monostatos [S] 149
Nun stolzer Jüngling, nur hieher,
Hier ist Sarastro, unser Herr.
Pamina
Er ist's! er ist's! ich glaub' es kaum.
Tamino
Sie ist's! sie ist's! es ist kein Traum.
Pamina
Mein Arm schlingt sich um ihn herum.   Es schling mein Arm sich um ihn
                                      her,

Tamino
Mein Arm schlingt sich um sie herum   Es schling mein Arm sich um sie
                                                her,

Tamino, Pamina
Und ich bin im Elisium.   Und wenn es auch mein Ende wär!
Chor
Was soll das heissen?
Monostatos
Welch eine Dreistigkeit!
Gleich auseinander, das geht zu weit.
Dein Sklave liegt zu deinen Füssen,
Lass den verwegnen Frevler büssen;

english

Sarastro
And a haughty woman.
A man must lead the hearts of women;
For without him every woman is apt
To step outside her proper sphere.

Monostatos [S] 149
So, proud youth, over here,
Here is Sarastro, our master.
Pamina
It is he! It is he! I can scarcely believe
    it.
Tamino
It is she! It is she! It is no dream.
Pamina
My arm embraces him,   My arm would embrace him,
Tamino
My arm embraces her,   My arm would embrace her,
Tamino, Pamina
And I am in Elysium.   Even if it meant my end!
Chorus
What is the meaning of this?
Monostatos
What audacity!
Separate immediately, that's going too
    far.

Your slave lies at your feet,
Make the bold transgressor pay;

Bedenk' wie frech der Knabe ist!
Durch dieses seltnen Vogels List
Wollt er Paminen dir entführen:
Allein ich wusst' ihn auszuspüren.
Du kennst mich—meine
   Wachsamkeit—
Sarastro
Verdient dass man ihr Lorbeern streut!
He! gebt dem Ehrenmann sogleich—
Monostatos
Schon deine Gnade macht mich reich.
Sarastro
Nur sieben und siebenzig Sohlenstreich.
Monostatos
Ach Herr! den Lohn verhoft' ich nicht.
Sarastro
Nicht Dank! es ist ja meine Pflicht.
Chor
Es lebe Sarastro der göttliche Weise,
Er lohnet und strafet in ähnlichem
   Kreise.
Sarastro
Führt diese beiden Fremdlinge
In unsern Prüfungstempel ein,
Bedecket ihre Häupter dann
Sie müssen erst gereinigt seyn.

Just think how insolent the boy is!
Through the cunning of this rare bird
He wanted to snatch Pamina from you:
But I was able to waylay him.
You know me—my vigilance—
Sarastro
Deserves that you be bedecked with laurel!

Hey! Give the honorable man
  immediately—
Monostatos
Just your favor makes me rich.
Sarastro
Just seventy-seven lashings of the slipper.
Monostatos
Oh master! I hardly expected that reward.
Sarastro
Nothing to thank! It's only my duty.
Chorus
Long live Sarastro, the divine sage,
He rewards and punishes within the
  same orbit.
Sarastro
Lead both these strangers
Into our temple of trials,
Then cover their heads
They must first be purified.

german

Chor   [S] 161
Wenn Tugend und Gerechtigkeit
Den Grossen Pfad mit Ruhm bestreut,   Der Grossen Pfad mit Ruhm
                                            bestreut

Dann ist die Erd' ein Himmelreich,
Und Sterbliche den Göttern gleich.

english

Chorus   [S] 161
When virtue and justice
Strews the broad path with fame,   Strews the path of the great with
                                           fame

Then earth is a heavenly kingdom,
And mortals like gods.

german

ZWEITER AKT (ACT II)
Nr. 9. Marcia [S] 169

Nr. 10   [S] 171
Sarastro
O Isis und Osiris schenket

Der Weisheit Geist dem neuen Paar!
Die ihr der Wandrer Schritte lenket,
Stärkt mit Geduld sie in Gefahr.
Chor der Priester
Stärkt mit Geduld sie in Gefahr.
Sarastro
Lasst sie der Prüfung Früchte sehen,
Doch sollten sie zu Grabe gehen,
So lohnt der Tugend kühnen Lauf;
Nehmt sie in euren Wohnsitz auf.
Chor der Priester
Nehmt sie in euren Wohnsitz auf.

Nr. 11   [S] 176
2 Priester
Bewahret euch vor Weiber=Tücken,
Dies ist des Bundes erste Pflicht!
Manch weiser Mann liess sich
    berücken,

english

ACT II
No. 9. Marcia [S] 169

No. 10   [S] 171
Sarastro
Oh Isis and Osiris grant
The spirit of wisdom to the new pair!
You who direct the wanderers' steps,
Strengthen them with patience at times
    of danger.
Chorus of Priests
Strengthen them with patience at times
    of danger.
Sarastro
Let them see the fruits of their trial,
Should they however go to the grave,
Then reward the bold course of virtue;
Take them up to your abode.
Chorus of Priests
Take them up to your abode.

No. 11   [S] 176
2 Priests
Beware of woman's wiles,
This is the first duty of the fellowship!
Many a wise man became ensnared,

german

Er fehlte und versah sichs nicht.
Verlassen sah er sich am Ende,
Vergolten seine Treu mit Hohn!
Vergebens rang er seine Hände.
Tod und Verzweiflung war sein Lohn.

Nr. 12   [S] 180
3 Damen
Wie? Wie? Wie?
Ihr an diesem Schreckensort?
Nie, nie, nie,
Kommt ihr wieder glücklich fort.
Tamino dir ist Tod geschworen,
Du Papageno bist verlohren.
Papageno
Nein, nein, nein, das wär' zu viel.
Tamino
Papageno, schweige still;
Willst du dein Gelübde brechen,
Nichts mit Weibern hier zu sprechen?
Papageno
Du hörst ja, wir sind beyde hin.
Tamino
Stille sag' ich, schweige still.

english

He failed, and was not aware of it.
In the end he saw himself forsaken,
His faithfulness repaid with mockery!
In vain he wrung his hands,
Death and despair were his reward.

No. 12   [S] 180
3 Ladies
What? What? What?

You in this place of terror?
Never, never, never,
Will you get safely away again.
Tamino, for you death is sworn,
You, Papageno, are lost.
Papageno
No, no, no, that would be too much.
Tamino
Papageno, be quiet;
Do you want to break your vow
Not to talk to women here?
Papageno
You hear, don't you, we're both
   finished.
Tamino
Quiet I say, be quiet.

german

Papageno
Immer still, und immer still.
3 Damen
Ganz nah ist euch die Königin,
Sie drang im Tempel heimlich ein.
Papageno
Wie? Was? sie soll im Tempel seyn?
Tamino
Stille, sag' ich! schweige still!
Wirst du immer so vermessen
Deiner Eidespflicht vergessen?
3 Damen
Tamino, hör' du bist verlohren,
Gedenke an die Königinn!
Man zischelt viel sich in die Ohren
Von dieser Priester falschem Sinn.
Tamino
Ein Weiser prüft und achtet nicht,
Was der gemeine Pöpel spricht,
3 Damen
Man sagt, wer ihrem Bunde schwört,
Ergiebt sich einer Mörderschaar.   Der fährt zur Höll mit Haut und
                                             Haar.

Papageno
Das wär der Teufel! unerhört!

english

Papageno
Always quiet, and always quiet.
3 Ladies
The Queen is very near to you,
She secretly forced her way into the
    temple.
Papageno
What? How? She is in the temple?
Tamino
Quiet, I say! Keep quiet!
Will you always so brazenly
Forget the duty of your oath?
3 Ladies
Tamino, listen you are lost,
Think of the queen!
There is much whispering in ears
Of the false nature of these priests.
Tamino
A wise man censors and disregards
What the common crowd say.
3 Ladies
It is said that he who swears into their
    fellowship
Gives himself over to a band of   Is dragged along to hell.
    murderers.
Papageno
That would be the very devil! Incredible!

german

Sag' an, Tamino, ist das wahr?
Tamino
Geschwätz von Weibern ausgedacht,   Geschwätz von Weibern nachgesagt
Und das ein weiser Mann verlacht.   Von Heuchlern aber ausgedacht.
Papageno
Doch sagt es auch die Königinn.
Tamino
Sie ist ein Weib, hat Weibersinn.
Sey still, mein Wort sey dir genug;

Denk' deiner Pflicht, und handle klug.
3 Damen
Warum bist du mit uns so spröde?
Auch Papageno schweigt? so rede!
Papageno
Ich möchte gerne—wohl—
Tamino
Still!
Papageno
Ihr seht dass ich nicht soll—
Tamino
Still!
Papageno, Tamino
Dass $_{du}^{ich}$) nicht $_{kannst}^{kann}$) das Plaudern
    lassen,
Ist wahrlich eine Schand für $_{dich}^{mich}$).

english

Tell me, Tamino, is that true?
Tamino
Gossip thought up by women   Gossip repeated by women
At which a wise man laughs.   But thought up by hypocrites.
Papageno
But the Queen says it too.
Tamino
She is a woman, has a woman's mind.
Be silent, let my word suffice for you;
Think of your duty, and act prudently.
3 Ladies
Why are you so shy with us?
Even Papageno is silent? Come on,
    speak!
Papageno
I'd like to—well—
Tamino
Quiet!
Papageno
You see that I must not—
Tamino
Quiet!

Papageno, Tamino
That _{you}I) cannot refrain from talking
Is truly a disgrace for _{you}me).

german

3 Damen, Papageno, Tamino
_{Sie}Wir) müssen _{uns}sie) mit Schaam
   verlassen,
Es plaudert keiner sicherlich.
Von festem Geiste ist ein Mann,
Er denket, was er sprechen kann.
Chor
Entweiht ist die heilige Schwelle,
Hinab mit den Weibern zur Hölle!
3 Damen
O weh! o weh! o weh!
Papageno
O weh! O weh! O weh!

Nr. 13   [S] 206
Monostatos
Alles fühlt der Liebe Freuden,
Schnäbelt, tändelt, herzt und küsst;   Schnäbelt, tändelt, herzet, küsst
Und ich soll die Liebe meiden,
Weil ein Schwarzer hässlich ist.
Ist mir denn kein Herz gegeben?
Ich bin auch den Mädchen gut!   Bin ich nicht von Fleisch und Blut?
Und ihr Blut giesst frisches leben [*sic*], Immer ohne Weibchen leben
Höh're Wärme durch mein Blut!   Wäre wahrlich Höllenglut

Drum so will ich, weil ich lebe,
Schnäbeln, küssen, zärtlich seyn,

english

3 Ladies, Papageno, Tamino
_{They}We) must leave _{us}them) with shame,
Certainly none will talk.
A man is firm in spirit,
He thinks about what he may say.
Chorus
The sacred threshold is defiled,

Down with the women to hell!
3 Ladies
Oh woe! Oh woe! Oh woe!
Papageno
Oh woe! Oh woe! Oh woe!

No. 13   [S] 206
Monostatos
Everyone feels the joys of love,
Pecks, pets, hugs and kisses;   Pecks, pets, hugs, kisses
And I must shun love,
Because a black man is ugly.
Don't I have a heart too?
I am also fond of girls!   Am I not of flesh and blood?
And their blood pours fresh life,   To live always without a woman
Greater warmth through my blood!   Would be truly the fire of hell.

And so I wish, because I am alive,
To peck, kiss, be tender,

german

Lieber guter Mond, vergebe,
Eine Weisse nahm mich ein.
Weiss ist schön, ich muss sie küssen,
Mond, verstecke dich dazu.
Soll es dich zu sehn verdrüssen,   Sollt' es dich zu sehr verdriessen,
O so mach die Augen zu.

Nr. 14   [S] 210
Königinn der Nacht
Der Hölle Rache kocht in meinem
   Herzen;
Tod und Verzweiflung toben um mich   Tod und Verzweiflung flammet um
   her,   mich her!
Fühlt nicht durch dich Sarastro
   Todesschmerzen,
Bist du mein Kind, bist mir nicht   So bist du, Nein! meine Tochter
   Tochter mehr.   nimmermehr:
Verstossen sey auf ewig! Verlassen
   sey auf ewig!
Zertrümmert sey auf ewig alle Bande
   der Natur,

Wenn nicht durch dich Sarastro wird
  erblassen!
Hört! Rachegötter! Hört! der Mutter
  Schwur!

Nr. 15   [S] 223
Sarastro
In diesen heil'gen Hallen
Kennt man die Rache nicht,
Und ist der Mensch gefallen,   Und ist ein Mensch gefallen,

english

Dear good moon, forgive,
A white girl captivated me.
White is beautiful, I must kiss her;
Moon, hide yourself from it.
If it vexes you to see it,   Should it vex you too much,
Well then, just close your eyes.

No. 14   [S] 210
Queen of Night
The vengeance of hell boils in my
  heart;
Death and despair rage around me,   Death and despair burns around me!
If Sarastro doesn't feel through you
  the pains of death
You are my child, my daughter no   So you are, No! my daughter
  more.   nevermore:
Be cast off forever! Be deserted
  forever!
All ties of nature be destroyed forever,
If, through you, Sarastro is not
  rendered lifeless!
Hear! Gods of vengeance! Hear! a
  mother's oath!

german

No. 15   [S] 223
Sarastro
In these hallowed halls
Vengeance is unknown,
And if a man has fallen,   And if a man has fallen

Ist Rath und Hülfe Pflicht.
Dann geht er heller an Verstand
Den Weg des Lichts an Freundes Hand.

Führt Liebe ihn zur Pflicht.
Dann wandelt er an Freundes Hand
Vergnügt und froh ins bessre Land.

Hier wo im heil'gen Bunde
Der Mensch den Menschen liebt,
Hier blutet keine Wunde,
Man duldet und vergiebt.
Dem Feinde seine Schuld verzeih'n,
Was kann des Weisen würd'ger seyn?

In diesen heilg'en [*sic*] Mauern
Wo Mensch den Menschen liebt –
Kann kein Verräther lauern
Weil man dem Feind vergiebt.
Wen solche Lehren nicht erfreun,
Verdienet nicht ein Mensch zu seyn.

Nr. 16   [S] 227
3 Knaben
Seyd uns zum zweitenmal
    willkommen,
Ihr Männer in Sarastros Reich.
Dies Glöckchen euch im Hain
    genommen,
Und diese Flöte schickt er euch;
Wollt ihr die Speisen nicht
    verschmähen,
So esset, trinket froh davon;
Wenn wir zum drittenmal uns sehen,
Ist Freiheit eures Muthes Lohn,
Tamino Muth! Nah ist das Ziel,
Du Papageno, schweige still.

Er schickt was man euch
    abgenommen,
Die Flöte und die Glöckchen euch.

Ist Freude eures Muthes Lohn!

english

Advice and help is a duty.
Then, clearer in understanding,
    he walks
The path of light on the hand of a
    friend
Here, where in the holy fellowship
A man loves brother man,
Here bleeds no wound,
One is tolerant and forgiving.
To forgive your enemy his guilt,

Love leads him back to duty.
Then he makes his way, on the hand
    of a friend,
Cheerful and happy into the better
    land.
Within these holy walls,
Where man loves brother man—
No traitor can lurk
Because the enemy is forgiven.
He who does not rejoice in such
    teachings

What can be more worthy of a wise
   man?

Does not deserve to be a man.

No. 16   [S] 227
3 Boys
Be welcome for the second time,
You men, in Sarastro's kingdom.
He sends you this bell, taken from you
   in the grove,
And this flute;
If you don't wish to disdain the dishes
Then eat, drink happily from them;
When we meet for the third time,
Freedom will be the reward for your
   courage,
Tamino courage! The objective is near,
You Papageno, be silent.

He sends you what was taken from
   you,
The flute and bells.

Joy will be the reward for your
   courage!

german

Nr. 17   [S] 231
Pamina
Ach ich fühl's, es ist verschwunden,
Ewig hin der Liebe Glück.
Nimmer kehrt ihr Wonnestunden
Hoher Freuden mir zurück.
Sieh Tamino, heisse Thränen
Strömen meine Wang' herab, die
   Wang herab,
Rührt dich nicht dies bange Sehnen?
Gut, ich kenn' den Weg ins Grab,
Ja, ich kenn' den Weg ins Grab.

Nimmer kömmt ihr Wonnestunden
Meinem Herzen mehr zurück!
Sieh Tamino! diese Thränen
Fliessen Trauter dir allein,

Fühlst du nicht der Liebe Sehnen
So wird Ruh im Tode seyn!
So wird Ruh im Tode seyn!

Nr. 18   [S] 235
Chor der Priester
O Isis! und Osiris! welche Wonne!
Die düstre Nacht verscheucht der
   Glanz der Sonne.
Bald fühlt der edle Jüngling neues Leben;
Bald ist er unserm Dienste ganz gegeben.
Sein Geist ist kühn, sein Herz ist rein.
Bald wird er unsrer würdig seyn.

Nr. 19   [S] 240
Pamina
Soll ich dich, Theurer! nicht mehr
    sehn?

english

No. 17   [S] 231
Pamina
Ah I feel it, it has vanished,
Gone forever the happiness of love.
You will never return to me,   You will never come back
Rapturous hours of sublime joy.   To my heart, rapturous hours!
See Tamino, hot tears   See Tamino! These tears
Stream down my cheek, down my   Flow for you alone, my beloved,
    cheek,
Does this distressed longing not move   If you don't feel the longing of love
    you?
All right, I know the path to the grave,   So there will be peace in death!
Yes, I know the path to the grave.   So there will be peace in death!

No. 18   [S] 235
Priests' Chorus
Oh Isis! and Osiris! what rapture!
The brightness of the sun drives away
    the shades of night.
Soon the noble youth will feel new life;
Soon he will be fully given over to our
    service.
His spirit is bold, his heart is pure.
Soon he will be worthy of us.

No. 19   [S] 240
Pamina
Shall I see you, dear one! no more?

german

Sarastro
Ihr werdet froh euch wiedersehn
Pamina
Dein warten tödliche Gefahren.

Tamino, Sarastro
Die Götter mögen ₍ᵢₕₙ/mich₎) bewahren!
Pamina
Du wirst dem Tode nicht entgehen,
Mir ahndet's, dich dem Grabe weihn.   Mir flüstert dieses Ahndung ein!
Tamino, Sarastro
Der Götter Wille mag geschehen,
Ihr Wille soll Gesetz ₍ᵢₕₘ/mir₎) seyn.   Ihr Wink soll mir Gesetze seyn.
Pamina
O, liebtest du, wie ich dich liebe,
Du würdest nicht so ruhig seyn.
Tamino, Sarastro
O glaub', ₍ₑᵣ fühlet/ich fühle₎) gleiche   Glaub mir ₍ₑᵣ fühlet/ich fühle₎) gleiche
    Triebe,   Triebe,
₍Wird/Werd'₎) ewig dein Getreuer seyn.
Sarastro
Die Stunde schlägt, nun müsst ihr
    scheiden.
Pamina, Tamino
Wie bitter sind der Trennung Leiden!
Sarastro
Tamino muss nun wirklich fort.   Tamino muss nun wieder fort!

english

Sarastro
You will see each other joyfully again.
Pamina
Mortal dangers await you.
Tamino, Sarastro
May the gods protect ₍ₕᵢₘ/me₎)!
Pamina
You will not escape death,
My foreboding is to see you to the   This foreboding whispers itself to
    grave.   me!
Tamino, Sarastro
May the will of the gods be done,
Their will shall be law to ₍ₕᵢₘ/me₎).   A sign from them shall be law to
                                                       me.

Pamina
Oh, if you loved as I love you,
You would not be so calm.

Tamino, Sarastro
Oh believe me, _{he feels} ^{I feel}) the same
   impulses,
_{He}^I) will be your faithful one forever.
Sarastro
The hour strikes, you must now part.
Pamina, Tamino
How bitter are the sorrows of parting!
Sarastro
Tamino must now really be away.

Believe me _{he feels} ^{I feel}) the same
   impulses,

Tamino must now be away again!

german

Tamino
Pamina, ich muss wirklich fort.
Pamina
Tamino muss nun wirklich fort!
Sarastro
Nun muss er fort,
Tamino
Nun muss ich fort!
Pamina
So musst du fort!
Tamino
Pamina, lebewohl!
Pamina
Tamino, lebewohl!
Sarastro
Nun eile fort!
Dich ruft dein Wort,
Die Stunde schlägt, wir sehn uns
   wieder.
Pamina, Tamino
Entflohnes Glück! Wann kehrst du
   wieder?
Ach wann kehrst du wieder?
Lebewohl! lebewohl!

O goldene Ruhe! kehre wieder!

english

Tamino
Pamina I must really be away.
Pamina
Tamino must now really be away!

Sarastro
He must now be away,
Tamino
I must now be away!
Pamina
So you must be away!
Tamino
Pamina, farewell!
Pamina
Tamino, farewell!
Sarastro
Now hurry away!
Your word calls you,
The hour strikes, we meet again.
Pamina, Tamino

Vanished happiness! When will you return?	Oh golden peace! Return again!
Ah when will you return?	
Farewell! Farewell!	

german

Nr. 20   [S] 246
Papageno
Ein Mädchen oder Weibchen
Wünscht Papageno sich.
O so ein sanftes Täubchen
Wär Seeligkeit für mich.

Dann schmeckte mir Trinken und Essen,	*[REIHENFOLGE DER STROPHEN UNGEWISS IM AUTOGRAPH]*
Dann könnt' ich mit Fürsten mich messen,	
Des Lebens als Weiser mich freu'n,	
Und wie im Elisium seyn.	

Ach, kann ich denn keiner von allen
Den reizenden Mädchen gefallen?
Helf eine mir nur aus der Noth,
Sonst gräm' ich mich wahrlich zu todt.

Ach, wird sich denn keine erbarmen,	Wird keine mir Liebe gewähren
Schon brechen die Augen mir Armen;	So muss mich die Flamme verzehren

Doch küsst mich ein weiblicher Mund,
Dann bin ich gleich wieder gesund.

So bin ich schon wieder gesund.

english

No. 20   [S] 246
Papageno
A girl or woman
Papageno wishes for himself.
Oh such a gentle little dove
Would be heaven for me.

Then drink and food would taste good,
Then I could compete with princes,
Rejoice in life as a wise man,
And be as in Elysium.

*[ORDER OF VERSES UNCLEAR
IN AUTOGRAPH]*

Ah, can I then be liked by none
Of all the charming girls?
Help me, one of them, in my need,
Or I shall truly pine to death.

Ah, will none have pity,
Poor me, my eyes already break;
Just a kiss from a woman's mouth,
And I'd then be immediately restored.

If none will grant me love
Then the flame must consume me;

Then I'd be once again restored.

german

Nr. 21   [S] 255
3 Knaben
Bald prangt den Morgen zu verkünden,
Die Sonn' auf goldner Bahn,
Bald werden Nacht und Irrthum
    schwinden;
Bald siegt der weise Mann.
O holde Wahrheit steig hernieder,
Kehr' in der Menschen Herzen wieder;
Mach diese Welt zum Himmel- Reich,
Und Sterbliche den Göttern gleich.
1ter Knabe
Doch seht, Verzweiflung quält
    Paminen!

Bald soll der Aberglaube schwinden

O holde Ruhe steig hernieder

Dann ist die Erd ein Himmelreich

2ᵗᵉʳ und 3ᵗᵉʳ Knabe
Trüb ist ihr Aug';   Wo ist sie denn?
1ᵗᵉʳ Knabe
Tod in den Mienen.   Sie ist von Sinnen!
3 Knaben
Sie quält verschmähter Liebe Leiden.
Ach, von Tamino soll sie scheiden,   Lasst uns der Armen Trost bereiten!
Fürwahr ihr Schicksal geht mir nah,   Fürwahr ihr Schicksal geht uns nah,
O wäre nur ihr Jüngling da;
Sie kömmt, lasst uns bei Seite gehn;
Wie ist sie selbst im Schmerz so   Damit wir, was sie mache, sehn.
    schön!
Pamina
Du also bist mein Bräutigam?   Du also bist mein Bräutigam

english

No. 21   [S] 255
3 Boys
Proclaiming the morning, the sun
Soon glitters on its golden path,
Soon night and error will disappear;   Soon superstition shall disappear,
Soon the wise man will triumph.
Oh, noble truth descend,   Oh, noble peace descend
Return into the hearts of men;
Make this world into a heavenly   Then the earth will be a heavenly
    kingdom,   kingdom
And mortals like gods.
1st Boy
But see, despair torments Pamina!
2nd and 3rd Boy
Troubled is her eye;   Where is she then?
1st Boy
Death in her looks.   She is out of her mind!
3 Boys
She suffers the pangs of disdained love.
Ah, from Tamino she must part,   Let us provide comfort for the poor
                                                  girl!
Truly her fate touches me,   Truly her fate touches us!
If only her young man were there;
She comes, let us step aside;

How beautiful she is, even in grief!
Pamina
Are you then my bridegroom?

So that we see what she does.

You are then my bridegroom

german

Willkommen! ende meinen Gram.

Durch dich vollend ich meinen
    Gram!

3 Knaben
Seht ihre Blicke wild und stier,
Vernahmt ihr's? Wahnsinn sprach aus
    ihr.
Pamina
Geduld, mein Trauter, ich bin dein,
Bald werden wir vereinigt seyn.
3 Knaben
Wahnsinn tobt ihr im Gehirne;
Selbstmord steht auf ihrer Stirne;
Holdes Mädchen! sieh uns an.
Pamina
Sterben will ich, von dem Mann,
Den ich nicht vermag zu hassen,
Weggeworfen und verlassen.
Dies gab meine Mutter mir.
3 Knaben
Wirf den Mörderstahl von dir.
Pamina
Lieber schnell das Leben lassen,
Als in langem Gram erblassen,
Tod ist Ende meiner Qual;

Mir willkommen Mörderstahl!
3 Knaben
Mädchen, willst du mit uns gehn?

Welch dunkle Worte sprach sie da!
Die Arme ist dem Wahnsinn nah!

Bald werden wir vermählet seyn!

Sterben will ich—weil der Mann,
Den ich nimmermehr kann hassen,
Seine Traute kann verlassen!

Selbstmord strafet Gott an dir!

Lieber durch dies Eisen sterben
Als durch Liebesgram verderben.-
Mutter, Mutter! durch dich leide
    ich,
Und dein Fluch verfolget mich!

english

Welcome! End my grief.
3 Boys
See her looks, wild and staring,
Did you observe? There was madness
    in her speech.

Through you I end my grief!

What dark words she spoke there!
The poor girl is near to madness!

Pamina
Patience, my beloved, I am yours,
We will soon be united.   We will soon be married!
3 Boys
Madness rages in her brain;
Suicide is written on her brow;
Sweet girl! Look at us.
Pamina
I want to die, by the man   I want to die, because the man
Whom I am unable to hate,   Whom I cannot bring myself to hate
Thrown away and deserted.   Can forsake his beloved!
This my mother gave me.
3 Boys
Throw the murder weapon away.   God will punish you for suicide!
Pamina
Better to leave this life quickly   Better to die by this iron [*dagger*]
Than to languish in sorrow,   Than to waste away in love-
                                               sickness.
Death is the end of my torture;   Mother, mother! Through you I
                                               suffer,
Welcome, murder weapon!   And your curse pursues me!
3 Boys
Maiden, do you want to go with us?

german

Pamina
Meines Jammers Maas ist voll!   Ja des Jammers Maas ist voll!
Falscher Jüngling, lebe wohl!
Sieh, Pamina stirbt durch dich;
Dieses Eisen tödte mich.

3 Knaben   [S] 272
Ha! Unglückliche, halt ein!
Dich verwirren deine Schmerzen!   Sollte dies dein Jüngling sehen
Weh thust du Taminos Herzen;   Würde er für Gram vergehen,
Dieses Herz, ganz ist es dein.   Denn er liebet dich allein.
Pamina
Was? er fühlte Gegenliebe,
Und verbarg mir seine Triebe,
Wandte sein Gesicht von mir?
Warum sprach er nicht mit mir?

3 Knaben

Schönes Kind! wir müssen schweigen;   Dieses müssen wir verschweigen
Doch wir wollen dir ihn zeigen,
Mit Entzücken wirst du sehn,   Und du wirst mit Staunen sehn
Dass sein Herz ganz dir geweiht,   Dass er dir sein Herz geweiht,
Selbst den Tod für dich nicht scheut.   Und den Tod für dich nicht scheut!
Komm, wir wollen zu ihm gehn.
Pamina
Führt mich hin, ich möcht' ihn sehn.

english

Pamina

The measure of my misery is full!   Yes, the measure of misery is full!
False youth, farewell!
See, Pamina dies through you;
May this iron kill me.

3 Boys   [S] 272

Ha! Unhappy one, stop!
Your grief confuses you!   Should your youth see this
You are causing anguish to Tamino's   He would die of grief,
    heart;
This heart is entirely yours.   For he loves you alone.
Pamina
What? He felt reciprocal love,
And hid his feelings from me,
Turned his face from me?
Why did he not speak with me?
3 Boys
Lovely child! We must be silent;   This we cannot reveal
Yet we want to show him to you,
With rapture you shall see   And you will see with astonishment
That his heart, devoted entirely to you,   That he has devoted his heart to
    you,
Shuns not even death for you.   And does not shun death for you!
Come, let us go to him.
Pamina
Lead me there, I want to see him.

german

Pamina, 3 Knäbchen

Zwey Herzen, die in Liebe brennen,	Zwei Herzen die von Liebe brennen,
Kann keine Macht der Erde trennen,	Kann Menschenohnmacht niemals trennen.
Sie halten fest in Schmerz und Leid.	Verloren ist der Feinde Müh
Ihr Bund ist Bund der Ewigkeit.	Die Götter selbsten schützen sie.

2 geharnischte Männer [S] 286

Der, welcher wandert diese Strasse voll Beschwerde,	Der welcher wandert diese Strasse voll Beschwerden
Wird rein durch Feuer, Wasser, Luft und Erde.	Wird rein durch Feuer, Wasser, Luft und Erden.
Wenn er des Todes Schrecken überwinden kann,	
Schwingt er sich von der Erde himmelan,	Schwingt er sich aus der Erde Himmel=an!
Er wird verklärt, geläutert, licht und rein,	Erleuchtet wird er dann im Stande seyn
Sich den Mysterien der Isis ganz zu weih'n.	

Tamino

Mich schreckt kein Tod, als Mann zu handeln,
Den Weg der Tugend fort zu wandeln,

Schliesst mir des Schreckenspforten auf!	Schliesst mir des Schreckens Pforten auf

Ich wage froh den kühnen Lauf.

Pamina

Tamino halt! ich muss dich sehn.

Tamino

Was hör ich? Paminens Stimme?

2 geharnischte Männer

Ja, ja! das ist Paminens Stimme;

english

Pamina, 3 Boys

Two hearts which burn in love,	Two hearts which burn of love,

No power on earth can part,

Can never be parted by human
  weakness.

They hold firm in pain and sorrow.
Their bond is the bond of eternity.

In vain is the enemies' effort,
The gods themselves protect them.

2 Armed Men [S] 286
He who wanders this path full of
  hardship
Becomes pure through fire, water, air
  and earth.
If he can overcome the terror of death,
He lifts himself from the earth
  heavenwards,
He becomes transfigured, purified,
  bright and clear,
To dedicate himself completely to the
  mysteries of Isis.

He who wanders this path full of
  hardships
Becomes pure through fire, water,
  air and earth.

He lifts himself from the earth
  heavenwards,
Enlightened, he will then be able

Tamino
Death does not frighten me from acting
  as a man,
From setting forth on the path of virtue,
Unlock for me the gates of terror!
I happily risk the bold journey.

Unlock for me the gates of terror

Pamina
Tamino, stop! I must see you.
Tamino
What do I hear? Pamina's voice?
2 Armed Men
Yes, yes! that is Pamina's voice;

german

Tamino, 2 geharnischte Männer
Wohl $_{dir}$ ^{mir}), nun kann sie mit $_{dir}$ ^{mir})
  gehn,
Nun trennet $_{euch}$ ^{uns}) kein Schiksal mehr,
Selbst wenn der Tod die Losung wär.

Wenn auch der Tod beschieden
  wär.

Tamino
Ist mir erlaubt mit ihr zu sprechen?
2 geharnischte Männer
Dir sey erlaubt mit ihr zu sprechen.

Dir ist erlaubt mit ihr zu sprechen!

Tamino, 2 geharnischte Männer

Welch Glück, wenn ~ihr euch~ ^wir uns^)
 wiedersehn [*sic*]
Froh Hand in Hand in Tempel gehn.
Ein Weib das Grab und Tod nicht
 scheut,
Ist würdig der Unsterblichkeit.

Pamina   [S] 294-95
Tamino mein! o welch ein Glück!
Tamino
Pamina mein! o welch ein Glück!
Tamino
Hier sind die Schreckens Pforten,
Die Noth und Tod mir dräu'n.
Pamina
Ich werd' an allen Orten an deiner
 Seite seyn.
Ich selber führe dich,
Die Liebe leite mich;

Welch Glück wenn wir ~euch~ ^uns^)
 wiedersehn
Froh Hand in Hand im Tempel gehn
Ein Weib das Nacht und Tod nicht
 scheut
Ist würdig, und wird eingeweiht.

Ich werde aller Orten an deiner
 Seite seyn.
Ich selbsten führe dich

english

Tamino, 2 Armed Men

How wonderful, now she can go
 with ~you~ ^me^),
Now no destiny can part ~you~ ^us^),
Even if death were the signal.

Tamino
Am I allowed to speak to her?
2 Armed Men
You are allowed to speak to her.
Tamino, 2 Armed Men
What happiness when ~you~ ^we^) meet
 again,
~Walking~ ^Walk^) happily hand in hand into
 the temple.
A woman who does not shun the grave
 and death
Is worthy of immortality.

Even if death were to be ~your~ ^our^)
 fate.

You are allowed to speak to her!

What happiness when we ~meet you~ ^meet^)
 again
~Walking~ ^Walk^) happily hand in hand in
 the temple.
A woman who does not shun night
 and death
Is worthy, and will be initiated.

Pamina [S] 294-95
Tamino mine! Oh what happiness!
Tamino
Pamina mine! Oh what happiness!
Tamino
Here are the gates of terror,
Which threaten danger and death.
Pamina
I will be at your side in all places.   I will be at your side in all places.
I myself will lead you,   I myself will lead you
May love guide me!

german

Sie streu' uns Rosen auf den Pfad,   Sie mag den Weg mit Rosen streun,
Den dornicht unser Fuss betrat;   Weil Rosen stets bei Dornen seyn.
Der Zauberflöte Himmelsklang   Spiel du die Zauberflöte an
Erleichtre unsern Heldengang: Sie schütze uns auf unsrer Bahn.
In seiner Zauberhöhle Schlunde   Es schnitt in einer Zauberstunde
Schnitt einst mein Vater sie tief in   Mein Vater sie aus tiefstem Grunde
   der Geisterstunde,
Aus einer ew'gen Zeder aus,   Der tausenjähr'gen Eiche aus
Bei Blitz und Donner, Sturm und
   Braus.
Lass tönen nun den Himmelsklang,   Nun komm und spiel die Flöte an!
Erleichtr'uns unsern Heldengang;   Sie leite uns auf grauser Bahn.
Pamina, Tamino, 2 geharnischte
   Männer
Ihr wandelt ^{Wir wandeln}) durch des Tones
   Macht,
Froh durch des Todes düstre Nacht.

Pamina, Tamino [S] 301-2
Wir wandelten durch Feuergluthen,
Bezähmten muthig die Gefahr.   Bekämpften muthig die Gefahr
Dein Ton sey Schutz in Wasserfluthen,
So wie er es im Feuer war.
Ihr Götter, welch ein Augenblick!
Gewährt ist uns der Weihe Glück.   Gewähret ist uns Isis Glück!

Chor [S] 307
Triumph! Triumph! du edles Paar!
Besieget hast du die Gefahr!
Geläutert bist du licht und rein!   Der Isis Weihe ist nun dein!

english

May she strew roses on the path	She may strew the path with roses,
Which our foot trod beset with thorns.	Since roses are always accompanied by thorns.
May the heavenly sound of the magic flute	Play the magic flute
Ease our heroic path:	It should protect us on our journey.
In the abyss of his magic cave	My father cut it in a magic hour
My father once cut it, deep in the hour of the spirits,	From the profoundest depths
From an eternal cedar,	Of the thousand-year-old oak
In lightning and thunder, storm and turbulence.	
Let it now play its heavenly sound,	Now come and play on the flute!
Ease for us our heroic path;	May it guide us on our grim pathway.

Pamina, Tamino, 2 Armed Men
Through the power of the sound _{you}^{we})
  walk
Joyfully through the gloomy night of
  death.

Pamina, Tamino [S] 301-2

We walked through burning fires,	
Bravely tamed the danger.	Bravely fought the danger
May your sound be protection in the water-torrents	
Just as it was in the fire.	
You gods, what a moment!	
The happiness of initiation is granted to us.	The happiness of Isis is granted to us!

Chorus [S] 307

Triumph! Triumph! You noble pair!	
You have conquered the danger!	
You are purified, bright and clear!	The initiation of Isis is now yours!

german

Komm, tritt nun in den Tempel ein.   Kommt, tretet in den Tempel ein.

Papageno [S] 311
Papagena, Papagena, Papagena.
Weibchen! Täubchen, meine Schöne!
Vergebens! Ach! sie ist verlohren!
Ich bin zum Unglück nur gebohren;

Schon fasst' ich sie ans runde Kinn;

Ich plauderte, mein Schatz war hin.

Ich schlürfte ächten Götterwein,
Ich sah ein Weiblein, jung und schön,
Nun ist mein Herz voll Liebespein,
Und ich will nichts als Mädchen sehn.
Papagena! Herzens Weibchen!
Papagena! liebes Täubchen!
S' ist umsonst, es ist vergebens!
Müde bin ich meines Lebens;
Aus dann meiner Augen Licht,
Denn wer todt ist, liebet nicht.
Diesen Baum da will ich zieren,
Mir an ihm den Hals zu schnüren.
Gute Nacht, du falsche Welt!
Die so arg mich Armen prellt;
Schiebst mein Glück mir vor die Nase,
Da ich's fasse, springt die Blase,
Fahre wohl, ich lasse dich!

Ich bin zum Unglück schon
 gebohren!
Ich plauderte—und das war
 schlecht,
Und drum geschieht es mir schon
 recht!
Seit ich gekostet diesen Wein
Seit ich das schöne Weibchen sah,
So brennts im Herzenskämmerlein,
So zwickets hier, so zwickets da!

Sterben macht der Lieb ein End,
Wenns im Herzen noch so brennt.

Mir an ihm den Hals zuschnüren,
Weil das Leben mir missfällt
Gute Nacht, du schwarze Welt!
Weil du böse an mir handelst
Mir kein schönes Kind zubandelst
So ists aus, so sterbe ich

english

Come, step now into the temple.

Come, step into the temple.

Papageno [S] 311
Papagena, Papagena, Papagena.
Little woman! Little dove, my lovely
 one!
In vain! Ah! She is lost!
I am just born for bad luck;
I already grabbed her by her round
 chin;

I am just born for bad luck!
I chattered—and that was bad,

I chattered, my sweetheart was gone.
I sipped a true wine of the gods,
I saw a damsel, young and beautiful,
My heart is now full of the pain of
    love,
And I want to see nothing but girls.

Papagena! Woman of my heart!
Papagena! Dear little dove!
It's useless, it's in vain!
I am tired of my life;
Out then light of my eyes,
For he who is dead does not love.
I will adorn this tree over there,
Hang from it by the neck.
Goodnight, you false world!
Which cheats poor me so badly;
You push happiness before my nose,
As I grasp it the bubble [*bladder*]
    bursts,
Farewell, I leave you!

And so it serves me right!
Since I tasted this wine
Since I saw the lovely woman,
So it burns in the chamber of my
    heart,
So it pinches here, so it pinches
    there!

Dying puts an end to love,
If it burns so much in the heart.

Since life displeases me
Good-night, you dark world!
Because you treat me badly
And don't send me a pretty young
    thing
So it's over, so I die

german

Schöne Mädchen, denkt an mich!
Doch will eine sich des Armen,
Der sich hängen will, erbarmen,
Wohl, so lass ich's diesmal seyn,
Rufet nur: Ja, oder Nein!
Keine hört mich, alles stille,
Also ist es euer Wille?
Papageno frisch hinauf!
Ende deinen Lebenslauf!
Nun, ich warte noch, es sey!
Bis man zählet eins, zwey, drey.
Eins, zwey, drey.
Nun wohlan es bleibt dabey
Weil mich nichts zurucke [*sic*] hält
Gute Nacht du falsche Welt.

Will sich eine um mich Armen
Eh ich hänge noch erbarmen

Weil mich nichts zurücke hält

3 Knaben [S] 322
Halt ein! O Papageno, und sey klug,
Man lebt nur einmal, dies sey dir genug.

Papageno
Ihr habt gut reden, habt gut scherzen,
Doch brennt es euch, wie mir im   Doch brennt' es euch wie mich im
    Herzen,   Herzen,
Ihr würdet auch nach Mädchen gehn.
3 Knaben
So lasse deine Glöckchen klingen,
Dies wird dein Weibchen zu dir
    bringen.

english

Beautiful girls, think of me!
However if one will have pity on the   If one for poor me,
    poor man
Who wants to hang himself,   Before I hang, will have pity
Then, all right, I'll leave it this time,
Just call: yes, or no!
No one hears me, all is still,
So is it your will?
Papageno don't delay!
End the course of your life!
Well, I'll just wait, let it be!
While one counts one, two, three.
One! Two! Three!
Well then that's how it is,
Since nothing holds me back   Since nothing holds me back
Goodnight false world.

3 Boys [S] 322
Stop! Papageno, and be wise,
One lives only once, let this be enough
    for you.
Papageno
It's all very well for you to talk and
    make fun,
If it were to burn in your heart, as in   If it were to burn in your heart as in
    mine,   mine,
You would also go after girls.
3 Boys
So let your bells ring,
This will bring your little woman to you.

german

Papageno
Ich Narr vergass der Zauberdinge.
Erklinge Glockenspiel, erklinge,
Ich muss mein liebes Mädchen sehn.
Klinget Glöckchen, klinget!
Schafft mein Mädchen her,
Klinget Glöckchen, klinget!
Bringt mein Weibchen her!
3 Knaben
Nun Papageno, sieh dich um.

Papageno [S] 330
Pa-Pa-Pa-Pa-Pa-Papagena.
Papagena
Pa-Pa-Pa-Pa-Pa-Papageno.
Papageno
Bist du mir nun ganz gegeben?
Papagena
Nun bin ich dir ganz gegeben.
Papageno
Nun so sey mein liebes Weibchen!
Papagena
Nun so sey mein liebes Täubchen,
Mein Herzens Täubchen.
Papageno, Papagena
Welche _{Freude} ^{Wonne}) wird das seyn,   Welche Freude wird das seyn

english

Papageno
Like a fool I forgot the magic things.
Resound, chimes, resound,
I must see my beloved girl.
Ring, bells, ring!
Produce my girl,
Ring, bells, ring!
Bring my little woman forth!
3 Boys
Now Papageno, look around you.

Papageno [S] 330
Pa-Pa-Pa-Pa-Pa-Papagena.
Papagena
Pa-Pa-Pa-Pa-Pa-Papageno.
Papageno
Are you now all mine?
Papagena
Now I am all yours.
Papageno
Well, then be my beloved little woman!
Papagena
Well, then be my dear little dove,
The little dove of my heart.
Papageno, Papagena

| What _{joy} ^{rapture}) it will be | What joy it will be |

german

Wenn die Götter uns bedenken,
Unsrer Liebe Kinder schenken,
So liebe kleine Kinderlein.
Papageno
Erst einen kleinen Papageno.
Papagena
Dann eine kleine Papagena.
Papageno
Dann wieder einen Papageno!
Papagena
Dann wieder eine Papagena!
Papageno, Papagena
Es ist das höchste der Gefühle,
Wenn viele Pa-Pa-Papagen _a^o)

| Der Seegen froher Eltern seyn. | Der Eltern Seegen werden seyn. |

Monostatos, Königin der Nacht,
  3 Damen [S] 340
Nur stille, stille, stille, stille,
Bald dringen wir in Tempel ein.
Monostatos
Doch Fürstin halte Wort; erfülle—
Dein Kind muss meine Gattin seyn.

Königin der Nacht
Ich halte Wort; es ist mein Wille.
Mein Kind soll deine Gattin seyn.

english

If the gods provide for us
And grant our love children,
Such dear little children.
Papageno
First a little Papageno.
Papagena
Then a little Papagena.
Papageno
Then again a Papageno!
Papagena
Then again a Papagena!
Papageno, Papagena
It is the sublimest of feelings
If many Pa-Pa-Papagen$_a^o$)s
Should be the blessing of happy   Will be the blessing of the parents.
   parents.

Monostatos, Queen of Night,
   3 Ladies [S] 340
Hush, hush, hush, hush,
We will soon be within the temple.
Monostatos
But princess, keep your word; see to
   it—
Your child must be my wife.
Queen of Night
I'll keep my word; it is my will
My child shall be your wife.

german

3 Damen
Ihr Kind soll deine Gattin seyn.
Monostatos
Doch still, ich höre schrecklich
   Rauschen,
Wie Donnerton und Wasserfall.

Königin der Nacht, 3 Damen
Ja, fürchterlich ist dieses Rauschen,
Wie fernen Donners Wiederhall!
Monostatos
Nun sind sie in des Tempels Hallen.
Königin der Nacht, 3 Damen,
   Monostatos
Dort wollen wir sie überfallen,
Die Frömmler tilgen von der Erd,
Mit Feuersglut und Dolch und   Mit Feuersglut und mächt'gem
  Schwerd.   Schwerdt!
3 Damen, Monostatos
Dir, grosse Königin der Nacht,
Sey unsrer Rache Opfer gebracht.
Königin der Nacht, 3 Damen,
   Monostatos
Zerschmettert, vernichtet ist unsre
  Macht!
Wir alle gestürzet in ewige Nacht.
Sarastro
Die Stralen der Sonne vertreiben die
  Nacht,
Vernichten der Heuchler erschlichene   Zernichten der Heuchler
  Macht   erschlichene Macht!

english

3 Ladies
Her child shall be your wife.
Monostatos
But quiet, I hear the sound of dreadful
  rushing,
Like thunder and waterfall.
Queen of Night, 3 Ladies
Yes, terrible is this rushing,
Like the echo of distant thunder!
Monostatos
Now they are in the halls of the temple.
Queen of Night, 3 Ladies, Monostatos
There we will take them by surprise,

Obliterate the sanctimonious ones
  from the earth
With burning fire and dagger and   With burning fire and powerful
  sword.   sword.
3 Ladies, Monostatos
To you, great Queen of Night,
Be brought the sacrifice of our
  vengeance.
Queen of Night, 3 Ladies, Monostatos
Shattered, annihilated is our power!
We are all plunged into eternal night.
Sarastro
The rays of the sun drive away the
  night,
Annihilate the surreptitious power of   Annihilate the surreptitious power
  dissemblers.   of dissemblers!

german

Chor   [S] 352
Heil sey euch Geweihten!
Ihr drangt durch die Nacht.   Ihr dranget durch Nacht!
Dank sey dir Osiris. Dank, dir Isis
  gebracht.
Es siegte die Wahrheit, in   Es siegte die Stärke und krönet zum
  himmlischem Glanz   Lohn
Strahlt Wahrheit und Liebe dein   Die Schönheit und Weisheit mit
  ewiger Kranz.   ewiger Kron!

english

Chorus   [S] 352
Hail to you, the initiated!
You forged your way through the night. You forged your way through night!
Thanks be given to you, Isis and Osiris.
Truth triumphed, in heavenly   Strength triumphed and crowns, as
  brightness   the reward
Your eternal garland streams truth and Beauty and wisdom with an eternal
  love.   crown!

Bibliography of Rarer Sources

Almanac de Gotha pour l'Année MDCCXCI. British Library P.P.2422.a.

Annalen der Physik, hrsg. Ludwig Wilhelm Gilbert. Bd. 62. (Bd. 32 Neueste Folge) (Leipzig, 1819). British Library P.P. 1487.

Annalen des Theaters. Staatsarchiv, Hamburg Z530 8.

Annals of Philosophy. Thomas Thomson, ed. British Library 439. e. 10. [Microfilm PB Mic C5360–5362].

Badener Zeitung. Stadtarchiv Baden bei Wien [Abth.MBNr.16], Städtische Sammlungen Archiv/Rollettmuseum der Stadtgemeinde Baden.

Beiträge zur Beethoven-Bibliographie, hrsg. Kurt Dorfmüller (München, 1978). British Library X.431/2997.

Berlinische Musikalische Zeitung. British Library Hirsch IV. 1133.

Bibliothèque Universelle, Geneva. British Library Science Reference and Information Service (P)Bx80-F(57).

Bonner Geschichtsblätter. Stadtarchiv und Stadthistorische Bibliothek Bonn I e 303.

Briefe an Schiller herausgegeben von L. Urlichs (Stuttgart, 1877). British Library 10910. cc. 10.

The Breitkopf Thematic Catalogue 1762–1787. (*Catalogo delle Sinfonie, che si trovano in manuscritto nella officina musica di Giovanno Gottlob Immanuel Breitkopf, in Lipsia.*) British Library MUS780.216.

Castelli, Ignaz Franz. *Memoiren meines Lebens* (1861). British Library 10707. bbb.43.

———. *Moderne Klassiker. Deutsche Literaturgeschichte der neueren Zeit in Biographien, Kritiken und Proben* (Ernst Balde, Cassel, 1854). British Library 816.a.6.

Chiarelli, Alessandra. "I Codici di Musica della Raccolta Estense,"*Quaderni della Rivista Italiana di Musicologia, Società Italiana di Musicologia* (Firenze, 1987). Biblioteca Estense Universitaria Modena CFI0050530.

Cornet. *Die Oper in Deutschland*, 24. British Library 7896.bb.39. Lorenzo da Ponte, *Memoirs of Lorenzo da Ponte*, trans. L. A. Sheppard (1929). British Library 12211. ss.2/1.

——. *Memorie di Lorenzo da Ponte.* (Nuova-Jorca, 1829), 7. British Library 1448. a.12.

Deile, Gotthold. *Freimaurerlieder als Quellen zu Schillers Lied "An die Freude"* (Leipzig, 1907), 10, n3. Warburg Institute Library, University of London FDD 352.

Dent, Edward J. Handwritten and typewritten notes on Giesecke; The Papers of Edward Joseph Dent, "'Mozart's operas' notes." King's College Library, Cambridge, EJD/2/3/1.

Deutsch, Otto Erich. "Der rätselhafte Gieseke." *Die Musikforschung.* V. Jahrgang (1952), British Library P.P.1946.aef.

——. *Musikverlags Nummern* (Berlin, 1961). British Library MUS 338.47.

Dramaturgische Blätter für Hamburg, hrsg. Fr.G. Zimmermann. (Hamburg, 1821). British Library P.P. 5243. i.

Dublin University Magazine. British Library P.P. 6155.

Ephemerides Politico-Litterariae (Pest). Országos Széchényi Könyvtár FM3/8111.

The Freeman's Journal and Daily Commercial Advertiser. British Library Newspaper Library IRL M19970–5; see also online at http://newspapers.bl.uk/blcs (10th August 2009).

Grandaur, Franz. *Der Text zu Mozart's "Zauberflöte" und Johann Georg Karl Giesecke.* (Separat-Abdruck aus den"Bayerischen Literaturblättern.") 1–2. Wienbibliothek im Rathaus (formerly Wiener Stadt- und Landesbibliothek) 31497A.

Hamburgischer Briefträger. Staatsarchiv, Hamburg, Z900 57, and Staats- und Universitätsbibliothek Hamburg Carl von Ossietzky X6565.

Hermathena. National Library of Ireland G 8805 h1.

The Hull Packet and Humber Mercury (Hull, England). British Library Newspaper Library EW M42333 1833-1834. See also online at http://newspapers.bl.uk/blcs (10th August 2009).

The Imperial Dictionary of Universal Biography. ed. John Francis Waller (London, Glasgow [printed], and Edinburgh, 1857–63). British Library 10601.y.2.

Jahrbuch für Theater und Theaterfreunde. Herausgegeben, von C. Lebrün. Erster Jahrgang (Hamburg, 1841). London University Institute of Germanic Studies C38.3 JTT1.

Jahresbericht der Geographischen Gesellschaft in München für 1877–1879 (München, 1880). British Library Ac.6059.

Johnstrup, F. *Gieseckes Mineralogiske Rejse I Grønland* (Copenhagen, 1878). British Library 7106.g.19.

Keller, Ludwig. *Schillers Stellung in der Entwicklungsgeschichte des Humanismus. Vorträge und Aufsätze aus der Comenius-Gesellschaft.* Dreizehnter Jahrgang. 3. Stück (Berlin, 1905). British Library Ac. 2622.

Leux, Irmgard. *Christian Gottlob Neefe (1748–1798).* Mit zwei Bildnissen und einer Handschrift-Nachbildung. Veröffentlichungen des Fürstlichen Institutes für musikwissenschaftliche Forschung zu Bückeburg. Fünfte Reihe. Stilkritische Studien. Zweiter Band. (Leipzig, 1925). British Library M.G. 1400. London University Warburg Institute DBE 90.

The London and Edinburgh Philosophical Magazine and Journal of Science. ed. Brewster. Vol. 4. June 1834. British Library P.P.1433.

Magazin der Musik. ed. C. F. Cramer. British Library P.P. 1945.

Masonic songbooks: *Freymäurerlieder mit Melodien, gedruckt bey G. L. Winter* (Berlin, 1771), C.424. *Allgemeines Gesangbuch für Freymäurer* (Danzig, 1784), 4785. bb. 61. *Gesänge für Frey-Maurer* (Leipzig, 1798) and *Sammlung auserlesener Freymaurer-Lieder* ([Kempten], 1790), 4785. aa. 48. (1–2.). *Vollständige Samlung von Freymaurerliedern zum Logengebrauch* (Leipzig, 1791–92), 4785. bb. 60. *Gesangbuch für Freymäurer* (Königsberg, 1800), 4785. bbb. 52.

Meenan, James, and Clarke, Desmond, eds. *The Royal Dublin Society 1731–1981* (Dublin, 1981). British Library X.800/31426.

Monumenta Chartae Papyracae Historiam Illustrantia, vol. I. ed. E. J. Labarre, *Watermarks by Edward Heawood, M. A.*, The Paper Publications Society (1950), British Library RAR 676.209 (open shelves), and 1950 [1957] offset reprint, corrected, L.R.402. f.12.

Moscheles, Ignaz. *Aus Moscheles' Leben nach Briefen und Tagebüchern herausgegeben von seiner Frau* (Leipzig, 1872). British Library 10705.ff.16 or Hirsch 3742.

Mozart, Wolfgang Amadé. *Verzeichnüss aller meiner Werke.* Facsimile edition of Mozart's thematic catalogue, British Library (London, 1990).

Musikalisches Wochenblatt. F. Ae. Kunzen and J. F. Reichardt, eds. (Berlin, 1793). British Library, Hirsch IV. 1125.

Neefe, Christian Gottlob. *Ein sächsischer Komponist wird Beethovens Lehrer.* (Schlossbergmuseum Chemnitz, 1997.) Beethoven-Haus, Bonn, Me 8 NEEF c / 1997 Schlo.

Nestler, Friedrich Hermann. Publisher of *Die Zauberflöte* libretto, undated. Staatsbibliothek zu Berlin Preussischer Kulturbesitz. Mus. T. 2077; New York Public Library +ZB *MG p.v. 285 [no. 6].

Neue Zeitschrift für Musik (Leipzig, 1856). Band 45. British Library P.P. 1946.

Niemetschek, Franz Xaver. *Lebensbeschreibung des k. k. Kapellmeisters Wolfgang Amadeus Mozart. 2. Aufl.* (Prague, 1808). British Library X.439/12075.

Nissen, Georg Nikolaus von, *Biographie W. A. Mozart's* (Leipzig, 1828). British Library 785.g.28.

Novello, Vincent, and Rosemary Hughes, eds. *A Mozart Pilgrimage. Being the Travel Diaries of Vincent and Mary Novello in the year 1829. Transcribed by Nerina Medici di Marignano* (London, 1955). British Library 7901.e.30.

Oberon (Frankfurt and Leipzig, 1780; British Library 11526.dd.30). *Neue und verbesserte Ausgabe* (Leipzig, 1789). British Library 11517.aa.52.

Privilegirte Wöchentliche gemeinnützige Nachrichten von und für Hamburg. Staatsarchiv, Hamburg, Z900 704.

Proben der Schrift-Sorten, welche in der Buchdruckerey von Friedrich Hermann Nestler wohnhaft in Hamburg auf den grossen Bleichen No. 323. [sic] befindlich sind (Hamburg, 1807). Staatsarchiv, Hamburg, A902 342.

Proben der vorzüglichsten Lettern in der Buchdruckerey von F. H. Nestler & Melle (Hamburg: Grosse Bleichen No. 29, 1834). Staatsbibliothek zu Berlin Preussischer Kulturbesitz, 1939.8938

Proceedings of The Geological Society of London November 1833 to June 1838, Vol. II (London, 1838). British Library Ac. 3171/4; also T. 1572.

The Proceedings of the (Royal) Dublin Society. National Library of Ireland IR 506 R9.

Proceedings of the Royal Irish Academy. National Library of Ireland IR 506.

Raisonirendes Journal vom deutschen Theater zu Hamburg (Hamburg, 1800). Bey Friedrich Hermann Nestler. Staatsarchiv, Hamburg, Z530 6.

Ratzel, Friedrich. *Jahresbericht der Geographischen Gesellschaft in München für 1877–1879. Zur Biographie des Augsburger Grönlandforschers Johann Georg Karl (oder Karl Ludwig) Metzler-Giesecke* (München, 1880). British Library Ac.6059.

Regensburgisches Diarium. Staatliche Bibliothek, Regensburg, 999 ZM Rat. civ. 439.

Regensburgisches Theater-Journal von 1784–1786. Stadtarchiv Regensburg. 332 Theatersammlung. Blank 3. Sign. 1872.

Rink, Hinrich Johannes. *Danish Greenland,* Dr. Robert Brown ed. (London, 1877). British Library 10460. cc. 14.

Salzburgisches Theater-Journal von 1786 den 1. Oktober bis 1787 den 20. Hornung, von Johann Georg Karl Giesecke, aus Augsburg, Mitglied der hiesigen Schauspielergesellschaft (Salzburg, 1787). Museum Carolino Augusteum, Salzburg, 19054/1.

Schink, Johann Friedrich. *Laune, Spott und Ernst, auf Kosten des Verfassers und in Kommisssion bei J. F. Hammerich zu Altona* (Hamburg, 1793), Landesbibliothek und Murhardsche Bibliothek der Stadt Kassel II 40a2/10.

Schmidt-Görg, Joseph. *Die Wasserzeichen in Beethovens Notenpapieren. Beiträge zur Beethoven-Bibliographie,* hrsg. Kurt Dorfmüller (München, 1978). British Library X.431/2997.

Schütze, Johann Friedrich. *Theater-Geschichte* (Hamburg, 1794). Reprinted Zentralantiquariat der Deutschen Demokratischen Republik (Leipzig, 1975). London University Institute of Germanic Studies C 38.53109 HAM 5 Scu.

Silfverstolpe, Fr. S. *Några Återblickar* (Stockholm, 1841). Kongl. Musikaliska Akademiens Bibliotek, Stockholm, C351.

Spinelli, A. G. In "Della Raccolta Musicale Estense" *Memorie della Regia Accademia di Scienze, Lettere, ed Arti in Modena,* Serie II, Volume IX (1893). Biblioteca Estense, Modena (I-MOe), S.C. Cat. 47 (Mus).

Steenstrup, K. J. V. *Meddelelser om Grønland.* Commmissionen O for Ledelsen af de geologiske og geographiske Undersøgelser i Grønland (Copenhagen, 1910). National Library of Ireland 549 G2.

Stephenson, Kurt. *Mozarts Meisteropern im aufklärerischen Hamburg* (Weimar, 1938). Staats- und Universitätsbibliothek Hamburg Carl von Ossietzky B1947/302.

———. *Hamburgische Oper zwischen Barock und Romantik.* Hamburger Theaterbücherei, hrsg. Paul Th. Hoffmann. Bd. 6. (Hamburg, 1948) Staats- und Universitätsbibliothek Hamburg Carl von Ossietzky X/8475–6.

Tausig, Paul. "Mozarts Beziehungen zu Baden." *Sonderabdruck aus Nr. 55–57 der Badener Zeitung* (1914), 9–15. Stadtarchiv Baden bei Wien [Abth.MBNr.16], Städtische Sammlungen Archiv/Rollettmuseum der Stadtgemeinde Baden.

Thalia. Herausgegeben von Schiller. Erster Band. Zweites Heft 1786. Leipzig, bey Georg Joachim, Göschen 1787. British Library P.P.4737.d.

Thematisches Verzeichniss derjenigen Originalhandschriften von W. A. Mozart . . . welche Hofrath André in Offenbach a. M. besitzt (1841). British Library Hirsch IV. 1064.

Thematisches Verzeichniss sämmtlicher Kompositionen von W. A. Mozart. Nach dem Original-Manuscripte herausgegeben von A.André. (1805). British Library Hirsch IV. 1062 and M.e.1.(2).

Walter, Friedrich Friedrich. *Archiv und Bibliothek des Grossh. Hof- und National theaters in Mannheim* (1899). British Library 011907.e.2.

Waterhouse, Gilbert. Notes and correspondence relating to his Giesecke researches; Institute of Germanic and Romance Studies, London University, IGS/Archives/ GWA boxes 111–113.

Wieland, Christoph Martin. *Lulu oder die Zauberflöte. Dschinnistan*, Dritter Band (Winterthur, 1789). British Library 12410.d.9.

Index

About the Author

A graduate of Cambridge University, Michael Freyhan combines musicological research with a concert and recording career, touring as a chamber music pianist and harpsichordist. He has been a repetiteur at Glyndebourne Opera House and held teaching appointments at the Royal Academy of Music, London; Reading University; and Birmingham Conservatoire. He has performed at London's Royal Festival Hall, Queen Elizabeth Hall, Barbican, and Wigmore Hall, as well as in recordings and broadcasts on radio and television in five continents. A recording of Spohr Piano Trios by the Beethoven Broadwood Trio, in which he played an 1823 Broadwood grand, won a Critics' Choice award in *The Gramophone*. In former years he was also active as a professional violinist and viola player, having been concertmaster of the National Youth Orchestra of Great Britain as a teenager.

Research into the history and authenticity of the first edition of Mozart's *Die Zauberflöte* has been an enduring obsession spanning more than three decades. His findings, the result of investigations in fifteen countries, have been published in the *Journal of the American Musicological Society*, *Mozart-Jahrbuch*, and *Musical Opinion*. He has lectured widely at American universities, including Harvard, Princeton, Stanford, and New York, and in Europe at Oxford, Cambridge, London, Leipzig, and Moscow.

He has written on a variety of musical topics in *The Strad*, *Strings* (formerly as London Corresponding Editor), *Piano Quarterly*, and *Brio, Journal of the UK Branch of the International Association of Music Libraries*. Other publications include a commissioned Toy Symphony and the completion of Süssmayr's Concerto Movement for basset clarinet, mentioned by Mozart in his letters, from autograph sketches in the British Library. The work has been performed at the Musikverein, Vienna, and recorded twice on CD.